A Companion to
The Magic

Studies in German Literature, Linguistics, and Culture

Edited by James Hardin
(*South Carolina*)

A COMPANION TO
THOMAS MANN'S
THE MAGIC MOUNTAIN

Edited by
Stephen D. Dowden

CAMDEN HOUSE

Copyright © the Contributors

Susan Sontag's "Pilgrimage" copyright 1996 by Susan Sontag,
reprinted with the permission of the Wylie Agency, Inc.

All Rights Reserved. Except as permitted under current legislation,
no part of this work may be photocopied, stored in a retrieval system,
published, performed in public, adapted, broadcast, transmitted,
recorded, or reproduced in any form or by any means,
without the prior permission of the copyright owner.

First published 1999 by Camden House.
Reprinted in paperback 2002.

Camden House is an imprint of Boydell & Brewer Inc.
PO Box 41026, Rochester, NY 14604–4126 USA
and of Boydell & Brewer Limited
PO Box 9, Woodbridge, Suffolk IP12 3DF, UK

ISBN
Cloth 1–57113–150–7
Paperback 1–57113–248–1

Library of Congress Cataloging-in-Publication Data

A companion to Thomas Mann's Magic Mountain / edited by Stephen D.
Dowden.
    p. cm. — (Studies in German literature, linguistics, and culture)
Includes bibliographical references and index.
    ISBN cloth 1–57113–150–7; paperback 1–57113–248–1 (both alk. paper)
    1. Mann, Thomas, 1875–1955. Zauberberg. I. Dowden, Stephen D.
II. Series: Studies in German literature, linguistics, and culture
(Unnumbered)
PT2625.Z38C66   1998
833'.912—dc21
                                                                          98–21803

A catalogue record for this title is available from the British Library.

This publication is printed on acid-free paper.
Printed in the United States of America.

Contents

Introduction		ix
1:	Transfiguration in Silence: Hans Castorp's Uncanny Awakening JOSEPH P. LAWRENCE	1
2:	Mann's Ethical Style STEPHEN D. DOWDEN	14
3:	Thomas Mann's Comic Spirit EUGENE GOODHEART	41
4:	War as Mentor: Thomas Mann and Germanness ÜLKER GÖKBERK	53
5:	From Muted Chords to Maddening Cacophony: Music in *The Magic Mountain* DAVID BLUMBERG	80
6:	Ambiguous Solitude: Hans Castorp's Sturm und Drang nach Osten EDWARD ENGELBERG	95
7:	Mortal Illness on the Magic Mountain STEPHEN C. MEREDITH	109
8:	Beyond Naphta: Thomas Mann's Jews and German-Jewish Writing MICHAEL BRENNER	141
9:	Technology as Desire: X-Ray Vision in *The Magic Mountain* KARLA SCHULTZ	158

10:	Distant Oil Rigs and Other Erections KENNETH WEISINGER	177
11:	Pilgrimage SUSAN SONTAG	221
Select Bibliography		241
Notes on the Contributors		243
Index		245

Acknowledgment

THANKS ARE DUE TO Karin Grundler-Whitacre, who helped greatly with the preparation of the manuscript for the publication of this volume.

Introduction

THOMAS MANN CONCEIVED THE IDEA of writing *The Magic Mountain* in 1912 and began his work in earnest only later, in 1915. When at last the book appeared in November of 1924, he was a few months short of his fiftieth birthday. It was his third novel.

Mann had published his first one, *Buddenbrooks,* in 1901, at the age of twenty-six. Subtitled "The Decline of a Family," it explores the spiritual (and physical) degeneration of a mercantile clan from its robust, burgherly beginnings into modern, art-vitiated decadence and extinction. This tale of a family's spiritual decline and death struck a nerve throughout a Europe that stood uncertainly on the cusp of a new century of urban culture and mass society. Mann's novels seemed to confirm the worst suspicions about what had been lost and what a nervous bourgeoisie might have to look forward to.

At one stroke, the novel's spectacular success with readers and critics elevated Mann to the status of modern master and gave to the German novel as form a new international prestige. And it sounded the basic, interwoven themes that would preoccupy Mann throughout his writing life: the exhaustion of nineteenth-century bourgeois culture, the morally ambivalent status of art in modern life — alternately figured either as sensual and corrupt or as liberating and form-giving — and the defining image of fatal disease.

Mann's creativity before the First World War had been intense. His best-known shorter works belong to this period, including "Tristan" (1903), "Tonio Kröger" (1903), and, especially, *Death in Venice* (1912). In 1909 *Royal Highness* appeared, which is perhaps his least-known novel — and in any case certainly less substantial than *Buddenbrooks* or *The Magic Mountain.* It tells the story of Klaus Heinrich, the prince of a fictional state in southern Germany that is materially impoverished, but thereby also romantically free of the encroachments of modern industrial society and the mass culture of urban life. In this fairy-story of a novel, Mann elegiacally celebrates the doomed privileges of more aristocratic, spiritually fuller times: taste, wealth, and entitlement. The prince, a figure who represents the artist's regal essence, marries the daughter of a prosperous American businessman who comes to the rescue of Klaus Heinrich's debt-ridden duchy. The resonances are biographical. In 1905 Mann himself had married Katia Pringsheim, daughter of a highly prestigious and well-to-do Munich family. Since the Mann clan had fallen on hard times, hard at least relative to their former wealth in Lübeck, her money came to him at an opportune moment.

Within a period of five years Katia bore four children and had two miscarriages. Her health suffered under the strain. During 1911 and 1912 a stubborn lung problem caused her to be absent from the family a good deal. Finally, Katia's doctor advised her to retire for an extended rest to a high-altitude sanatorium in the Swiss alps. Thomas Mann spent four weeks with her at Davos during May and June of 1912. Specializing in the treatment of tuberculosis, the clinic had been a fashionable health resort since the 1870s. Robert Louis Stevenson, to name only one tubercular celebrity, had sojourned there. Its head physician even cautioned Mann himself about a "moist spot" on one of his lungs, solemnly advising him to stay for a course of treatment. The skeptical novelist did not succumb to the temptation that would later hold Hans Castorp under the mountain's spell. But Mann's four-week visit supplied him the images, thoughts, and impulses that he later poured into *The Magic Mountain*.

After *Death in Venice* appeared, Mann felt inclined to work up his sanatorium observations into a humorous story, which he intended to call "Der verzauberte Berg" ("The Enchanted Mountain"). He envisioned it as a comic complement to *Death in Venice*. As he worked on the tale his intentions changed and expanded. The project soon grew into a full-scale novel in which he intended to explore the interrelatedness of sexual love, disease, and death, and their ethical meanings. The advent of the First World War, however, interrupted his progress. Thomas Mann was a deeply conservative German patriot, a romantically pessimistic chauvinist, while his brother Heinrich had strong leanings toward the democratic West and its Enlightenment tradition. The ensuing rift between the brothers caused both a great deal of pain and provoked Thomas Mann to write his long and tortuous anti-Western diatribe, *Reflections of a Nonpolitical Man*, much of which is directed against his brother's views. He finished the book in 1918, just in time for the final Allied victory.

Consequently, the *Reflections* was more or less an immediate anachronism, a work of backward-looking *ressentiment*. But many of his fellow intellectuals, embittered over imperial Germany's humiliation and in fear of a communist revolution, took solace in its aggressive defense of Germany's supposed spiritual superiority over the forces of Western democracy and what they saw as its culture of mass mediocrity. Hans Castorp's explicit mediocrity, much like that of Leopold Bloom or Josef K., no doubt reflects Mann's own perception of twentieth-century selfhood.

Mann returned to the manuscript of *The Magic Mountain* in April of 1919. Rereading his work, he saw that the war had made some of it obsolete. Above all, Settembrini's irrationalist rival for Hans Castorp's attentions, a Protestant minister named Bunge, made way for a new presence. Mann replaced him with the strange figure of Naphta, an unlikely combination of Jew, Jesuit, and Communist. Certainly the Russian revolution and the Spartacus Union's threat of widespread communist uprisings in Germany disturbed the sleep of the middle and upper classes, not least in Bavaria, where Thomas Mann lived. His Munich was the scene of street battles and a short-lived Soviet Republic. In his diaries of May 1919, Mann voices fears that were not his alone. He sees Bolshevism as "the most horrific cultural catastrophe that has ever threatened the world." He wonders if the "old world" can be saved and transformed "or whether the Kirghiz-idea of rampaging and annihilation will prevail." (Perhaps we are meant to see Hans Castorp's Kirghiz-eyed seductress as his sexual nemesis: Madame Chauchat annihilates his manly willpower, reduces him to abject dependence.) Mann's diaries also show that he viewed Bolshevik activity in Munich as a peculiarly Jewish operation. He fears the unwashed masses, a "great migration from below," and maligns "the Russian-Jewish type" as a carrier of the revolution. Presumably he intended the Galician Jew Naphta to suggest this category to his readers. Certainly the place of Jews in German society was undergoing baleful transformation. And at least for Mann's imagination, steeped in the Protestant Prussian tradition, the idea of Jesuitical Catholicism contained an undercurrent of threat to the reigning order of things.

But perhaps the most important and most general transformation was one that Mann perceived in himself after the war. It was a shift away from his mood of apocalypse and what he thought of as his sympathy with death, a change that would influence the gradual development of *The Magic Mountain* between 1919 and 1924. The bluster and unfocused sermonizing of the *Reflections* betray in Thomas Mann an underlying sense of doubt, one that he had sought to overcome with sheer verbal bravado.

The transformation is a much-discussed moment in Thomas Mann's biography. It is the traditional view that he abandons his former chauvinism to embrace democracy and life-affirming Western virtues. In the notes for his humanistic essay "Goethe and Tolstoy," he is explicit about the affirmation of life: "Happiness consists in striving in a reasonable way for the true values, lasting goodness, not for that which belongs only to appearance, to the moment, or even contradicts the laws of reason. That means to renounce indulgence in fleeting appetites and approval in the present. Renunciation." Hans Castorp, drawn on by the intermingled pleasures of sexual love and death, must learn to renounce his dark yearnings and affirm life. At least this is the view that Mann himself, who in 1921 began to think of the novel as a Bildungsroman, endorses.

Hans Castorp

Hans Castorp, seemingly so practical and worldly, suffers from a lack of connection to the world. He is a student, and as in Kafka, the student is a condition that embodies incompleteness. Moreover, the practicality he pretends to masks his lack of spiritual orientation. The main concern evident in Hans Castorp's way of life is a concern for himself, his creature comforts. Rather like Josef K. and K. of the castle, Hans Castorp (the curious ritual of always stating his full name seems somehow necessary, as if to fortify his insufficiently firm grip on the will to exist), is thrown back on himself and the meager resources of his inner life. He seems unable or unwilling to assert the fullness of personal individuality. Schopenhauer's negation of the will and Zarathustra's news that God is dead belong to the immediate background of Mann's vision of Hans Castorp's world. So does the bottomless *ennui moderne* that Flaubert diagnosed in the bourgeois culture of the nineteenth century. Hans Castorp inherits this sad world.

The origin of this condition is the generalized malaise of a culture in which tradition has broken down into disconnected fragments and in which people lack a binding sense of larger purpose, unity, and identity. Kierkegaard solved the problem with a leap into faith, but the secular imagination must make do with other means. As the endless and pointedly modern disputations of Settembrini and Naphta suggest, no constellation of ideas or beliefs exists according to which the world can be confidently ordered. The time itself has broken down. The consequence of this collapse is a low-grade but chronic sense of emptiness, a malaise experienced by the individual — by Emma Bovary, to name a salient example — as boredom. She seeks relief from it in erotic adventure. Hans Castorp's boredom, and the underlying melancholy of which it is the primary symptom, keep him on the lookout for physiological causes. Mann's narrator, though, maintains a critical detachment. He is eager for the reader to understand the fuller implications of the protagonist's situation:

> a human being lives out not only his personal life as an individual, but also, consciously or subconsciously, the lives of his epoch and contemporaries; and although he may regard the general and impersonal foundations of his existence as unequivocal givens and take them for granted, having as little intention of ever subjecting them to critique as our good Hans Castorp himself had, it is nevertheless quite possible that he senses

his own moral well-being to be somehow impaired by the lack of critique.

Hans Castorp's situation embodies the modern condition, and the novel explores his limitations and possibilities. The principal limitations are time and death.

Time

What kind of time does Hans Castorp have on his hands? It is leisure time, for he is a man with an ample private income. It is leisure in the sense that he is freed *from* the need to work for a living, and therefore free *for* — what? A more detached relation to essential things, such as the erotic pursuit of Madame Chauchat and the contemplation of death? The pursuit of elevated cultural matters, perhaps, in the higher sense of understanding the world through the liberal arts. Yet Castorp is something of a philistine, too. He has no active intention of lofty cultural pursuits or spiritual self-perfection. His preferred reading matter is a technical textbook, *Ocean Steamships*. His leisure is also simple idleness, devoid of any save biological meaning. Still, whatever limitations may handicap him, Castorp is free for the world. So Castorp's leisure is literally of the higher sort. He has ascended, traveled upward to the magic mountain where, as in King Mark's Wagnerian court, time becomes space. On the mountain Castorp has broken free of time itself. And even though reminders of individual mortality are all around him, he scarcely takes them seriously.

Just as Mann's novel escapes literal reality by hollowing out a fictional space in which to work, so also Hans Castorp pulls off the neat trick of escaping from linear time and history — personified in the the figure of Hans's grandfather and the dynastic element in nineteenth-century Germany's *Grossbürgertum* that he represents. Seen from this angle of vision, old Senator Castorp looks rather like Father Time himself: especially in the formal, life-size portrait that Hans views as his true identity, an identity that outlives the old man's death.

> It showed Hans Lorenz Castorp in his official dress as a Lord Councillor of the city: the sober, even pious costume of burghers from a vanished century, habiliment that simultaneously conducted a dignified and adventurous community through the ages — lending its support on lofty occasions in order ceremoniously to make the past present and the present past — and also to proclaim the fixed order of things, the venerable security of their signature in transactions.

For Hans, the painting expresses the grandfather's true and abiding form. History fathers the present, and it is the tyranny of the past from which we seek to free ourselves. Thomas Mann, the close student of Schopenhauer and Nietzsche, shares with them and many other modernists a fundamental hostility to the idea that the force of history must dominate our existence. Its vicissitudes and fluctuations are not the truest indicators of human identity; indeed, they may mask it, as Schopenhauer believed.

History and time are the enemy of essential humanity, a recurring theme in the novel of modernism. Ulrich, the protagonist of Musil's *Man Without Qualities*, seeks refuge from the contingencies of temporality in a mystical sphere that he and his sister call the "Other Condition." Art can produce a similar liberation. In a crucial passage of *The Sleepwalkers* the narrator declares that a cello sonata — played by a man in memory of his dead wife — has this extraordinary effect: "Time itself was canceled and shaped itself into space which enclosed them all while Kessel's cello rang out, uprearing sound, upbuilding space, fulfilling space, fulfilling them also."

Nothing is more common in literary modernism than the attempt to undo time. Conrad's bumbling anarchist in *The Secret Agent* conspires to blow up the clock at Greenwich, central timepiece of modernity. Goethe warns Harry Haller not to take time seriously in Hesse's *Steppenwolf*. In *Ulysses*, Stephen Daedalus declares history to be a nightmare from which he is trying to awake. And modern German history, as Mann was intensely aware, had by 1914 become unmistakably nightmarish. His countryman Walter Benjamin, who likewise experienced the nineteenth century's bourgeois progress as spiritually empty, sought to blast open the continuum of history.

Hans Castorp, whose childhood has been saturated in death and displacement, and who feels no sense of calling for a future in shipbuilding (drearily embodied in his bedside reading, *Ocean Steamships*), instinctively seeks a space in which to maneuver toward a heightened sense of personal authenticity. Rather like the more urbane, self-aware protagonist of Musil's *Man Without Qualities*, Hans Castorp decides to take a vacation from life. He withdraws from the contingencies of quotidian routine and retreats to the magic mountain for seven years of contemplation. There he hovers among competing intellectual, spiritual, and carnal possibilities.

Love and Death

Hans Castorp goes to visit his cousin for three weeks, but he ends up staying seven years. What makes him stay? It is the double seduction of both eros and death, fused irresistibly in the voluptuously exotic figure of Madame Chauchat. She seduces him to forgetfulness of what one must do in the life of work, family, state, and the other institutions of orderly life,

life lived down in the flatlands. Erotic bliss is a finite moment of forgetting; death is the real thing.

Death has tugged at Hans Castorp ever since his childhood. Twice orphaned — first by his parents and then by his grandfather — he gravitates toward the living dead. Their mountain is a enchanted realm, one that towers above ordinary life. It is the place in which life's great chthonic forces, sex and death, thrust themselves into view. Hans is caught between indulgence in his darkest desires and the sense of responsibility.

At least since Rabelais, sex and death have been the novel's special territory. Except in extraordinary cases (Sade, for example), the novel does not attempt to persuade us that the promptings of our darker nature are beyond good and evil. The suppression and repression of evil is not philistinism, or at least not most of the time in serious fiction. However, it is not always so easy to tell the difference between good and evil. Bad fiction, kitsch, declares that it knows the difference with certainty. Yet surely it is a central task of the novel not to legislate the difference but to explore it. The novel, as a way of knowing the world, can reveal that there is something in our minds that finds it necessary to challenge and test the inevitably imperfect definitions of good and evil we may inhabit at a given historical moment or in a given cultural setting. This skeptical impulse is a defining feature of good fiction, often expressed stylistically as ambivalence and irony. It is the literary trope much prized by poets and novelists, always spurned by politicians and ideologues such as Settembrini. He warns Hans Castorp never to accept it as a habit of mind: "Where irony is not a forthright device of classical rhetoric whose meaning is not for one moment unclear to common sense, it makes for depravity," he warns Hans Castorp. "It becomes an impediment to civilization, an unclean flirtation with the forces of stagnation, spiritual squalor, and corruption." Settembrini's apprehension notwithstanding, the effect of irony should be to open the imagination to new ways of seeing and thinking about good and evil, codes of virtue always also imperfect and susceptible of change. Creditably, even Hans Castorp wonders what sort of irony there might be that is not for a moment unclear.

The position of the contemporary liberal admirer of Mann's novel must be open to irony and ambivalence. One wants to be right-thinking about ethnicity, gender, class, and oppression in general. The aesthetic impulse, however — as Thomas Mann repeatedly reminds us — is no respecter of the conformist, bourgeois niceties in contemporary liberal culture. And this is not because fiction passively mirrors prevailing ideologies and prejudices — though sometimes it does; one thinks of Mann and his fraught attitude toward Jews. But even here, once prejudice finds its way into a novel, the genre's built-in ethic of ironic or dialogical form opens prejudice to question. The novel as a genre, when it rises to its highest standard, challenges all fixed ideologies, those reigning and those not. Seen from the perspective of the contemporary discomfort about admiring a book that may not be completely egalitarian in spirit, *The Magic Mountain* is still powerful enough to break taboos of the bourgeoisie. This is not a weakness but is much more a part of the claim the novel has on us. "As a spontaneous utterance of life," wrote Bruno Schulz, "a work of art poses a task for ethics, not the reverse. If art were merely to confirm what had already been established elsewhere, it would be superfluous."

The Translations

Alfred A. Knopf published *The Magic Mountain* translation in 1927. It was he who urged Thomas Mann to accept Helen T. Lowe-Porter as the book's translator. She had already translated his *Buddenbrooks*, but Mann — whose English was not strong — lacked enthusiasm for Knopf's choice. He had another translator in mind for *The Magic Mountain*. Knopf's will prevailed, however. Indeed, Lowe-Porter became the English-language conduit for nearly all of Mann's works during his lifetime.

Not all readers of the English versions have been satisfied. For many years the quality of Lowe-Porter's translations has been under siege. Mann's ironic tone, syntactic complexity, and elaborately mannered style are a major challenge to any translator. Certainly it is no challenge to find errors and misjudgments of various sorts in Lowe-Porter's Mann. In chapter two of *The Magic Mountain*, for example, steam-driven cranes unload goods into railway cars and warehouses: "Eisenbahnwagen und Schuppen." Lowe-Porter writes "into waiting trains and scales," conjuring the "waiting" part out of thin air and evidently supposing "der Schuppen" (shed or storage building) to be "die Schuppen" — the scales of a fish — and then confounding fish scales with the kind of scales that weigh freight. Not a fine moment in the history of Mann translation, nor an isolated one.

Still, Lowe-Porter's accomplishment is not to be doubted, if only for reasons of priority and familiarity. In the unstable universe of thoughts and images uprooted from one language and replanted in another, there is a sense in which even corrigible error can become canonical. Kafka's late aphorism has some explanatory force here: "Leopards break into the temple and drain the sacrificial vessels; this occurs repeatedly, again and again: finally it can be reckoned on in advance, and it becomes a part of the ceremony." One need not look far to find such desecrations of the text. The Bible is the outstanding instance of the strange process through which the authority of inaccurate translation transcends that of scholarly precision. The New English Bible is no doubt a "better" translation than the Authorized Version, but it will never acquire the canonical authority of the "original" King James translation. The New English is a Bible that does not ring with the same poetic truth that generations of familiarity have invested in its great predecessor. Therefore, if Lowe-Porter's waiting trains and scales have somehow become a part of the ceremony, they may as well stay put.

So it is at least in principle possible that an aura of authority and authenticity may accrue to a classic translation, or to a translated classic such as Lowe-Porter's *Magic Mountain* — not because of its beauty or accuracy (though there are passages in Lowe-Porter that possess both of these qualities), but simply because her impersonation of Mann's voices is the one that has for decades been in our ear. Perhaps this explains why the new translation by John E. Woods, which appeared in 1995, retains the title that Lowe-Porter gave to Mann's novel. It might have been convenient if Woods had called his translation *The Enchanted Mountain*. The contributors to this volume, for example, would find it simple to distinguish between the two versions in their references. More to the point, though, is that *The Enchanted Mountain* would also have altered the resonance of the title, making it suggestive of the fairy-tale tradition upon which it draws. Recent research by Michael Maar has shown that Mann's imagination was lastingly and pervasively influenced by the severe moral vision of Hans Christian Andersen's fairytales. Even *The Magic Mountain* shows traces of Andersen's world. Joachim, for example, is nothing if not a steadfast tin soldier.

In general Woods has been able to correct the various errors of Lowe-Porter's translation. None is of major significance, but it is reassuring just the same to have increased accuracy. However, the new translation has taken a giant step backward in one instance. The crucial dialogue between Hans Castorp and Madame Chauchat at the end of chapter six — which Mann wrote and published in French, and which Lowe-Porter retains in the original French — has now been rendered in English. This is certainly an unimprovement, and one with which even the editors who made the decision seem ill at ease: comically, they have had these pages printed in italics, as if through typographical convention to suggest the foreignness of the exchange between amorous Hans Castorp and Madame Chauchat.

And, inevitably, some things slip through the nets of translation altogether. One of these is Mann's identification of Hans Castorp with the *Siebenschläfer*. Both Lowe-Porter and Woods translate this common word with the neologism "Sevensleeper," echoing the seven years of Hans Castorp's withdrawal from flatland reality. The translators' choice is no doubt correct, as far as it goes. Mann's enthusiasm for number symbolism is well known. But *Siebenschläfer* also, and primarily, means dormouse. Of course, this European creature is not a mouse at all, but a shy nocturnal beastie, familiar in children's literature, who seems able to exist for long periods in a dormant state. Hans Castorp spends a good deal of his time prone, snoozing his life away in a "rest cure" for a disease he never even contracted. The dormouse allusion disappears in English.

A third resonance, possibly the most important one, also enters the work — or, rather, fails to in translation. In German the "Siebenschläfer," now to be understood literally in the plural as "Seven Sleepers," refers to a medieval martyr legend in which seven Christians are condemned to die by being walled up in a cave. When the cave is opened some centuries later, they have miraculously survived the death sentence to reemerge intact into life. This image of death and redemption, also explored by Goethe in a poem of 1815 entitled "Siebenschläfer," holds obvious significance for the novel. Mann certainly intended his readers, as many passages in his letters attest, to understand Hans Castorp's descent from the magic mountain down into real life and the First World War as the hero's rebirth.

Thomas Mann Now

Thomas Mann's place in the canon of modernist classics may not be as secure as those of Kafka, Joyce, and Proust, at least among academic critics. For Mann seems now to have more detractors among contemporary critics than the other three. This may, in part, have to do with the formal character of Mann's accomplishment. While Kafka and Joyce were both stylistic innovators of startling originality — and Proust, too, is certainly stylistically unique in his own right — Mann's style seems linked to the past. In *Doctor Faustus*, a novel in which Mann explores this question of form and innovation, he invents a composer who shatters the style barrier, creating a new form that is adequate to modern experience. Mann himself, closer in many ways to his narrator Zeitblom, never achieved the breakthrough into a new and original expression of the modern experience. He relied instead on parody and an ironically, often comically heightened, version of nineteenth-century realism. In this mode he simultaneously seeks not only to celebrate the traditional novel and exploit its narrative possibilities but also to detach himself critically from that tradition. And certainly this is an underlying compact that Mann makes with his readers in *The Magic Mountain*. The language of the novel, like its setting, belongs to a world and a way of life that disappeared forever after 1914.

Another factor that has militated against Thomas Mann's standing among academics critics since 1989 — which is to say, since the end of the Cold War — may be the reception that his work has traditionally received. Mann has always been the darling of liberal Western critics, who found in him a German writer of the first rank who seemed to embody a German intellectual tradition not compromised by Nazism. Mann's activities on behalf of democracy during the war, and his hostility to the forces of McCarthyism in the United States after the war, made him seem to be a lion, like his Settembrini, of right-thinking democratic values. The Cold War kept alive the centrality of political categories in literary criticism. Consequently, Mann remained in the forefront of the academic canon.

But since the fall of the Berlin Wall, there has been no reason to engage with Marxist critics such as Georg Lukács over the question of Kafka's supposedly decadent modernism vs. Mann's supposedly wholesome realism. In addition, the publication of Mann's diaries since the 1970s has clarified his early chauvinism, his anti-Jewish prejudices, and the full extent of his homosexual proclivities. This richer, more complex vision of Mann — far more interesting than the older and relatively one-dimensional image of Mann the good democrat — has jolted him loose from the position that he has hitherto held on the syllabi of literature courses.

Consequently, we stand now at a interesting moment in the study of Thomas Mann and of literary modernism in general. The essays in this book — all of which, with the exception of Susan Sontag's memoir, were written expressly for it — should suggest new paths in the understanding of both. If Thomas Mann and his books have turned out to be not exactly what they have hitherto seemed to be, it is no cause for disappointment. We are instead prompted to seek fuller knowledge, greater clarity, and deeper understanding.

— S. D. D.
September 1998

JOSEPH P. LAWRENCE

1: Transfiguration in Silence: Hans Castorp's Uncanny Awakening

"It was, to speak in subdued, respectful tones, a historic thunderclap that shook the foundations of the earth, but for us it is the thunderbolt that bursts open the magic mountain and rudely sets its entranced sleeper outside the gates. There he sits in the grass, sheepishly rubbing his eyes, like a man who, despite many an admonition, has failed to read the daily papers."

UNLIKE *BUDDENBROOKS*, A NOVEL SO open to the world that, like a good piece of cultural history, it summons the reflections of any generally educated reader, *The Magic Mountain* is more remote and forbidding. Although it contains a rather straightforward account of the state of the European soul at the brink of the First World War, the novel still manages to cast doubt on the inviting realism of its own language. No work of realistic fiction would have everything unfold by sevens. In the end, the entire novel seems to be artfully — even too artfully — contrived. Living in a trustworthy world, one in which objects remain (or seem to remain) simply themselves, we at first experience a kind of vertigo when we encounter the inner world of the novel, where even the most everyday object doubles as a symbol of the whole. Our situation is not unlike that of Hans Castorp himself, who, when he first arrives on the mountain, makes himself dizzy in the realization that he has left the trustworthy world of hardwood forests and songbirds behind.

In the novel, anything can be anything else. A cigar, for example, is a woman. It even delivers something of that great challenge that so overwhelmed Peeperkorn, for without the skill and attention of a man its fire is easily extinguished. Its body is lithe and organic, its skin laced with veins. It breathes. The air it draws sustains the fire of life. It produces its ash through oxidation. It becomes, through its peculiar mode of dying, a metaphor for the life process itself. Its description plays into the descriptions of other objects, as well: a thermometer, a pencil, even a gramophone. And, as a metaphor of living through dying, it mirrors every tubercular patient at the sanatorium. Above all, however, it evokes the figure of Madame Chauchat, desirable and temperamental, willing to return love once she is satisfied with the love she receives.

This fluctuation of meaning is intensified by the free play of irony that Mann adopts. The same cigar that is life may just as well represent a coffin. Sealed in a jar, it loses its taste and character. This in turn constitutes a warning about how *The Magic Mountain* is to be read. If the work is hermetic, it is also something more. In other words, if Mann posted a sign, "For Experts Alone," he did so in good humor. The broadest network of inter-reflecting symbols could never yield more than the dull monotony Hans Castorp encounters in a snowstorm, the monotony of tiny ice crystals that vary their hexagonal symmetry into infinity. This is the trope of death, not life. For the novel itself to live, it must be open to the lived reality that unfolds beyond the text. As a result, it contains meanings that must prove hermetic even to the most learned of hermeticists. The most secret of meanings is not the one that is based on obscure allusion, but the one that derives from direct openness to the world. Reading between the lines is a skill taught only by life itself.

If Mann's intention was as life-affirming as I believe it to have been, I have already justified the nonexpert's right to speak. The nonexpert is, on my understanding, the philosopher — one who, instead of possessing wisdom, is consumed by the desire for it. As Socrates always insisted, the idea of a professional philosopher, or the philosopher as expert, is a contradiction in terms. The philosopher is characterized less by ambition, the "flatland" desire for validation within an institutional order, than by what Settembrini was getting at when he called Hans Castorp "life's problem child." The desire for high-mountain air, for fields of frozen forms that never melt, has more in common with the agoraphobic desire to cling to the eternal repetition of place and routine than with the saint's desire to take heaven by storm. As such, it is characteristic of all of those who are too sensitive to immerse themselves in the stream of life.

Mann's conviction is that such delicacy still contains a potential for a truly healthy and vibrant life. This goes, moreover, beyond an assertion of diffuse and desperate optimism. Instead, it represents a sober assessment of one of the truly interesting inner relationships: that between the complete social reject, in this case the taciturn, bearded Hans, who, at the end of his stay on the Mountain, is seated at the "bad" Russian table, and the philosopher, or even better, the philosopher warrior, the one whose indifference to life has been magically transmogrified into a readiness to confront whatever the world throws into his path, even if that be the utter hell of trench warfare. Tying these two moments together is something that commentaries on *The Magic Mountain* have generally failed to do.

IT IS, OF COURSE, impossible to deliver the reflections of the nonexpert with complete confidence. Instead of being proclaimed, they have to be "hazarded." This is a procedure that has its drawbacks. For every Hans Castorp, there are thousands of Herr Albins and Frau Stöhrs, any one of whom might lay claim to a hidden philosophical talent. The philosopher, after all, is simultaneously everyone and no one. Still, with luck, our reflections need not be as arbitrary as the movement of a drinking glass sliding over the surface of a ouija board. Reason itself has roots as obscure as those of Naphta's *Pietà*, not the work of any "Mr. Individual Creator" but an anonymous work that culls together the dreams and sufferings of an entire age. Some dreams, we must remember, are wrought with meaning. Buried in ashes, the flame of the cigar suddenly flares forth. Can it have been fanned by anything but the winds of desire?

If Hans Castorp is the recipient of a philosophical education, it should be possible to determine what it is he has learned. Yet adherence to this principle has tended to lead readers of the novel astray. Mistaking the hero's awakening interest in ideas for an indication that the goal of his education is to be found in whatever beliefs he ultimately espouses, the reader is led into a guessing game as to which idea he has appropriated from which of his pedagogues. One discovers, for instance, a pendulum swing from the influence of Settembrini, the liberal humanist, to Naphta, the reactionary romantic, a movement that leads back again to the safer (and more politically correct) views of Settembrini. This movement is supposed to be "confirmed" by reference to Mann's own movement from the Naphta-like *Reflections of a Nonpolitical Man* to his later rejection of such dangerously "Germanic" ideas. Speaking against this "influence" model of interpretation, itself deeply rooted in the presuppositions of liberal humanism, is the entire theme of hermetic pedagogy: Hans Castorp's famous "receptivity" is a peculiar one, for it is bound together with an astonishing capacity to maintain skeptical distance from what he is being told. While his teachers intend to brainwash, his refusal to play along, his persistence in carefully "weighing" whatever he is told, transforms them into unsuspecting midwives of a genius that, though obscured by the very humility that makes it possible, is far greater than the capacities they themselves command.

Another way of trying to show that Hans Castorp becomes "safely" bourgeois by the end of the novel lays less emphasis on his political commitments. According to this reading, the education of Hans Castorp culminates in his long-deferred decision simply to do his duty. In this case, it is not only Settembrini but also his cousin Joachim, who represents the ideal. Once again, the key to the interpretation is supposed to be the resemblance between Hans Castorp and Thomas Mann himself: the artist who bourgeois-slavishly sits at his desk, effecting through hard work what others might consider the gift of inspiration.

But seven years is too much out of a man's life for the point to be that simple. Even if the interpretation were correct, we would have to understand what differentiates Hans's realization that he owes something to the world from the dull stupidity of those who simply do (and think) whatever they are told. The work ethic seems to function well enough with its system of external rewards. Someone who came to it out of an earnest search for meaning would represent no more than a peculiar anomaly.

A more sophisticated reading emphasizes Hans Castorp's fundamental detachment from all of the ideas with which he is bombarded. This reading also tries to justify itself by referring to Mann's own intellectual situation, this time his famous use of "irony." The task it leaves us with is evocative of contemporary discussions of Derrida: one tries to decide whether Mann's irony represents the despairing voice of philosophical nihilism or the reassuring voice of magnanimity and tolerance that characterize the ethically enlightened. What strikes me as significantly improved in this reading is that instead of focusing on "new beliefs that Hans Castorp has attained," it focuses on the real concern of a philosophical education, the state of the hero's soul. If Hans were simply gathering beliefs, then the longer he stays on the mountain, the more he should have to say. In fact, the opposite is true. In the beginning he chatters, nervously and nonstop. After he immerses himself in his researches, he comes to speak carefully and with commendable elegance. His growth is a growth into silence. By the end of the novel, he has nothing left to say. It would seem that we are being shown not the intellectual development of a scholar so much as the *via negativa* of the mystic. Sickness humbles the spirit, opening up access to forces more vital than those it itself commands.

To understand this rightly, we should resist the temptation to identify Hans Castorp too closely with Thomas Mann. The hero of *The Magic Mountain* became a warrior, not a writer. Whereas the ironist frees himself from attachment to particular ideas in order to move more easily and reflectively through the whole world of ideas, what Hans Castorp has done goes much further: he has freed himself from the world of ideas in order to facilitate his return back into "the stream of life." This is something very different from "doing one's duty." The latter, by placing strict boundaries upon our action (the distinction between good and evil), refuses to meet reality on its own terms. Genuine wisdom differs sharply from the outlook of the moralist, who is in love not with reality but with its idealized form, the idea of the "should," reality released into its completion. Wisdom, by contrast, is the love of reality itself. It is in terms of an approach to real wisdom that I would like to discuss Hans Castorp's final transformation.

To understand what happens to him, it may be helpful to direct attention away from the specific beliefs he endorses. Instead of focusing on what he thinks about, we have to look at what he is. A simple example is his growing resistance to the cold, one of the things that so intimidated his elder cousin, James Tienappel. In this regard, the real importance of the conversations with Settembrini and Naphta is the fact that they took place at all. Throwing one's soul before two such obstinate and dogmatic pedagogues is not unlike skiing into the face of a blizzard. Hans's fervor for "experimentation" goes beyond the speculative zeal that awakened Settembrini's interest. "Trying on ideas" does not take one to the very brink of the abyss.

It is his zeal for radical experimentation that wins Hans Castorp the designation "philosopher." When Clavdia, after her return to the mountain, refers to him as a philosopher and an *homme de génie*, she is responding not to his dialectical capacity, but to his willingness, even in the face of the intensity of love he feels for her, to recognize and affirm her freedom. It is a willingness that, irreconcilable with the intrinsic possessiveness of the ego, can only be understood if the ego has undergone some kind of death. To explain Hans Castorp's education by reference to his conversations with Settembrini and Naphta is to accept Settembrini's assertion that there are only two possible kinds of pedagogues, the humanist or the priest. In contrast, Hans has discovered another teacher entirely: the love of death. It is this love, he tells Clavdia, that is the real *lapis philosophorum*, the core of true hermetic pedagogy. This is not as far-fetched an idea as it might seem. It is Plato's Socrates, after all, who insisted that true philosophy arises not from the doctrines of a "teacher" but from the resolute anticipation of death. It is the same Socrates who affirmed his own philosophical stature not by articulating a new doctrine, but by the courage with which he met his own death. All of this is of immediate relevance to the story told in *The Magic Mountain*.

HANS'S *BILDUNG*, precisely to the degree that it is philosophical, is not developmental. He does not "accumulate" a specific series of ideas and insights. If he grows into the strength to take on life, he does so by the resilience with which he retreats from it. This accounts for the peculiar structure of Mann's novel. The "ascent" of Hans Castorp is always simultaneously a "descent." We have to take quite seriously Settembrini's warning that instead of climbing into the heavens (Davos Dorf is a mile high), Hans has in fact descended into Hades.

The descent brings with it a progressive opening of the self. The young man who first arrives on the mountain is nervous and fidgety, maintaining only with an effort his conventionally rigid facade. As the "lax" atmosphere of the sanatorium slowly enables him to release his grip on himself, it becomes apparent that the nervousness he displayed in the beginning hid something more powerful and serious at its core. He experiences his initial awakening in the form of a pounding heart and a racing mind. That he relates to the world around him with fear does not, however, mean that he lacks courage. Indeed, the readiness to encounter fear is the seed of the courage that Hans Castorp ultimately brings to the battlefield (which is why Mann, in the "Snow" chapter, calls fear the "prerequisite" of courage). Settembrini's advice, soon after Hans's arrival, that he return immediately to Hamburg is tantamount to the suggestion that he flee from the encounter with himself. This becomes apparent when, later in the novel, James Tienappel not only makes the return that Hans fails to make, but does so in an overtly cowardly manner. The reader is thus being asked to appreciate the real degree of courage it takes to accept and actively cultivate the kind of mental and emotional lability with which Hans has to contend. His natural sensitivity is intensified into a kind of anxious hysteria by the mountain's physical isolation from the rest of the world. To view this response as having anything to do with courage will seem highly paradoxical. One whose heart begins to pound whenever he conceives a penetrating idea will appear more cowardly than courageous. Yet Mann's conception retains a degree of plausibility. In the high-mountain void in which Hans Castorp is suspended, hidden feelings and repressed memories surge up within him. He does not shy away. Soon enough, he has let himself become totally absorbed in the mystery of being. It is in this condition that he falls in love — feverishly so.

He is visibly caught in a double movement. On the one hand, by opening himself to new experiences, both inner and outer, he gains a fuller and renewed sense of time. That is to say, he becomes stronger and healthier. On the other hand, by thus exposing himself, by becoming more receptive to the world around him, his entire system is thrown out of balance. He becomes chronically ill.

Settembrini, a philosophical materialist, is incapable of understanding the nature of Hans Castorp's sickness. For Settembrini, sickness is no more than an unfortunate physical aberration. It is more akin to stupidity than to slumbering genius. Indeed, this is the basis of his rejection of the compassion Hans displays by visiting the terminally ill. Such compassion, from Settembrini's viewpoint, is simply unnecessary. Nature protects itself by a kind of dialectic of stupidity: when pain is heightened, consciousness is reduced. Only a healthy organism can be genuinely aware. Those who suffer hallucinations, for example, are, by the very weakness that allows them to hallucinate, protected from the terror that we ourselves imagine would be ours if we suddenly began to see demons dancing in our midst. It is a reassuring thought. Hans's violent reaction, toward the end of the novel, to seeing the ghost of his dead cousin would suggest that it is not always true.

In contrast to Settembrini, Hans respects sickness, for he knows from personal experience that it can grow out of a hyperactive psyche just as well as from organic decay. In other words, it is bound to a "more" rather than a "less" of sensibility and consciousness. When Hans is lost in the snow he momentarily hopes for the merciful self-narcosis that Settembrini had promised. But the narcosis never comes. Instead, anxiety extends his awareness so dramatically that minutes unfold as hours. Even his sleep in the snow fails to bring with it the promised reduction of consciousness. Hans has a dream that is more vivid and intense than his normal state of awareness. It culminates in the revelation that a savage and unspeakable monstrosity underlies even the Settembrini world of light. The sanitary and hygienic health that is the goal of all Enlightenment rationality has disease at its own core.

What might be surprising is that Hans does not collapse into insanity when he peers into that awful truth, given in the nightmare image of witches gorging themselves on the raw flesh of dismembered infants. Instead, he is prepared for a "healthier" state of health than the one Settembrini, who has made himself oblivious to the dark ground of all Enlightenment, is ever able to envision.

It is, however, hard to say just what constitutes this new state of health. It is this difficulty which creates the illusion that *The Magic Mountain* is not about health at all, but about sickness. According to Krokowski (the sanatorium doctor who represents Freud on his way to becoming Jung), a healthy man is as self-contradictory as a square circle. One does not have to be a Settembrini to doubt the correctness of the slogan. It seems impossible, of course, that life, if it is the continual dissolution of form, could ever attain form's full perfection. But what, we may ask, if the highest life-giving form is the indeterminate form of death itself? A life that could somehow hold itself "in" death, if by no other means than by a full recognition of death's essential unknowability, would be the healthy life. Were this recognition simultaneously the basis of a reconciliation (this is what Hans Castorp seems to suggest when he refers to an active "love" of death), then there would no longer be anything to fear. Socratic ignorance, knowing we do not know, would serve as the conduit of Socratic courage. The dialectic is, however, an obscure one. For death to lose its sting, one would have to do more than know its unknowability. After all, a dog knows the unfamiliarity of a stranger when he sees one. Yet his knowledge hardly constitutes a reconciliation. When he barks, he barks in fear.

For Hans to solve this problem, he will have to do more than simply recognize the limits of reason. He will have to find some way to assure that death itself is no longer a stranger. While it is most unlikely that he can achieve any communicable knowledge of death, it remains a possibility that he can grow into an ever-deeper, if irrevocably private, awareness of death. "Barking" may represent a reflex that one can successfully overcome.

IN A WAY, death has never been a stranger to him. While he was still a child, he experienced the deaths, one after the other, of his mother, his father, and his grandfather. His life in the sanatorium, moreover, provides him with an opportunity to witness death on a routine basis. This includes some of those who were closest to him. His cousin Joachim dies of tuberculosis. Peeperkorn and Naphta both kill themselves — Naphta before his very eyes.

In his one "highly questionable" act, an act of boredom and confusion, Hans even defies the rule according to which there is something greater than "the pain of the impossibility of ever seeing the dead return to life," namely, "the pain of not being able to wish it." He, at any rate, has the nerve (and the gall) to summon forth, in a midnight séance conducted by Krokowski, the apparition of his dead cousin. In that moment, Settembrini's image of Odysseus's descent into Hades has become all too real. Hans Castorp has fed blood to Joachim, an act he immediately repents. The dead must be allowed to rest in their "beyond."

But what is that beyond? What is death? Hans is no closer to knowing the answer for all of the deaths he has witnessed. Even the apparition from the abyss provides no answer, for it is the apparition we see, not the abyss itself. Where has it come from? From Hades? From the hidden depths of the subconscious? Or from the dark ground of reality itself?

The novel presents us with two interpretive possibilities. Behrens and Settembrini, metaphysical materialists, maintain that death is a bogey, "vastly overrated," and that it is real only to the degree that our fears make it real. This is the old argument of Lucretius, according to which, because we die when we die, death is not anything we could possibly experience. It is simply of no concern to us. Krokowski and Naphta, metaphysical idealists, are just as convinced of the opposite. From their point of view, materialism is itself constituted by an act of denial. The pretense that there is nothing to fear is the most eloquent demonstration of the tremendous hold fear has upon us: we live in illusions because we are incapable of facing the horror of existence. Indeed, as they see it, the entire edifice of modernity — the attempt politically and technologically to control and stabilize reality — is nothing other than the sham construction of those who flee from the inevitability of death and human loss.

Even the stability of indissoluble matter, the foundation upon which the Enlightenment view rests, can be thrown into question. The true idealist regards what appears to be simply "given," nature itself, as a construction. This view seems not even to require any theological reduction of nature to a God speaking forth his creation. In the chapter entitled "Research," Hans not only speculates that the life process is a corruption (a disease) of matter, but he goes on to envision matter as a corruption (the dead husk) of energy. He has some good science to back him up. The issue is not, however, to be resolved on that level. The nature of the ultimate ground of reality cannot be pieced together. Thoughts only serve to camouflage it. Reality itself cannot be inferred, it must be seen. To be seen, it must show itself.

It would seem that precisely this is impossible. We are left simply with opposing metaphysical options. Coherent views of reality can be built on either materialist or idealist presuppositions. Recognizing the impossibility of deciding between the alternatives leads us to ironic detachment. The most that Hans Castorp can do, according to this viewpoint, is to remain hovering in a state of suspension between Settembrini and Naphta, at least until death itself answers the question. If the self disappears and the world remains, Settembrini will be proven right (though no one will be there to acknowledge the fact). If the world disappears and the self remains, Naphta will be proven right (in this case alone will genuine knowledge be possible). The death that decides the issue, moreover, can only be one's own death. The view from the outside settles nothing.

The possibility of a knowing death suggests, however, that irony need not have the final word. It is true, of course, that the distorting mediation of the self constitutes an insurmountable barrier to the full and complete self-manifestation of reality. Death alone holds out the possibility of eliminating the distortion. The decisive issue becomes, then, whether or not it is possible to die and to be reborn. If Hans Castorp's descent into Hades were more than a metaphorical one, the issue could be resolved — and in a manner that would escape the dogmatisms of both Settembrini and Naphta. Only one who has seen the truth could successfully dispense with all unwarranted assumptions.

The way in which literature traditionally depicts the self-manifestation of truth is in tragedy. Consider *King Lear*. The Gonerils, Regans, and Edmunds of the world spin their webs of hypocrisy and lies. The Lears and Cordelias get caught in the trap. When truth is revealed, as it always will be in the end (or the lie would not be a lie), the innocent are made to suffer. Some of them (like Lear) are in fact guilty — but without ever having willed the misdeeds they enacted. Others (like Cordelia) are innocent in every respect, for they understood the truth from the beginning. The suffering they undergo is anything but beautiful. Yet there is beauty in the victory of truth that makes what otherwise would be a fully gratuitous suffering necessary. It would be too much to suggest that such beauty could redeem an absurdity beyond redemption. It does, however, make it possible to face — and ultimately to accept — even that level of absurdity. Tragedies not only lift the veil that disguises truth, they also provide us with the strength to bear it.

While Settembrini is too droll a character to merit a tragic end, *The Magic Mountain* does effectively unmask the lie by which he has lived. The psychosomatic roots of Settembrini's illness become visible through the impact of Naphta's suicide on his "sensitive nature." He has become, despite his best intentions, a case for Krokowski rather than Behrens. This means, moreover, as already suggested, a "more" rather than a "less" in illness. The prophet of action is the only man who is so sick he has to remain on the Mountain. What one believes is not what one is.

The real tragedy has to do, of course, not with Settembrini, but with the whole world Settembrini represents. Having conceived the lie that death is a bogey (and that humanity can elevate itself above nature), the Settembrini world must be destroyed in the conflagration of universal warfare. Nor does it help that the ideology of Enlightenment is dedicated to the cause of world peace. The tragedy of being human is that an innocent heart does not leave the hands unstained (here, Oedipus is a better example than Lear). The very self-righteousness of the Enlightenment's commitment to peace, the arrogant certainty with which it distinguishes between good and evil, implicates it fully in the catastrophe that ensues. In the words of Naphta (whom Hans Castorp comes to regard as not only abhorrent but "almost always right" in his judgments), what the age of Enlightenment really desires is not what it preaches, the liberation of the individual, but rather the opposite, total destruction, the unimpeded reign of terror. Better stated, perhaps, it is the very liberation of the individual — his separation from the community — that is itself the destruction. Hans Castorp lives the separation. He attains complete "freedom" when, towards the end of his stay on the mountain, he receives word that his foster father has died. Having attained such freedom, he dies his death.

The deep depression (or is it simply a profound sense of peace?) that descends upon him after Naphta's suicide is the hermetic seal that cuts him off from the world entirely — and thus facilitates the slow maturation of his hidden strength and light. Hans Castorp's depression, his utter lack of connection to the "world," is the decisive moment in his long struggle for real health.

It would be a serious mistake to take any of this as suggesting that Naphta's reactionary fanaticism represents the true alternative to the fanaticism of the Enlightenment. The only alternative to fanaticism is no fanaticism at all. It is Hans Castorp who (besides being the true genius) is the true "child of peace." He is kept pure by his ability to refrain from exercising his judgment. His purity is his refusal to succumb to the attempt of his pedagogues to "politicize" him. By adopting the position of the pure observer, he is able to withstand the divisiveness that sustains all politics (which is always already warfare of one sort or the other). Humanity does not have to be polarized into good and evil. Ultimately, it is what it is. When, in the end of the novel, Hans enters the fight, he has no mission or cause whatsoever. Instead of fighting for one "side" or the other, he has become an agent of truth itself. This truth is absolute and unqualified. As such, it is antithetical to any judgment whatsoever (anyone who believes that it is possible to "speak" the truth has not even begun to fathom what truth itself is). Truth is visible only to the mind and heart that, sufficiently schooled in suffering, have become fully open to reality: able to bear the apocalypse itself.

In the parting image of *The Magic Mountain*, we find the thirty-year-old Hans Castorp enlisted in a regiment of younger and (one would think) much fitter men. The five-meal-and-nap-forever form of existence that had determined his previous seven years has come to an abrupt end. Deprived of food and sleep, Hans Castorp dodges shrapnel and treads upon the body of a fallen comrade. Victoriously "awakened," he has risen above the world by extending his shadow-world Hades into full-fledged, raging Hell. Nor does he "grant death dominion over his thoughts." He is not among those who succumb to fear by "lying down where it is not wise to lie down." He is, in other words, no longer the same man who, when his runaway imagination transformed a brief snow squall into a raging blizzard, lay down and surrendered himself to death. He, who once routinely terrified himself by listening, in the silence of the night, to the drumbeat of his own racing heart, is now racing across the battlefield to the rolling sound of drums that are real. Indeed, the lunatic sage is not only running, but singing. Between versus of Schubert's "Lindenbaum," an enormous shell explodes several yards in front of him. He dives to the ground and is hit by a large clod of dirt. Our old hypochondriac declares the pain to be "nothing" and gets up, not only to continue running but also to go on with his song.

Whether he lives or dies is undisclosed. The author himself does not know. In other words, the final fate of Hans Castorp is unimportant. It does not belong to the story. Hans's story ends precisely at the point where it ceases to matter whether he lives or dies. This "ceasing to matter" is Hans Castorp's final attainment, providing full confirmation of his battlefield courage.

It is not as negative as it might sound. Instead, it is the perfect mirror of Thomas Mann's own attainment, his dogged portrayal of reality, simply as it is, beyond all pessimism or optimism. This is not to say that Hans Castorp is, once again, simply a double of Thomas Mann. Quite the contrary. He is utterly and completely different from his author. He is, in other words, unthinkable as a projection of the authorial "self." It is, in fact, the gap between them that is the most essential issue. For only one who has died to oneself is capable of letting the other stand forth from its own ground. Just as Hans let Clavdia be Clavdia, he now let a war be a war. This is the secret of wisdom, the genuine love of reality, that it draws together the profoundest humility and the purest form of creative genius. Thomas Mann created Hans Castorp not by using him as a vehicle of his own self-expression, but by stepping aside, allowing Hans Castorp to become Hans Castorp.

What makes Mann's work so compelling is that it fully achieves that place beyond pessimism and optimism — and thereby beyond all judgment and all ego. We can fathom the greatness of this accomplishment when we recall the proximity of optimism to the contrived cheerfulness of those who are depressed but unable to bear the silence. It is fearfulness that needs to obliterate fear — courage takes fear into its heart. When we understand this, we are able to realize that Mann's resigned "neither-nor" bears witness to the reality of a Good that is situated above and beyond whatever it is that we make of reality. It is what gives us the strength to face even the possibility of eternal recurrence, our enslavement in a world that must sink, again and again, into the nightmare of its own formative chaos. The strength to face reality is the mark of the warrior. The ability not only to grit one's teeth and assume one's stand but also to reach out in love, to respond to the world in song, is the mark of something more. It is the mark of the philosopher, one who has learned not only to face but to love reality, as well. Where there is love, there is no need to contain and constrict and control. The power of such love is so great that even renewed descent into chaos will not stifle its song.

"Silence separates," Settembrini fears — and his fear is our fear, the fear of anyone who, insisting upon "the social constitution of the self," makes of newspaper reading a somber duty. It is the fear of the entire "age of information," the fear of all of those who flee relentlessly into garrulousness, in the vain hope that we will thereby find release from the solipsistic confines of the self.

What Settembrini does not know is that the inability of our generation to provide a sense of meaning (so akin to the inability which left Hans Castorp cast aside and abandoned on the top of a mountain) is an inability that arises when words have been "used up," when they have been spoken too often, dealt with as too self-evident, mechanically reproduced and thrown at us in a relentless flow of information that this is happening and that is happening, that this has happened and that has happened, that this will happen and that will happen, that this, that that, until finally meaning itself has dissipated like so much smoke blown to the wind. To retain their meaning, words have to be reforged in silence.

And silence there is. In the upper reaches of the mountain, where everything is frozen in eternal snow and ice, there is a silence so deep that it can only awaken fear and holy dread. To enter into it requires courage, for it is a silence capable of quelling our very identity. One can become lost in it for years, until every bond with the outer world is broken. It appears as the deepest of depressions, one that sinks into the awful finality of the grave. Hermetic elevation begins only after the elements are let apart, after the self dissipates and the body begins (as it has always already begun) to decay. Here, in the innermost depths, in the sanctuary of the Divine Himself, a Word slowly goes forth, a Word that can and will provide illumination and meaning, awakening not only life but the desire to live. Even the horrors of trench warfare will not put a stop to it. It is the novel itself which is the song. To the battle! With drums that beat and trumpets that blare! Resurrection from death and tomb! The message is an old one. By communicating it through the story of a hero as "ordinary" as Hans Castorp, Thomas Mann was able to make it available even to such as we ourselves are.

STEPHEN D. DOWDEN

2: Mann's Ethical Style

WRITING IN THE MID 1950S, Marguerite Yourcenar matter-of-factly points out what most literary readers of the time accepted as self-evident: "Thomas Mann's works have attained to that very rare category, the modern classic."[1] Since then Mann's reputation has lost some ground, in particular among academic critics. "The only provocative aspect of Thomas Mann's fiction today," writes one contemporary skeptic, "is their former success."[2]

Could it be that *The Magic Mountain*, like old Peeperkorn, has lost its potency? More circumspect skeptics have spoken of the need to demystify Thomas Mann and the "affirmative" criticism that has too long celebrated him uncritically as a modern classic. The demystification typically takes one of two tacks, or a combination of the two. It either attempts to assess the depths of Mann's social and political conservatism after his democratic turn, his residual anti-Semitism, and the antifeminist presuppositions that inform his imagination; or it takes up the homosexual revelations of his diaries to explore the bearing that Mann's obstructed desire may have had on his fiction and other writing.

Part of the demystification is no doubt fueled by the Cold War image of Thomas Mann among academics and literary liberals. Mann's larger-than-life presence as a one-man cultural institution seemed comforting to those who felt the need for a presiding intellectual presence in German letters, one that could serve to reconnect postwar Germany to its pre-Nazi tradition. Though Mann explicitly warned against dividing Germany into good Germans and bad Germans,[3] he still epitomized for many the good, politically respectable German. One thinks of Hans Castorp distinguishing between the Good Russians and the Bad Russians in the dining room of the International Sanatorium Berghof. As Good German laureate, Mann served as the most prominent representative of twentieth-century Germany's continuity with its classical tradition, and of Germany's integration into the larger scene of European and American letters. The reasons for this are well known. He had opposed the Nazis as early as 1923 (in his public letters to *The Dial* in New York), had eventually gone into exile rather than lend support to the Hitler regime (in 1933), and had spoken out against it from his strongholds in Switzerland and Southern California. Whatever his reservations about good vs. bad Germans may have been, Mann always cherished and cultivated his role as the representative of German culture: "Where I am, there is Germany," he famously declared to *The New York Times*.[4] Even if there is an element of wry self-mockery in the allusion to Louis XIV, few would doubt that he meant what he said.

Debunkers of the Mann myth point out that it took a great deal of time — until 1936 — before the writer could be brought to denounce the Nazis emphatically, in public, and without equivocation. That was three years after he had gone into exile, three long years after the Nazi seizure of power. Mann had worried about forfeiting his property and bank accounts in Germany, and about losing his readership to the Nazi censors and, with it, future income. Still, when he took the decisive step, he left no room for reconciliation. The break was complete — and not only with Nazi Germany. Even after the war Mann never returned to the Germanies except to visit and lecture. He continued to live in the United States but moved back to Switzerland when McCarthyism transformed the face of the America he had admired under Roosevelt into something alien and sinister.

A return to the land of the magic mountain was apt. He lived there in a world apart, the seemingly timeless, autonomous realm of his art and international reputation. Mann no longer took sides in the burning political issues of the day. He remained studiously aloof from practical politics, content to accept the honors heaped on him from both sides of the Cold War. It is true, as his last diaries show, that the novelist still longed to be *representative*. Of the many essays Mann wrote about the predecessor he most envied and emulated, the one entitled "Goethe as Representative of the Bourgeois Age" may best suggest a perspective on the amplitude of his own ambition. Mann would have liked to be representative for his era in a way that Goethe once had been for his own. Yet it is not clear, now that the Cold War has receded into history, of precisely what the postwar Thomas Mann was to be representative.

He was as out of sympathy with postwar Germany as his Serenus Zeitblom is by the end of *Doctor Faustus*. The postwar novel in Germany (it is probably reasonable to speak of the post-Mann novel) took new paths. The world of his old age was hardly touched by realities other than his legendary vanity (at his audience with the pope Mann's mind turned to Goethe's famous meeting with Napoleon, as a sort of standard of measure) and his lifelong preoccupation with death. Mortal fear of illness and death dogged him. He died in 1955, wondering if his achievement would be a timeless one or one bound to its historical moment.

Time and death, major themes in *The Magic Mountain*, are also major themes in modernism as a whole. They impinge directly on the status of his novel as modernist classic. Yourcenar, for one, perceives *The Magic Mountain* as a novel above all about the eternal human struggle between life and death. Mann's own way of thinking about secular modernity's relation to myth and eternity, concerning which present critics take a dim view, resonate with Yourcenar's.[5] Academic critics have more often sought the novel's durability in reading it as an expression of its time and its author's (representative) life. It bears the imprint of a crucial moment in German history.

Mann's private exertions against his own darkly romantic and reactionary impulses, and toward a liberal Western way of thinking, register especially in *The Magic Mountain*. As he wrote he gravitated more and more toward the enlightened political views of his clownish Settembrini. So it is that *The Magic Mountain* has been useful to critics in Germany and the United States who felt a need to fuse modernism with a democratic sensibility. Much has been written about his conversion, which took place in the middle of writing *The Magic Mountain* (1915–1924), from his idiosyncratically German cultural conservatism to a more cosmopolitan, more democratic, and then eventually anti-Nazi stance.

However, it is not unproblematical to anchor literary modernism — Thomas Mann's or anybody else's — in enlightened Western values. Contemporary critics who focus our attention on matters of race, gender, and class in the novel have often been severely critical of the modernist canon. The impulse is not new. Such misgivings are only the contemporary mode of a more general trend. As early as 1950, perhaps the high point of Mann's international prestige, Lionel Trilling expressed qualms about the politics of modernism. He worried that if

> we name those writers who, by the general consent of the most serious criticism, . . . are to be thought of as the monumental figures of our time, we see that to these writers the liberal ideology has been at best a matter of indifference. Proust, Joyce, Lawrence, Eliot, Yeats, Mann (in his creative work), Kafka, Rilke, Gide — all have their own love of justice and the good life, but not for one of them does it take the form of a love of the ideas and emotions which liberal democracy, as known by our educated class, has declared respectable.[6]

Interestingly, Trilling feels obliged to distinguish between Mann's essays — he would have known the anti-Nazi activist Mann of the 1930s-1940s rather than the pre-First World War reactionary — and the fiction.

The novels, he implies, have a subversive cast that troubles him. Trilling's misgivings about Mann's modernism are not without basis. Thomas Mann's bourgeois respectability and the respectable classicism of his fiction were an elaborate pretense (which, properly speaking, is what art is anyway), an attempt to stave off chaos. But how radical is Mann's imagination now, in the 1990s? Familiarity has blunted the edge of his fiction. Its classic status, exacerbated by the routine character of much academic criticism, has made Mann's modernism seem quaintly out of date to some in our era of unbuttoned sex and pornographic violence in film and fiction. Think of Hans Castorp's fit of discomposure early in the novel, brought on by the boisterous copulations of the Bad Russians staying in the room next to his. Mann is discretely oblique about erotic doings. We will never know exactly what happened when Hans Castorp went to get his pencil from Madame Chauchat. Times, mores, and fiction have all changed. Yet Mann's modernism remains, as I will argue, subversive.

His conflicted sense of his own sexuality, like Hans Castorp's ambivalence about settling his affections on Clavdia or Hippe, is not so remote from the postmodern era, or any other. Utterly to flout convention by yielding to the flesh is as pernicious to social order in, say, the fiction of Flaubert or Tolstoy, or in that of John Updike or Martin Walser, as it is in Euripides' *Bacchants*. For Thomas Mann, it was in part an immediately personal question. Since the publication of his diaries (1975–1996), we have gained clear insight into the true depths of his inner conflict concerning what he called, in the parlance of the day, his "inversion."[7] He was sexually attracted to young men throughout his adult life, yet — so far as we are able to judge from the extant diaries (he destroyed a few) — Mann never consummated his erotic fantasies, promptings of the sort that mean ruin for his artist figure, Gustav Aschenbach. A man of firm will (a virtue embodied in the pivotal image of the clenched fist in his *Death in Venice*), Mann mastered these urges, renouncing the dark satisfactions that beckoned to him.

He married, raised a large family of children (or, rather, was usually nearby while his wife raised them), and did not stray from the middle-class patriciate's conventions of decorum. The concept of marriage comes under scrutiny from time to time in his work. Mann believes wedlock drives its roots into demonic ground. In *Doctor Faustus*, Adrian Leverkühn scoffs at the sacrament of matrimony as a way of trying to swindle the devil. It serves the burgherly world, he says, by curbing the disorderly effects of carnal appetites.[8] Similarly, the Berghof's resident connoisseur of the demonic, Naphta, ranks marriage not among absolute goods but merely as civilization's stratagem for holding in check the flood tide of desire. Wedlock serves "solely to limit sensual desire and instill moderation, so that the ascetic principle, the ideal of chastity, might be affirmed without defying the flesh with impolitic severity."[9] Marriage is the institution that regulates the torrent of erotic passion by diverting its flow into socially productive channels.

One senses, in the commentaries of Naphta and Leverkühn, Mann's close attention to Goethe's *Elective Affinities*, a novel in which the nuptial floodgates of passion are figured literally. The catastrophe of a dam bursting coincides with the failure of the marital bond to contain the passions of Goethe's protagonists. The damage that an uncontrolled flood causes to the civic world resembles the damage threatened when the stability of marriage as a public institution comes unstuck. Each is a natural disaster, a failure of man to control nature.

In his own life Mann took great care to avoid any untidiness in matters of style or "bourgeois form," from the solidity of his marriage to his other domestic arrangements, down to and including the regimen of his stern workday. It comes as no surprise that his various biographers report the interior order of his household, like that of his stylish outward appearance, to have been fastidious. The judicious observance of style and form is, as Settembrini frequently points out, a symbolically significant, if slight, victory of civilization over chaos.

It is only a minor exaggeration to seek a parallel in Mann's sense of social and political order. Though he was as ineluctably drawn to the dark romanticism of illiberal German *Kultur* as he was to the forbidden pleasures of homoerotic sexual release, Mann prudently chose the security of modern, Western, middle-class values. In this commitment to order and moderation, as in much else, Goethe was his model. Goethe famously shunned the reckless sweetness of the artist's life in Italy in order to return to his station as a provincial German bureaucrat. Mann's comments on Goethe's pessimistic ethic of renunciation (*Entsagung*) are suggestive of his own life:

> The pathos of Goethe's renunciation — or, since it is a matter of something constant, something that suffuses and governs existence — his ethos of renunciation is of a personal sort. It is fate, the instinctual mandate of his particular national mission, which was essentially civilizing [*sittigend*].[10]

Though celebrated for his "pagan" nonconformism, Goethe renounced the transgressive pleasures the free spirit. He willingly, if not exactly gladly, acquiesced in the conventions of Europe's Christian morality. So argues Mann in his essay on *The Elective Affinities*, a piece he composed shortly after completing *The Magic Mountain*. Goethe forswears the artist's hedonism, Mann suggests, out of a sense of national responsibility. In his public life Mann felt called upon (and was often literally called upon) to shoulder a similar burden of civic responsibility, even national mission. From the middle 1920s through the late 1930s Mann did what he could to civilize his fractious nation with the means at his disposal: essays, lectures, open letters, newspaper pieces. However harshly moralists of the present may in retrospect judge his views, suppositions, and omissions (or the extraordinary strangeness of his emulation of Goethe), the civilizing intent is unmistakable.

Yet his imagination was not dead to the potential obstacles to and, especially, limitations of a victory of enlightened reason. After his murky tirade of 1915–1919, *Reflections of a Nonpolitical Man*, he did not express these reservations about liberal values in the lectures and essays that are the venue of his role as national pedagogue. Instead, the doubts and darker promptings of Mann's soul overflowed not into the public or even private life he lived but into the relatively contained space of his novels. Like marriage, the novel is a cultural institution — a "form," to use a key word from *The Magic Mountain* — in which the rich and potentially threatening disorder of human desire and fear may flow into productive channels or, at least, not be destructive. The novel is a theater of Dionysus.

The novelist imposes form on chaos not with story or plot so decisively as with the style of his narrative. For style, as Susan Sontag observes, "is the principal decision in a work of art, the signature of the artist's will."[11] The galvanic energy of Mann's literary style, like the urbanity of his personal style, expresses discipline and renunciation. Though an unbeliever, he was in his moral reflexes Protestant to the bone. Hard-won literary form is the point at which his ethics and aesthetics converge. He regarded the artist's need to achieve form as a moral imperative. It is on this imperative that Aschenbach founders, succumbing to the deadly allure of formlessness (the morally impossible homoerotic love for a boy) represented in the novella as the beckoning sea. Form holds disorder at bay. Consequently, Mann's prose is the occasion for a decorous, elegantly ironic, but also elegaic display of stylistic virtuosity. Its basic gesture is this: to recover for the twentieth century — the age of mass society and the concomitant sense of declining human worth — something of the nineteenth century's moral clarity and self-confidence.

It is reasonable to speculate that Mann's enduring appeal rests in significant measure on his stylistic achievement — but only insofar as its peculiar vitality is intrinsic to the tale he tells, as the embodiment of its consciousness. In *The Magic Mountain* Mann was able to define specifically modern perplexities in a style that was original and highly individual, yet drew its force from the gently ironic appropriation of conventions and norms of an earlier, reassuringly secure era. There is nothing similar in English-language modernism (with the exceptions, only remotely similar, of Ezra Pound's earnest parodies of medieval and ancient forms or Joyce's not-so-earnest contrafaction of *The Odyssey*).

The concern for style crosses over into character. Hans Castorp's grandfather embodies the burgherly solidity and moral clarity that Mann (and modernism in general) imputes to the nineteenth century, sometimes nostalgically, sometimes damningly. A disinterested look at the nineteenth century does not support either view, obviously, but it is easy to see how novelists of Mann's era perceived their own world by comparison with the one presented in, say, Trollope or Fontane, George Eliot or Tolstoy. In *The Magic Mountain* the figure that embodies the lost world is Hans Castorp's venerable grandfather. Though old and stodgy — and unabashedly reactionary — the old man has an emphatic sense of style and decorum that is intrinsically connected to the moral order of his world.

The text invites us to contrast Hans Castorp's dandyism with the sense of permanence that old Tienappel's ceremonial councilman's habiliment suggests: frock coat, broad starched and pleated ruff collar, fluted jabot, old-style wide-brimmed hat, silver-buckled shoes, and all the other traditional regalia. For Hans Castorp this image of his grandfather, captured and made permanent in an imposing full-length portrait, more or less guarantees the continuity of past and present. The ruff, especially, has symbolic importance for him. Its style is no incidental affectation but a symbol of form, power, and permanence. In it the grandfather stands above time. Hans Castorp's garb is of the moment. The modern style of wearing a necktie, naturally, is the merest vestige of that starched ruff's imposing expression of authority and authenticity. Hans's own sense of personal style is fastidious, but it also runs to bourgeois affectation and decadent triviality: monogrammed underwear and the like. "It was his maxim that no one in the empire except residents of Hamburg knew how to iron — and a badly creased cuff on one of his pretty pastel shirts filled him with a terrible unease." Such externalities do not express the underlying form of his existence; instead, they impose from without a tentative sense of order. His rotten teeth, mentioned in the same paragraph — always a telling feature in Mann's universe — suggest the rottenness of his inner life. For he is a child of material, not spiritual, values: "he dearly and truly loved living well, and despite his thin-blooded, refined appearance, he clung to the cruder pleasures of life as a gluttonous baby clings to its mother's breast" (30). His Maria Mancini fetish serves to keep this aspect of his character in view.

Mann's novel has most often been perceived as his statement about morals in the Weimar era, as an "argument" in the philosophical sense about making affirmative ethical choices. Ever eager to guide the reception of his novels, Mann has himself abetted this misprision. In one of his official pronouncements on *The Magic Mountain* he throws in his lot with the party of humanity, represented by the clownish Settembrini, without irony:

> This book, which has the ambition to be a European book, is a book of good will and resolve, a book of ideal renunciation of much that is beloved, many perilous sympathies, enchantments, and seductions to which the European soul has been and is disposed and which, all in all, has only *one* piously majestic name — a book of departure, I say, and pedagogical self-discipline; its service is to life, its will to health, its goal is the future.... Does Hans Castorp degenerate? Does he go under? He in fact rises up! [He] is brought to think about things and awakened to a sense of duty to his government in a way that in the "flatland" (and do we not have an ear for the ironic deprecation sounded in that word?) he would never have attained in his whole life.[12]

Hans Castorp learns to be a good German, do his duty, and serve his government. Well, there we have it. But *what* we have, perhaps, is the public man seeking to deflect criticism and channel into wholesome, even politically correct, categories a work of substantially more demonic force than its author was willing to admit or even see.

The basic thrust of modernism was (and remains) its subversion of the comfortable, self-satisfied, middle-class way of life that has simultaneously enhanced our material well-being as it continues to corrode the life of the spirit. This theme is not, in the parlance of postmodern criticism of the modern, "exhausted." It is the fundamental gesture of critique as central for Mann and Kafka as it remains now for Don DeLillo or William Gass, Milan Kundera or William Burroughs. Postmodernists continue to struggle with the hollowness of modern spiritual life that their modernist precursors were the first to explore in fiction. And the principal weapon in this struggle is not any particular inventory of ideas that distinguishes them from their predecessors but the artistic naming and taming of chaos by imposing form on it. The style of Kafka is as unrepeatable as the style of Thomas Mann — all of Mann's parody and irony notwithstanding. Postmodernists must naturally reject them to craft ironies of their own.

In *White Noise* (1985) — to take now a single but perhaps representative example (with the added appeal of being a novel that has attained that rare category, the "postmodern classic") — Don DeLillo abstracts his style from the well-worn idioms of science, technology, journalism, corporate jargon, and advertising, with all attendant euphemisms, verbal evasions, and inflations. Here is an exchange between the novel's protagonist, Jack Gladney, who is a death-haunted professor of "Hitler Studies," and his wife, Babette. Like almost everyone else in *White Noise* (because they have been exposed to a toxic spill) and in *The Magic Mountain* (because they have been exposed to tuberculosis), Babette is unwholesomely preoccupied with death. Her fear is so intense that she has submitted to the sexual demands of a research-and-development scientist who is illegally manufacturing a product called Dylar. Descended, perhaps, from the soma of Huxley's *Brave New World* or the Murti Bing pill of Witkiewicz's *Insatiability*, Dylar functions to anesthetize the fear of death.

In this exchange with his wife, Jack forces her to talk about her addiction to Dylar and her seedy affair with the renegade researcher who developed the drug. She describes the situation to her husband as an "indiscretion":

> "You call this an indiscretion, as if we haven't had a revolution in frank and bold language. Call it what it was, describe it honestly, give it the credit it deserves. You entered a motel room, excited by its impersonality, the functionalism and bad taste of the furnishings. You walked barefoot on fireretardent carpet. Mr. Gray went around opening doors, looking at the full-length mirror. He watched you undress. You lay on the bed, embracing. Then he entered you."
>
> "Don't use that term. You know how I feel about that usage."
>
> "He effected what is called entry. In other words he inserted himself. One minute he was fully dressed, putting the car rental keys on the dresser. The next minute he was inside you."
>
> "No one was inside anyone. That is a stupid usage. I did what I had to do. I was remote. I was operating outside myself. It was a capitalist transaction."[13]

And so forth. Jack and Babette communicate in the vernacular of technologically sophisticated, well-educated, middle-class consumers. It is "bold and frank" in a sense, but also hilariously disabled and remote from lived experience. Even sex, traditional stronghold of human spontaneity, has been colonized here by rational utility and its overcivilized, warped idiom. When Babette begins to weep softly, the radio intrudes (its automatic timer is broken). Seeking to comfort her, Jack plies his wife with food — banana slices suspended in Jell-O.

Verbal style embodies the impaired, disoriented lives of these people. Style and sense would be seamless here, were they not already identical. Jack and Babette are aware of their ironic way of talking. DeLillo is not making fun of them. He contrives that we see the humor is not his but theirs. Ironic wit, even at so tense a moment, is their defensive reflex against the language they find themselves forced to inhabit. Their habitual humor in deploying their damaged language is an aesthetic bulwark against the emptiness of lives dominated by consumer products, marketing slogans, product names, and transnational corporations. To mock the banalities of administered "usage" is almost as good as breaking through into a new, fresh, honest way of talking — but not quite. They know this and do the best they can with the language their culture puts at their disposal. DeLillo, like Thomas Mann before him, knows that modern language has to be treated ironically.

The form of DeLillo's prose is distant from Mann's, but its origin in aesthetic-ethical discipline and the desire to impose significant order on "a world full of abandoned meanings"[14] is identical. The centrality of death is identical, too, since death is the bedrock limit that brooks no denial. Jack at first refuses to accept Babette's dread of death, arguing that there must be some underlying cause for her condition, her weight problem, for example, or her height. With sublime candor she replies: "What could be more underlying than death?"[15]

Whether the threat is the double-edged sword of contemporary technology or the more ancient peril of infectious sickness, death remains the novelist's point of orientation. It is the vanishing point of enlightened reason and the discourse of science, an experience with its own set of fragile meanings. Mann uses the idea (if it is an idea) of disease and the specific conceit of tuberculosis to order these ideas. There are three separate, intertwined strands that are easily identifiable. Two are familiar, the Romantic and the psychoanalytic, and the third, though obvious, has remained curiously underdeveloped by readers of the novel.

In our era tuberculosis is no longer the threat that it was in Mann's day, at least in the West, though worldwide it remains a menace. In the nineteenth century and well into our own, "consumption" had a literary and artistic meaning as an ennobling, purifying disease: it spiritualizes the body as it consumes its material part, so that the soul's inner glow can shine forth. We may (or may not) see this light on the face of steadfast Joachim when he returns from below, now mortally touched by the disease. His eyes, "although they had sunk deep in their bony sockets, were larger and more beautiful than ever. Hans Castorp took comfort in that, because all the worry, gloom, and unsteadiness had vanished from them now that his cousin was bedfast, and only the light he had noticed early on was visible in their calm, dark — and, to be sure, *ominous* — depths" (524–525). Among the afflicted at the Berghof, only Joachim seems to have been granted the sentimental privilege of this traditional, romantic meaning.

His death, highly individual and thus filled with traces of some hidden sweetness, would not have been possible had he survived to go under among faceless millions after 1914. Looking back on the war in *Doctor*

Faustus, Serenus Zeitblom stresses the individual's loss of significance, but he does not ascribe that consequence to the war itself:

> This carelessness, this indifference to the individual fate, might appear to the be the result of the four years' carnival of blood just behind us; but appearances were deceptive. As in many another respect here too the war only completed, defined, and drastically put in practice a process that had been on the way long before.[16]

The Magic Mountain is largely concerned with these processes. Joachim's romantic death suggests, I think, that he must die because he is morally out of place in the debased modern world. He belongs to another era. But perhaps another factor weighs more heavily. The coming war would not belong to the professional soldier. It was the first war in history (after the much smaller American Civil War) to be fought by masses of middle-class, civilian volunteers like Hans Castorp. Not Joachim but Hans is the man of the future.

A second mythology of morals that Mann draws from tuberculosis finds expression in Krokowski's seriocomic pontifications about love and disease. He reverses the older romantic theme, adding an analytically intellectual twist and a widened cultural resonance. The disease-stricken body expresses not a pure spirit but a will blighted by needless self-denial. The symptoms of disease screen the suppressed, underlying "love." Illness is only love transmuted, the spiritual made physical (126) by means of what resembles a Kafkan metamorphosis. Unsatisfied inward need revenges itself on the abstemious flesh. When Madame Chauchat inflames Hans Castorp's sluggish Northern blood, he interprets his elevated temperature as fever, a symptom of illness.

Unrequited love does make you sick. We may think of Kitty Shtcherbatsky's debilitating illness after Count Vronsky jilts her in *Anna Karenina*. No one needs Krokowski to learn that lesson. But his Berghof auditors gather from their guru that the TB from which they suffer must be the body's response above all to sexual inhibition and frustration.[17] The message he is sending, of course, is that to recover they must let themselves go, open themselves to passion, and so be freed from the debilitating fear of sensuality.[18] Berghofians require little encouragement to heed his call. The sanatorium is jumping with amorous intrigue on balcony passageways, nocturnal bedhopping, adultery, and sensual indulgences of every sort, from institutionalized gluttony (five heavy meals daily) and sloth (the "rest cure"), to fads for spiritualism, dancing, photography, stamp collecting, cards, parlor games, chocolate, and any other passing craze that may momentarily serve, like Babette Gladney's Dylar, to blot out the laming knowledge of death.

The third meaning that Mann extracts from the disease metaphor is more complex. It has to do with how life and death are intertwined. More specifically it has to do with how Hans Castorp's life is interlocked with that of Madame Chauchat and with that of his cousin, Joachim. Each is marked by the disease, each represents death, but each does so in a different way. Before turning to them, it should help to clarify the general meaning of Mann's use of tuberculosis as metaphor. Its meaning is taken for granted: tuberculosis at the pan-European sanatorium is a metaphor for the spiritual malaise of European culture. Moral and spiritual decadence is expressed as somatic degeneration, especially of the lungs. The word *spirit*, after all, comes from the Latin for *breath*.

That tuberculosis should be the most appropriate metaphor, as opposed to, say, syphilis, typhus (as in *Buddenbrooks*), cholera (as in *Death in Venice*) or diphtheria, may require a few words of explanation. Consumption of the pre-First World War era, then also known as phthisis, involved the degeneration of the organism, often but not always the lungs. Joachim dies of laryngeal TB. When tuberculosis affected the respiratory system, the lung gradually became honeycombed with ragged, bleeding cavities. Hence the blood on the handkerchief of the coughing victim. More to the point, however, is the fact that TB was thought to have been unknown to the pre-urban world. Its appearance coincided with the rise of modern, urban society. So it was regarded as an affliction characteristic of mass civilization. As a disease endemic to city life, tuberculosis flourished in badly ventilated, crowded, unsanitary, industrial centers of the nineteenth century. And since the disease's true causes remained long unknown, and could not be treated anyway, a cure was sought in rest and above all in a "change of air." So it is that Zane Grey sends his enfeebled Easterners "out West." The tubercular protagonist, for instance, of *The Heritage of the Desert* (1910) must leave the morally and spiritually corrupt city to regain his health and manly vigor in the fresh air and moral purity of the great outdoors. It is against this well-worn background that Mann sends Hans Castorp up the Magic Mountain.

Because the unwholesome air of the teeming city seemed to be a precondition of the disease, and since observers had long noted the absence of TB in the Swiss Alps (and the Andes and the Rockies of New Mexico), medical authorities supposed the dryness of mountain air and its freedom from impurities — along with increased sunshine — to be beneficial to the disease's urban victims. The so-called open-air cures became common as of the 1830s and persisted until antibiotics defeated the disease in Europe and North America from the late 1920s until the 1950s. Before antibiotics, though, the way to treat TB was with clean, dry mountain air, a great deal of rest, copious food, drink, and sunshine. The rest was up to the wisdom of the body.

If tuberculosis was the disease endemic to nineteenth-century mass society, Hans Castorp and his cousin Joachim are the characteristic young men of mass culture: not powerful individualists but middlebrow figures shaped by the climate of the times, without strong moral sensibilities and with banal prospects for the future.[19] Mann repeatedly stresses his central protagonist's status as the product of modern mass society. Hans Castorp's comfortable private income does not save him from the curse of being average. For being of the mass is a qualitative, not a quantitative distinction.[20] Like his literary cousins Josef K. and Leopold Bloom, Hans Castorp is not supposed to point to what we might achieve, but where we really stand: he is *middling* ("mittelmäßig") in every way that counts — morally, intellectually, sexually, socially, politically. His desires and ideas are those of the broad, undistinguished average. He asks for little more than the tribal comforts of the *Grossbürgertum* to which he belongs, and these he regards as entitlements. His Maria Mancinis, his carefully tailored clothes, and other such consumer luxuries define him to himself more than does any sense of larger purpose or calling. He idles away his time unaware of the "crippling effect" that the historical moment exercises on his spirit and soul (31). He experiences the hollowness of mass society only as a vague sense of boredom. But the narrator clarifies for us its precise meaning:

> We have as much right as anyone to private thoughts about the story unfolding here, and we would like to suggest that Hans Castorp would not have stayed with the people up here ... beyond his originally planned date of departure, if only some sort of satisfactory answer about the meaning and purpose of life had been supplied to his prosaic soul from out of the depths of [the] time. (226)

Why does he stay? He is engaged in an unconscious search for a proper mode of being. His dalliance with disease and death eventually supplies one. With her voluptuous slam of the dining room door, Madame Chauchat awakens the slumbering burgher to the human condition's deepest sensual pleasures. She touches his primordial essence. Similarly, Joachim's death drives home to him a primordial sense of life's fragility and limit, perhaps its meaning or, possibly, its lack thereof — which is in any case also an orientation of sorts.

LET US TURN FIRST to his relationship with Clavdia Chauchat. She vividly embodies the erotic vitality that in this novel is paradoxically linked to disease, decay, formlessness, and death. Sexual desire goes its way without benefit of reason, and reason is the principle that underlies the logic of forms such as good government, marriage, and civilized social norms.

Clavdia, who flouts all of these (and does so naturally, casually, without even exerting herself), is usually likened by the men in the novel to animals of various sorts: kitten, thoroughbred mare, and she-wolf (Settembrini talks balefully about her "lone-wolf eyes"). Her animal nature and animal spirits set her apart from more domestic female varieties. Fräulein Engelhart, the novel's schoolmarm, wistfully covets Chauchat's freedom ("Russian women are by their very nature so very free and liberal" [134]). And of course Clavdia's free and easy ways especially draw men to her. Her door-slamming entrance to the dining room jolts Hans Castorp out his bourgeois torpor. Above all, conventional social forms cannot contain Madame Chauchat's large spirit; not even marriage — the institution that for Mann, as for Goethe and Tolstoy, embodies the good housekeeping of civilization itself — can. As a free spirit, Madame Chauchat is a living, breathing threat to the moral order of European life.

For this reason, seemingly, Settembrini cannot abide her. She radiates an exotic, undisciplined, unconstrained "Oriental" sexual power — and freedom — that imperils reason, the male principle of constraint. Madame Chauchat has many irrepressible sisters in modernist fiction. We think, for example, of Kurtz's wild African mistress in Conrad's *Heart of Darkness*, of the Slavic seductresses who are ubiquitous threats to men in the works of Broch, Musil, and Roth. In German literature this figure is perhaps most familiar in Kafka. Madame Chauchat has a lot in common with Leni of *The Trial*. Walter Benjamin has observed that Leni's webbed fingers mark her as antediluvian — water is her element and the ancient sign of universal femininity. She is a modern river nixie. Like Undine or Melusine or even Andersen's little mermaid, she must take possession of a man (because his element is the spirit) in order to obtain a soul. Josef K. succumbs readily to her more powerful desire.

The woman-fish's webbed fingers find an analogue in Clavdia's anatomy, insofar as it marks a certain primitive element in her character. Clavdia Chauchat's most Asiatic feature, the epicanthic fold of her Kirghiz eyes, is, as Hofrat Behrens assures Hans Castorp, an "atavistic vestige" (258) and as such a sign of her primitive, perhaps man-devouring nature. Settembrini is characteristically harsher in his view of her. He dehumanizes her, referring to her eyes as wolflike. The metaphor is telling. He sees her, more or less literally, as a predatory bitch. "Asia is devouring us," warns Settembrini in a dig at Madame Chauchat.

His meaning is double. The "us" refers to "us Europeans," first of all, insofar as he is trying to persuade Hans Castorp that insatiable Asia is somehow consuming Europe. In his view the sanatorium, Europe in miniature, is inundated with "Mongolian Muscovites," feminine and feminized predators from beyond the enfeebled pale of Western civilization. There is implicit in his caveat a sexual and racial innuendo, implying that Hans Castorp's unconcealed wish to offer up his healthy young European seed to the "lovely, contaminate creature" (209) points toward the dilution of what Settembrini has referred to as "our race."

In addition, this "us" refers to "us men" as fathers of the bloodline. Men must guard against this creeping, feminine, Asiatic degeneration of the white European male. The "International League for the Organization of Progress," a eugenic alliance of which he is proud to be a member, has taken up the problem of degeneration: "We are studying the problem of our health as a race, and the means for combating the degeneration which is a regrettable accompanying phenomenon of our increasing industrialization" (241). The apologetic subtext of his phrasing admits the mixed blessings of technological progress. As Settembrini sees it, progress toward the "perfect state" (242) involves "perfecting the human organism" (241).

There is an interesting problem of translation involved in this passage. Helen Lowe-Porter seems not to have believed her eyes. She engages in a bit of interpretive sleight of hand when she writes "our health as a race," which implies the German word *Geschlecht*, suggestive of the *human race*. Settembrini uses the word *Rasse*. What he actually says is distinctly sinister:

> A large-scale scientific program of reform has been drawn up, embracing all presently known possibilities for perfecting the human organism. The problem of the health of *our race* is being studied, including the examination of methods for combating its degeneration, which doubtless is one lamentable side effect of increasing industrialization. (241; my italics)

Settembrini, who lays emphatic claim to the high prestige of the word, takes care with what he says. Literary language is, as he expounds to Hans Castorp, the source of human dignity and moral discipline, the very foundation of Western civility. Consequently, we must take him at his word when he proudly declares that *all* methods for improving human bloodstock are being considered. The end in view is progress toward the *perfect state*, a monstrous fallacy by any sane political standard. Settembrini's utopian, even fanatic vision of final perfection has the makings of a totalitarian nightmare. And the evidence, in particular his undisguised animosity toward the Slavic and Eurasian patients at the Berghof, suggests that by "our race" he really does mean white people in Europe.

He is blunt about the threat from the East. "Asia surrounds us," he complains in the Lowe-Porter translation (241). Actually he says rather more sensuously — and obviously with Clavdia Chauchat in mind —

"Asia is devouring us. Tartar faces in every direction you look" (238). He feels called on to lecture Hans Castorp about the way one ought best to talk about things, especially time:

> "Do not ape the words you hear floating in the air around you, young man, but speak a language appropriate to your civilized European life. A great deal of Asia hangs in the air here. It is not for nothing that the place teems with Mongolian Muscovites — people like these." And Herr Settembrini pointed back over his shoulder with his chin. "Do not model yourself on them, do not let them infect you with their ideas, but instead compare your own nature, your *higher* nature to theirs, and as a son of the West, of the divine West, hold sacred those things that by both nature and heritage are sacred to you." (239)

In the figure of Settembrini various discourses of the era converge: race, contagion, sickness, degeneration, and the fear of mass society that is figured abstractly in the metaphor "Asia" and is deliciously incarnate in Clavdia's enticing body.

The irrational underpinnings of his enlightened rationality are showing. The "divine" West of Settembrini's unabashedly passionate, even romantic idyll concerns "our race," which excludes the likes of the Eurasian witchwoman (Settembrini's classical imagination figures her as a Circe). He fears that Hans Castorp will betray the superior, masculine, which is to say, more spiritual attentions that he has bestowed on him. Better to lose Hans Castorp altogether than to lose him to *her*.

> "I urge you: Consider your self-respect, your pride. Do not lose yourself in an alien world. Avoid this swamp, this isle of Circe — for you are not Odysseus enough to dwell here unharmed. You will walk on all fours, you are tipping down onto your front limbs already, and will soon begin to grunt — beware!" (243)

Madame Chauchat is the conduit for a force that wells up through her from the mountain below their feet. It is the telluric female power to sever the bond that joins brothers in the fraternity of men.

The rant against Clavdia and Asian blood discloses the nightside of Settembrini's instrumental reason. His impotent resentment of her (Nietzsche's rather stronger notion of *ressentiment* would not be out of place in this context[21]) is grounded in the irrational within him, which he fails to acknowledge. Pleasure is not his element; he dislikes women and music; he lacks true gusto, joie de vivre: "one could not even imagine his ever laughing heartily" (238). Clavdia brings out his irrational side as surely as she does Hans Castorp's, though in a different way. Lodovico may not exactly have a crush on Hans Castorp, but his attraction is plainly of the erotically tinged male-to-male sort that Thomas Mann knew so well: erotic but not sexual, in the jargon of the day. A hint of sexual jealousy flavors his hostility to Madame Chauchat. She is encroaching; Hans belongs to him. When Hans chooses Clavdia over him on carnival night, Settembrini sulks for many weeks. When he at last speaks again to his wayward pet, he is tactless and aggressive in his defensively superior way: "Well, my good engineer, how did you like the pomegranate?" (349).[22]

Originally Mann had conceived Settembrini as the figure of fun, an Italian organ-grinder, cranking out the same tune — reason, science, mass democracy, progress — over and over. However, by 1919 he had warmed up somewhat to Settembrini's point of view. In a diary entry of October 14, 1919, he wrote that Settembrini's doctrines remained "problematical." But he also had to admit to himself that Settembrini's was the only voice in the book that resists the general submission to death. This view of Settembrini, popular among advocates of a politically comfortable reading of the novel, does not persuade.

Like everyone else on the enchanted mountain, Settembrini cannot escape the claims of the irrational: death, desire, the sweet enticements of formlessness. Hans Castorp is right when he accuses Settembrini of hypocrisy and cowardice for refusing to leave the mountain (244–245). To the end his "mentor" remains an embittered and resentful ascetic, leading a loveless, hermitlike existence away from the give and take of life lived in real time, not on the magic mountain. He has no wife (even Socrates had a wife), no lover — man or woman — no family, no friend closer than Hans Castorp, no correspondents other than professional colleagues. He represents disembodied intellect, which is a strange ideal for a man only in his thirties. (Settembrini is not so much older than Hans Castorp, yet he affects the manner of a wizened sage.) Reason is his Dylar, and the body is his enemy, "because the body is nature, and nature — as an opposing force, I repeat, to mind, to reason — is evil, mystical and evil" (246). Small wonder that Mann expressed a certain reservation toward his views.

Clavdia Chauchat, by contrast, is not the force of corruption, lust, and disgrace that Settembrini imagines her to be. Her antibourgeois temperament is highly individual and has nothing in common with Naphta's cult of absolutist violence, cruelty, and terror.[23] His contempt for the flesh as seducer of the spirit outstrips even that of Settembrini. Both of them reject the carnal body as unspiritual, as feminine, as corrupt. Clavdia Chauchat embodies everything this pair of misogynists cannot abide. Though she is plainly intelligent (she holds her own even in conversation with Naphta, who, as we have good reason to believe, does not suffer fools gladly), her wisdom is of the body. She is open to life and pleasure, accepting of its costs and risks. She is no reckless, man-devouring voluptuary. In fact, the evidence shows her to be principled and reserved. We have every reason to believe that she is discriminating in her choice of lover. Even our luckless hero manages only one night of lovemaking with the elusive beloved — not much to show for seven years of passionate devotion. But then she also brings Peeperkorn to him, a towering embodiment of the life-force who, even dying, dwarfs the cerebral influence of Settembrini and Naphta.

Curiously, Peeperkorn arrives as a gift from Clavdia. His mighty presence draws them closer together — whether in chaste sanctity or carnal desire, though, the narrator wisely declines to say,

> for love cannot be disembodied even in its most sanctified forms, nor is it without sanctity even at its most fleshly. Love is always simply itself, both as a subtle affirmation of life and as the highest passion; love is our sympathy with organic life, the touchingly lustful embrace of what is destined to decay. (590)

Clavdia's untrammeled yet principled nature shows in other ways. Unlike the principal male characters, she is no joiner of organizations. There is an element of conformism in Naphta's need to belong among the Jesuit brethren and Settembrini's adherence to the rites of Masonic brotherhood. More important, she adamantly insists on certain forms, in particular the formal form of address. It is a small but telling detail. Eros has its own customs, etiquette, and protocols. Hans Castorp's relationship to her is joyful, a way of seizing life's beauty. Transcendence, freedom, and beauty, like Madame Chauchat's affection, are elusive, ephemeral, and not entirely respectable by conventional standards. For all his intellect, Settembrini has no comprehension of such love and pleasure. His vulgar catcalls to embarrassed village girls (a characterizing leitmotif in the novel) serve as an index to his impotence, repressions, and self-deceptions. His grotesque ogling ineptly parodies erotic flirtation. Settembrini has no sense of feminine companionship or authentic interest in it. His hooting whistles, kiss-blowing and leering, which occur only when he is in the company of male companions, serve more as a signal for male-to-male bonding than as an appeal to women.

I AM ARGUING that Hans Castorp's tryst with Madame Chauchat is an epiphanic experience for him, fully in the tradition of classic modernism — "as one of the last stands of belief in a secular age."[24] The "wicked, riotously sweet hour" (344) with Clavdia nourishes, liberates, and expands his hitherto prissy soul, opening it to the sublime mystery of self-transcendence, offering him a glimpse of the abyss. The thread of Mann's allegiance to Schopenhauer calls attention to itself here. Hans Castorp overcomes, however briefly, the subjectively unitary reasoning self to reach toward the unindividuated and timeless will. Clavdia speaks of self-forgetfulness (587). She awakens his prosaic soul to its own inner depths and to nature — and this is the mountain's magic — as the source of irrational power. To be cut off from the magic means to be shriveled, empty, narrow, dull, uncreative, i.e., the kind of complacent burgher that Hans Castorp had been.

But the erotic is potentially destructive, too. Pressed beyond the bounds that Madame Chauchat seems instinctively to respect, the urge to dissolve the self in erotic union closely resembles, or perhaps prefigures, the dissolution of the self in death. Hans Castorp — no Odysseus, as Settembrini has emphatically averred — could lose himself in such an experience. The danger is that his passion would become little more than a Dylar treatment. It does not because Mann qualifies it by linking it with one other defining epiphany. The second one is the death of Joachim.

Mann, as the consistent dualist he was, casts Joachim as Hans Castorp's counterpart and complement, that is to say, a double of sorts. The military cousin, straitlaced and unapologetically tied to the flatland, is Hans Castorp's second self. They are the same age, similarly middling in their blue-eyed qualities and defects of character, brotherly in their dealings with each other (Behrens calls them the Gemini twins), and in similar erotic dilemmas. Hans loves his slim-hipped, small-breasted Russian seductress; Joachim pines stoically for the more undividedly female Marusya, also a Russian — she of the orange-scented handkerchiefs, rounded hips, and ample, maternal breasts. Hans, destined by his flexible character (or perhaps characterlessness) to survive, yields to his passion. "Honor-loving" Joachim, marked for death by the brittle intransigence of his inner life, refuses to listen to his body. The steadfast tin soldier abandons the mountain clinic to stand his post down below. He does not act on his love for Marusya. He ignores the needs of his own flesh and returns to active duty with his regiment. But the "body triumphs, has other plans than the soul" (490). Joachim succumbs to the disease.

Up to that point Hans Castorp had willingly admitted to his enthusiasm for death and its rituals:

> "Don't you love the look of coffins? I've always enjoyed looking at one now and then. I think of a coffin as an absolutely lovely piece of furniture, even when it's empty, and if there's someone lying in it, it's really quite sublime in my eyes." (107)

His attitude toward death could be described as voyeuristic, even pornographic. During his do-gooder phase of the "Danse macabre" chapter, he takes a less than admirable interest in the terminal patients. There is a vulgar element to his intrusions on them. Young Karen Karstedt, for example, enjoys his fickle ministrations for a while. But even she, favored though she is, manages to die without his notice. This is remarkable in the tiny world they share and does not reflect well on Hans's character. "Hans Castorp had been unaware of her sudden turn for the worse and exitus; otherwise he would gladly have taken part in her burial, both out of friendship and his admitted love of funerals" (441). The enthusiasm for funerals is jaded. It helps give the measure of his decadence. But one event brings about a change in him. Losing Joachim, a cousin as close as a brother, unsettles Hans — gradually, but eventually with a profound impact.

Up to that point Hans Castorp had somehow contrived to live his life in death's proximity and yet repress the knowledge that he, too, must die. He had literally forgotten death. Interestingly, Hans Castorp's relationship to Joachim significantly echoes a death in *Anna Karenina*. In Tolstoy's novel the male protagonist of its parallel plot, Konstantin Levin, has a consumptive brother, Nikolay. The brother, a difficult man, plays only a small role in the novel, and that role is to die, as it were, in order to remind his brother, Kostya, to live. Kostya had been lost in gloom and self-pity because of a disappointment in love. His brother's death gives him the shock that puts his life, indeed life itself, back into perspective:

> His thoughts were of the most various, but the end of all his thoughts was the same — death. Death, the inevitable end of all, for the first time presented itself to him with irresistible force. And death, which was here in this loved brother . . . was not so remote as it had hitherto seemed to him.[25]

With the approach of his brother's death he grasps his own mortality. At first the "insoluble question" of death lames his spirit, but the affirmative — and fundamentally erotic — will to live rises powerfully within him. As tuberculosis gradually consumes his brother, Levin manages after all to link his life to that of his beloved Kitty Shtcherbatsky in marriage.

At his brother's deathbed — when, as a sign of the end, Nikolay begins to tug at his covers (Joachim echoes the gesture) — Levin falls again into the sense of horror he had known before at the "insoluble enigma" of death:

> its inevitability rose up before him more terrible than ever. But now, thanks to his wife's presence, that feeling did not reduce him to despair. In spite of death, he felt the need of life and love. He felt that love saved him from despair, and that this love, under the menace of despair, had become still stronger and purer. (593)

When Nikolay dies, Levin finds himself confronted with a new, equally insoluble mystery, one "urging him to love and to life": Kitty is pregnant.

How different, yet how similar, is Hans Castorp's tale of love and death. Joachim's cruel passing (and that awful rictus smirk that takes over his face) drives home all that is truly at stake in life — or almost does. Understanding ripens in Hans Castorp's limited imagination only later, in the famous séance chapter. He frivolously calls on Joachim to return from the dead (Settembrini, long years before, had likened Hans to an Odysseus among the shades). Joachim, who materializes in the field garb of the coming war, heeds his cousin's call. The effect of this desecration on our protagonist is stunning. Hans Castorp, chastened at last, whispers "Forgive me!" and weeps.

The moment is crucial. The novel's two basic stitches — Love (Clavdia) and Death (Joachim) — are now sewn, completed so far as shaping the spiritual life of the protagonist is concerned. The deaths of Peeperkorn and Naphta are mere variations on the theme.

The comparison with *Anna Karenina* remains instructive. For Tolstoy, the sacrament of marriage gives life shape, direction, and meaning. Hans Castorp, as our narrator tells us, is also seeking "some sort of satisfactory answer about the meaning and purpose of life" (226). Unlike Mann, Tolstoy vouchsafes his protagonist just such a sense of orientation, though he, too, is alert to the dark alternative. Tolstoy contrasts the wholesome, life-affirming love of Kitty and Levin — erotic but also spiritual — with the adulterous, merely carnal, and therefore death-haunted passion of Anna and Count Vronsky. In one of the novel's central (and grossly sensual) images, Vronsky recklessly races a thoroughbred mare to her death. Anna, of course, is the mare. In the end Levin lives a full life with his family, and Vronsky flings himself into a faraway war against the Turks. Love (wife and family) and Death (the Balkan Wars) dominate still, but each in its own domain.

Mann's world, the world of modernism, lacks the clarity of Tolstoy's moral universe. Hans Castorp's passion for Madame Chauchat is explicitly adulterous, echoing in a more or less comic register Vronsky's erotic love for his Anna. However, aside from nationality, the seductive, playful, elusive Clavdia shares little with Anna Karenina or Kitty Shtcherbatsky. For Thomas Mann, writing after the colossal bloodbath of the First World War, a conjugal solution to Hans Castorp's search for meaning would have seemed trivial and ridiculous. Consequently, it makes sense that Castorp's eroticism, like Vronsky's, is more closely entwined with death than with marriage, children, and the affirmation of life.

WHERE, THEN, do we stand at the end of the novel? Has Hans profited from his experiences and emerged from his seven-year sleep wiser, morally sound, with independent judgment? Mann himself suggests that this is the case, and perhaps it is true. However, the undertow of the novel's subversive irony — emphatically a matter of its style more than of its author's conscious intent — is powerful. It militates against the more comforting certainties that Mann seems to intend.

Perhaps a reversal of the erotic flow takes place: Hans, like Vronsky (and Eduard in *The Elective Affinities*), redirects his erotic energy, putting it in the service of death. Swept along with the passions of the time, he joins the German war effort. However benign Mann's considered intentions may have been, the end of the novel fuses eros (the will to life, creativity, and pleasure) with Hans Castorp's long-standing sympathy for the abyss. Warlike aggression may save him from his own self-absorbed morbidity by extroverting the attraction to death. Sexual feeling is easily transformed into aggression, replacing the desire (or at least the passive willingness) to die with the will also to kill.

Is this the old conservative Mann, seduced by the glory of service to the Fatherland? Possibly, but probably not. And though the Freudian element of this is also plain, it is probably not traceable to Mann's reading of Freud. This turn is simply implicit in the compelling logic of Mann's own novelistic thought. The novelist, nostalgic for the world of Goethe and Tolstoy, would like to identify his hero with love. Yet his analytical vision is clear and unsentimental. He cannot keep from identifying him also with death. Love, as Thomas Mann knew, does not make history. Death, expressed as violence and war, does. So Hans Castorp, Mann's harmless little dormouse, emerges from his seven-year reverie into a larger, more intense dying. This is the novel's ironic, subversive power: it tells the tale not of democracy's coming victory, but of death's.

"*For the sake of goodness and love, man shall grant death no dominion over his thoughts*" (487). Mann's high-sounding, heartfelt moral is hard to uphold in the lethal ruck of a World War. Irony, the basic tool in the ethical style of the novel, governs the conclusion of *The Magic Mountain*. Does Hans Castorp do the right thing? Does he show his true colors, express his hard-won spiritual maturity by answering the call of the Fatherland? Or is Hans Castorp's erotic attraction to nothingness simply turned outward by historical circumstance, extroverted into the deadly action of war — which is manifestly where the novel had been headed since its beginning? Joining the lemminglike rush of average men into the patriotic abyss, Hans willingly, even enthusiastically, becomes the cannon fodder of the historical moment. It is difficult to take seriously the idea that Hans Castorp's post-mountain self mirrors the image of a social and political ideal. The First World War was a famously spurious answer to the era's ennui, and so also to Hans Castorp's emptiness, his yearning for a sense of life's purpose and meaning. The war gave full vent to Europe's most deep-seated, destructive impulses.

In *The Magic Mountain* Mann has little to say about the manifold political, economic, and social forces of that historical moment. He concentrates his novelist's X-ray vision on the interior forces that move Hans Castorp, who, like most others in modern mass society, is a man of not very independent judgment. It may not be the ideal of duty and patriotism that underlies his service to the fatherland (in this he is, as in all other ways, middling) so much as a native sympathy for annihilation that makes death, violence, and war seem the logical, even inevitable form of his self-expression. By this transmutation of nothingness into action — violence and destruction — death comes to seem affirmative: killing the enemy, dying for one's country. The novel's pessimism, and its subversive force, rest on this view of our likeable protagonist as mass man ineluctably attracted to mass death in the First World War. The war was widely perceived as an opportunity for Europe's moral regeneration.[26] By 1924 Mann knew the folly of this thought. He knew where it had led Europe and Germany. His Hans Castorp, in his deluded eagerness to take part in the great killing, is in no way extraordinary.

Mann, as I have pointed out, resisted the kind of dark reading I have offered here. His classic essays of the period — "Goethe and Tolstoy" (1921), for example — attempt to celebrate the classic humanism of his predecessors. Mann aligns himself with that life-affirming tradition. Perhaps Hans Castorp has learned to do his duty, or perhaps — as seems more likely to me — a more complex irony is at work. *The Magic Mountain* may not bear out the humanistic optimism of Mann's public stance. Certainly his novel does not luxuriate decadently in the thought of death. It reluctantly pays death its due at the beginning of an era that would see unprecedented heaps of corpses. Mann knew the human cost of the First World War, which — as he could not know, but which we do know — was only the beginning.

Still, its horrors were sufficiently impressive. The novel's analytic pessimism, characteristic of subversive modernism, need not collapse into decadent aestheticism. Mann did not invent the eros of war and death; he was only trying to write a novel that might comprehend it. Moreover, the novel as a form — especially when coupled with the individual accomplishment of Mann's endlessly resourceful, highly wrought, playful style as a writer in that form — are themselves an act of resistance. If death means the dissolution of form, as Mann's figures repeatedly aver, then the cultivation of literary form can be a way of maintaining a sense of hardened resolve in the face of death's inevitability. Mann's characteristically ironic style is a way of looking at profound and unsettling truths about human ephemerality and imperfection without being reduced to the kind of morally paralyzing horror that Konstantin Levin experiences when confronted with the certainty of his brother's death.

Notes

[1] Marguerite Yourcenar, "Humanism and Occultism in Thomas Mann," in *The Dark Brain of Piranesi and Other Essays*, trans. Richard Howard (New York: Farrar Straus Giroux, 1984), 199.

[2] Dagmar Barnouw, *Weimar Intellectuals and the Threat of Modernity* (Bloomington: Indiana UP, 1988), 121. Among German writers, Mann's reputation declined immediately after the Second World War. Many were angered by Mann's criticism of those who remained in Hitler's Germany and by his refusal to return to Germany to live. But more significantly, many younger writers were seeking a new literary idiom and naturally had to free themselves from the preeminence of that established by Mann. Martin Walser's critiques of Mann, such as that in his Frankfurt lectures, *Selbstbewußtsein und Ironie* (Frankfurt am Main, 1981) are the best known. Among critics (and especially among the senior dignitaries of public literary criticism, such as Hans Mayer and Marcel Reich-Ranicki) Mann's reputation remained unclouded. But among the younger critical generation of the 1980s and 1990s Mann's prestige is, as in the United States, regarded with suspicion.

[3] "Deutschland und die Deutschen," *Gesammelte Werke*, 11 (Frankfurt am Main: S. Fischer, 1960), 1126ff.

[4] "Mann Finds U.S. Sole Peace Hope," *The New York Times*, February 22, 1938, p. 13.

[5] New Age forefather Joseph Campbell argues that in *The Magic Mountain* and in other works by Mann ancient motifs persist "in such a way as to suggest that in our lives today, largely unrecognized at present, the archetypes of mythic revelation are manifest and operative still." Joseph Campbell, *The Masks of God: Creative Mythology* (New York: Viking, 1968), 321–348, here p. 325.

[6] Lionel Trilling, *The Liberal Imagination: Essays on Literature and Society* (London: Mercury Books, 1961), 98.

[7] Among the drift of books that accumulated around the manuscript of Thomas Mann's *Magic Mountain* was Hans Blüher's widely read *Role of the Erotic in Male Society*. Blüher speaks explicitly of the "Typus inversus," the homoerotic man. The male-to-male bond produces society's creative component, he argues, while the family serves not culture, spirit, and achievement but simply the propagation of the species. Hans Blüher, *Die Rolle der Erotik in der männlichen Gesellschaft: Eine Theorie der menschlichen Staatsbildung nach Wesen und Wert*, 2 vols. (Jena: Eugen Diederichs, 1917–1919). In a diary entry of September 17, 1919, Mann recorded: "Read Blüher in the evening. One-sided, but true. There is no doubt in my mind that 'even' my *Reflections of a Nonpolitical Man* are an

expression of my sexual inversion." Thomas Mann, *Tagebücher 1918–1921*, ed. Peter de Mendelssohn (Frankfurt am Main: S. Fischer, 1979), 303.

[8] Thomas Mann, *Doctor Faustus*, trans. Helen T. Lowe-Porter (New York: Knopf, 1948), 186–187.

[9] Thomas Mann, *The Magic Mountain*, trans. John E. Woods (New York: Vintage, 1996), 579.

[10] Thomas Mann, "Zu Goethes *Wahlverwandtschaften*," in *Goethes Laufbahn als Schriftsteller* (Frankfurt am Main: Fischer Taschenbuch, 1982), 175. The essay was originally published in 1925.

[11] Susan Sontag, "On Style," in *A Susan Sontag Reader* (New York: Vintage, 1983), 152.

[12] Thomas Mann, "Vom Geist der Medizin," *Gesammelte Werke,* 11 (Frankfurt am Main: S. Fischer, 1960), 595–596.

[13] Don DeLillo, *White Noise* (New York: Penguin, 1986), 194.

[14] *White Noise*, 184. In *The Magic Mountain* the narrator connects Hans Castorp's plight to the absence of meanings: "We would like to suggest that Hans Castorp would not have stayed with the people up here even this long beyond his original date of departure, if only some sort of satisfactory answer about the meaning and purpose of life [*Sinn und Zweck des Lebensdienstes*] had been supplied to his prosaic soul from out of the depths of time." *The Magic Mountain*, 226.

[15] *White Noise*, 197.

[16] *Doctor Faustus*, 365.

[17] Mann's Dr. Krokowski interestingly links *The Magic Mountain* to the present. His comic Freudianizing among the suggestible Berghof population anticipates the later, highly lucrative, and not so funny Freudianizing of the latter-day Krokowskis of the mass media and self-help rackets who have made social epidemics of recovered memory, chronic fatigue, satanic ritual abuse, multiple personality disorder, alien abduction and other psychogenic "syndromes." See Elaine Showalter, *Hystories: Hysterical Epidemics and Culture* (New York: Columbia UP, 1997).

[18] "As much as TB was celebrated as a disease of passion, it was also regarded as a disease of repression. The high-minded hero of Gide's *The Immoralist* contracts TB (parallelling what Gide perceived as his own story) because he has repressed his true sexual nature; when Michel accepts Life, he recovers. With this scenario, today Michel would have to get cancer." Susan Sontag, *Illness as Metaphor* (New York: Farrar Straus Giroux, 1977), 21.

[19] "Geistige Zeitbestimmtheit, . . . geistige-sittliche Indifferenz, Glaubenslosigkeit und Aussichtslosigkeit." *Tagebücher*, June 9, 1919.

[20] "By masses," wrote Ortega in his decisive study of 1930, "is not to be understood, solely or mainly, 'the working masses.' The mass is the average man. In this way what was mere quantity — the multitude — is converted into a qualita-

tive determination: it becomes the common social quality, man as undifferentiated from other men, but as repeating in himself a generic type." José Ortega y Gasset, *The Revolt of the Masses*, trans. anonymous (New York: Norton, 1993), 13–14.

[21] Settembrini suffers from what Nietzsche describes as a life-negating asceticism. It has a hatred of the human, especially all that is animal in human beings, a rejection of the senses, of happiness and beauty and a longing for escape from "appearance, change, becoming, death, wishing, from longing itself — all this means — let us dare to grasp it — a *will to nothingness*, an aversion to life, a rebellion against the most fundamental presuppositions of life. . . ." *On the Genealogy of Morals and Ecce Homo*, ed. and trans. Walter Kaufmann (New York: Vintage, 1967), 162–163.

[22] Settembrini likens Hans Castorp to the ravished maiden Persephone, all but lost to the upper world. She belongs among the dead. But just how might Settembrini know that Hans Castorp has tasted of the pomegranate? Gossip? Spying? Conjecture? None of the possible answers suggests the disinterested commentary of an uninvolved party. There are limits to his intellectual detachment: "Despite his contemptuous attitude toward the society of the place, he always knew everything that went on" (151). Settembrini's pique here stems from an ill-concealed, probably sexual jealousy.

[23] Naphta's theocratic "communism" (though radical communalism would be closer to conventional usage, since no Marxists of his or any other day would likely have claimed him as one of their own) rejects the sovereignty of the self-reliant, rational individual. This man-centered humanism he regards as the self-aggrandizing ideology of bourgeois culture. History is relegated to the domain of the inessential. Not unlike the French antihumanists of the 1960s and 1970s, Naphta sees "man" as a Western mystification, an historically contingent construct whose dissolution is drawing near. And his cold-blooded embrace of terror, the solvent to be employed in the dissolution of subjective autonomy and individual freedom, anticipates the actual policies of subsequent regimes. Hitler, Stalin, Mao, and Pol Pot sought to eradicate the various ideas and institutions in which the ideology of man had established itself as self-evident: liberalism, democracy, individualism, constitutionalism, and human rights. Similarly, the return of theocracy to the Islamic world since the Shah of Iran was deposed gives a certain currency to Naphta's seemingly remote pontifications.

[24] Charles Baxter, "Against Epiphanies," in his *Burning Down the House* (Saint Paul: Graywolf, 1997), 62. Baxter observes that overuse has devalued epiphany as a literary device, especially since modernism. I would argue that *The Magic Mountain* contains both authentic epiphany (that of eros) and the more familiar inflated form, embodied in the conceptually overburdened "Snow" chapter. In it Thomas Mann says too much. He attempts to give his readers a vocabulary of images overly freighted with reference to prefabricated ideas and concepts. Because of its nature — philosophical propositions thinly disguised as poetic images — this chapter has assumed an exaggerated importance among interpreters.

It is eminently interpretable. Words, speaking, writing, and literature are, as Settembrini avers, "a splendid and republican achievement" (348) that belongs to the world of the intellect. Hans Castorp's epiphany is of another order entirely, recalling his experience with Pribislav Hippe: "From the start, there was not the least reason to give it a name; the furthest thing from his mind was ever to talk about the matter — that would have been most unlike him and he felt no need to do so. Besides, to give a name would have meant, if not to judge it, at least to define it, to classify it as one of life's familiar, commonplace items, whereas Hans Castorp was thoroughly convinced at some subconscious level that anything so personal should always be shielded from definition and classification" (119). Madame Chauchat herself, and not some laborious description of Hans Castorp's feelings about her, is the metaphor that transfuses meaning to the reader. She is visible spirit, the epiphanic object that is a solid body yet achieves in this novel a rare kind of poetic transparence (emblematized in the X-ray she gives Hans as a keepsake) that frames a meaning that is otherwise beyond words. The figure of Madame Chauchat functions as a lightning rod that attracts meanings from namelessness.

[25] Leo Tolstoy, *Anna Karenina*, trans. Constance Garnett (New York: Modern Library, 1950), 413.

[26] Roland N. Stromberg, *Redemption by War: The Intellectuals and 1914* (Lawrence: U of Kansas P, 1982).

EUGENE GOODHEART

3: Thomas Mann's Comic Spirit

THE NARRATOR OF *THE MAGIC MOUNTAIN* begins by urging patience in the reader. The journey to the mountain will be a long one, the stay, though anticipated to be short, will be much longer (seven years in duration). The eventful uneventfulness of Hans Castorp's visit to this tubercular cousin, Joachim Ziemssin, occurs in slow time. The passage of time is of course one of the great themes of the novel, endlessly and oppressively reflected upon by the narrator. The reader needs to be patient, if he is to be rewarded. The narrator remarks: "and so this storyteller will not be finished telling our Hans's story in only a moment or two."[1]

We have lost the habit of slow time. Our attention span, conditioned and exemplified by television, demands speedy delivery, rapid change, instant gratification. *The Magic Mountain* requires an audience that will find relief from the speed with which things pass in contemporary society. Slow time is the time of illness. For the chronically ill, excluded from the pressures of the workaday world, there are no deadlines to be met, no responsibility to others. There is only the narcissistic concern with one's own body: the schedule of doctor's visits and the taking of medicine, the routine of meals. The sick person must learn patience. In the Berghof sanatorium, the site of the novel, one aspires to be a patient.

It has been often said of the novel that the illness of the residents of the sanatorium (drawn from a cross section of Europeans: Germans, Italians, Austrians, Russians, etc.) reflects a civilization in crisis. The novel is set at a time immediately before the Great War. At the end, the residents leave the sanatorium as the alarums of war are sounded, and the last view we have of Hans Castorp is in battle fatigues trudging through the mud in a hail of fire. The publication date is 1924, three years after the publication date of *Civilization and Its Discontents*. The ending of the novel has an uncanny resemblance to the ending of Freud's essay. "And out of this worldwide festival of death, this rutting fever that inflames the rainy evening sky all around — will love someday rise up out of this too?" (706). Freud writes: "And now it is to be expected that the other of the two

'Heavenly Powers,' eternal Eros, will make an effort to assert himself in the struggle with his equally immortal adversary [Thanatos]. But who can foresee with what success and with what result?"[2]

This may be taking the novel more seriously or rather with a different kind of seriousness than intended. Certainly the characters themselves seem not to sense crisis or take their illness as an omen of impending catastrophe. Castorp explains to his uncle, James Tienappel, who on a visit to the sanatorium cannot understand Hans's infatuation with it. The "first effect of [the mountain air] was greatly to enhance illness to exuberant eruption, so to speak. . . . Had he never noticed that there is something exuberant about the eruption of illness, as if the body were celebrating" (422). The narrator's view is by no means certain, but Castorp's self-possession in the scene and his uncle's bewildered retreat (he arrives with confidence that he can take Castorp back with him to the flatlands and departs alone in haste) suggests the narrator's complicity with Castorp. Reading *The Magic Mountain* is like the experience of the patient who awaits the diagnosis of the doctor as he probes the body and listens for symptoms of disease. And it is, curiously enough, free of anxiety. Both the reader and the patient perversely do not want to have a clean bill of health, for illness as it turns out is a sign of vitality.

The concluding sentence about love rising up is suspect — and not simply for its sentimentality. The opposition between love and death in the last sentence is belied by the narrative, which identifies love with disease and death. Castorp falls passionately in love with Clavdia Chauchat, the fascinating "Asiatic" woman with the Kirghiz eyes. She embodies "the genius of illness," which confers upon her a "freedom" to be herself. Illness is not a misfortune that befalls Madame Chauchat, but her very essence. "For she is a woman of genius, [Hans Castorp said], and her husband has . . . granted her freedom to make use of her genius, either because he is very stupid or very intelligent, I cannot say, not knowing the fellow. In any case, it was wise of him, for it is her illness that confers such freedom on her, it is the genius of illness that she serves" (600). In falling in love with her, Castorp must overcome a revulsion that he initially experiences from her bad manners (she slams the door on entering the dining room). And he can overcome it only when he accustoms himself to the sanatorium as the habitation of illness. Castorp not only has to accept the fact that he is ill (he resists the diagnosis in the early days of his visit), he has to experience it as a celebration of his body. The illness arouses his desire for Clavdia, whose presence makes him feverish. Mann is, of course, exploiting familiar knowledge about the erotic effects of tuberculosis. We know that the feverishness of the imaginations of Keats and Lawrence, for example, owed a great deal to their tubercular condition.

Illness, like everything else in the novel, becomes an idea. It figures prominently in the philosophical debates between Settembrini, the exponent of Enlightenment, and Naphta, the Jesuitical exponent of a paradoxical combination of medievalism and communism. As one might expect from an Enlightened reasoner, Settembrini views illness as a form of irrationality that can be cured and ultimately banished from the world. Health is the reason of the body.

> Illness is definitely not elegant, and certainly not venerable — such a view is itself a sickness, or leads to it. Perhaps I can best arouse your abhorrence of that idea by telling you that it is outdated and ugly. It comes from an era of superstitious contrition, when harmony and health were demeaned and distorted into caricature, a fearful era, when harmony and health were considered suspicious and devilish, whereas infirmity in those days was as good as a passport to heaven. Reason and enlightenment, however, have banished those shadows, which once lay encamped in the human soul. (96)

Castorp listens respectfully to Settembrini's eloquent speech ("a regular aria"), "both bewildered and abashed" (97). In a sense, the argument is out of place, for it denies what is the pervasive condition of the scene of the novel — the illness, latent or manifest, of all its residents.

Settembrini's own condition belies the argument, confirming, as it were, its abstract and utopian character. (We know that Mann was settling scores with his brother Heinrich, a writer in the liberal Enlightenment tradition, in his satiric though not unaffectionate depiction of Settembrini. In "The Making of the Magic Mountain," his commentary on the novel appended to the Lowe-Porter translation, Mann speaks of Settembrini as "sometimes a mouthpiece for the author, but by no means the author himself."[3] This sounds like a second thought about a character who seems more clown than spokesman for Mann's ideas.)

Naphta's affinity for illness alone would make him the more compelling figure. It is not simply a matter of who is right and who wrong, but the way the imagination of illness energizes argument, making it more interesting in its complication. To return man to a healthy nature is to dehumanize him and turn him into an animal. Felix culpa. To fall from grace is to fall into disease and death, a human condition.

> Illness was supremely human, Naphta immediately rebutted, because to be human was to be ill. Indeed, man was ill by nature, his illness was what made him human, and whoever sought to make him healthy and attempted to get him to make peace with nature, to "return to nature" (whereas he had never been natural) . . . wanted nothing more than to dehumanize man and turn him into an animal. Humanity? Nobility? The Spirit was what distinguished man — a creature very much set apart from

nature — from the rest of organic life. Therefore, the dignity and nobility of a man was based in the spirit, in illness. In a word, the more ill a man was the more highly human a man was and the genius of illness was more human than that of health. (456)

The Christian doctrine of humility is implicit in this affirmation of illness; the sick body is a confession of the body's mortality. Health only cultivates the illusion that we will live forever, effectively averting our gaze from the reality of death. In defending the Inquisition, Naphta implicitly draws an analogy between the use of torture to obtain a confession and illness as God's and nature's way of obtaining an acknowledgment of the body's mortality. Naphta, less sympathetic than Settembrini, nevertheless wins the debate. Castorp in his thoughts while lost in the snow reluctantly concedes to Naphta: "You [Settembrini] are a windbag... you mean well... I like you better, although [Naphta] is almost always right" (468).

What accounts for Mann's fascination with disease? Naphta's argument, powerful as it is, is not the argument that Mann himself would make. There is no evidence that he would follow Naphta's Christian logic of the transcendence of suffering through suffering. Though the theme is not developed in the novel, there is the suggestion of a symbiosis between illness and creativity that would have appealed to Mann, the artist. "Any man who recognizes an organic symptom of illness to be the product of forbidden emotions that assume hysterical form in conscious psychic life also recognizes the creative power of the psyche in the material world" (645). The healthy body, unconscious of itself, does not experience its own activity. Without errancy, it has no story to tell; like the state of innocence, health is the condition before the fall, before individuation and consciousness. It offers no challenge to the mind and the soul. It cannot lead to wisdom, which as the ancient Greeks knew comes through suffering. Settembrini's Enlightenment view doesn't even acknowledge sickness as a passage to a regained healthy state, a necessary memory of the susceptibility of even the healthy body. The Enlightenment will "have banished those shadows."

For Castorp as for Mann, the sanatorium at Davos is not so much a site of cure as it is a spectacle of illness and the variousness with which its patients experience it. The sanatorium for Castorp is the place that liberates illness from its repressed or denied condition in the "normal" life he leads in the flatlands. He breaks the rules of the sanatorium, visiting the other patients with a combination of compassion and curiosity. The ostensible reason for Castorp's visit is to see his cousin Joachim; the real reason is to discover himself or the fact that he is ill, which may be the same thing. Like Freud, Mann could respond to the question of what is man with the answer: "Man is a sick creature." And the discovery is attended with a sense of liberation, not dismay. Castorp revels in it. It becomes his bond with others.

In *Intoxicated by My Illness*, Anatole Broyard writes of his affinity for *The Magic Mountain*, "the grand definitive romance of illness, a portrait that, I would say, speaking as a connoisseur now, will never be equaled. His description of life itself showed how precarious it was: 'a form-preserving instability, a fever of matter . . . the existence of the impossible-to-exist, of a half-sweet, half-painful balancing, or scarcely balancing, in this restricted and feverish process of decay and renewal, upon the point of existence.'"[4] For Broyard, dying is a creative, voluptuous and even hilarious experience. Like Castorp in *The Magic Mountain*, he is filled with a perverse excitement at the discovery that he is ill, the condition for all sorts of discoveries about himself.

The novel has been read as a *Bildungsroman*, the sanatorium being a sort of university with a varied curriculum. Castorp becomes a student not only of Naphta and Settembrini, who is relentlessly described as a pedagogue, but of the Drs. Behrens and Krokowski, who represent different views of the relationship between the flesh and the spirit, body and soul or mind. (Behrens is a materialist, discovering causes in the soma, whereas Krokowski is a psychoanalytic idealist looking to the psyche for explanations.) The inarticulate but impressive Mynheer Peeperkorn and his lover Madame Chauchat are teachers of Eros and feeling, a love for life beyond ideas. Castorp comes across as the eternal undergraduate who would prolong his stay indefinitely in the hermetically sealed world of the mountain if it weren't for the war, which forces him to return to the flatlands, where he will presumably be educated in other ways.

This is a familiar and attractive reading of the novel, but I confess to sharing Jill Anne Kowalik's skepticism about the significance of Castorp's education. What does he learn from his mentors? As Kowalik remarks, he does not seem to achieve "an increase in moral consciousness." She also notes an absence of "acceptance and appreciation of the seriousness of suffering."[5] If anything, in the climactic chapter, "Snow," there seems to be a rejection of what he is being taught. "My two pedagogues! Their arguments and contradictions are nothing but a *guzzabuglio*, the hubbub and alarm of battle, and no one whose head is a little clear and heart a little devout will let himself be dazed by that" (486). The curriculum at Davos engenders confusion rather than clarity, which some would say is what a curriculum should do: create *guzzabuglio* (a favorite word in the novel, meaning mess or muddle) to unsettle the student in all his views. Whenever Castorp philosophizes on his own he deservedly encounters ridicule, and not only from his philosophical mentors. Here is Castorp on love and death: "But irrational love is a mark of genius, because death, you see, is the principle of genius, the *res bina*, the *lapis philosophorum*, and it is also the pedagogic principle. For the love of death leads to the love of life and humanity. That is how it is. It came to me on my balcony, and I am delighted to be able to tell it to you." And Clavdia's response is definitive: "You are a silly philosopher, Hans Castorp" (587). Did Mann mean to represent the mountain as the site of education or in effect parody it? His famous irony makes it difficult to answer one way or the other. Mann suggests that "Hans Castorp would not have stayed with people up here even this long beyond his originally planned date of departure, if only some sort of satisfactory answer about the meaning and purpose of life had been supplied to his prosaic soul from out of the depths of time" (226). He does stay, but it would be hard to say what he learns about the point and purpose of the business of living.

Castorp acquires a good deal of medical information about the body. He is exposed to the conflict of ideas, which he struggles without much success to relate to his own experience. The love affair with Mme. Chauchat is a brief episode that makes him feverish and provides him with a long memory. It is as hard to make sense of the charismatic effect of Peeperkorn on Castorp as it is difficult for Peeperkorn to express himself.

Castorp has the air of a serious student, an overachiever, if there was something to achieve. If he (and the reader) learn anything, it is that the ideas that occupy such a large space in the novel are untrustworthy and worse. Settembrini in particular provides no guide even for his own life. "Ah, this Settembrini — it was not for nothing he was a man of letters, grandson of a politician and son of a humanist! He had lofty ideas about emancipation and criticism — and chirruped at the girls in the street" (468).

But the failure of ideas is not confined to Settembrini. In a memorable passage, Mann describes what happens to ideas as they develop in debate.

> "Form!" [Settembrini] said. And Naphta grandiloquently responded, "Logos!" But he who would not hear of the logos, said, "reason!" And the man of the logos defended "Passion!" Confusion reigned. "Objective reality," shouted one; "the self!" cried the other. Finally one side was talking about "Art!" and the other about "Criticism!" And both constantly returned to "Nature!" And "Spirit" and to which of them was more noble, and to the issue of "free aristocracy." But there was no clarity, no order, not even of a dualistic and militant sort, for it was all not only contradictory, but also topsy-turvy, and the disputants not only contradicted one another, but also themselves. (457)

A veritable carnival! Mann is not simply indicating the intellectual incoherence of Settembrini and Naphta. His target is the character of ideas per se. Mann here performs like a deconstructionist *avant la lettre*, dramatizing the self-contradictoriness to which all ideas are susceptible.

In his foreword to *Women in Love*, D. H. Lawrence speaks of the struggle for verbal consciousness as "a very great part of life." "Any man of real individuality tries to know and to understand what is happening, even in himself, as he goes along." "Verbal consciousness" (Lawrence means by that phrase ideas that one has about oneself and the world) may be false as well as true. It should not be the "superimposition of a theory" but rather "the passionate struggle into conscious being." How do the ideas of Mann's characters measure up to the Lawrentian standard?

One certainly hears in the impassioned debates between Naphta and Settembrini the sounds of "passionate struggle." But they are not "struggl[ing] into conscious being." They have already achieved it — and their intellectual passion is, so to speak, the epiphenomenon of their achieved beings. Passion is partly in their beliefs and partly in their scorn for each other's views. For Lawrence, ideas must be tested by experience and therefore are open to refutation. Neither Settembrini nor Naphta tests ideas: they inhabit closed systems to be fought for and defended. If there is a testing, it is in the relatively open mind of Castorp, and presumably in the mind of the sensitive reader. Who then is in the right, Settembrini or Naphta? Neither — though, as I have already said, Naphta is the more compelling figure. Neither, because their ideas do not survive the test that the novel itself provides: the mortality of the body. Settembrini's Enlightenment optimism is useless against the facts of disease and death. The technological advances in medicine, which have effected so many cures (and in particular for the diseases which afflict patients of the Berghof sanatorium) do not confirm that optimism. The whole panoply of antibiotics, it appears, cannot ultimately outwit the cunning of viruses capable of transmuting themselves into even more formidable antagonists of the body. We in the developed world may have become healthier and longer lived, but there is still the ineluctable prospect of bodily deterioration and death. The future of mankind contains the proliferation of sanatoria for the elderly. Our defenses against disease and death may be only in degree more effective than our efforts to create lasting peace in the world.

Naphta may have come closer to surviving the test, because he embraces disease, suffering and death, but he too is finally the captive of a faith that is immune to testing: the homeopathic belief that one can transcend suffering through suffering. Naphta's doctrine of suffering applies only to himself; it is a retrograde vision of the world, undesirable as an ideal and realizable only as oppression. It is, finally, the dream of the torturer and self-torturer. What would Naphta had made of modern totalitarian societies? It is, at least, a question whether he would have found them congenial. As Alexander Nehamas remarks, both Naphta and Settembrini reject the "low, material or animal"[6] — Settembrini in the name of reason, Naphta in the name of faith. The philosophies of both men lead away from reality or to a destructive vision of it.

Nothing is more telling against the moral authority of ideas than the brilliant penultimate chapter, "The Great Petulance," in which Naphta, insulted by Settembrini, challenges him to a duel. In the duel, Settembrini fires in the air, enraging Naphta, who calls out "Coward!" and turns his gun upon himself. The event deposes Reason, the very medium of ideas, from its pedestal above the fray and shows that in its most abstract manifestations it "contains far more profound and radical possibilities for hatred, for categorical and irreconcilable hostility than are found in social life" and that in its very rigor it can lead "inexorably to bestial deeds" (689–690). (The most devastating critique of Enlightenment Reason is made by the champion of the Enlightenment.) This is Settembrini's lesson to Castorp, and it effectively collapses the intellectual opposition between Naphta and Settembrini. It produces in Castorp an understanding that exceeds that of his mentor: "[Settembrini's] thoughts were not his thoughts — just as he would never have taken the notion to fight a duel on his own, but had only adopted it from Naphta, the little terrorist; they merely showed that he, too, was enveloped by the same inner state that had possession of them all — it had enslaved Herr Settembrini's beautiful reason, had made it its tool" (690). The novel in effect concludes with an acknowledgment of the power of ideas to destroy rather than create. Rather than an alternative to violence (Reason's dream of itself), ideas are the source of violence. We should speak not only of the ineffectuality of Reason, but of its destructiveness. It is not fortuitous that the chapter that follows and concludes the novel, "Thunderbolt," gives us the scene of the Great War and Castorp's participation in it.

So we have the paradox of a novel of ideas which dramatizes their ineffectuality, or their destructive effectuality. They can neither explain nor transform the world. What is the attraction of these ideas? Ideas for the novelist do not have a life of their own. They do not exist, as they do for the philosopher in an abstract space, free of "the genetic fallacy." "It is remarkable how a man cannot summarize his thoughts in even the most general way without betraying himself completely, without putting his whole self into it, quite unawares presenting as in allegory the basic themes and problems of his own existence" (35). Ideas are a medium in which a character performs and reveals or conceals what he is. However confused the ideas may be, what emerges are characters who betray themselves in the expression and acting out of the ideas. Dostoyevsky was the master of the novel of ideas, because so much was at stake for his characters (Stavrogin, Kirilov, Ivan Karamazov, etc.) in their commitment to ideas. I would not make the same claim for Mann's characters.

Mann's interest in ideas has a strong theatrical element. Naphta, Settembrini and to a lesser extent Behrens and Krokowski are performers of ideas. In his *Italian Journey* Goethe jests that the hospital could become the dominant institution of modern life. I imagine Mann, who regarded himself as Goethe's successor as Germany's greatest Man of Letters, was aware of the prophecy. In any case, *The Magic Mountain* is in a sense a realization of the prophecy in a way that anticipates future realizations. The Berghof sanatorium is both a hospital and a theatrical spectacle, a scene of entertainment both for its residents and for its readers. (In our time, Goethe's prophecy has been realized at the level of popular culture in TV dramas. "General Hospital," "ER," and "Chicago Hope" provide a kind of anesthetizing experience of bodily harm, not unlike the pleasures of violence in detective dramas.) The asthmatic attack of the hunchbacked Mexican is a hilarious performance: "he suddenly could not get his breath and would then grab his neighbor, man or woman, in the iron grip of one of his long hands, hold on tight as a vise, and drag his struggling, panicky victim, now shouting for help, down into the pool of dread with him" (201). Or consider the director, Dr. Behrens's relishing the decomposing body:

> First of all, your guts burst . . . there you are lying on your wood shavings and sawdust, and the gases, you see, swell you up, blow you up until you're immense, the way frogs look when naughty boys blow air into them, until you're a regular balloon, and then your abdomen can no longer take the pressure and bursts. Bang! You relieve yourself noticeably . . . your bowels gush out. Yes, and after that you're actually socially acceptable again. If granted a holiday, you could visit your heirs without causing much offense. You stink yourself out, so to speak. (431)

Symptoms of the mind, the ideas exuberantly celebrate its energy.

The scene of war that concludes the novel might have provided a genuine test of the seriousness of its ideas. But it does not. The terrible devastations of the Great War in Paul Fussell's *The Great War and Modern Memory* and Pat Barker's novels are given to us by Mann in a nostalgically heroic evocation:

> There are three thousand of them, so that they can be two thousand when they reach the hills and the valleys — that is the meaning of their numbers. They are a single body, so constructed that even after great losses it can act and triumph, even greet its victory with a thousand-voiced hurrah — despite those who are severed from it and fall away.
>
> Youngsters with their backpacks and bayoneted rifles, with their filthy coats and boots — and in watching, one might also see with a humanis-

> tic, beatific eye, might dream of other scenes. One might imagine such a lad spurring a horse on or swimming in a bay, strolling the shore with a girlfriend, his lips pressed to his gentle beloved's ear, or in happy friendship instructing another lad to string a bow. And instead there they all lie, noses in the fiery filth. That they do it with joy, and also with boundless fear and an unalterable longing for home, is both shameful and sublime, but surely no reason to bring them here to this. (704)

This is the war told in a moment or two that deprives it of its reality, the kind of story he does not tell about the mountain. It is written from the vantage point of someone who stands upon a hill (a magic mountain?), observing and not participating — and observing in a very diminished sense of the word. He understands the need to deploy three thousand troops, because one thousand are sure to fall by the way. Literary memories of epic wars construct an image of a collective sense of triumph, despite the killing (no signs of torn limbs or entrails in the description), which even the heroically-minded Homer encompassed in his descriptions. The contrast between the scene of war, the idyl of the lad and his girlfriend (seen with "a beatific humanistic eye") is hardly sustained as a contrast; in reverting to the scene of war, the narrator insists that the soldiers lie, noses in the filth, with joy. Both idyl and war are scenes of joy. (Even if one hears the note of irony in the juxtaposition of joy and mud, it doesn't overcome the stronger lyric note in the passage.) Mann acknowledges the horror of war but blurs it with aesthetic evocations of the glory of battle. There is a touch of what Primo Levi, characterizing certain writing about World War II, calls the "lechery of aestheticism." Such a compromised view of the war might explain Mann's complacent farewell to Hans Castorp: "Your chances are not good. The wicked dance in which you are caught up will last many a little sinful year yet, and we would not wager much that you will come out whole. To be honest, we are not really bothered about leaving the question open. Adventures in the flesh and spirit, which enhanced and heightened your ordinariness, allowed you to survive in the spirit what you will probably not survive in the flesh" (706). Could the "adventures in the flesh and spirit" in the sanatorium possibly prepare Castorp for the devastations of the Great War? Those who survived the war physically unharmed were often spiritually destroyed. The war, with its consequences for nations and humanity in general, was not merely a staging ground for the progress of one particular soul.

Which returns us to the question of Mann's seriousness in representing disease and death. One doesn't have to be in a war to have the experience of being ravaged by a fatal illness. Rarely in the novel, however, do we get a sense of the terrible ravages of illness, of the devastating loneliness of death. We do get such a glimpse, more than a glimpse, in Joachim's death: not only in Joachim's admirable stoicism but in his mother's and Hans's sense of loss. The main spirit of the novel I think is elsewhere — in a kind of theatrical display of symptoms, of the knowledge of the etiology of illness and of political, moral and religious ideas. The magic mountain is an ivory tower of virtuosos, displaying their talents, sometimes pedantically, at other times brilliantly, but in a comic spirit. The contemptible Frau Stöhr may be close to the spirit of the novel in her unwitting puns — for instance, when she mistakes "deceased" for diseased[7] and premises for primroses. Doesn't the novel itself identify disease with death? And doesn't one vacate the primroses in vacating the premises? Frau Stöhr gives us the comedy of the perishing body. Even Joachim, perhaps the most serious character in the novel, refuses to take life on the mountain seriously: "I sometimes think that illness and death aren't really serious matters, that it's all more like loafing around, and that strictly speaking, things are serious only down below in real life" (50).

Reviewing *Death in Venice*, a young D. H. Lawrence (age twenty-four) saw the novella as a work at the end of a line. Mann was "the last sick sufferer from the complaint of Flaubert, "resisting life's "disordered corruption" with "his fine aesthetic sense, his feeling for beauty, for perfection."[8] Though *The Magic Mountain* does not contain an artist figure comparable to Aschenbach, it represents the bourgeois values that Aschenbach embodies before his "fall." The world of Mann's characters is an achieved world. The ideas that circulate in it represent forms of existence for which there is no real future. The irony of Settembrini's progressivism is that it has become an obsolete idea with no prospects, whereas Naphta's outlook is openly reactionary. The world of the novel is poised on the brink of disaster, and yet the narrative seems oddly insulated from it — as if Mann simply refuses to allow anything to disturb his equilibrium. Published in 1924, the novel comes across as a retrospective celebration of a world that had already passed away. Once upon a time . . .

Mann's attraction to the Dionysian is evident throughout his work. We find it in the dream of the Bacchantes in *Death in Venice*, in the Walpurgisnacht in *The Magic Mountain* and briefly in his evocations of the Great War. But his sensibility is Apollonian. He is the ironic master of extreme situations, experiencing danger at a safe distance. This reading of *The Magic Mountain* goes counter to its gravitas, though it is consistent with its irony. It is very much in the spirit of Mann's own comment upon his intention. "[The novel] was meant as a humorous companion-piece to *Death in Venice* [the work that immediately preceded it] and was to be about the same length: a sort of satire on the tragedy just finished. The atmosphere was to be that strange mixture of death and lightheadedness I found at Davos."[9]

Notes

[1] Thomas Mann, *The Magic Mountain*, trans. John E. Woods (New York: Alfred A. Knopf, 1995), xii. Unless otherwise indicated, citations are from this edition.

[2] Sigmund Freud, *Civilization and Its Discontents* (1930; New York: Norton, 1962).

[3] "The Making of *The Magic Mountain*," in *The Magic Mountain*, trans. H. T. Lowe-Porter (New York: Alfred A. Knopf, 1958), 726.

[4] Anatole Broyard, *Intoxicated by My Illness and Other Writings on Life and Death* (New York: Fawcett Columbine, 1992), 13.

[5] Jill Anne Kowalik, "'Sympathy with Death': Hans Castorp's Nietzschean Resentment," *German Quarterly* 58 (1985), 28.

[6] Alexander Nehamas, "Getting Used to Not Getting Used to It: Nietzsche on *The Magic Mountain*," *Philosophy and Literature* 5 (1981): 83.

[7] The pun in the Lowe-Porter translation disappears in the Woods version which has Frau Stöhr speak unaccountably of "decentifiction."

[8] D. H. Lawrence, "German Books: Thomas Mann," *Phoenix: The Posthumous Papers of D. H. Lawrence*, edited by E. D. McDonald (New York: Viking, 1950), 312.

[9] "The Making of *The Magic Mountain*," in *The Magic Mountain*, trans. H. T. Lowe-Porter (New York: Alfred A. Knopf, 1958), 722.

ÜLKER GÖKBERK

4: War as Mentor: Thomas Mann and Germanness

USING ADORNO'S ESSAY "ON THE QUESTION: What is German?" to introduce representations of Germanness in Thomas Mann's works during the First World War and the early 1920s may at first appear anachronistic. Adorno's essay was written in the 1960s, long after the author's shared experience of exile in the United States with Thomas Mann. The repatriated exile's reflection on the question of Germanness is informed by the self-fragmentation imposed by exile and at the same time by Adorno's effort to remedy that fragmentation via a return to the medium of the German language. Adorno calls the latter the objective factor in his decision to return even though he acknowledges an accompanying subjective need (*Heimweh*). Interestingly, the argumentation of the essay, up to the above-described biographical reflections, undermines essentialist constructions of Germanness but then turns to a description of some essential characteristics of the German language. Adorno writes of his motivations for repatriation as follows:

> Not only because in the newly acquired language one can never quite convey the intended meaning as exactly, with all the nuances and with the rhythm of the train of thought, as one could in one's own. What is more, the German language seems to have a special elective affinity for philosophy and especially for its speculative element [*Moment*] which is so easily distrusted in the West as dangerously unclear — and not entirely without justification.... German is not merely the signification of fixed meanings; rather, it has retained more of the power of expression, in any case, than would be attributed to Western languages by someone who did not grow up in them, for whom they are not second nature.[1]

Even though Adorno considers the possibility that the entire question of expressing oneself fully may simply lie in the relationship of any mother tongue to a foreign language, he nevertheless insists on some specific, objective traits of the German language. For Adorno, not only highly speculative ideas but also particular German concepts, such as *Geist, Moment,* and *Erfahrung,* with all their finely nuanced connotations, are untranslatable.

While Adorno's reconstruction of self-identity through the medium of language is historically remote from Thomas Mann's earlier self-search via the concept of Germanness from the First World War up to the time of the publication of *The Magic Mountain* (1924), the strategy of constituting the self through identification with a supraindividual mental domain (the German language or the German cultural heritage) is shared by both. Yet, my aim here is not to explore these strategies as affirmations of a particular self with respect to hypostatized group identities. Both Mann and Adorno are rather inclined either to play with such notions or, as in Adorno's case, to think them through dialectically and historically. Consequently, it is perhaps most instructive to see how both in Adorno and in Mann the force of essentialist definitions of Germanness is counteracted by specific methods of argumentation.

Adorno's dialectical thinking in his essay "On the Question: What is German?" manifests itself clearly when the author turns against the speculative capacity of the German language, which he had moments before defined as its distinguishing attribute. Notwithstanding his own desire to participate in this specificity of his native language, Adorno warns of any swindle with truth which could result from the "metaphysical surplus of the German language." He thus maintains that "the metaphysical character of language is no privilege. One must not borrow from it the idea of depth which becomes suspicious the moment it engages in self-glorification."[2] Adorno's critique, here directed at manipulation of and by language, runs through the entire essay, targeting "the fabrication of national collectivities," as he calls it. Germanness is, as such, a stereotype, but so similarly are others (the Russian, the American, and so forth). Their fabrication results in nothing but binary oppositions: "Those qualities with which one identifies oneself — imperceptibly become the Good; the foreign group, the others, Bad."[3]

Yet Adorno does not stop at this point. In the public sphere of 1960s Germany he sees an uncritical invocation of the German tradition. The reclaiming of Kant, Goethe, or Beethoven as German possessions means for Adorno nothing but a betrayal of their works. Nevertheless, Adorno embarks on a path, both on historical and dialectical grounds, seeking a truth content in stereotypical representations of Germanness which either result from or appeal to collective narcissisms. Taking Wagner's notorious formulation, "to be German means to do something for its own sake," Adorno explores the premises of such thinking in the idealist systems of the eighteenth and nineteenth centuries.[4] He concludes that not only did this "For-its-own-sake" inevitably become intertwined with expansionist state politics but it also resulted, by arrogantly granting primacy to spiritual creations, in an inhumanity of some sort. The great concept of autonomy (of ideas), then, implies violence in its will to dominate, even if this domination is to be understood in intellectual terms: "If one dares to assume something that is specifically German, then it is this intertwining of the magnificent — unwilling to hold itself to any conventionally established border — with the monstrous."[5]

When Adorno proceeds finally to address the question of whether Hitler was a quintessentially German phenomenon, his answer is again embedded in a dialectical mode of thinking. He claims that "while it is inexact to ascribe Hitler to the German national character as its fate, it is also no coincidence that he rose to power in Germany."[6] What crystallizes out of Adorno's essay is finally the concept of *equivocality* pertaining to all answers to the question "What is German?" The impossibility of an unequivocal answer results, for Adorno, from the *complexity* he locates in "the insight that in whatever is German the one cannot be had without the other."[7]

The affinity of such an insight with similar representations in Thomas Mann's 1947 novel *Doctor Faustus* is obvious.[8] The parallel between the protagonist-composer Adrian Leverkühn's pact with the devil and Adorno's depiction of Germanness as the intertwinement of the magnificent and the monstrous is unavoidable. Less obvious, however, is the intellectual proximity of Mann's reflections on Germanness during the First World War to Adorno's stance in his later essay. The following analysis will demonstrate that such proximity exists as a *complexity* in the definition of Germanness. This kinship of argument will be explored to the end of deepening our understanding of *The Magic Mountain*.[9] Furthermore, Mann's earlier treatment of Germanness during the Great War, his discourse on aesthetics and politics as exemplified in his essayistic work from that period, most notably in the voluminous *Reflections of a Nonpolitical Man*, stands as more than mere background to *The Magic Mountain*.[10] The latter represents for Mann a revisitation of issues of concern in the war essays.

The conception of *The Magic Mountain* was occasioned by Mann's visit to a sanatorium at Davos, Switzerland, during his wife Katia's stay there. The year was 1912, and Mann had just completed his novella *Death in Venice*. In his 1939 introductory lecture to *The Magic Mountain* at Princeton University, Mann explained his initial sense of the novel with the often-cited words: "It was meant as a humorous companion-piece to *Death in Venice* and was to be about the same length: a sort of satire on the tragedy just finished. The atmosphere was to be that strange mixture of death and lightheadedness I had found at Davos. *Death in Venice* portrays the fascination of the death idea, the triumph of drunken disorder over the forces of a life consecrated to rule and discipline. In *The Magic Mountain* the same theme was to be humorously treated."[11]

With the outbreak of war, however, Thomas Mann's artistic career, which already had reached maturity, underwent a crisis. After producing significant works in his early period, including *Buddenbrooks*, *Tonio Kröger*, and the recently completed *Death in Venice*, Mann found writing fiction impossible. He was compelled to postpone his work on two novels, *Felix Krull* and *The Magic Mountain*, in favor of essayistic efforts. In the preface to his *Reflections of a Nonpolitical Man* Mann relates his own stagnation to the crisis of the times. In response, he sets for himself as his major task gaining insight into Germany's social and political upheaval. Giving meaning to this external turmoil was at the same time linked for him to a critical review of his own artistic foundations. These foundations, parallel to the sociopolitical circumstances, had to be reevaluated in order for Mann to return to creative work.[12]

The caesura of the First World War marked for Thomas Mann the end of the cultural ascendancy of an educated European bourgeoisie and moved the author to work on a series of essays in an attempt to solve his personal consciousness of crisis. Consequently, these writings, in which the question of Germanness is central, should rightly be viewed as integral to the genesis of *The Magic Mountain*. Whether the novel later to be written finally bears witness to an overcoming of the positions its author defended during the war years, or whether the issues of the 1910s were revisited on the fictional plane in *The Magic Mountain* without coming to a substantially different conclusion, is a much disputed point in the literature on *The Magic Mountain*.[13] I would suggest that a closer look at Thomas Mann's discourse in the war years might be productively pursued from a different perspective. Unlike the practice in much critical commentary on *The Magic Mountain*, the aim here is to explore segments of the war essays to the end of shedding light on interpretive questions in the later novel, rather than using the essays as mere supportive devices. Thus, Mann's earlier intellectual positions will be seen to constitute an outlook directed toward the discourse of *The Magic Mountain*.

An examination of Thomas Mann's work during the First World War should also prove instructive to the nonspecialist, since the Thomas Mann best known to the American audience is the Thomas Mann in exile from the Hitler dictatorship, the artist as champion of democracy and brilliant expounder of the "demonic" in modern German culture and politics. During the war, however, a considerably more obscure figure than the democrat of 1933–1947 published a series of profoundly conservative essays, among them the aforementioned volume, *Reflections of a Nonpolitical Man*. In them Mann apparently justifies both the untempered monarchical rule of the German emperor and the German war effort itself by appeals to the needs of a superior *Kultur*. His claim to be "unpolitical" reveals itself to be, if not a mask for reaction, at least a gesture of complicity with it.

In his study of the development of German conservatism since the French Revolution, Karl Mannheim establishes a relative autonomy for individual thought, although he sees it as fundamentally conditioned by collective patterns of thought (*Denkintentionen*). A nationalistic-conservative posture prevailed among the German intelligentsia of the Wilhelminian epoch. Among its diverse representatives were figures such as German ideologue Paul de Lagarde; historians Jacob Burckhardt, Ernst Troeltsch, and Oswald Spengler; sociologists Ferdinand Tönnies and Max Weber; and, finally, Wagner and Nietzsche. In order to understand the common feature of thought within this divergent group, Mannheim's category of reflectivity proves useful. Mannheim situates conservatism's reflective posture on historical grounds, pointing to conservatism's origins as a specific reaction to the French Revolution. He argues convincingly that in the antithesis between the idea of progress and conservatism, the latter constitutes the secondary element, since it finds its raison d'être in the former.[14] A central issue in this polarity revolves around the philosophy of history. The Enlightenment designs a model of history based on the concept of linear progress, whereas the conservative opposition, especially in Germany, develops a historical model based on a theory of organic growth, or the cyclical view of history. The specific concepts that constitute the core of Wilhelminian conservatism's anticapitalist, antiliberal opposition, such as *Lebensphilosphie* and the polarities *Volk* and the masses, *Kultur* and civilization, *Geist* and politics, *Gemeinschaft* and *Gesellschaft*, were all inspired by this model of organic growth.

While Thomas Mann's indebtedness to the leading conservative discourse of the age is evident in his war essays, his deviation from it is equally obtrusive. This rather peculiar stance becomes most markedly transparent in Mann's complex position on the single issue of war. In the essayistic work from the 1910s, the issue is intrinsically linked to the representation of Germanness. The transfiguration of war as the *defender* of the values of the sphere of *Geist* (intellect, fine arts, and the spiritual) was a premise that Thomas Mann shared with the proponents of German conservatism. In Mann's wartime writings, this transfiguration results from an analogy drawn between this intellectual (spiritual) realm and the reality of the war. Consequently, the artistic and the military mode of life are seen as correlative to the extent that the former is considered an allegory of the latter. Mann exemplifies this idea by referring not only to the protagonists of his fiction, such as Thomas Buddenbrook, Gustav Aschenbach, and Klaus Heinrich of *Royal Highness*, but also to historical figures ranging from Frederick the Great to Kant and Nietzsche, and last but not least to himself. All represent a soldierly mode of life. The common ground of their existence rests in discipline and austerity.

Thomas Mann contrasts this mode of existence, which he deems specifically German, to that of the liberal activist of the time, typified in the *Reflections* as Civilization's Literary Man (*Zivilisationsliterat*). He traces the roots of the former back to the Lutheran-burgherly tradition, while rejecting the latter as alien to Germanness, rooted in the *bourgeois* — distinct from the German *burgherly* — tradition of Western democracies. Further analysis of Mann's antithetical thinking in his discussion of ostensible polarities between Germany and the West — culture (the sphere of creative forces, including the demonic and the antirational) and civilization, art and politics — reveals again the transposition of the meaning of the war from the realm of power politics and related interests to the defense of cultural values, which Thomas Mann identifies with the German tradition. Thus by asserting his own prowar attitude as an apology for preserving German values, Mann bestows upon his own artistic existence a higher meaning. He regards himself as a successor in the great spiritual tradition of Germany.[15]

At this point, Thomas Mann's theses on Germanness seem to perform precisely the function that Adorno calls "the fabrication of national collectivities." No wonder, then, that Thomas Mann scholarship has traditionally regarded these essays as the expression of a regressive element in Mann's development as a liberal, progressive thinker and later champion of humanism.[16] Does Mann participate in such collective narcissism to the end of self-affirmation? A critical overview of the reception of the *Reflections* indicates how far from unitary this reception has been. At the founding of the Weimar Republic, the essays were welcomed only by one faction of the right wing. Democrats, however, were united in deeming the essays reactionary.[17] The divergence of opinion has continued unabated, with critics in the main treating the war book only peripherally and citing particularly Mann's democratic speech of 1922, "The German Republic," as a decisive turning point in Mann's development. If the *Reflections* are viewed somewhat mildly, this is done in the light of the essays' autobiographical value and as a reaction not primarily to the First World War but to the "war of the brothers," the dramatic ideological break between Thomas and his brother, Heinrich Mann, a vocal defender of progressive politics. As Kurt Sontheimer has commented, without the

Reflections the overall evaluation of Mann's political essays would have been, to some extent, easier.[18]

The controversy surrounding the *Reflections of a Nonpolitical Man* renders it necessary to explore further Mann's relation to the First World War, for the divergence of opinions is in fact symptomatic of Mann's own indeterminate stance at the outbreak of the war. It should be added here that Mann's justification of the war as the preservation of German *Kultur* forms only one part of his discourse; his perspective in general can best be described as ambivalent, a response shared with other prominent writers, including Gerhart Hauptmann, Rudolf Dehmel, Ernst Bertram, and Stefan George. Along with the *Reflections of a Nonpolitical Man*, Mann's peculiar comments on war can be traced in essays such as "Thoughts in War" (1914) and "Frederick and the Grand Coalition: A Sketch for Our Times," whose publication in 1915 immediately preceded work on the *Reflections*. Mann's letters and diaries at the outset of the war are in the same vein, revealing the ecstasy of war along with shock and anxiety. Significantly, "The Thunderbolt," concluding *The Magic Mountain*, attests to a similar ambivalence. That such ambivalence still inhered in Mann's stance while he was looking backward, i.e., from the 1920s, to the war renders problematical the notion of definitive breaks in the author's thinking. Mann seems rather to follow consistently throughout his career Adorno's dictum that all answers to the question "What is German?" (or here, "What is the German war?") are permeated with *equivocality*. "The Thunderbolt" thus warrants closer examination.

The narrator of *The Magic Mountain* refers to the outbreak of the war as "a historic thunderclap that shook the foundations of the earth" at the same time he reassures the reader that he will keep his voice lowered and humbly hold back from "turning that thundering rumble into a blustering narrative. No bombast, no rodomontade, here" (699). These words not only suggest that the dimensions of the event bring the narrator to an awesome standstill but also that the (bourgeois) narrative has no vocabulary to represent the event. Thus the thunderbolt surfaces as a force which bodes the end of narration itself. Nevertheless, at this point the narrator is still capable of practicing his interpretative skills to bestow meaning upon the thunderclap. He muses that besides the shattering effect of this explosion on the global plane, "for us it is the thunderbolt that bursts open the magic mountain and rudely sets its entranced sleeper outside the gates" (699). According to the interpretive scheme presented, it is only due to the overwhelming turn of events that Castorp finally liberates himself from the spell of the hermetic sanatorium society. The narrator observes that the awakening sleeper "drew his legs back under him, stood up, looked around. He saw that the enchantment was broken, that he was released, set free — not by his own actions, as he had to admit to his shame, but set free by elementary external forces, for whom his liberation was a very irrelevant matter." Abandoning "the great stupor" resulting from his contemplative life at high altitude, the young hero rushes toward the battlefield, the realm of action and masculinity (702).[19]

The war here represents the last instance in the chain of experiments Hans Castorp undergoes and experiences on the magic mountain; it concludes the humanistic notion of *placet experiri*. The novel, then, ascribes to the war the role of ultimate mentor, by means of which Hans rounds out his education. He indeed seems to have reached some kind of inner certainty before he leaves the sanatorium, even if the narrator attempts to destabilize this certainty by pointing to Hans's past confusions about dream and reality and by maintaining that "that relationship [between dream and reality] has never been definitively decided." Based on this certainty, the mentor-disciple constellation of Herrn Settembrini and Hans Castorp is *conspicuously* reversed. Earlier, Castorp's superior position to the antithetical thinking represented in the disputes between the Enlightenment proponent Settembrini and the totalitarian reactionary Naphta had merely been implied:

> Things were no longer as they had been once, when, after first establishing sudden clarity, Herr Settembrini would sit down at the bedside of a horizontal Hans Castorp and attempt to influence him by correcting his opinions about matters of life and death. It was the other way around now; with hands tucked between his knees, the student now sat beside the bed of the humanist, . . . kept him company and listened politely to his presentations of the world situation. (699–700)

While the narrator attributes Settembrini's exhaustion to the overwhelming shock of Naphta's suicide, the symbolic undertones here are unmistakable. That Settembrini now assumes the horizontal posture suggests his downfall as mentor, if not consciously for himself, at least for Hans Castorp and the reader.

It is, therefore, not surprising that in the final analysis the narrator detects inconsistencies in Settembrini's way of thinking. But unexpectedly, the inconsistencies pertain to the Italian's perception of the war. The narrator takes Settembrini's blending of humanity and politics, humanistic ideals and civilization's final victory, as the grounds justifying peace and war at the same time: "Yes, Herr Settembrini's own inner state meant that in his world of beautiful views, the element of the eagle's boldness prevailed more and more over the dove's mildness." Settembrini's state of mind as transmitted through the narrative instance indicates an imbalance, a shift from a discourse "on dove's feet" toward "the rushing pinions of eagles," caused by the chaos of war (700). It is, however, true that the thunderbolt not only triggers confusions, it also unmasks previous ones. Consequently, it is only in light of the thunderbolt that the narrator can convey to the reader that Settembrini all along had been conscious of and perplexed by his own attitudes toward the world's recent political conflicts. Humanitarian pacifism and belligerent political activism are no longer discrete categories. The Italian's reactions are *complex*, an indication of some level of identification on the author's part. The novel's discourse ultimately remains equivocal. Does the reader encounter in these last pages a confused Settembrini, or does she or he confront the "true" nature of the humanist? The apperception of war functions on two planes at the same time: it both perplexes and provides clarity.

Yet the narrator chooses to emphasize the cathartic function of war on Hans Castorp, and he does so magniloquently, seeming himself to participate in something of an ecstasy: "And so he sank back down on his knees, his face and hands raised toward a heaven darkened by sulfurous fumes, but no longer the ceiling of the grotto of sinful delight." Settembrini joins the same ecstasy as he sends his pupil out to the battlefield with the words: "Fight bravely out there where blood joins men together" (702). Soon after this the narrator appears oblivious to his previous promise to remain modest and refrain from giving an exact account of the war. In the final pages of the book the narrator proves himself quite adept at doing precisely what his promises had ruled out, that is, "turning that thundering rumble into a blustering narrative." The reader suddenly finds the narrator by a roadside at the battlefield. He again assures himself and the reader that he will not use "rodomontade," not attempt to provide a vocabulary for this overwhelming scene beyond both his expertise and his comprehension. Clearly, Mann is playing with his narrator when he nevertheless allows him to describe the battlefield. But there is a further irony, for the depiction is powerful both in technical detail and in dramatic force. This suggests that perhaps the narrative has in some sense transcended the voice of the traditional bourgeois narrator of a bygone era.

An ambivalence vis-à-vis the war manifests itself also here, in the fusion of detail with dramatic overtones. The battlefield is described naturalistically evoking, with powerful imagery a most horrifying inferno. Hans Castorp

> has thrown himself on his stomach at the approach of a howling hound of hell, a large explosive shell, a hideous sugarloaf from the abyss. He lies there, face in the cool muck, legs spread, feet twisted until the heels press the earth. Laden with horror, this product of science gone berserk crosses thirty yards in front of him, buries itself into the ground, and explodes like the Devil himself, bursts inside the earth with ghastly superstrength

and casts up a house-high fountain of soil, fire, iron, lead, and dismembered humanity. (705)

At the same time, the image of thousands of youngsters forcibly marching is presented as an organic whole, recalling associations with concepts such as *Gemeinschaft* (community) and *Volk*, central values of German conservatism. The narrator remarks with fascination that "they are a single body, so constructed that even after great losses it can act and triumph, even greet its victory with a thousand-voiced-hurrah — despite those who are severed from it and fall away." Allusions are repeatedly made to the flushed faces of the young soldiers, calling them "feverish lads." Castorp, too, has a flushed face, recalling the *heightened* state he experienced while on the mountain. He now runs, singing Schubert's romantic *Lied* "The Lindentree," a much scrutinized aspect of the last chapter. The significance of this passage in the present framework of analysis lies in the *way* Castorp sings, comparable to "the way a man sings to himself in moments of dazed, thoughtless excitement, without even knowing. . . ." The battlefield as it is represented is permeated with both the most horrifying images of death and an ecstatic energy. It is true that the narrative instance does not himself succumb to the ecstasy of the soldiers: "That they do it with joy, and also with boundless fear and unutterable longing for home, is both shameful and sublime, but surely no reason to bring them here to this" (704–705). In "The Thunderbolt," then, the sum of depictions and commentaries betrays a profound ambivalence toward the war. The concluding lines of the novel, which leave the question open whether "love" will ever emerge out of this universal "festival of death," do not resolve the ambivalence. That these lines echo the vision of the "Snow" chapter adds to the complexity which underlies the meaning of war in *The Magic Mountain*.

Such complexities are most aptly subsumed under the category of the problematizing attitude which provides substance and continuity in Thomas Mann's writings.[20] A reexamination of the wartime essays reveals that under the layers of Mann's conservative discourse a similar attitude prevails. A method analogous to the notion of experiment in *The Magic Mountain* surprisingly looms beneath the surface of the German-conservative theses of the *Reflections*. The multiplicity of perspectives through which the former probes the overcoming of binary oppositions can also be detected in the latter. This strategic parallel indicates that locating a conclusive break or a turning point, as a number of scholars posit between Mann's stance during the First World War and the 1920s, is not necessary. Mann's avoidance of direct commitment in his fiction and essayistic work is a signal aspect suggesting consistency within his oeuvre.

As suggested earlier, Mann's ambivalent disposition in the *Reflections* toward progress and conservatism in the years surrounding the First World War is articulated precisely around the question of Germanness. Conventional wisdom has generally taken the conservative-nationalistic assertions of the war essays to illuminate Mann's response to this question. As a concept, then, it becomes the foundation of Mann's polemic against Germany's entrance into a democratic phase. Mann begins his *Reflections* by posing his primary conservative thesis: "Germanness as protest." At this point, however, he raises a crucial question: How does an artist, who until this time has served as a chronicler and analyst of decadence, transform himself into a patriot with the outbreak of war? From his own ambiguous response to his public self-questioning it is clear that Mann did not want absolutely to define and justify his patriotic stance. Two formal qualities inform his argument throughout the essays in a significant manner: 1) the weaving of a position out of argument and counterargument and 2) the discrepancy between a critical-analytical form and a politically engaged content. The force of this rhetorical strategy, structurally the very foundation of the *Reflections*, sublates the truth-content of one assertion and replaces it, however tentatively, with another. The result is a discourse in suspension. The ambivalence animating such a method finally leaves the ultimate truth-content of the *Reflections* highly questionable.

Dostoyevsky's 1877 essay "The German Question" serves as Mann's point of departure. The Russian writer deems Germany "the protesting empire" and identifies the object of the protest as the legacy of Rome, identified now with the West. The protesting-empire identity does not refer only to Luther's Protestantism. Germany is, rather, understood by Dostoyevsky as an *eternal* land of protest. And "eternal" here assumes both historical and typological significance. Mann's own determination of Germany begins the first chapter of the *Reflections*, "Protest," with his acknowledgment of Dostoyevsky and introduction of an antithetical structure, the fundamental polarity of Germany and the West. The strategy enables Mann to broach the theme of war, whose justification forms the second section of the chapter. Carrying Dostoyevsky's formulation of eternal protest over to the war, Mann asserts that it is in a spiritual sense that Germany conducts the war effort:

> In my opinion, then, there has been the most complete unanimity from the first moment that the intellectual roots of this war, "the German war," as it is called with every possible justification, lie in the inborn and historical "protestantism," that this war is essentially a new outbreak, perhaps the grandest, the final one, as some believe, of Germany's ancient struggle against the spirit of the West, as well as the struggle of the Roman world against stubborn Germany.[21]

Provocative content aside, it is most illuminating to trace the form of the thesis to the categories of conservative thought which are manifest in the gesture of opposition. So it is no accident that the positive content of Germany's mission is elided. That Germany has not spoken its final word, that Luther's protest also remained a negative one, can for this reason be traced back to the fact that Germany's destiny, according to the conservative logic, is located in the oppositional stance per se and not in the content of its opposition. While liberalism's polemic confronts the old order, it at the same time offers a positive content in its worldview (the principles of the French Revolution). With conservatism the protesting posture, negativity toward the threat of the new, outweighs all else. Thus as Karl Mannheim has argued, progressive thought is both chronologically and logically prior. In our context, the West assumes both historical and ideological primacy vis-à-vis a protesting Germany.

Surprisingly, however, this chapter of the *Reflections* both posits the nature of Germanness and implies a counter-discourse. While Mann holds to the double meaning of "eternal" as both historical and typological, in his definition of Germanness he at the same time historicizes the issue by questioning the general validity of Dostoyevsky's thesis, hence relativizing it. Stating that Dostoyevsky was greatly influenced by Bismarck's personality when he wrote his essay after the Franco-Prussian war, Mann notes: "In the intervening time it lost some of the intensity of its truth.... Today we do not need to read it to be fully aware of its message and contemplate its truth."[22] The fact that the thoughts of the Russian writer have regained their truth-value in changed historical circumstances can be explained, according to Mann, by the war. War confirms for all the now-historicized validity of Dostoyevsky's "warlike truth." In the middle of his polemical formulation of Germanness as protest it becomes clear that Mann is also interested in maintaining a certain distance to the crown prince of this thesis, Dostoyevsky. He vacillates between recognition of the historical relativity of Dostoyevsky's formulation of Germanness and its ideological relevance for the present day. There is no doubt that Mann no longer invokes Dostoyevsky unequivocally, but is, rather, determined to stress the pragmatic, ideological relevance of these ideas. It therefore becomes questionable how well Mann's worldview accommodates such truth-content as these assertions offer. Even as he formulates that conservative standpoint, his point of view is not transparent.

Ambivalence in the determination of Germanness is deepened when Mann distinguishes this concept from that of the West, of Civilization and Enlightenment. In this contrast the unarticulated character of Germany's oppositional stance is underscored. The lack of voice is perceived on the side of the representatives of Civilization as barbaric: "The Roman West is literary: this separates it from the Germanic — or more exactly — from the German world, which, whatever else it is, is definitely not literary."[23] The essence of the latter manifests itself for Mann in music, a realm not linked to humanitarianism. While constructing such binary oppositions, Mann proceeds rather descriptively and casts few aspersions against the principles of literary humanitarianism as such. His polemic only begins with the distinction between the ideas of classical humanity and their application. In other words, he does not so much confront the ideas of the French Revolution as their degeneration in practice, as concretized in the rigid Jacobin doctrine. That the new distinction is not completely consistent with the polemic earlier engaged against the West would seem to suggest that Mann either conflates or wavers between two ideas in the *Reflections*: first, the dismissal of the idea of progress as such, and second, the rejection of its distorted form, represented by a Robespierre, which he now sees resurrected in liberalism's battle to win over Germany.

Mann offers an analysis of the liberal spirit, whose real task he determines to be a passionate protest *against* protest, in his third chapter, "Civilization's Literary Man." The radical literator type, Mann argues, wishes Germany's defeat because he desires its conversion. How would a Europe freed from the "German protest" look? In Mann's view it would be "a somewhat amusing, somewhat insipidly humane, trivially depraved, femininely elegant Europe that was already all too 'human,' somewhat implausibly adventurous and loud-mouthed democratic, a Europe of tango and two-step manners, a Europe of business and pleasure *à la* Edward the Seventh, a Monte-Carlo Europe, literary as a Parisian cocotte."[24] In a manner recalling his rejection of the petrified Jacobin revolutionary ideal, Mann here opposes another form of the same idea, a degenerated and shallow notion of progress. The radical literary man is actually a German himself, but insofar as he advances such a degeneration, his inclination tends toward the nationally French rather than the German-national. He indeed represents for Mann the "classically unbroken" French national being "that has as yet reached no critical self-reflection, no resignation."[25]

In literary terms, civilization's literary man has been regarded as a somewhat distorted prototype for *The Magic Mountain*'s Settembrini. Mann's representation of the inconsistencies in the former's attitude toward war coincides almost verbatim with Settembrini's portrayal in "The Thunderbolt." Mann maintains in the *Reflections* "that civilization's literary man is not really an opponent of war, not absolutely a pacifist, that he acknowledges incontestable intellectual validity in the decision to wage war, and that he sees in war an *ultima ratio*, yes, something like God's judgement. . . . The truth is that civilization's literary man does not denigrate war when it is waged in the service of civilization."[26] Mann alludes to the lineage of Italian republicans, Freemasons, radicals, and literati, in short to Settembrini's ancestors. In *The Magic Mountain* Naphta elucidates to Hans Castorp the dark background of Freemasonry. The Illuminati order in the eighteenth century, he explains, had incorporated ritual aspects of medieval religious orders and implied some linkage to Oriental mysticisms, which gave the secret society a new power of fascination. Naphta concludes that the purely humanitarian character of Freemasonry, as Settembrini understood it in his time, was actually mixed with a past of "Jesuitical obscurantism," and that Herr Settembrini, even if not intentionally, participated in it (498–504). The information, conveyed through his antagonist, relativizes Settembrini's representative role. In light of the irrational element informing Freemasonry's past, Settembrini's philanthropy and his commitment to Enlightenment ideas become more problematical than a purely rationalist position suggests. As Settembrini's ambivalence toward war evinces, oppositions such as pro-war/antiwar or irrational/rational lose their validity. When Castorp sits between the two mentors and listens to their controversy which included Freemasonry and its cabalistic past, "thoughts and images tumbled topsy-turvy in Hans's mental workshop. There sat death, a humanistic rhetorician clad in a blue coat; and when you focused on this philanthropic and pedagogic god of literature, what you saw crouching there had a monkey face, with the symbols of night and sorcery on its brow" (514).

Notwithstanding the confusion of images in the above scene, it should be recalled that Mann's overall representation of the Italian humanist engenders sympathy, despite the ironic distance accompanying Settembrini's Enlightenment rhetoric.[27] Furthermore, the concluding chapter of *The Magic Mountain* entails such ambiguity toward the war that Settembrini's contradictions are complementary and not at all averse to the general vagueness of the discourse. In the *Reflections* a strikingly similar discrepancy is attributed to the radical literary man of Germany; but the initial polarity posed between this type and Mann himself is gradually blurred. For Mann admits that he, too, has a part in the democratization of Germany. Thus, both in the literary and the essayistic form, war becomes a cipher of complexity; the positions of its proponents and opponents shift.

The aforementioned critique of the literator's lack of self-reflection, his "unbroken" French mentality, indicates that Mann's critique, his conservative polemic, is directed against an optimism grounded in a largely unreflected faith in progress.[28] Mann is unable to recognize in the self-assertion of civilization's literary man the painful sense of fragmentation he himself experienced:

> Not that he [civilization's literary man] has had to struggle with himself, that the times have torn him in painful spiritual conflict; not that his heart

is bound here *and* there, that he is trying by admonishing, punishing, appeasing, and preaching to pacify both sides, placing himself, like gentle Romain Rolland, above the fray. With full passion, he thrusts himself *into* the fray — but on the side of the enemy.[29]

But how is the critique of this unproblematic posture, of this throwing-oneself-in-the-fray, connected with Germanness? With its initial distinction as protest, deeply embedded in music and metaphysics, is Mann's definition of Germanness not also an engaged posture? By the third chapter of his work Mann has relinquished this definition. With a new determination of substance of Germanness the conservative discourse itself changes into one intent on *problematizing*. From this new position Mann turns against the unreflective posture of the civilization literator. And what is the content of this new determination? While the "eternal protest" of Dostoyevsky was a pure negation with no positive sense, the new connotation of Germanness dissolves all substantive content, including that of "eternal protest." By capturing Germanness in a problematizing attitude Mann transforms it into an empty concept, enabling him to operate with it from a variety of perspectives: "The concept 'German' is an abyss, bottomless, and one should be extremely careful with its negative, the judgement of 'un-German,' so that one is not tripped up and hurt."[30]

This assertion is highly significant regarding the ambivalence informing the *Reflections*. From this point on the book's entire dichotomous manner of argument is undermined. The now deconstructed concept of *Germanness* simply precludes a mode of argumentation based on polarities such as the familiar culture/civilization, music/literature, spirit/politics, in short, German/un-German. In other words, the antipodal levels of understanding in the text retain only a relativized validity. The actual process of argumentation is exposed in the correction of the antipodal mode on the text's surface.

Yet Mann does not linger in this totally reflective, self-questioning writing posture. After thoroughly deconstructing the concept "Germanness" Mann ascribes to it new, transformed content which no longer turns on the notion of a mute land: "In Germany's soul, *Europe's* intellectual antitheses are carried to the end — 'carried to the end' — in a maternal and in a warlike sense. This is truly her real national destiny."[31] The conservative demarcation of Germany as distinct from the enlightened West is blurred. Beyond this, the conflict between the two diverging worldviews is transposed to a point within Germany itself. With this shift in meaning, Germany now not only entails resistance to progressive thought but, itself implies, paradoxically, the principles of progress. For Mann no longer perceives Germany's uniqueness in its "eternal protest" but in its *problematic* being, in which the European conflicts reside. In light of this redefinition the critique of the civilization literator is refocused. The pro-Western type goes awry because of his inability to recognize Germany's peculiar characteristic as the battleground of European contradictions; he instead attempts to resolve the contradictions. Mann, on the other hand, alludes to Germany as the vessel of European intellectual oppositions when he insists that indeterminacy is Germany's national characteristic and that these very oppositions render the notion of a united Germany extremely tenuous. Of course, there are intellectual conflicts in Western countries, in France and England, but these are enveloped within the national integrity of each. In contrast, these conflicts emerge in Germany "completely without national coloration, without national synthesis."[32]

Mann's steadfast insistence on the peculiarly German problematic becomes decisive for him when he projects this national fate into the realm of the individual intellectual. For Mann as artist his fate is to remain mired in the problematic and to share the tragedy uniquely ordained for Germany. The intertwinement of national and individual destinies is further explored through the concept of "burgherly nature." His analysis of this concept relies heavily on Georg Lukács's depiction of *Bürgerlichkeit* in *Soul and Form* (1911) and comes to the conclusion that the *German* artist shares the same ethical sensibility as the burgher: "An artist is burgherly when he transfers the ethical characteristics of the burgherly way of life: order, sequence, rest, 'diligence' — not in the sense of industriousness, but of faithful workmanship — to the exercise of art."[33] Adopting Lukács's premise of the primacy of ethics over aesthetics in his discussion of nineteenth-century German realism, Mann thus establishes "the Germanic figure of the burgherly artist" in contradistinction to the European aesthete.[34]

The new determination of Germanness evincing the lifestyle of the burgher and based on stability and order might at first seem diametrically opposed to the previous allusions to Germanness as the battleground of European intellectual conflicts. A closer examination of "burgherly artist" reveals, however, that the concept itself is anything but free from contradictions. While the surprising combination of the adjective "burgherly" with the noun "artist" was first employed by Lukács in his discussion of German realism, Mann uses it as the paradoxical basis from which to proceed on the disharmonious aspects of the German burgherly artist. Mann does not, then, use the concept to confirm the unproblematic equilibrium suggested in the initial equation of the burgherly and the artistic forms of life: "Burgherly artistic genius, a paradox come true, but a paradox just the same, a duality and inner conflict at any rate, in spite of the legitimacy that this intellectual way of life has, precisely in Germany."[35] The "duality" here does not necessarily (or only) refer to Mann's own burgherly way of life as an artist. According to Mann such a split occurs, for example, in Wagner's art by virtue of the composer's "ability that arose from the need not only to capture and fascinate the most sophisticated people — this is obvious — but also the wide mass of simple ones."[36]

In all of these considerations of the burgherly artist the obtrusiveness of terms such as "paradox," "split," and "duality" suggests interesting projections on Mann's part. The idiosyncratic destinies of both Germany and himself (as artist), function in both directions: Mann understands his own fate as an artist mirroring his country's intellectual destiny, while at the same time construing Germanness as a projection of the premises of his own artistic stance. While the initial definition of the "burgherly artist" only identifies the adjective "burgherly" with "German," soon it is the paradoxical connotation itself which is transferred to the nature of Germanness. Mann deems the unresolved tension stemming from the simultaneous claim on being a burgher and an artist as "Tonio Kröger's old song," raising at the same time a telling question:

> But is one perhaps precisely for this reason *German*? Is not the German character the middle, the medium and the mediating one, and the German the central human being in the grand style? If it is already German to be a burgher, then it is perhaps even more German to be something between a burgher and an artist, and also something between a patriot and a European, between a protestor and a Westerner, a conservative and a nihilist...?[37]

Definitions of Germanness as the vessel of both European antitheses and of the burgherly artistic nature have complementary semantic functions. However, with Germanness occupying the *middle position*, a new identity is ascribed both to the German nation and the artist Mann. The mediating role of the German character does not dissolve the antinomies in favor of one side or the other; on the contrary, its *causa essendi* is grounded in the existence of these polarities. Again, what is interesting here is the manner in which Mann transfers the categories informing his fictional work into sociopolitical discourse. As it remains Tonio Kröger's task to play the mediator between "life" and the "intellect," despite his ironic consciousness of their irreconcilability, Mann imagines that being German implies a middle ground between the protestor and the Westerner, conservatism and the idea of progress.

The decisive question that needs to be addressed in this context is whether Germany's mediating role would foster the sublation (*Aufhebung*) of those antitheses which Mann designates as European; would it lead to a kind of Hegelian synthesis? The passage from the *Reflections* cited above, as might be expected, is not definitive in regard to this question. The idea of Germanness as the middle part appears rather as a blueprint and is in fact proposed on an experimental basis. For this reason Mann calls this last shift in the series of definitions of the German nature a "musing" (*Grübelei*).[38] Nevertheless, the new definition unmistakably anticipates the concept of "humanity" which Mann was to develop in the 1920s. During the Weimar era he locates the idea of humanity precisely where the above-discussed definition of Germanness led: to the arena of intellectual conflicts. (In the war essays the concept "humanity" itself remains primarily linked to the unpolitical nature of the educated German bourgeoisie.) In this sense "humanity" as the middle position reveals itself in the much-disputed section of the "Snow" chapter in *The Magic Mountain*.

Castorp's reflections, following his dream in the snow of the "sunny people" and the atrocious temple, revolve around "man," "*homo Dei*," and "humankind" until the seemingly revelatory conclusion, conspicuously conveyed in the novel in italics: "*For the sake of goodness and love, man shall grant death no dominion over his thoughts.*" The pondering that leads to this proposition reveals Castorp circumscribing humanity in a series of tentative formulations. His thoughts wander from "life's problem child" to "*homo Dei*'s state" as the middle of opposite forces (of life and death and their variations); from the concept of the "middle" he proceeds to the more dramatic formulation portraying man as "the master of contradictions, they occur through him, and so he is more noble than they." It is thus plausible to argue that the definition of Germanness as the middle, a definition which Mann articulates musingly in the war essays in question form, is transferred to Castorp's idea of humanity as heralded in his snow vision. In the episode on Freemasonry, Castorp finds the endless disputes between his mentors wearisome: "They carried everything to extremes, these two, as was probably necessary for the sake of argument, and squabbled fiercely over the most extreme choices, whereas it seemed to him that what one might, in a spirit of conciliation, declare truly human or humane had to lie somewhere in the middle of this intolerant contentiousness, somewhere between rhetorical humanism and illiterate barbarism" (513). The use of the term "middle" clearly reiterates Castorp's insight in the snow. More important, however, are the phrases "in a spirit of conciliation" and "one might . . . declare," for they confirm the premise of the italicized sentence in "Snow" contained in the ethical proclamation of the phrase "for the sake of." It is not a coincidence that Hans's Freemasonry reflection is situated in the chapter "A Good Soldier," which immediately follows "Snow." Assuming a middle position is not an epistemic but an ethical necessity; not because one would grasp 'truth' in the middle of binary oppositions but because only through this conciliatory state would one liberate the "human" from victimization by intellectual or political extremes. Thus, in "A Good Soldier," the remark of his dying cousin, Joachim, that he was feeling feverish turns Hans's attention in human terms to his cousin and away from the contentious debaters Naphta and Settembrini.

Finally, while in Mann's use of the "middle" in the *Reflections* and *The Magic Mountain* merely the terms "German" and "*homo Dei*" seem to have been transposed, Castorp's designation of man as "the master of contradictions" in "Snow" reiterates, more subtly than in the above equation, another definition of Germanness from the *Reflections*, that of Germanness as the battleground of European oppositions. These connections between the *Reflections* and *The Magic Mountain* are illuminating in that they reveal that the blueprint for Mann's attempt in the 1920s to overcome the antithetical mode of thinking had already been drafted in what is ostensibly his most antithetical work, *Reflections of a Nonpolitical Man*. Even though Mann's representation of the German character as the middle presupposes a field of oppositions, Germanness denies itself any partisanship.

The definition of Germanness as the middle ground, then, implies a crucial anticipatory foundation. But the middle-ground determination also significantly intensifies the sense of ambivalence underlying the concept of Germanness. At no point does Germanness as mediation coincide with any of the previous definitions presented in the war essays, even if it complements the idea of Germanness as battlefield. Mann's strategic shift from one definition of the German national character to another finally means that grasping the core of the concept "German" is impossible.

The lack of definitive conclusions both in the war essays and *The Magic Mountain* is rooted in Mann's essentially modernist posture, a stance which implies an assault on the concept of absolute truth. As early as the 1906 essay "Bilse and I" Mann sketches the contours of this posture. In contrast to direct expression, which Mann regards as self-exposure, he posits the freedom of the artist as aloof from presuppositions. With this definition, Mann proclaims the principles of his own artistic stance.[39] I would suggest, however, that the major function of irony in Thomas Mann's fiction is not the avoidance of commitment for its own sake. Mann problematizes issues using the tools of cognitive critique in a manner not unlike Adorno's dialectical strategies in his exploration of Germanness. The ambivalence animating Mann's shifting definitions of Germanness in the *Reflections of a Nonpolitical Man* betrays a decided affinity with the mode of representation in Mann's literary work. Analogously to "The Thunderbolt," where the author's perception of war could not be reduced to one definitive formula, the argumentation of the war essays leaves a clear identification of the author's stance with neither progressive nor conservative thought. The affinity of strategies in the fictional and essayistic realms lies in their exploratory critical premises.

As several statements from 1917–1918 attest, essay writing makes Thomas Mann rather uncomfortable. In a letter from this period the author alludes to his recently completed *Reflections of a Nonpolitical Man* in a manner recalling the "Prologue" to the war essays, that is, as a book imposed upon him by the times themselves.[40] Immediately before the publication of the *Reflections* he describes the publication as an adventure which would expose him to the public in a much different, more immediate way than could ever happen with a novel.[41] There is no doubt that Mann's hesitations here stem in part from the uneasy — perhaps unsuitable — role he played in the wartime essays as a nationalistic polemicist. Yet, as noted above, another cause of this uneasiness can be traced to the historical need to express himself in an essay rather than in narrative fiction, for this means the inevitability of direct speech, of immediate engagement, in short, the necessity of taking a position. The *Reflections*, then, becomes a "true adventure" for Mann by virtue of his having to speak himself instead of having others speak, as Mann formulates the problem in his "Prologue." Mann's claim that a residue of role-playing can be detected throughout the *Reflections*, even if the whole matter was quite serious for him, supports the assumption that he had not fully adjusted to this new discourse. The allusion to role-playing indicates that Mann has not abandoned artistic premises as he enters a realm which demanded direct engagement with the events of the time. Mann himself realizes the problematical aspect of this new task and admits that the *Reflections*, a political confession, retains in spite of the nonfiction mode in which it is written, a "poetic sophistry" that Mann attributes to his artistic identity. He sees a paradox in this discrepancy, but leaves all further speculation aside.[42]

An all-too-often clichéd reception of the *Reflections* does little to acknowledge this paradox. What is worse, the German-nationalistic theses of the book have been frequently attached to the person Thomas Mann in an uncritical fashion. Such readings rely, on the one hand, on the seemingly confessional character of the war essays and, on the other hand, on a superficial correlation between author and work. It is precisely such "preconceived ideas that stubbornly persist in being attached to Mann as a person" which Adorno attempts to undo in his essay "Toward a Portrait of Thomas Mann."[43] According to Adorno, it would be wrong to transfer the formulaic ideas from Mann's work (such as the conflict between the burgher and the artist) expressly to the person of the artist himself: "I believe that the substance of a work of art begins precisely where the author's intention stops; the intention is extinguished by the substance.... Understanding Thomas Mann: his work will truly begin to unfold only when people start paying attention to the things that are not in the guidebooks."[44]

The concept of substance stands conspicuously at the center of Adorno's argument. Substance, described as the sedimentation of a historico-philosophical meaning in the *form* of a work of art, carries Hegelian connotations in Adorno's argument. Such a definition clearly detaches substance from the author's intention. In his comment on Thomas Mann, Adorno contrasts concrete elements of Mann's novels, such as the depiction of events and fictional characters, in which Adorno recognizes the substance, with general ideas which are presumed to contain the meaning. For Adorno, "even the last boldface sentence in the snow chapter of *The Magic Mountain*" is such a general idea which is outweighed by those elements forming the substance.[45]

This compelling distinction between substance and intention may be used to shed light on the question of Mann's intellectual stance in the FirstWorld War. Adorno's thought demonstrates that the image of Thomas Mann as the representative of conservative Germanness is largely inferred by means which ignore the separation, evident in Mann's oeuvre, between linguistic form and personal origin. Adorno maintains that such a procedure encourages critics "to take out of [the oeuvre] as its substance what the author put in. This procedure is not very productive, of course, but nobody has to think very much, and it puts even stupidity on solid philological ground, for, as it says in *Figaro*, he is the father, he says so himself."[46] Understanding Mann's wartime oeuvre, especially the *Reflections*, only in terms of the disparate assertions in it, without taking into consideration the *form* of argument by virtue of which the discourse destabilizes itself, might consequently result in some kind of *Figaro* logic: he is the conservative, he himself says so.

Refuting such an argument is rendered difficult by the fact that the *Reflections* is understood solely as a confessional book. Could a similar notion of substance similar to what Adorno sees in Mann's fiction be the question here? In two letters from 1918 Mann suggests that *Reflections of a Nonpolitical Man* should not be read as a "book" which aims at convincing the reader of certain opinions but, rather, as a novel. In this sense, Mann maintains, the *Reflections* is to be understood as the representation of an intellectual fate which its author experienced, and from which he later — by virtue of representing it — distanced himself.[47] However, if we were to take this utterance alone as evidence of the point to be demonstrated, we would be trapped in the same *Figaro* logic that Adorno invokes. Focusing on the formal-compositional elements of argument in the war essays rather than relying solely on Mann's own commentary thus proves more productive for exploring their substance in Adorno's sense. The shifting definitions of Germanness, outlined earlier, bear witness to this substance.

Furthermore, it must be remembered that the private person often remains concealed behind masks. For Adorno, masks emerge not only from the clichés of the public sphere, but also from the self-dissimulation of the artist. The mask of the genius in modern literature attests to this dual aspect. As for Thomas Mann, Adorno writes: "Masks can be switched and the many-sided Mann had more than one. The best known is that of the Hanseatic, the cool and reserved senator's son from Lübeck."[48] It is not easy to determine to what extent the image of the German-conservative Thomas Mann, an image suggested by Mann himself in the *Reflections* and his correspondence in the First World War, implies a mask. Instead of merely focusing on the question of masks, then, the task is to explore — in Adorno's sense — the substance of the *Reflections of a Nonpolitical Man* and to pose the question of how the representation of the conservative artist is undermined by the discourse of the war essays.

Clearly, written from beyond the experience of the Third Reich, Adorno's "On the Question: What is German?" counteracts constructions of Germanness more forcefully than Thomas Mann's political vision would ever allow during the First World War. At the outset of his essay Adorno writes: "It is uncertain whether there even is such a thing as the German person or a specifically German quality or anything analogous in other nations. The True and the Better in every people is much more likely that which does *not* adapt itself to the collective subject but, wherever possible, even resists it."[49] While in the *Reflections* one definition of Germanness is "an abyss," Mann does not thematize the problem of constructing collective identities as Adorno does. On the contrary, he attributes to other nations — even if for the sake of depicting intellectual or political positions — fixed characteristics, contrasting them to the elusiveness of Germanness. Adorno's "resistance" reveals itself in Mann primarily around the concept of Germanness.

Even though Adorno's defiant attitude toward the collective subject is more expansive, his strategy of argument circles around Germanness. He resists hypostatizations through a myriad of points which at times appear incompatible, including his focus on the nature of the German language. But as mentioned earlier, the author's attachment to and distance from the realm of the German language reveals a crucial aspect of his dialectical method. While Adorno's native tongue functions in the essay as the signifier of the intellectual collectivity of a nation, thus serving as a palliative for his fragmented self in exile, Adorno also makes clear the kind of pitfalls hypostatizing this linguistic realm might entail. Yet, in Adorno's undercutting of collective identities, one aspect of "what is German" stands out as a given: the *complexity* of the question, that is, the impossibility of an unequivocal answer. Precisely this insight is the most resounding echo of Thomas Mann's treatment of the same question in the *Reflections*. Notwithstanding the danger of stereotyping, we may conclude here that such complexity permeates the thought of both Mann and Adorno as authors working with the German language. Adorno comments on Mann:

> The rhythm of his sense of life was unbourgeois: it was not continuity but rather an oscillation between extremes, an alternation of rigidity and illumination. That may have been irritating to friends who were not very close to him. For in this rhythm, where one state negated the other, the ambiguity [*Doppelbödigkeit*] of his character was revealed. I can think of scarcely a statement he made that was not accompanied by this ambiguity. Everything he said sounded as though it had a secret double meaning which, with a devilishness that went far beyond his ironic stance, he left it to the other person to figure out.[50]

Notes

[1] Theodor W. Adorno, "On the Question: 'What is German,'" trans. Thomas Y. Levin, *New German Critique* 36 (1985): 121–131, here 129. Cited as Adorno.

[2] Adorno, 130.

[3] Adorno, 121.

[4] Adorno, 123–125.

[5] Adorno, 124.

[6] Adorno, 125.

[7] Adorno, 125.

[8] As is known from the "Author's Note" following the *Faustus* text, Thomas Mann borrowed quite freely, at times verbatim, from Adorno's writings on their contemporary, composer and theoretician Arnold Schönberg, and the twelve-tone system developed theoretically in the latter's *Harmonielehre*.

[9] All further references will be to, *The Magic Mountain*, trans. John E. Woods (New York: Alfred A. Knopf, 1995).

[10] Thomas Mann, *Reflections of a Nonpolitical Man*, trans. Walter Morris (New York: Frederick Ungar, 1983).

[11] Thomas Mann, "The Making of *The Magic Mountain*," trans. H.T. Lowe-Porter in *The Magic Mountain*, trans. H.T. Lowe-Porter (New York: Vintage, 1969), 716–27, here 720.

[12] Mann, *Reflections*, "Prologue," 3–4. In the critical literature on Mann numerous accounts describe the impact of this shattering realization on the author's intellectual development. Hans Mayer, for example, draws on Mann's own words to note the crucial temporal play informing *The Magic Mountain*. Temporal perspectives seem to be transposed. The narrative moves inexorably toward the First World War, while the composition of the narrative looks backward, taking the war as the narrated genesis and the 1920s as the authorial vantage point. Hans Mayer, *Thomas Mann*, 2d ed. (Frankfurt am Main: Suhrkamp, 1983), 119.

[13] For an overview of this dispute see Hugh Ridley, *The Problematic Bourgeois: Twentieth-Century Criticism on Thomas Mann's "Buddenbrooks" and "The Magic Mountain"* (Columbia, SC: Camden House, 1994), especially Chapter 6, "Lost in the Snow," 109–120.

[14] Karl Mannheim, *Konservatismus: Ein Beitrag zur Soziologie des Wissens*, eds. David Kettler, Volker Meja, and Nico Stehr (Frankfurt am Main: Suhrkamp, 1984), 68. Mannheim's definition of the term "conservatism" on historical grounds enables a significant distinction to be drawn between the concept of "traditionalism," which he borrows from Max Weber, and conservatism.While the former manifests itself as an unreflective adherence to established customs and life forms, the reflectivity of conservatism is its crucial characteristic. Klaus Epstein in his *The Genesis of German Conservatism* (Princeton: Princeton UP, 1966) draws on Mannheim's designation of "old conservatism" (*Altkonservatismus*) when he states: "Conservative attitudes have existed throughout recorded history, in the sense that men have felt hostile to changes in their accustomed and cherished world. They are correlative with the fact of change itself, and are basically rooted in the human fear of the unknown and desire for a predictable environment. There have been many changes throughout history which have provoked not only a psychological uneasiness but an articulate expression of Conservative defense.... What is significant in the eighteenth century — in Germany around 1770 — is that Conservatism, while remaining in substance a defense of concrete institutions *ad hoc*, developed for the first time the *self-conscious* attitude of a distinctive *Weltanschauung*" (65). While the above formulations reflect an older conservatism identified with particular historical epochs, crucial qualities of these political dispositions are carried over into new conservative forms in Wilhelmine Germany at the turn of the twentieth century. For models of new conservatism see, among others, Armin Mohler, *Die konservative Revolution in Deutschland 1918–1932*, 4th ed. (Darmstadt: Wissenschaftliche Buchgesellschaft, 1994); Clemens von Klemperer, *Germany's New Conservatism: Its History and Dilemma in the Twentieth Century* (Princeton: Princeton UP, 1968); Fritz Stern, *The Politics of Cultural Despair* (New York: Anchor, 1965).

[15] Three figures prevail within this tradition as "a triple constellation of eternally united spirits": Schopenhauer, Wagner, and Nietzsche (*Reflections* 54). Their

impact on Mann's self-understanding as an artist remains a major theme throughout the *Reflections*.

[16] In the Thomas Mann scholarship, especially since the 1980s, there has been an increasing tendency to refocus on the *Reflections of a Nonpolitical Man* as a work of primary significance for Mann's overall intellectual development and worldview. By exploring the war essays more thoroughly than earlier these recent studies have laid out new and differentiated aspects of the *Reflections*. Especially informative for my framework of analysis here are Irving Stock, "Ironic Conservatism: Thomas Mann's *Reflections of a Nonpolitical Man*," *Salmagundi* 68–69 (1985–86): 166–85; John Evan Seery, "Political Irony and World War: A Reading of Thomas Mann's *Betrachtungen*," *Soundings* 63.1 (1990): 5–29; and Herbert Lehnert, Eva Wessel, *Nihilismus der Menschenfreundlichkeit: Thomas Manns "Wandlung" und sein Essay "Goethe und Tolstoi*," Thomas-Mann-Studien, 9 (Frankfurt am Main: Vittorio Klostermann, 1991), 11–110. These works also share points of contact with my earlier study "Konservatismus, Skepsis, Fortschrittsdenken: Thomas Manns *Betrachtungen eines Unpolitischen*," diss., U of Washington, 1986. Compare also, among others, Hellmann, *Das Geschichtsdenken des frühen Thomas Mann: 1906–1918* (Tübingen: Max Niemeyer, 1972); Klaus Bohnen, "Argumentationsverfahren und politische Kritik bei Thomas Mann," in *Gedenkschrift für Thomas Mann 1875–1975*, ed. Rolf Wiecker (Copenhagen: Text und Kontext, 1975), 171–91; Hermann Kurzke, *Auf der Suche nach der verlorenen Irrationalität: Thomas Mann und der Konservatismus* (Würzburg: Königshausen und Neumann, 1980); Hubert Ohl, "Künstlerwerk: Zu Thomas Mann's 'Betrachtungen eines Unpolitischen,'" *Heinrich Mann: Sein Werk in der Weimarer Republik*, eds. Helmut Koopmann and Peter-Paul Schneider (Frankfurt am Main: Vittorio Klostermann, 1983), 41–53.

[17] For a complete overview of these incompatible contemporary receptions see Klaus Schröter, ed., *Thomas Mann im Urteil seiner Zeit: Dokumente 1891–1955* (Hamburg: Christian Wegner, 1969), 77–102.

[18] Kurt Sontheimer, *Thomas Mann und die Deutschen* (Munich: Nymphenburger Verlag, 1961), 11.

[19] See Bernd Widdig, "Mann unter Männern: Männerbünde und die Angst vor der Masse in der Rede *Von deutscher Republik*," *German Quarterly* 66.4 (1993): 524–36. The study focuses on the homoerotic subtext of Mann's 1922 speech *The German Republic*. Widdig concludes that, because of the exclusive nature of the male bond as portrayed in the 1922 speech, Mann's turn to democracy had not yet taken place at that point. Widdig argues that Mann saw the beginning of the Republic not in its official declaration in 1918 but, rather, in the departure point of 1914. "In the community of the young German warriors, the first unification of state and culture takes place" (527).

[20] See Stanley Corngold, "Mann as a Reader of Nietzsche," *The Fate of the Self: German Writers and French Theory* (New York: Columbia UP, 1986), 129–159.

[21] Mann, *Reflections*, 29.

[22] Mann, *Reflections*, 28.

[23] Mann, *Reflections*, 32.

[24] Mann, *Reflections*, 44–45.

[25] Mann, *Reflections*, 39.

[26] Mann, *Reflections*, 42.

[27] See Irving Stock, "The Magic Mountain," *Modern Fiction Studies* 32.4 (1986): 487–520, here 509.

[28] The lack of self-critique which Mann detects here in the optimism of the literator type, is explored on a much larger historical and theoretical scale by Adorno. See especially Max Horkheimer and Theodor W. Adorno, *Dialectic of Enlightenment*, trans. John Cumming (New York: Continuum, 1972).

[29] Mann, *Reflections*, 38.

[30] Mann, *Reflections*, 37. Compare with Louis Dumont, *German Ideology: From France to Germany and Back* (Chicago and London: U of Chicago P, 1991), 53–65, here 64.

[31] Mann, *Reflections*, 36. It should be noted here that in this new determination of Germanness as the battleground of European currents, Mann refers only to the realm of the intellect; he ignores all social and historical currents which give rise to them. That Germany might develop out of its problematic vacillation through changes in the social, historical dynamic, appears in Mann's consciousness only negatively as a degenerated image of society. Mann rejects it out of hand.

[32] Mann, *Reflections*, 36.

[33] Mann, *Reflections*, 73.

[34] Mann, *Reflections*, 72.

[35] Mann, *Reflections*, 76.

[36] Mann, *Reflections*, 77.

[37] Mann, *Reflections*, 78.

[38] Mann, *Reflections*, 78.

[39] See also Harald Höbusch, "Kunst und Kritik beim frühen Thomas Mann: Thomas Manns Ästhetik, 1893–1913," diss., U of California, Irvine, 1996, 152–170.

[40] Erika Mann, ed., *Thomas Mann: Briefe 1889–1936* (Frankfurt am Main: Fischer, 1961), 133–34.

[41] *Thomas Mann: Briefe*, 149.

[42] Mann, *Reflections*, "Prologue," 3.

[43] Adorno, "Toward a Portrait of Thomas Mann," *Notes To Literature*, vol. 2, ed. Rolf Tiedemann, trans. Shierry Weber Nicholsen (New York: Columbia UP, 1992), 12–19, here 12.

[44] Adorno, "Thomas Mann," 13.
[45] Adorno, "Thomas Mann," 13.
[46] Adorno, "Thomas Mann," 13.
[47] *Thomas Mann: Briefe*, 148.
[48] Adorno, "Thomas Mann," 14.
[49] Adorno, "What is German?" 121.
[50] Adorno, "What is German?" 16.

DAVID BLUMBERG

5: From Muted Chords to Maddening Cacophony: Music in *The Magic Mountain*

WRAPPED IN FURS AND WOOLENS, HANS CASTORP lies on the balcony of room 34 in his beloved lounge chair on a winter night. Out of the darkness music comes to him, "drifting up, now near, now far, from the valley."[1] Music without musicians, its source remains invisible, suggesting what we already know — that it belongs to Hans Castorp, to his story, his world, and like the hovering female body teeming with life which will soon appear, it is a projection of his desire. The vacillating strains of music presage the moist breathing and "lacelike pounding of her heart" (281). Carried by the wind, Hans's night music resembles the suspended image which seems "remote and yet as near as his senses" (272). The music's ebb and flow becomes a metaphor for Hans's fluctuating perception of the cosmic vision of life which excites both analytical and passionate responses. Following an extended colloquy on the origins of life and detailed analysis of the body's biology, the floating image bends toward the now enraptured visionary, enveloping him in a "hot and tender" embrace (281).

In Nietzsche's *The Birth of Tragedy* the Dionysian spirit of music engenders a similar image of a "primordial mother," eternally procreative and "eternally finding satisfaction in [the ceaseless flux] of phenomena."[2] Nietzsche derives the connection between a primal life force and music from Schopenhauer, for whom music was the direct expression of the will itself. Although both philosophers see music as potentially breaking the illusion of the *principium individuationis*, they disagree on the final goal toward which such insight is the first step. For Schopenhauer, music "enables us to survey and comprehend" the essence of the will and thus escape it temporarily.[3] The permanent form of such escape corresponds to the complete quelling of "the will-to-live" and is achieved only by holy men through extreme asceticism. In contrast, Nietzsche emphasizes music's ability to arouse passion for life and sensual experience. At the heart of Nietzsche's "optimistic" justification of life and attendant critique of life-denying morality lies the Dionysian spirit of music. According to Mann, Schopenhauer's denial of the will implies a privileging of metaphysics, of the "idea" of man over his physical manifestation. Mann terms such privileging "Apolline" and contrasts it to Nietzsche's "Dionysism."[4] Echoing Nietzsche, who, despite his enthusiasm for a Dionysian intoxication revealed as truth, recognized the necessity of its rational, objective counterpart, Mann posits art as the reciprocal interpenetration of spiritual objectivity with sensuality, of "Geschlecht" with "Geist."[5]

This dialectic conception of art informs *The Magic Mountain* — including the novel's music, charged as it is with the affirmation and denial of the will articulated by Schopenhauer and Nietzsche. The following discussion of this music and its reception in the ears of Hans Castorp moves through a series of scenes from the novel. From popular ditty to sublime aria, Hans's musical experiences consistently expose an unconscious level of the text.

In a scene from early in the book, "muted chords" from a morning concert at the hotel below the sanatorium make their way up the mountain slope and in through the balcony doors of Hans Castorp's room. As he listens to the music Hans watches a pale woman dressed in black walking in the garden below who "matched her long, somber strides, apparently without realizing it, to the rhythm of the march music in the distance" (37). By setting the movement of this somber figure to march music, Mann invokes the allegorical image of death, resolutely advancing. Even before Hans, and with him the reader, learns of *Tous-les-deux's* two deathly ill sons, her walk through the garden is inflected as a funeral march. Yet she herself remains unconscious of the music. The march music functions in a way similar to the chorus in Greek tragedy — invoked by Mann through *Tous-les-deux's* resemblance to "a famous tragedian" — by giving universal resonance to an individual action. Like the chorus, the music originates in a space outside of the narrative's immediate confines: while audible to the audience — which here includes Hans Castorp — it remains unknown to the dramatic figures. Cast as a universal symbol of suffering, the woman arouses Hans's sympathy. For a moment he sees through the illusion of the "I" and "You," the veil of the Maya. Her suffering becomes his suffering and colors his perception of the world: "it seemed [to Hans] as if her sad appearance darkened the morning sun" (37). Through contemplation of the tragic figure Hans seems temporarily to overcome his will, to recognize his oneness with the world; and yet his selfless sympathy, as is shown later in the novel, belies an infatuation with the signs of inner decay and death. As a symbol of war and the military the march also hints at the young protagonist's ultimate fate on the battlefield, where such desire finds its highest fulfillment.

The exposition of Hans's feelings concerning death is suspended in this scene by his simultaneous perception of sounds of an "indelicate nature" emanating from an adjoining room. In an instant the scene's focus shifts from the moribund to the sexual, with a corresponding change in the musical accompaniment. Just as it had with the figure of death in the garden, music brings out the essence of this new image.

> An apparent chase around the furniture, the crash of an upturned chair, a grab, an embrace, slaps and kisses — and then . . . to accompany the invisible scene, a waltz was struck up in the distance, the tired melody of a popular ballad. Hans Castorp stood, towel in hand, and listened against his best intentions. (38)

Upon initial consideration, the gliding rhythm of the waltz appears strangely incongruous to the indelicate, aperiodic movements of Hans's neighbors. As a symbol of grace, sophistication, and elegance, the waltz poses a sharp contrast to their raucous behavior. However, it is not the elegant dance of the Viennese ballroom that is invoked here, but rather "the tired melody" of a *Gassenhauer*, to use Mann's original German designation. Defined as a popular street-song with humorous or even crude lyrics and a banal melody, the *Gassenhauer* becomes in this passage an icon for the lower classes to which — in the eyes of Hans Castorp and of the majority of the Berghof's inhabitants — this "Bad Russian" couple belongs. By associating the waltz with the Bad Russian couple and their indiscretion, Mann intimates the waltz's origin as a daring, even risque, intrusion from the lower classes into the polite world.[6] Since it presents a base, inferior form of the waltz, the scene's musical accompaniment also reflects Hans's condescending attitude toward his "low-class" neighbors and their indiscretion. Yet despite his outrage at the couple's moral impropriety, Hans cannot help but stand and listen. By presenting the young protagonist thus betrayed by his own desires, Mann exposes the fraudulence of his moralistic snobbery and prudishness. With this turn the scene becomes a critique of the bourgeois who indulges voyeuristically in the eroticism and open sexuality associated with the lower classes while intent on maintaining a moral position from which he can damn the very actions he secretly wants to observe. The reader can laugh knowingly at young Hans Castorp and his vulnerability to the power of the will.

In a similarly critical fashion Gustav Mahler integrates waltz forms into his symphonies, composed at the beginning of the century. With biting sarcasm the composer pokes fun at Austrian society through shrill and highly exaggerated waltzlike themes — invoking Vienna's popular musical heritage while pointing out its obsolescence. In the third movement of his Ninth Symphony, completed in 1910, Mahler strips the modern waltz of its elegance and sophistication by combining it with a "Ländler," the waltz's plebeian predecessor. But it is not through "contamination" that the unrefined, folksy style of the "Ländler," brings the waltz down from its lofty heights; instead, the "Ländler" with its coarse, unreserved quality, exposes the waltz and its pretension of refinement, in effect removing the glitter that conceals the vulgarity and morbidity of the world of the operetta with which the waltz had become associated. Music becomes the vehicle through which Mahler, like Mann, exposes the repressed desires of the bourgeoisie.[7]

One character in particular captures the "vulgarity and morbidity" underlying the cheery facade of the operetta. Lady Overblown, one of the Berghof's "high-ranking" patients visited by Hans Castorp during his tour of charity, is in a permanent state of excitement and titillation. She fidgets, churns her legs, and punctuates her speech with "a very high, silvery-bright, bubbly laugh" (300). Brimming with sexual energy, the ill young woman is depicted as desirous despite (or perhaps because of) her moribund state. The narrator makes special note of her girlish neck, dimpled collarbone, and breasts — "soft and young under the linen sheets" (301). Her theatrical laughter, rhythmically articulated in the text ("ha ha ha, hee hee hee"), keeps her breast constantly fluttering as she struggles for air. Filled with ornamental trills, grace notes, and silvery arpeggios, Lady Overblown's incessant laughter turns her utterances into musical passes and brings to mind an aria from the most famous of Viennese operettas, *Die Fledermaus*, composed by the "Waltz King" Johann Strauss Jr. in 1874. Commonly known as the "laughing song," "Mein Herr Marquis" is sung by Adele, a chambermaid who is attending a ball disguised in her lady's best dress and posing as a famous actress. When recognized by Herr von Eisenstein, her employer, Adele successfully laughs off what she knows to be the truth by suggesting the utter absurdity of his claim: "Ja, sehr komisch, / Ha ha ha, / Ist die Sache, / Ha ha ha." With the help of the guests who also find Eisenstein's faux pas funny, the chambermaid maintains her illusion. Her performance more than simply convinces her accuser; it enchants him and inspires an amorous kiss.

Quivering breasts and musical flourish, however, leave Hans Castorp unmoved. Lady Overblown's mirth disturbs him; it — like the "waltzing" of his neighbors — strikes him as inappropriate to someone "hovering between life and death" (302). Insulted by her nonchalance in the face of death, Hans disapproves of Lady Overblown, whose behavior makes comedy out of tragedy. He condemns her glittery purls of laughter as products of "childish giddiness and silly ignorance" (302). Wrapped up in his condescending judgment, Hans fails to consider a psychological interpretation of her behavior.

Such interpretation is, however, close at hand and even has a representative within the novel. Dr. Krokowski would surely recognize the cycle of repression manifest in Lady Overblown's neurotic laughter and its function as a defense mechanism against the knowledge of her very serious condition. She, like Adele, uses laughter as means of deception. However, by presenting his "Adele" on her deathbed, where the only deception possible is self-deception, Mann turns farce into bitter satire. On the eve of the "Thunderbolt's" massive destruction, Lady Overblown becomes the symbol of a society happily oblivious to its own imminent demise. Her singing represents the "silvery twilight" of the Viennese operetta and its gay society still intent on forgetting the world and its problems through escapist entertainment. With its underlying principle of repression, operetta glosses over dissonances in both story and score with bubbly melodies and garish dance scenes; the *Gassenhauer* and the waltz — the era's true *Danse Macabre* — are the art form's dominant forces. Instead of leading to a deeper, more analytical understanding of the Schopenhauerian will, or to genuine passion (as opposed to Lady Overblown's theatrics), operetta represses knowledge of the life — and death — behind the veil of appearances by closing each performance with the illusion of a perfect world.

Contributing to the decline of the operetta was the advent of film — even before its shadowy inhabitants were given voices. Cheaper ticket prices and the allure of technology helped the cinema secure an increasingly large share of the entertainment industry. In the company of another deathly ill young woman, the cavalier cousins visit the Bioscope Theater in Platz to view movies projected "to the accompaniment of trivial music, which offered present rhythms to match vanishing phantoms from the past" (311). Prefiguring music's role in the invocation of the dead Joachim later in the book, the musical accompaniment appears to help summon the "phantoms" into the here and now. Through its immediacy music is intended to counteract the projections' cryptic quality, which results largely from their lack of sound. And indeed music facilitates film's illusion of reality, but it does this by concealing signs of death. Just as the séance functions not to recognize and accept death but, rather, to deny death's claim on the deceased, the cinema's music masks the image's deathly silence. Akin to Lady Overblown's silvery laughter, this music represents a distinctly repressive psychological mechanism.

In *Composing for the Films* Eisler and Adorno liken motion-picture music to a "singing child in the dark" who sings to break the silence, which on an unconscious level signals muteness and death. Music serves as an "antidote against the picture" and its threatening silence.

> The need was felt to spare the spectator the unpleasantness involved in seeing effigies of living, acting, and even speaking persons, who were at the same time silent. The fact that they are living and nonliving at the same time is what constitutes their ghostly character, and music was introduced not to supply them with the life they lacked . . . but to exorcise fear or help the spectator absorb the shock.[8]

Such appeasement of fear allows the viewer to respond to the cinematic experience like Frau Stöhr — also present in the Bioscope movie house — who, as Hans Castorp observes, "abandoned herself to the film" (311). The object of fear quickly becomes a source of pleasure which provides temporary fulfillment of "civilization's secret wishes" (311) and lures the spectator into a silent stupor marked by the same mute impotence originally feared. Although this stupor is not unlike Hans's own musically induced trances, the cinematic presentation leaves him relatively unaffected. Kept "sober" by thoughts of how his mentor Settembrini would respond to such a "misuse of technology," Hans steers clear of the celluloid sirens. Perhaps even more significant in this respect is the presence of Frau Stöhr, whose "red, uneducated face was contorted with pleasure" (311). As the novel's foremost representative and most avid consumer of low culture, Frau Stöhr functions as a negative example to Hans Castorp: if she is so taken in by the movies, then they must surely be of no value to him. Hans seeks deeper, more profound experiences of life and death and thus rejects the cinema's projected "phantoms" and "trivial music" for the very reason that they disturb the "silence, the solitude, the serenity" of death (315). Hans consequently experiences such serenity when at the close of the *Danse Macabre* he stands with Karen Karstedt at her future grave "with open mouth and sleepy eyes" (316).

We have seen this reaction before. Coupled early in the book with the effects of alcohol, music washes over Hans, leaving him in a highly relaxed, trancelike state. The intoxicating influence of music is written on Hans's face in physical symptoms which bear a strong resemblance to those witnessed at the grave site.

> Hans Castorp loved music with all his heart, its effect being much like that of the porter he drank with his morning snack — profoundly calming, numbing, and "doze"-inducing — and he listened now with pleasure, his head tilted to one side, mouth open, eyes slightly bloodshot. (36–37)

The signs of enervation (submissiveness, loss of speech, and reduction of visual acuity) indicate a general lowering of both physical and psychological defenses. Hans loses himself in both body and soul to the music, which does not appear to hold his attention by virtue of its structural cohesion or its emotional intensity (if, indeed, it can be said to *hold* his attention at all); his is neither a critical nor an impassioned listening. Through its "'doze'-inducing" power music reduces Hans to a dreamer "without a single firm thought in his head" (29) and neutralizes his reasoning capacity — shutting down all goal-oriented thought processes and opening the door to the unconscious and its primitive drives.

For Mann, Sigmund Freud's division of the human psyche into the id, ego, and superego represents the "translation of [Schopenhauer's] metaphysics into psychology," with the id corresponding "to a hair" with Schopenhauer's will.[9] Through Freud the will gains a more precise articulation as the locus of the two most basic human drives: *Eros*, the sex drive, and *Thanatos*, the death drive. These drives merge in Hans Castorp's love for Clavdia Chauchat which, significantly, is early on signaled by music. Before Hans is fully conscious of the extent of his feelings for the ill and exotic woman, he finds himself humming "a little song that he had heard sung in a light soprano voice, who knew where or when... that had turned up now in his memory" (137). The song, a piece of popular salon music by the Czech composer Franz Bendel,[10] speaks in clichéd lyrics of the binding power of love:

> Wie berührt mich wundersam
> Oft ein Wort von dir,
> Das von deiner Lippe kam,
> Und vom Herzen mir!

Like the recently remembered homoerotic love for Pribislav Hippe, the song contributes to the emergence of thoughts and desires whose object is Madame Chauchat. Music acts as catalyst, stimulating the conscious manifestation of a secret passion. Despite finally turning his nose up at the "silly" little song, Hans takes some satisfaction in the message it imparts — a message close to his own heart:

> One could no longer say that it thudded on its own accord, for no reason, and without any connection to his soul. There was a connection now.... Hans Castorp needed only to think of Frau Chauchat — and he did think of her — and his heart had a suitable emotion to make it pound. (138)

Lifted out of the realm of animal instinct, the heart is recast as the complement to the soul. As euphemistic metonym for his sexual drive, the accelerated pounding of Hans's heart now has a basis in his love for Clavdia; it has been given a "reason." But Hans is not satisfied with such simple harmony between "Geist" and "Geschlecht" and thus rejects the song.

While appropriate to a calm, pedestrian love "down there in the flatlands," the song fails to capture what Hans sees (with no little pride) as the reckless nature of his now quite conscious obsession with a married woman with tuberculosis. Serving as a negative definition every time the topic of his love is invoked, the "little song" becomes a leitmotif.[11] Its "amiable, tender melancholy" is contrasted to the irreconcilable extremes of "frost and heat," of an amorphous dreaminess and feverish desire governing Hans's love (226). Hans even refers to the song in his passionate speech to Clavdia on Walpurgis Night, using it as a foil for his rapturous musings: "Oh, love is nothing if not foolish, something mad and forbidden, an adventure in evil. Otherwise it is merely a pleasant banality, good for singing calm little songs down on the plains" (336). There, on his bourgeois "Brocken," at the peak of his passion (at least of the passion we are privy to), Hans cannot resist looking down for a moment, far down, to the "calm little song," his whipping boy of "low" art, appropriate for the "flatlands," but not for his sublime, elevated feelings. For Hans's truly tragic love only grand opera will do.

Mann borrows generously from the operatic repertoire in forming the dramatic conception of love adhered to by his impressionable protagonist. Two works prove particularly significant in this respect. Hinted at in passing references throughout the novel, the operatic subtext is fully developed in the final chapters. Left behind by Clavdia for the second and final time, Hans discovers "a new passion and enchantment, a new burden of love" (630) aroused by the modern gramophone and its "ghostly music." The specter of Hans's love for Clavdia appears most distinctly in Bizet's *Carmen* (1874), a fragment of which drifts up to Hans's balcony (161) long before he describes the work in a discussion with Pieter Peeperkorn (602). Hans's identification with the story of *Carmen* is first hinted at following an early triumph in the trivial love games with Madame Chauchat. Whipped into a state of ecstasy by a friendly nod from his would-be seductress, Hans suggests to Joachim that they attend a Kurhaus concert that afternoon in the hope that they will hear "that aria from *Carmen*" (232). The aria referred to (from the opera's second act) is sung by Don José, the unlucky soldier who falls under Carmen's spell. In this scene distant bugles have sounded, calling Don José away from his tryst with Carmen and back to his regiment. Intent on fulfilling his duty, he pleads with the fuming Gypsy to understand his predicament. Holding the wilted flower which she had given him at their first meeting, months earlier, Don José sings the story of his love, of the fantasies he entertained while in prison, in an attempt to convince her of his devotion. His song has little effect on Carmen, the sultry dancer, who desires sensual pleasure, not spiritual devotion.

In her analysis of Bizet's opera, Susan McClary points out the fundamental difference in the two characters' conceptions of love:

> Carmen's is firmly grounded in sensuality and the body, while José's attempts to transcend the body through violent striving, conquests, climaxes. Hers involves opening up to another human being; his demands single-minded control and possession.[12]

This extreme disparity lies at the heart of the opera's ever mounting tension, which ultimately leads to Carmen's brutal death. Don José's true object of desire is the dead flower, symbol of his own idealized love, which, unlike the fiercely independent Carmen, he can control and possess. In *The Magic Mountain* such dead symbols are all that remain of Clavdia Chauchat after her departure: her inner portrait and the gramophone records — both securely in the possession of Hans Castorp — are the objects of a devotion which rivals that expressed by his operatic alterego. In order to heighten his "rapt sympathy" with "the little soldier's aria," Hans often listens to it in isolation from the opera's dissonant context (638). In this way he can preserve the aria's bourgeois ethos, the fantasy of transcendent love, which is otherwise undercut by Carmen's cold response.[13] When Hans does venture further into the opera, as in the chapter "Fullness of Harmony," he stalls out at the end of the second act which culminates in the Gypsy band's paean to freedom — a freedom which Don José can also enjoy if he escapes with the outlaws into the mountains. Hans Castorp — sitting for hours on end in a comfortable armchair listening to music streaming from the Berghof's new gramophone — is not yet ready for this opera's violent ending.

At the same sitting Hans has already listened to a different finale, that of Verdi's *Aïda* (1871). It too ends in death, but in a death which is much more compatible with Hans's romantic vision of love. Without Aïda, believed to have returned to her homeland, the hero Radames resigns himself to death. The daughter of the king, Amneris, who is also in love with Radames, pleads with him to renounce Aida and allow her to save him. He refuses. Unwilling to defend himself against charges of treason, Radames is sentenced by the high priest to be buried alive in the crypt underneath the temple of Vulcan. In the opera's final scene, containing the "most admirable music [Hans] had ever heard" (635), Radames is unexpectedly joined in the crypt by his beloved Aïda. Transported by "the ecstasy of an immortal love," they die in each other's arms.

In light of Clavdia's return to the Berghof accompanied by Pieter Peeperkorn, Hans's position resembles that of the rejected lover Amneris, who at the end of the opera throws herself onto Radames's tomb crying out for her "beloved corpse." Acting on morbid tendencies of his own,

Hans throws himself into his "new passion" for the gramophone, the "little truncated coffin of fiddlewood," and its acoustic traces of a living body (633). A twofold desire for possession of and union with the lover's body and soul fuels both characters' passion. For Amneris the unmovable stone that immures Radames, while satisfying the one desire, makes satisfaction of the other impossible. But unlike the crypt's hermetically sealed entrance, the doors of the "small, dull-black temple" are "flung wide" [633]), allowing the heavenly voices to fill the small salon. Housing neatly packaged versions of his operatic lovers embalmed on "treasured disks," the listening room affords Hans a clean and controlled union with death. Here he can experience the allure of the crypt without the stench of its gases, the glory of eternity without the "crude horrors of reality." And it is thanks to "the victorious ideality of music," "the consoling power of beauty to gloss things over" (636) that our hero can enjoy a death as beautiful and sweet as he had always known it could be.

Considering Mann's professed indebtedness to the most famous German opera composer of the nineteenth century, Richard Wagner, it is surprising that no direct reference is made to him in *The Magic Mountain*.[14] Having Hans Castorp choose Italian and French operas as his favorites (a fact that seems to embarrass the narrator [639]) signals Mann's increasingly critical view of the German composer and his art — an attitude nourished by Nietzsche's view of Wagner.[15] Yet, just as with Nietzsche, for whom Wagner — despite the philosopher's scathing critique of him — always remained the Romantic artist *par excellence*, the master of Bayreuth proves omnipresent in Mann's novel even when unnamed.[16]

One of the subtle references to Wagner occurs during Hans's "ill advised" hike, which culminates in the memory of Pribislav Hippe. As he ascends into the mountains behind the sanatorium, the young German *Wanderer* begins to sing "sentimental folk melodies . . . including one that contained the lines: The bards do praise both love and wine, / Yet virtue still more often — " (115). Mann extracts these lines from a student song composed by Albrecht Methfessel in 1818.[17] The text of "Des Vaterlandes Hochgesang," adapted from a poem by Matthias Claudius, speaks of the German *Volk*'s dedication to the fatherland of the old bards and preservation of German virtue. Although surely shared by Wagner (modern champion of the German "Meistersinger"), the nationalist sentiment of the folk song alone does not imply his presence in this scene. However, as Hans continues up the mountain he enhances his musical number with "theatrical gestures" and "the splendid back-rolled *r* and well-rounded vowels of opera singers" (116). Through operatic inflection in what has degenerated into "nonsense syllables and words" Hans's performance becomes a subtle parody of the Wagnerian hero. Reminiscent of

Siegmund and Siegfried, who in consecutive chapters of the *Ring* cycle race up a mountain pass to the Valkyr rock to meet with death or passionate love, Hans pushes his body to its limit as he climbs while singing at the top of his lungs. Brought to exhaustion by his combined artistic and athletic activity, he collapses, "totally out of breath and gasping, half-blind, with only bright patterns dancing before his eyes" (116).

Hans's physical reaction bears the symptoms of the authentic musical experience described by Wagner in *The Artwork of the Future*. After invoking visions of the natural world (including the same "hanging pasture land" and "towering mountain walls" characteristic of the young hiker's surrounding landscape), Wagner names the organ of true insight, the ear, through which "the inmost essence of all the eye has held suspended in the cheat of scattered show" is revealed. Moving quickly from nature to art, he asserts that "our eyesight is paralyzed to such a degree by the effect of music upon us, that with eyes wide open we no longer intensively see."[18] Far from a symptom of illness, such impairment is a positive development within Wagner's musical experience for it signals the recession of the superficial world of "Schein." By directly expressing the underlying essence of the world, music cuts through the spectacle of appearance and individuality and reveals our oneness with the "universal will."[19] Thus, read through Wagner, Hans's half-blindness signals his predisposition to submit to a collective will. "Des Vaterlandes Hochgesang" also promotes such submission, moving from a metaphorical representation of the *Volk* as "Waldthal," which echoes the patriotic song in the first strophe, to a renewed vow of allegiance to the fatherland in the second.[20]

In his treatise Wagner further illustrates music's universality by comparing it to the prelinguistic utterance, to "the cry for help, the wail, the shout of joy" which we understand "without any reasoning go-between."[21] The transformation of the lyrics sung by Hans into "nonsense syllables and words" (116) reminiscent of Wagner's primal utterance similarly suggests that the state of "hypnotic clairvoyance" — the pinnacle of Wagner's musical experience[22] — is not accessible through reason. Its attainment requires surrender to the irrational power of nature which includes man's innermost feelings and drives. Hans submits himself to such power when, having moved on to an idyllic spot near a mountain stream, he lies down and enters a dreamlike state. With "his eyes closed, his ears filled with the rushing of the water," Hans is "transported to an earlier stage of life" to relive his adventure with Pribislav Hippe (117). By losing himself in the "idyllic chatter" of the water, which he loves "as much as he loved music, perhaps even more," the enervated dreamer achieves the "clairvoyant ecstasy" imagined by Wagner. But unlike Wagner, Mann sees danger in such complete surrender of self. In an image that brings out the potentially violent power of music as a natural force, the stream becomes a "torrent" beside which Hans's body — abandoned by his ecstatic spirit — lies "lifeless."

Whether lulling the listener to sleep or whipping him into a frenzy, music does not sit well with Hans's moral guardian Herr Settembrini, for it precludes rational thought processes. On an outing to a nearby waterfall some seven years after the eventful hike, the enlightened humanist warns against the dangers of nature's irrational force. As the circle of acquaintances led by Pieter Peeperkorn nears the waterfall, Settembrini remarks: "It sounds timid enough now. . . . Just be prepared — you won't be able to hear yourself think" (610). Having reached their goal, the visitors stand awestruck before the "pandemonium of hell." More than the visual effect, it is the waterfall's deafening roar that so impresses them — a roar with a raw musicality:

> Water plunged in a maddening cacophony of every conceivable noise and tone: thunders and hisses, howlings, boomings, tattoos, cracks, rattles, throbbings, and chimings. . . . They thought they could hear — from behind, from above, from every side — menacing, threatening trumpet calls and brutal male voices. (610)

A far cry from the brook's "idyllic chatter," Mynheer Peeperkorn, the "heathen priest," has led them to the catastrophic music of Dionysian frenzy. As the charismatic, impassioned antipode to Herr Settembrini, Peeperkorn teaches Hans of his "*religious* duty to feel" (594), while emphasizing that such feeling does not originate in the individual; the individual is simply the vessel through which it passes. The cacophonous rush of the waterfall symbolizes a source of inspiration so powerful that even Peeperkorn is threatened by it. After insisting on picnicking directly before the massive waterfall, he surrenders his voice to the thundering din in a prefigurement of his impending suicide. The dense sound mass consumes his words, drowning out the bitter disclosure of the "Man of Sorrows." Like the mouthings of a cinematic phantom, Peeperkorn's announcement of self-annihilation blends with the "music's" subliminal content.

Short of the last-ditch effort at romanticizing murder (*Carmen*) and self-sacrifice (*Aïda*) in "Fullness of Harmony," death has a distinctly atonal articulation at the end of the book. There, music no longer engages in the play of seduction which Hans hears in his favorite recordings and in the distant strains born on evening breezes. It assaults its listeners with a violence that is painfully direct. Instead of revealing humankind's harmonious oneness with the world, it presents nature as an uncontrollable force antagonistic to life. In a passage that echoes the cataract's thunderous crash, a new force emerges as elemental as nature but manmade, and articulated as dissonant music:

> Dusk, rain, and mud, fire reddening a murky sky that bellows incessantly with dull thunder, the damp air rent by piercing, singsong whines and raging, onrushing, hellhound howls that end their arc in a splintering, spraying, fiery crash filled with groans and screams, with brass blaring, about to burst, and drumbeats urging onward, faster, faster. (703)

Mann's visceral depiction of modern warfare relates the failure of reason and breakdown of structure (both social and linguistic) in some of the most poetic, indeed, most "musical" lines found in the entire novel. For a moment, the language adopts the dissonant imagery and rhythmic urgency of Expressionist art. As the ultimate challenge to literary representation, the Great War threatens to explode the confines of conventional syntax. On the textual battlefield we witness not only the end of the "problem child" Hans Castorp and the bourgeois-humanist epoch which he represents but also the beginning of modern art and culture.

In music this cathartic shift corresponds to the break with tonal harmony. Arnold Schoenberg describes his move into atonality in 1907 (the first year of Hans's stay on the "Magic Mountain") through a vision of a demonized nature: "I had the feeling as if I had fallen into an ocean of boiling water."[23] Like Hans Castorp's enlistment, the composer's "fall" is driven more by historical necessity than personal will: Schoenberg does not dive into modernity, he falls into it. Far from reveling in the demise of the old conventions, he regrets their passing and suffers from the loss of stability they provided. But instead of indulging in romantic nostalgia and its obsession with the dead, Schoenberg's art unflinchingly relates the psychological pain and fear accompanying such loss. It renounces the backward gaze of late Romanticism and expresses the dissonant here and now of the modern world. Dependent on the same musical narcotic consumed by Hans Castorp, the bourgeois audience rejected atonal music, sensing its "phenomenal, dangerous capability to undermine the easy pleasurability of music for all time."[24] Like Hans, they wanted a music they could love, a music that would "gloss over the crude horrors of reality" (636), not represent them.

Notes

[1] Thomas Mann, *The Magic Mountain* (New York: Vintage, 1996), 267. All subsequent quotations are from this new translation by John E. Woods, with page numbers indicated in the text.

[2] Friedrich Nietzsche, *The Birth of Tragedy and The Case of Wagner*, trans. Walter Kaufmann (New York: Vintage, 1967), 104.

[3] Arthur Schopenhauer, *The World as Will and Representation*, trans. E. F. J. Payne, 2 vols. (New York: Dover, 1966), 1:267.

[4] Thomas Mann, "Schopenhauer," *Essays of Three Decades*, trans. H. T. Lowe-Porter (New York: Knopf, 1947), 404.

[5] Mann, "Schopenhauer" 406.

[6] The dangers of the waltz were early recognized as witnessed by a pamphlet entitled *Beweis daß das Walzen eine Hauptquelle der Schwäche des Körpers und des Geistes unserer Generation sey* published in Halle in 1799. See Eduard Reeser, *The History of the Waltz* (Stockholm: Continental Book Co., n.d.), 20.

[7] In his monograph *Mahler: Eine musikalische Physiognomik* (Frankfurt am Main: Suhrkamp, 1960), Theodor W. Adorno underscores the sharp contrast in this symphonic movement between a Ländler section, a much faster Walzer section, and "einem quasi überösterreichischen, zeitlupenhaften Ländlerthema" (209). Crucial to the movement's bitter humor are the "überenergische Harmonik des 'Trunkenen im Frühling'" and "wüste Vulgarismen" heard by Adorno in the Walzer section (210).

[8] Hanns Eisler and Theodor W. Adorno, *Composing for the Films* (New York: Oxford UP, 1947), 75.

[9] Thomas Mann, "Freud and the Future," *Essays of Three Decades*, trans. H. T. Lowe-Porter (New York: Knopf, 1947), 417.

[10] Bendel (b. 1833, Schönlinde, North Bohemia — d. 1874, Berlin), who studied with Proksch in Prague and Liszt in Weimar, composed high-class, drawing-room pianoforte pieces and songs which attained great popularity. Originally entitled "Wie berührt mich wundersam," the song quoted by Mann also became popular in the United States as "Heart-Throbs" (New York: G. Schirmer, 1882).

[11] The authority of the soul over the yearnings of the heart is expressed further in the song's fourth strophe, which reads: "O welch tief Geheimniss trägt / Still der Seele Bund, / Das aus beider Herzen schlägt, / Was ein Herz empfand." The lover's deep secret, with its sexual undertones, remains unarticulated in the song. The novel echoes this moralizing ethos, positing an ideal love for the sake of which "*man shall grant death no dominion over his thoughts*" (487) while leaving the central scene of carnal love unarticulated. Although *The Magic Mountain* has the dimensions of a symphony, it also exhibits the bourgeois prudishness and "tender melancholy" of the "sentimental little song." Perhaps this is why Mann, through Hans Castorp, rejects it with such repetitive insistence.

[12] Susan McClary, *George Bizet, Carmen* (Cambridge: Cambridge UP, 1992), 98.

[13] Carmen's response is antagonistic to Don José's aria in musical terms, as well. Her "deft tritone move to g^1" on the words "Non! tu ne m'aimes pas" challenges the aria's "normative," albeit tenuous "tonality" (McClary, 98).

[14] In *Reflections of a Nonpolitical Man*, trans. Walter D. Morris (New York: Frederick Ungar, 1983), Mann lists Wagner with Schopenhauer and Nietzsche as his most important artistic and intellectual influences. There he states: "Seldom, I think, has Wagner's influence been as strong and decisive upon one who is not a musician . . . as I must admit it has been on me" (55).

[15] Cf. above all *The Case of Wagner*, in which Nietzsche sings the praises of Bizet's *Carmen* while railing against Wagner, who "has made music sick" (trans. Walter Kaufmann [New York: Vintage, 1967] 164).

[16] In her study *Mythos und Symbolik im Zauberberg von Thomas Mann* (Bern: Verlag Paul Haupt, 1979), which includes the most detailed (while not always most daring) account of the novel's music to date, Lotti Sandt convincingly establishes Wagner's "Allgegenwärtigkeit" (155–157).

[17] Albrecht Methfessel, "Des Vaterlandes Hochgesang," in *Volksthümliche Lieder der Deutschen im 18. und 19. Jahrhundert*, ed. Franz Magnus Böhme (Leipzig: Breitkopf und Härtel, 1895), 5.

[18] Richard Wagner, *The Artwork of the Future*, trans. H. Ashton Ellis, *Wagner on Music and Drama*, eds. Albert Goldman and Evert Sprinchorn (New York: Da Capo, 1964), 186. Such impairment of vision is hinted at through mention of "bloodshot eyes" every time Hans listens to music.

[19] Wagner borrows from Schopenhauer, but, as Mann recognizes, in a way which leaves the philosopher's "wisdom" untouched ("Schopenhauer" 397). Instead of leading to a "denial of the will" Wagner's ideal music inflames the will to the point that it perceives in itself "the almighty will of all things" (*Artwork* 184).

[20] The song's complete text reads: Stimmt an mit hellem hohen Klang, / Stimmt an das Lied der Lieder, / Des Vaterlandes Hochgesang, / Das Waldthal hall ihn wider. / Der alten Barden Vaterland, / Dem Vaterland der Treue, / Dir, freies unbezwungenes Land, / Dir weihn wir uns aufs neue. / Zur Ahnentugend wir uns weihn, / Zum Schutze deiner Hütten: / Wir lieben deutsches Fröhlichsein / Und alte deutsche Sitten. // Die Barden sollen Lieb und Wein, / Doch öfter Tugend preisen / Und sollen biedre Männer sein / In Thaten und in Weisen. // Ihr Kraftgesang soll himmelan / Mit Ungestüm sich reißen, / Und jeder echte deutsche Mann / Soll Freund und Bruder heißen."

[21] Wagner, *Artwork*, 183.

[22] Wagner, *Artwork*, 186.

[23] See Paul Griffiths, *Modern Music: A Concise History* (New York: Thames and Hudson, 1994), 25.

[24] Norman Lebrecht, *The Companion to 20th-Century Music* (New York: Simon and Schuster, 1992), 309.

EDWARD ENGELBERG

6: Ambiguous Solitude: Hans Castorp's Sturm und Drang nach Osten

> *For solitude sometimes is best society*
> *And short retirement urges sweet return.*
> —Milton, *Paradise Lost*
>
> *The ideal of the Karamazovs, an ancient Asian and occult ideal, begins to become European, begins to devour the spirit of Europe.*
> —Hermann Hesse, "The *Brothers Karamazov* or the Decline of Europe"

THERE ARE MERGING PARALLEL MOTIFS IN *The Magic Mountain* that crystallize some conclusions about Mann's work and make possible the reading of the novel that follows. Two such motifs are the inherent ambiguity[1] of the state of solitude that pervades the sanatorium and its patients, especially Hans Castorp, and the principal force (other than the illness itself) that overcomes and eventually directs Castorp's life on the mountain and drives him into solitude — namely, the ominous and threatening spirit of solitude itself: the East. That spirit beckons to the hero, for far from being its victim, Hans Castorp arrives at the mountain both predisposed to be seduced by the East and even eager to pursue his seducers. The first of these seducers was his childhood friend and male counterpart to Clavdia Chauchat, the Slav boy Pribislav Hippe — the "blending of Germanic blood with Slavic-Wendish, or vice versa" (118). Toward the latter half of the novel, Mann characterizes Castorp's self-abandonment to Eastern lures as a falling into "self-narcosis," likening its spell to that most Eastern of potions — opium. Despite all kinds of ominous warning signals to Castorp for him to resist these Eastern seductions, he increasingly surrenders to his "Drang nach Osten," which is centered on, but by no means exclusive to, his pursuit of Clavdia Chauchat. It is this Russian woman with her "slightly Asiatic" eyes who embodies most, if not all, the allurements and dangers of the East.

And so Hans Castorp will discover that the enticements of the East serve as a defining measure of his alienation, however temporary, as he sheds the West imprinted in him when he arrives on the mountain. Further, it is that very East that will situate the ambiguity of his solitude, his need to be connected contravened by his need to be "lost" in the abysses of the void that defines the East in this novel: the far-away Daghestan (where Clavdia Chauchat comes from) becoming the equivalent of the amorphous, vast, spaceless and timeless whiteness he encounters in "Snow."

IT IS OBVIOUS THAT, among other things, *The Magic Mountain* is "about" solitude. Both in the life of its hero, Hans Castorp, and in the lives of his fellow patients solitude is the accompanying condition (or consequence) of their collective illness. As a disease, none fitted Mann's purposes of depicting isolation from the world better than tuberculosis; indeed the Berghof is in certain respects a perfect parallel to a monastery/nunnery. The patients have come to this isolated mountain retreat from "down there" to live what we are repeatedly told is an "hermetic" existence. True, some are more cut off from the world than others; some resist their sealed-up lives; some return periodically to the "flatland" for respites. But the thrice-orphaned Hans Castorp (that is what he calls himself when his uncle, the last male relative, dies) becomes the consummate isolato. Ultimately he severs all relations with the "other" world: he ceases to read newspapers, has little or no contact with what family is left, stops ordering his beloved Maria Mancini cigars from "below," and increasingly becomes self-absorbed and isolated even from his own companion sufferers. Indeed, as Hofrat Behrens predicts from the start, Castorp has a "talent" for illness that makes him a perfect patient; even when pronounced well enough to leave, he resists. And in time he develops a superiority and contempt that allow him to use his isolation as a basis for small, but significant, acts of high-handed behavior. His isolation, cultivated and flaunted, begins to convey a stern message: 'Watch out! I am no one to mess with; my space is mine, and no one is permitted near it.' From convivial and polite innocent, Castorp becomes something of an intellectual and social snob, a harsh judge of his fellow patients. Such snobbery is no longer that earlier, more charming bourgeois sense of "right" (everyone should wear a hat in order to take it off in reverence when necessary) but a contemptuous, sometimes sneering, attitude of righteousness. Only *he* will defy the rules and ski the mountains (almost at peril of death); only *he* will play the third party in that morality play of Peeperkorn and Clavdia Chauchat; only *he* will become the proprietor of the gramophone and its records; only *he* will take the risk of first raising the ghost of his cousin, Joachim, and then abruptly terminating the séance. Such behavior signals an inherent impatience that becomes a source for turning Castorp into a solitary malcontent. But this, too, is unfair and incomplete, for Castorp, even to the end, preserves compassionate impulses and cares deeply for those he respects or admires: his cousin Joachim, Clavdia Chauchat, Peeperkorn, even Settembrini. So the case of Hans Castorp's state of solitude — like so much else on the magic mountain — is ambiguous.

Still, all the accompanying fetishes of illness on the magic mountain necessitate a variety of solitary acts. There are the daily rest cures taken on one's balcony, sealed (hermetically) in one's mummylike blankets; the "measuring" of one's temperature; the occasional necessity for privacy to use the "Blue Peter"; and, of course, the state of becoming moribund and facing that final solitary act, death itself. Yet, again, all this is counterbalanced by a conviviality, however forced it may be, among the patients. Transcending their aloneness, their solitariness, they seek each other out in a variety of social and sexual liaisons that create a kind of counterculture both to the "flatland" and the prescribed "rules"-culture of the sanatorium. We hear of games played, of riotous behavior, of overeating and too much drinking, of excursions to waterfalls, of parties, séances, sexual affairs. By and large these violations are known to the establishment and are most often winked at as necessary outlets. Perhaps reactions of defiance, these desperate attempts to normalize the life of illness bespeak something communal. To be sure, it is not the sort of community envisioned by Settembrini or Naphta, or that dreamt of by Hans Castorp in "Snow," but it is community of a kind. "In solitude for company," to quote from a refrain in an Auden poem — that is the true perspective of solitude and the attempts to ameliorate it, and even Castorp is not exempted, though certainly he carries out this ambiguous existence in a way unique to himself.

A major component of solitude is time: how the individual fills it, or makes attempts to *ful*fill it; how time is separated out from spatial intrusions, so as to isolate the "flow" itself, unhindered by clocks or calendar constrictions. Again illness suits itself to temporal isolation, especially such extended isolation as is meted out to so many of the patients on the magic mountain. And with a loss of "normal" indicators of time, we become ensnared, seduced as Settembrini asserts, so that we adopt a uniquely different view of life. For Settembrini, the slovenly, loose, vague, unstructured, dangerous, and even demonic nature of this acquired world-view — which he resists — comes from the East, is palpably contrasted to the normal, measured, sane sense of time championed in the "civilized" West. Among many modernists this fear of the East was common: Yeats placed unflattering "vague Asiatic immensities" in contrast to Phidian "measurement"; Eliot envisioned "hooded hordes" threatening Western civilization; Hesse asserted that *The Brothers Karamazov* was the "cause" of Europe's "Untergang"; and, in *The Magic Mountain,* Mann plays out the contrast in so many ways that the subject commands attention.[2] For indeed it is Asia and the West and their respective perspectives of time that define, insofar as this is possible, the nature of solitude and its often ambiguous role in Mann's novel.

In his critical chapter on the narration of Time ("A Stroll by the Shore") Mann writes:

> The diaries of opium-eaters record how, during the brief period of ecstasy, the drugged person's dreams have a temporal scope of ten, thirty, sometimes sixty years or even surpass all limits of man's ability to experience time . . . with images thronging past so swiftly that, as one hashish-smoker puts it, the intoxicated user's brain seems to "have had something removed, like the mainspring of a broken watch." (532)

In some sense this description, reminiscent both of De Quincey and Baudelaire (who translated him), describes the somnambulant atmosphere of the whole novel. Mann's emphasis on time and space echoes De Quincey (and Baudelaire), especially the temporal distortions Castorp experiences almost from the start. The dreams that mark a duration of great length when in fact they may be very brief in *real* time parallel, as Mann points out, the long narrative time of the first three weeks, three months, the first year of Castorp's stay. "Snow," which occurs two thirds of the way into the novel, occurs in the *second* winter of Castorp's stay — he will remain five more years. Those dreams that "surpass all limits of man's ability to experience time" are also described by De Quincey: "I sometimes seemed to have lived for seventy or one hundred years in one night; nay, sometimes had feelings . . . of a millennium passed . . . of a duration far beyond the limits of any human experience" (68).[3] Whether Mann's echo is direct or accidental is of no importance; what is clear is the common druglike experience of enchantment. Castorp often behaves as if under the spell of opium, and his sojourn on this magic mountain is like a long dream fugue, like the "L'Après-Midi d'un Faune," which becomes one of his favorites when he assumes control of the gramophone records. But enchantment has many faces. Offering its lures all too readily, the magic mountain's enticement is one elongated dream, a timeless vista where one may not merely "forget" but, as Mann suggests in "Walpurgisnacht," play the pig, like Odysseus stranded on Circe's island.

Though Hans Castorp sheds no tears for home and makes no effort to return until the war awakens his sense of "duty," his journey has many parallels with Odysseus's. It is long, it is full of seductions, it has its own Hades, and it, too, ends in battle. Mann was certainly not averse to "epic" thinking.

In his metaphysical quests, his "research," Castorp operates like a solitary, a captive of narcotic trance. Of course, Settembrini and Naphta are the putative father-teachers, but each has an agenda; cousin Joachim has no inclinations toward philosophizing, and Clavdia Chauchat, if anything, is the antiphilosophe, while Peeperkorn is incapable of formulating coherent sentences. Krokowski may be the analyst of the psyche, but about Castorp's analytic sessions we hear nothing; Behrens's jovial public mask covers deep private grief— he reveals little of what he really thinks or feels. So Castorp's isolation is fairly complete, and one of the few connections with the flatland is his beloved Maria Mancini cigar: "Did not Maria act as a kind of connection between him, a man withdrawn from the world, and his former home in the flatlands?" (381). As Freud did not say, sometimes a cigar is *not* a cigar: this religious, feminine-named phallic object links Castorp not merely to the flatland but to Clavdia Chauchat, for it ultimately serves as a rival's symbol to the cigars that Behrens sports.

When Castorp contemplates Joachim's departure, it causes him fear and anxiety: "Can it be that he'll leave me alone up here...?" (408); but in the end Castorp reacts as he did when Clavdia Chauchat left: "It was all of no interest to Hans Castorp" (415). His often indulgent self-isolation, masked as inhibition, irritates the sense of urgency Clavdia expects from a pursuing lover. Twice in the novel — during Walpurgisnacht and during her talk with him about Peeperkorn — she reproaches his failure to declare himself sooner: "'I was annoyed by your detachment'" (589). Although a certain reserve in young Castorp played a role in his sideline passion, it seems also apparent that his cultivated sense of isolation was quite deliberate. Also, he knew that surrender to Clavdia signaled a much broader giving in to impulses better kept at some distance. Here is what he tells Peeperkorn:

> For the sake of [Clavdia's] love and in spite of Herr Settembrini, I subordinated myself to the principle of irrationality, the principle behind the genius of illness, to which, admittedly, I had long since ... submitted myself and to which I have remained true up here.... [The] flatlands is entirely lost to me now, and in its eyes I am as good as dead. (601–602)

With the deaths of Joachim and Peeperkorn and the final departure of Clavdia Chauchat, Castorp's solitude takes on a more "jaded" aspect; the word is Behrens's, who correctly diagnoses: "'Castorp, old pal, you're bored'" (616). He succumbs, like others, to the "demon" called "stupor"; he begins playing solitaire obsessively until the solitary ritual of music-listening on the newly acquired gramophone, for which he anoints himself guardian, "rescued... [him] from his mania for solitaire..." (626). Still he maintains his "good nature," which makes him the "confidant" of individual fellow patients; yet "sadly [he was] unable to find a hearing among the easygoing majority" (622). Uncle Tienappel's death makes for finality: he feels orphaned a third time, though he experiences a new freedom which liberates him finally to sever his last link with the world — the Maria Mancinis that become replaced with a local Russian brand, thus maintaining at least a faint link to Clavdia Chauchat.

So Castorp's ambiguous solitude, accompanied by an equally ambiguous freedom, make him increasingly sensitive to time. Now "he no longer carried his pocket watch. It had stopped, having fallen from his nightstand... [and] he had long ago dispensed with calendars.... It was his way of honoring the stroll by the shore, the abiding ever-and-always, the hermetic magic, to which, once withdrawn from the world, he had proved so susceptible" (699). (The broken watch recalls Mann's description of the opium dreamer's brain, which feels as if something "has been removed, like the mainspring of a broken clock.") At the very moment, then, of Castorp's highest achievement of "freedom" (from time) and isolation (in space), of dreaming "anonymously," the abstract "communal" call of nation and war shakes him loose from his self-narcosis to navigate the dubious and even more ambiguous battlefield, all too much time-oriented and space-specific. It will turn out to be the novel's final irony.

FROM THE MOMENT Hans Castorp arrives at the Berghof, he senses that he has entered a new dimension where "Space, like time, gives birth to forgetfulness...."[4] This dreaded Lethe, which Settembrini cautions against so vehemently, so often, begins to assert itself in small matters and ends in the wholesale forgetting of that other world, the flatland. Some, like cousin Joachim, experience the "everlasting, endless monotony" (14) impatiently, as something to endure; but Hans Castorp will be a sojourner at the Berghof for years before he even begins to feel any sense of stagnant monotony. For a long time he relishes the routine of the patient, eager for just that respite from the world; and though he cannot consciously know that three weeks will turn into seven years, his "talent" for illness quickly asserts itself, and it takes no time at all for the casual visitor to become a professional patient, transformed into "a veritable mummy," taking his rest cures even before an official diagnosis exiles him to three weeks of solitary confinement in his bed.

Late in the novel, after Clavdia Chauchat's return to the Berghof, her archenemy, Settembrini, tells Castorp not without sarcasm, "Of course, your weakness for things Asian is well-known" (575). There is little doubt that the major element of this "weakness" is his hopeless surrender to Clavdia Chauchat. Yet Castorp often displays many of the characteristics Settembrini associates, in a state of dread, with the East. One reason, argues Settembrini, why the Berghof attracts so many patrons from the East is that their life-style, already predisposed to languor, needs little adjusting. From all the arguments about the vastly superior culture of Western Enlightenment compared with Eastern chaos and irrationality, perhaps one might pluck the following as the most inclusive indictment Settembrini offers:

> . . . two principles were locked in combat for the world: might and right, tyranny and freedom, superstition and knowledge, the law of obduracy and the law of ferment, change and progress. One could call the first the Asiatic principle, the other the European, for Europe was the continent of rebellion, critique, and transforming action, whereas the continent to the east embodied inertia and inactivity. (154)

However sweeping such a map of antinomies may read, it accurately reflects some of the contending forces within Hans Castorp. While he, too, strives for "freedom" it will turn out to be not the active Faustian spirit (which Settembrini clearly has in mind) but that ambiguous and contingent freedom of Dostoyevsky, Nietzsche, and Freud, in danger — if one is not careful — more of imprisoning than liberating the self. The freedom of "negative capability," vouchsafed to Castorp in his solitude in the snow, is a heavy burden. Castorp tells his cousin Joachim that Settembrini's "freedom and courage are somewhat namby-pamby concepts" (379). Indeed, he then repeats what Clavdia Chauchat had once asked (in French): does Settembrini have sufficient courage to "'*lose himself or to let himself be ruined?*'" [*se perdre ou même de se laisser dépérir?*] (379). As it concerns Settembrini the question is rhetorical; just as clearly Castorp implies that *he* may have such courage. What Clavdia Chauchat had said during Walpurgisnacht, "that one ought not to search for morality in virtue . . . but in just the opposite . . . in sin, in abandoning oneself to danger" (334), has not been forgotten. When Clavdia returns with Peeperkorn, Castorp means to prove that point to her, for had he not already "lost" himself by waiting for her return? In a manner of speaking, had he not "ruined" himself, abandoned himself — yes, to danger? "'We had a folk song in school, that went, 'The world is lost to me now,'" he tells Clavdia. "That's how it is with me" (584). Therefore he cannot lend her a postage stamp, for he has no contact with the world below: "I have no feeling whatever for the flatlands anymore" (584).

WHO, THEN, is this young man with this "weakness for things Asian"? Deep into the novel Naphta argues that "Illness was supremely human," while Settembrini retorts that "Illness ... was inhuman" (456). This difference between their concepts of illness and death forms the center of their antagonism, but Castorp arrives at the mountain much more sympathetic to Naphta's position than to Settembrini's. He has a reverence for death that reinforces his talent for illness; he refuses to accept the humanist's assertion that illness is not "elegant ... [or] venerable," that "illness is rather a *debasement*," that "illness and despair are only forms of depravity" (96–97; 218). Now it is true that these views are deep-seated in Castorp's "Urerlebnisse" — the death, in quick succession, of his parents and grandfather — and that his position will be reinforced by more experiences as an adult patient at the Berghof. Nevertheless, his whole nature, like those of many of Mann's characters, is inhibited, repressed, wound into protective denials, so that he is ripe for a version of Dionysian rebellion. The affinities he feels for the dead and dying, translated for a time into his ritual visitations with the moribund, are clearly in concert with his desire for a solitude that beckons to him from his own inner need to be "ill" and thus severed from his "health" of the flatlands. Falling in love with Clavdia Chauchat is in all ways contrary to his upbringing: her bitten fingernails, her Asian slit eyes, her unkempt appearance, her unladylike entrance into the dining room — all these are the very features that attract. It is a classic case of reaction-formation.

Castorp's almost immediate attempts to distance himself from family is a conscious break with exterior ties in order to clear the way for the searching *interior* inquiries to come. In addition to asking *What is life?* and *What is time?* he will also ask *Who am I?* For these questions his illness and the sanatorium provide the perfect condition and venue:

> "Contemplation, retreat — there's something to it.... One could say that we live at a rather high level of retreat from the world up here.... To tell the truth, now that I stop and think about it, my bed, and by that I mean my lounge chair, you understand — has made me think more about things than I ever did in all my years down in the flatlands." (370)

Castorp's seemingly uncharacteristic behavior during Walpurgisnacht, which includes the first public rejection of Settembrini and a carnal consummation with Clavdia Chauchat, is the first clear indication to himself of his surrender to the spirit of the East. On his knees, speaking a better French than he has a right to, his biologically worded *blazon* of his conquest is absurd and significant. It is not only that he must express his "passion" in a neutral language (as has often been noted); in addition, the comic disguise of scientific terminology for love language transforms a passionate longing for body into a feat of accomplished displacement. This gentlemanly, cultivated Western exemplar pursues his Eastern conquest within the linguistic context of a covert military maneuver. As each passionate description of Clavdia's body parts is couched in the textbook language of biology and related sciences, the total impression takes on the characteristics of unbridled Eastern passion wrapped (and trapped?) in a Western exterior. Mann slyly refuses to recount what later in the evening becomes, at last, *overt*.

Chauchat's absence, however, does not generate any pining. At one point Castorp declares himself relieved to be distanced both from Settembrini (who has moved to the village) and from Chauchat. What he cultivates is a solitude that will culminate in his dangerous excursus into the void in the chapter "Snow." When Behrens pronounces him cured and fit to leave, he refuses: "a departure seemed impossible, because . . . he had to wait for Clavdia Chauchat" (413). This is the first of many self-deceptions that will keep him on the mountain for seven long years.

DESPITE THE IRONIC TURN of Castorp's dream vision in "Snow" — namely, that he forgets it by the time he returns "home" — this chapter remains pivotal, as Mann himself indicated. For the dream vision is not all that informs this episode. Castorp's rebellious initiative to go skiing and contravene the sanatorium regimen is initially applauded by Settembrini; but even he cautions against the folly of skiing off into the unknown, what turns out to be Castorp's *descensus averno*. But that journey into the unknown whiteness is a semiconscious immersion into the "destructive element."[5] The ensuing experience of his encounter with the blizzard generates not only his ambiguous solitude but also the choices between life and death that lie beneath it. The "dare" he offers the void of whiteness embodies all the features of submission to a spaceless, timeless surrender to the very East that so horrifies Settembrini. "Snow" has been criticized as a sudden insight unprepared for or an event that settles nothing, since Castorp remains for years after his experience. Neither criticism is justified: though the chapter comes "late" in the novel in terms of page counting, it is still relatively early in Castorp's stay, and its emphasis on solitude and surrender to irrationality has been amply prepared for from the first week, when Castorp's solitary walk ends up in a swoon and a hefty nosebleed. In addition, the fact that much time elapses after the episode is in no way anticlimactic; Castorp's "forgetting" is partly a function of allowing Mann the space for further developments of the same themes of solitude and surrender.

Shortly before "Snow" Uncle Tienappel flees from the snares of the magic mountain, and for Castorp this has special significance. His uncle's arrival evokes no conversations about home and family: they "said nothing about personal and family affairs" (423). When only days later Tienappel beats a hasty retreat, it signals a certain finality: "And that was the end of the attempt by the flatlands to reclaim Hans Castorp... for him, however, it meant freedom finally won, and by now his heart no longer fluttered at the thought" (432). This freedom is quickly translated into the purchase of skis and his determination to learn how to use them. And that "permitted him the solitude he sought, the profoundest solitude imaginable, touching his heart with a precarious savagery beyond human understanding" (466). Indeed, watching people ski and sled inspires in Castorp a new admiration, a "sense of dignity" he recognizes in activities that made for a "deeper, wider, less comfortable solitude than that afforded by his hotel balcony" (468). This mummy has unwound itself and is now prepared for his own "deeper, wider" experience.

As he skis away from familiar markers he is soon "deep in his solitude," headed for the "icy void" (469). We learn that Castorp has "secretly" been trying to get lost, fearful but with "defiance," until he is "staring into nothing, into white, whirling nothing" (474). (Now he resembles Wallace Stevens's "Snowman" "who listens in the snow / And, nothing himself, beholds / Nothing that is not there and the nothing that is.") Lost in the sudden snowstorm he faces self-annihilation, a gradual death, "self-narcosis" — a condition described as "highly ambiguous" (475). Everything hangs in the balance: either surrender to "self-narcosis" or engage the battle, stay awake, move, fight your way from dream-death back to life:

> All this came from those ambiguous attacks, which he fought off only feebly now. The familiar blend of languor and excitement... had grown so strong in both component parts that it was no longer even a question of his taking prudent action against such attacks.... [H]e came to excuse his own inertia in fighting off such attacks of self-narcosis. (476)

Although Castorp nearly succumbs, eventually he musters sufficient strength to engage his will to live. Before that, in that twilight between death and life, he has his dream-vision, "anonymously, communally" — each word itself a description of an aspect of ambiguity. What he dreams has often been described and analyzed; suffice it to say that the duality central to the dream — the Arcadian vision disturbed by death and terror not far off — is neither new nor startling. For Hans Castorp the dream validates what had not revealed itself to him clearly — namely, not only the existence but also the necessity of ambiguity. It becomes Mann's version of Keats's "negative capability": "Man is the master of contradictions" (487).

Back from his excursion, the dream already fled from memory, Castorp does not quit the hermetic mountain for the flatland world. He will stay many years beyond this experience, and in that expanse of time he will become increasingly prone to isolation, moodiness, and mummification quite different from the kind that required wrapping oneself in blankets. But the essential difference of this solitude from that before "Snow" is that now he has a grasp of its necessary ambiguity, and for years he will live comfortably within it rather than feel it as a tug-of-war between contending forces. Internal strife is transformed into a balancing act, and he, too, becomes a "master of contradiction." Castorp warms to Naphta's word "hermetic" — "a magic word with vague, vast associations" (501). Indeed, "hermetic" fittingly describes Castorp's remaining years on the mountain. Settembrini notices a new kind of silence: "Wordlessness isolates. One presumes," he urges, "that you will seek to break out of your isolation with deeds" (508). But he may misunderstand; and in fact we hear no more of any skiing excursions. Henceforth Castorp will spend his solitary time in "safer" surroundings; one kind of "icy void" has been encountered, if not conquered. Still, more than before "Snow," Castorp falls under the spell of "self-narcosis"; all latent inclinations toward Asia become manifest. Slowly, inexorably, Castorp is absorbed into the final "stupor," where "anonymous" and "communal" no longer stand as equal ends of a single antinomy but where they collapse into each other as wilful, if domesticated, inertia.

THE PRINCIPAL ARGUMENT of this essay has focused on the undulations of Hans Castorp's ambiguous solitude (which resembles the ups and downs of his fever chart) and has seized on how that solitude's ambiguity was shaped. It takes shape with Castorp's inclinations — his fastidious burgher upbringing notwithstanding — to pursue the irresponsibility inherent in his perception of the infinite and timeless East, where Western individual and communal certitude succumb to Eastern anonymous timelessness — and, one must add, from Castorp's perspective, slovenliness. The Spenglerian Faustian view is, after all, infinite, too, but infinite action, not Eastern superfluity, inertia, the Underground Man. Castorp's solitude, however ambiguous, has taught him both the reward and pain of solitude and the self-consciousness it engenders. Octavio Paz writes, "Hence the feeling that we are alone has a double significance: on the one hand it is self-awareness, and on the other it is a longing to escape from ourselves."[6] Thus it is with Hans Castorp. His pursuit of the East essentially embodied both drives: self-awareness, it may be argued, can only be achieved in alien territory, and for that purpose the East (transplanted onto the mountain) served him well. Yet self-awareness, itself a form of solitude, eventually can become sufficiently dangerous to prompt an exit that reunites the self with the world. As Nietzsche wrote in *Beyond Good and Evil* (§146): "If you gaze long into an abyss, the abyss will gaze back into you."

In his spectacularly popular mid-eighteenth-century tome on solitude, Johann Georg Zimmermann wrote, "Retirement from the world may prove peculiarly beneficial . . . [in] youth . . . to lay the foundation of the character"; but also, "Solitude . . . is equally unfriendly to the happiness and foreign to the nature of mankind."[7] Or, as Octavio Paz reminds us, the human "is the only one who seeks out another. . . . [He] is nostalgia and a search for communion . . . aware of his lack of another . . . of his solitude" (195). We pay a price for our solitude, and of that Castorp becomes keenly aware.

During the course of his experience of near annihilation in the snow, much is revealed to Castorp, not all of which he forgets. He and Clavdia Chauchat become bound in a common friendship formed to protect a helpless Peeperkorn, and he tells her, "There are two ways to life: the one is the regular, direct, and good way. The other is bad, it leads through death" (587). This "ambiguity," though he sees it clearly, continues to dominate his life on the mountain long after Peeperkorn is dead and Clavdia Chauchat has left for good. We may believe he resolves it when he breaks the spell and joins the mass exodus for the nations at war. Yet which road Castorp finally takes is more open to question than it may appear. Singing the favorite Schubert *Lied* (about love and death) on the battlefield, where his creator gives him precious little chance of survival, is Hans Castorp following the "good" road to life — "regular" and "direct"? Or has his "weakness for things Asian" won against all odds, and by dispatching him into the hopeless battlefield has Mann hurled him from the enchantment of one irrationality to the seduction by yet another — the "irrational streams of blood," as Yeats called them? At best, these questions leave us in a state of ambiguity.

Notes

[1] I use the word "ambiguous" rather than "ambivalent" although a case might be made that Castorp's attitude toward solitude is both. Yet "ambiguous" better suits the argument made here, since ambivalent comes with too much psychoanalytical baggage and has other, less fitting, connotations.

[2] See Yeats's "The Statues" and comments in *On the Boiler* and elsewhere; Eliot, *The Waste Land*; Hesse, "Die Brüder Karamasoff, oder der Untergang Eu-

ropas," *Betrachtungen und Briefe* (Frankfurt am Main: Suhrkamp, 1957). The fear of the East was widespread among "Western" writers, especially after the Russian Revolution. On 15 March 1922, Eliot wrote Hesse that he would like to have some of his *Blick ins Chaos* translated, as he considered it to have "a seriousness the like of which has not yet occurred in England," and he was "keen to spread the reputation of the book." *The Letters of T. S. Eliot, 1898–1922*, ed. Valerie Eliot, 1 (London: Faber and Faber, 1988), 509–519. Sidney Schiff, under the pseudonym Stephen Hudson, published translations of two essays in *The Dial* in 1922: "The Brothers Karamazoff— The Downfall of Europe," 62.6 (June 1922), 607–618, and "Thoughts on the Idiot of Dostoevsky," 63.2 (August 1922), 199–204. Chris Ackerley has written a brief essay on this matter, "'Who Are These Hooded Hordes...': Eliot's *The Waste Land* and Hesse's *Blick ins Chaos*," *AUMLA*, 32 (November 1994): 103–106. I am indebted to Haskell M. Block for bringing some of these details to my attention.

[3] Mann's quotation, and the general effects of opium and hashish, sound as if they come from De Quincey or Baudelaire, who translated De Quincey. I have been unable to find the precise quotation in either, though Mann was familiar with Baudelaire's *Journaux Intimes* and quoted a relevant passage from it (see below). De Quincey lingers on the change in perception of time and space under the influence of opium. "Space swelled and [was] amplified to... unutterable infinity." This disturbed him less, however, than the "vast expansion of time." In addition De Quincey connected these space/time effects to Asia and its heavy burden of geographical space and temporal history: "Southern Asia is the seat of awful images and associations... [T]o me the vast age of the race... overpowers the sense of youth in the individual" (*Confessions of an English Opium-Eater and Other Writings*, ed. Grevel Lindop [New York: Oxford UP, 1985], 72–73). His haunting dreams of the Malay remind one, even if accidentally, of Peeperkorn's mysterious Malay servant. In *Artificial Paradises*, Baudelaire confirms that drug-induced dreams are distorting: "all notion of time [has] vanished"; a "minute will seem an eternity"; "the proportions of time and existence are distorted..." (*Artificial Paradises*, trans. Stacy Diamond [New York, Carol, 1996], 57, 52, 29). In a letter to Ernst Bertram (1920, four years before the publication of *Der Zauberberg*), Mann wrote: "It is touching to see how the weak-willed, decaying Baudelaire, already succumbing to hashish, attempts to encourage himself to work" [translation mine], and then Mann quotes a passage toward the end of the *Journaux Intimes*, which invokes Baudelaire's self-command to work six hours a day, to seize on an *idée fixe* that will sustain him. *Thomas Mann an Ernst Bertram, Briefe aus den Jahren 1910–1955* (Pfullingen: Neske, 1960), 91; for the original see Baudelaire, *Ouevres Complètes* 1:673. For an analysis of Western perceptions (and misperceptions) of the East see Edward W. Said, *Orientalism* (New York: Pantheon, 1978).

[4] I have addressed this question elsewhere. See *Elegiac Fictions: The Motif of the Unlived Life* (University Park and London: Pennsylvania State UP, 1989), 173–191.

[5] "Destructive element": this phrase comes from Conrad's *Lord Jim*, where Stein says, in what became an icon passage for Modernism, "The way is to the destructive element submit yourself, and with the exertions of your hands and feet in the water make the deep, deep sea keep you up" — keep you from drowning. Although Hans Castorp and Lord Jim live very different lives they have in common a necessity to submit to the "destructive element" in order not merely to survive but to face squarely the coexistence of life and death. The whiteness-void is a literary motif especially rich in nineteenth- and twentieth-century Western European and American literature: for a few examples, see Mary Shelley's *Frankenstein*, Poe's *Narrative of A. Gordon Pym*, Melville's *Moby-Dick*, Joyce's "The Dead," and Lawrence's *Women in Love*.

[6] Octavio Paz, *The Labyrinth of Solitude* (New York: Grove Press, 1985), 195.

[7] Johann Georg Zimmerman[n], *Solitude* (London, 1827), 4 and 193. No translator is noted. The original German title is *Über die Einsamkeit*, 1756.

STEPHEN C. MEREDITH

7: Mortal Illness on the Magic Mountain

AT THE BEGINNING OF *THE MAGIC MOUNTAIN*, a mediocre young man — who will prove to be not so extremely mediocre, if such an expression is possible — arrives in a world of the sick for a three-week visit. He stays for seven years, at first denying that he belongs but gradually becoming accustomed to, even dependent upon the ways of the mountain.

Several themes are announced in the first few pages — musically, as leitmotifs, to be re-sounded and elaborated throughout the course of the novel. Hans Castorp is mortal, like all of us, though he is at first loathe to admit it. This is one sense in which he is mediocre, for he does indeed belong to the world of people who will die. Mediocre though he may be, he is also capable of flashes of brilliance, however transient — which also makes him the same as everyone else. His "organic matter" is prone to decay; he is tainted; and the taint of disease is akin to the taint of Original Sin. He is a man of the middle, not only in being mediocre in many ordinary senses — he is of middling abilities and of the middle class, for example — but also in being a German: midway, to use the Spenglerian construct, between the decaying orient and the nascent frontier to the West. And at the Berghof, he will be a German among Russians good and bad, Poles, Italians, Spaniards, and other members of the international community.

In addition to the metaphorical uses of the sanatorium, Mann also intends for these people to be ill — literally. The denizens of the mountain, whatever else they may be, are all ill, including the director, Dr. Behrens — some quite seriously, and some fatally. Joachim Ziemssen, Hans Castorp's cousin, dies. Naphta, too, dies, though by his own hand. Clavdia Chauchat, we may infer, is also fatally ill, from "bouchement tuberculeux des vases de lymphe" — tubercular blockage of the lymphatic vessels. Settembrini is said (by Clavdia) to be seriously ill as well, and along the way, we are introduced, however briefly, to numerous other "moribundi."

Had Mann intended to use disease only as a surrogate for "mortality," any number of diseases could have been used. His choice of tuberculosis, however, was anything but haphazard. He reports how he, like Hans Castorp, once visited a tuberculosis sanatorium at Davos and was threatened by the idea that he too might be ill. Where Hans Castorp succumbed to the charms of love and the mountain, Thomas Mann, one might infer, fled in terror like Hans's uncle James Tienappel. So Mann had the personal experience of tuberculosis and, indeed, believed himself to have weak lungs. In the following, we note the use of the verb "threatened", and his use of the term — in the psychoanalytic sense? — of the word "transference":

> In the year 1912 — over a generation ago now — my wife was suffering from a lung complaint, fortunately not a serious one; yet it was necessary for her to spend six months at a high altitude, in a sanatorium at Davos, Switzerland. . . . There is a chapter in *The Magic Mountain*, entitled "Arrival," where Hans Castorp dines with his cousin Joachim in the sanatorium restaurant, and tastes not only the excellent Berghof cuisine but also the atmosphere of the place and the life "*bei uns hier oben*." If you read that chapter, you will have a fairly accurate picture of our meeting in this sphere and my own strange impressions of it.
>
> The impressions grew stronger and stronger during the three weeks I spent at Davos visiting my wife while she was a patient. They are the same three weeks Hans Castorp originally meant to spend at Davos — though for him they turned into the seven fairy-tale years of his enchanted stay. I may say that they threatened to do the same for me. At least *one* of his experiences is a pretty exact transference to my hero of things that happened to me; I mean the examination of the carefree visitor from the "flatland," and the resulting discovery that he himself is to become a patient too! [1]

Beyond his personal experience with tuberculosis, there is the obvious fact, pregnant of metaphors, that the ill with tuberculosis congregate in sanatoria — obvious, but in need of interpretation. From the perspective of modern medicine, there is, perhaps, no worse way to treat people suffering from tuberculosis than to concentrate them in a small area where they can reinfect one another. But in *The Magic Mountain*, the ill form a society apart, a society of the tainted — a society at one and the same time apart and yet resembling the decaying monarchist political system that came to an end after World War I.

But wherefore "tainted"? Is it a sin to be ill? And again, why ill with tuberculosis? Mann had a lifelong interest — some would say obsession —

with illness. We may note, en passant and in a partial list, that Christian Buddenbrook suffered from a nervous disorder; Thomas Buddenbrook, like many of Mann's characters, had weak teeth, from which, somewhat ludicrously, he dies; Frau Klöterjahn and Herr Spinell, in *Tristan*, had tuberculosis; von Aschenbach succumbs, in Venice, to the plague; Rosalie von Tümmler, in *The Black Swan*, dies of cancer; the scabs on Müller-Rosé's back (*Felix Krull*) are from secondary syphilis; and Adrian Leverkühn (*Doctor Faustus*) goes Müller-Rosé one better by developing a florid case, described in painstaking detail, of tertiary syphilis.[2] But the fullest exploration of disease comes in *The Magic Mountain*, and here the specific case chosen by Mann was tuberculosis. We are, today, accustomed to viewing infectious illnesses as environmentally determined. In the interminable nature versus nurture debate we are nowadays committed nurturists all.[3] We blame the current resurgence of tuberculosis, and rightly, on crowded housing, inadequate medical care, poor nutrition, or concurrent illnesses, especially AIDS. We are condescending toward the view — unenlightened, as it appears to our eyes — that there may be individuals with a proclivity for tuberculosis — or, as Hofrat Behrens put it, a "talent" for the illness. Behrens's statement does not even address the notion that such a talent might be inherited. This was, however, precisely the notion that guided Mann and, indeed, was a commonplace of medical practice at the time. Mann is not subtle about this idea. We are told, for example, that the protagonist's father, Hans Hermann Castorp, while grieving for his recently dead wife, caught pneumonia on a windy spring day and died five days later. While Hans Hermann was "not the most robust man," his father and the protagonist's grandfather, Hans Lorenz Castorp, "was a man rooted firmly in life, a tree hard to fell" (18–19); nevertheless, he too caught pneumonia; and though he "struggled amid great agony," he too died of this disease. We have already mentioned that Hans's cousin, Joachim Ziemssen, dies of tuberculosis, and Hans's uncle, James Tienappel, flees the Berghof in panic from the incipient realization that he too is infected. The protagonist of *The Magic Mountain* inherited the weak lungs of his forebears and was, moreover, a "delicate child of life." That is, he bore an ambivalent relationship to life, and carried within him, like an inherited birthmark, a small moist spot in his lungs.

But . . . back up a step. Ambivalent relationship to life? Exactly what is the alternative? If there are "teams" or "sides," and Hans Castorp is not quite fully committed to the life "team," then whose side is he on? Hans Castorp is far from the only one of Mann's characters who is less than fully committed to "life." Indeed, the decline of the Buddenbrook family is, in essence, a loosening and abatement of each successive generation's commitment to life. We can cite any number of other neurasthenic characters, especially in early to middle Mann, who seem less than fully committed to living, but von Aschenbach and Thomas and Hanno Buddenbrook come immediately to mind.

To overstate the issue for the sake of clarification, Mann plays fast and loose with several parallels, which he connected through drastic, at times even egregious leaps of transitive logic. Mann asks repeatedly, in the chapter "Humaniora": "What is life?" We can ask: what is opposed to life? Life, it would seem, means the unreflective, doughtily acquisitive life of the upper-middle-class burgher. Thomas Buddenbrook, elected senator would *seem* to embody this life, but we know better: in him the decay is already evident — in his choice of an exotic wife, for example. The life force ebbs, and Thomas Buddenbrook — or von Aschenbach or numerous other characters — strains under the tense demands of keeping up the drudgery of having to live. "I would sleep . . ." as the enervated, overly sensitive Tonio Kröger says, albeit in a slightly different context. No, to see the life force at work it would be better to look not at Thomas Buddenbrook but his grandfather, old Johann Buddenbrook, with nary an idea in his head save the building of his firm and fortune. Opposed to this "life" which the Tonio Krögers of the world only watch, and the Thomas Buddenbrooks and Hans Castorps live only with strain and difficulty, what do we find? Illness. Artistic creativity. Criminality. Sin. We find illness in Hans Castorp, Joachim Ziemssen and others on the list given above; artistic creativity in von Aschenbach, Tonio Kröger, and Adrian Leverkühn, among many others; sin in the supposed life of Pope Gregory (*The Holy Sinner*); and criminality in *Confessions of Felix Krull*. And we have the distinct impression, sometimes a certainty, explicitly stated by Mann, that by a weird transitive logic all of the opposites of Life can be equated.

Tuberculosis was called consumption because the flesh of the patient with tuberculosis appeared to consume itself. We understand this phenomenon — the fever, the weight loss, the muscle wasting — as resulting from the elaboration of cytokines: protein mediators of the immune response to tuberculosis. Cytokines activate the cells that ingest and kill the bacteria that cause tuberculosis: mainly lymphocytes and macrophages. When these same cytokines are secreted in very large quantities in patients with progressive tuberculous lesions,[4] they have strong metabolic effects as well: they cause fever, muscle wasting, and so forth — all of the "consumptive" signs of tuberculosis. From the point of view of pathophysiology, there are things yet to learn, but little mystery in these changes. It is nevertheless striking that an often fatal illness should have the aspect of life burning bright: the hectic flush and fever seeming to betoken the acceleration of the fire of life. It is, then, also no mystery that Mann could find tuberculosis a congenial object on which to affix an ironical gaze: for this is illusory life, life that only appears to burn bright in the actually moribund. As such, this illusion is similar to the apparent summit of Thomas Buddenbrook's life, when he was elected senator. The Buddenbrook family would *seem* to be at the height of its trajectory, but Thomas, who has been feeling the strain of trying, against his real inclination, to carry on with "Life," knows that his family's current glory is, like the glorious color of leaves in autumn, only a prelude to death:

> "Why, Tony — it is a mood, certainly. It may pass. But just now I feel older than I am.... Often and often, in these days, I have thought of a Turkish proverb; it says *'When the house is finished, death comes.'* It doesn't need to be death. But the decline, the falling-off, the beginning of the end. You know, Tony," he went on, in a still lower voice, putting his arm underneath his sister's, "when Hanno was christened, you said: 'It looks as if quite a new life would dawn for us all!' I can still hear you say it, and I thought you were right, for I was elected Senator, and was fortunate in my business, and this house seemed to spring up out of the ground. But the 'Senator' and this house are superficial, after all. I know, from life and from history, something you have not thought of: often, the outward and visible material signs and symbols of happiness and success only show themselves when the process of decline has already set in. The outer manifestations take time — like the light of that star up there, which in reality may already be quenched, when it looks to us to be shining its brightest."[5]

Later in the novel, Thomas "happens upon" a philosophy book in his room — seemingly an unlikely finding in this particular household, but not really so unlikely as it might first seem, for the interest in philosophy is yet another sign of decay. Exactly who put this book in Thomas's drawer? We are not told. Nevertheless, though the title is not named, we have no trouble in surmising that it is Schopenhauer's *The World as Will and Representation*: we surmise, so that if this is not exactly the correct guess, it might just as well have been that paragon of metaphysical pessimism.

And so it is in *The Magic Mountain*: illness and death are less than The Enemy. But to say that illness is a comfort, and a relief from the exigencies of the will, only tells half the story. *We* might be content to oppose illness to Life, but Thomas Mann was not. For him, illness was adumbrated with association to art, sensuality, and sin. Illness, in its literal form an unforgivable sin to the doughty burgher, is also the portal to the greater sins of sexual licentiousness, and artistic and intellectual creativity. And of these, it would seem that artistic creativity is the greatest sin. In the chapter "Snow," Hans Castorp declares his right to dream his nightmare vision of the human condition. Though Mann undercuts this forthright declaration with irony, informing us that after he takes a hearty meal, Hans's adventure recedes into oblivion, and also by noting of Hans's peroration that "he babbled," we note that no such forthright declaration was needed[6] for Hans's sexual adventure with Clavdia Chauchat. Given the slim pretext of the carnival ("Walpurgis Night"), Hans Castorp is happily launched into a trajectory of pencil-borrowing, paeans to the body and medicine, French speaking, and unsafe sex.

Hans Castorp experienced illness and death early and often. It was a family tradition. Hans's fond recollection of the baptismal font — in which he was baptized, like his father and grandfather, and great doubled, tripled, quadrupled — was intimately tied to the recollection of death. The young boy of eight, like many children, thrilled in repetition of a favorite story, especially one that "locates" the child, but this was a story of *both* baptism and death:

> There were seven names in all now, each rounded out with the date of inheritance, and the old man in the white necktie pointed with his ringed forefinger as he read off each of them to his grandson. His father's name was there, as was in fact his grandfather's, and his great-grandfather's; and now that syllable came doubled, tripled, and quadrupled from the storyteller's mouth; and the boy would lay his head to one side, his eyes fixed and full of thought, yet somehow dreamily thoughtless, his lips parted in drowsy devotion, and he would listen to the great-great-great-great — that somber sound of the crypt and buried time, which nevertheless both expressed a reverently preserved connection of his own life in the present to things now sunk deep beneath the earth and simultaneously had a curious effect on him: the same effect visible in the look on his face. The sound made him feel as if he were breathing the moldy, cool air of Saint Catherine's Church or the crypt in Saint Michael's, as if he could sense the gentle draft of places where as you walked, hat in hand, you fell into a certain reverential, forward rocking motion, your heels never touching the ground; and he also thought he could hear the remote, cloistered silence of those reverberating spaces. At the sound of those somber syllables, religious feelings got mixed up with a sense of death and history, and all of it together somehow left the boy with a pleasant sensation — indeed, it may well have been that it was solely for the sake of that sound, just to hear it and join in reciting it, that he had once again asked to be allowed to see the baptismal bowl. (21)

When his grandfather died and was laid to rest, "Hans Castorp was relieved to see his grandfather decked out in his authentic perfection." For there were two grandfathers, or, as the title of this chapter put it "Grandfather in his Two Forms": the everyday "temporary, imperfectly adapted improvisation," which contrasted with the true grandfather, decked out in his senatorial garb, "clad in a robe like black jacket, hanging open at the front, edged in fur along the lapels," and depicted in the "splendid portrait, painted in the style of the old masters," showing his grandfather amid "columns and Gothic arches."

Like grandfather who died, death itself had a twofold form, a theme repeated often throughout the novel, but first stated explicitly here. Hans Castorp, though too young to formulate these sentences, vaguely apprehended the twofold form of illness and death:

> Analyzed and put into words, his feelings might have been expressed as follows: there was something religious, gripping, and sadly beautiful, which was to say, spiritual about death and at the same time something that was the direct opposite, something very material, physical, which one could not really describe as beautiful, or gripping, or religious, or even as sad. The religious, spiritual side was expressed by the pretentious lying-in-state, by the pomp of flowers and palm fronds — which he knew signified heavenly peace — and also, and more to the point, by the cross between the dead fingers of what had been his grandfather, by the blessings a copy of Thorvaldsen's Christ extended from the head of the coffin, and by two towering candelabra on either side, which on an occasion like this also took on an ecclesiastical character. The explicit and well-intended purpose of all these arrangements was apparently to show that Grandfather had now passed on forever to his authentic and true form. But they also served another purpose — one that little Hans Castorp likewise noted, if not admitting it to himself in so many words; in particular, the masses of flowers and more especially the very well represented tuberoses were there for a more sobering reason — and that was to gloss over the other side of death, the one that is neither beautiful nor sad, but almost indecent in its base physicality, to make people forget it or at least not be reminded of it. (26)

Later, on the mountain, the ill and the dead will be seen as objects of shame. The dead are carried down from the mountain, somewhat absurdly, by bobsled when the roads become impassable in the winter, usually in the wee hours so they are not observed. Hans's and Joachim's visits to the moribundi are announced with the *anonymous* gift of flowers. In the quote given above, tuberoses (what else?) cover the odor of corruption. Rooms are fumigated with formaldehyde,[7] H_2CO, not only to kill physical bacilli, but to erase a taint. Such modesty before death might appear old-fashioned to us or not, though we have not completely overcome such inhibitions.[8]

The sense, in some of Mann's pages, that illness is morally wrong, or a sign of weak character is expressed by the German proverb "Krankheit ist eine unverzeihliche Sünde": illness is an unforgivable sin.[9] This saying, ostensibly, is in the spirit of stoical self-denial: only the weak and (morally) lame succumb to an illness, but the strong (and virtuous) do not. This sentiment is also shared by Settembrini (showing that it is not limited to

Germans) who rebukes Castorp by telling him that his attitude toward suffering should be a European one, not the weak Eastern one.[10] Yet, to cite this "proverb" only begs the question: whence comes the sense, in some German popular sayings and elsewhere, that illness is a sin? Behind the sense of sin — and really, not very far behind it — is a sense of temptation, and of something to be resisted, something that draws one forth into corruption. A similar theme is announced in a different context in Mann's late masterpiece, *Doctor Faustus*. The devil is belittled as a remnant of the "medieval" — read: "superstitious" — past, a childish belief. But Kaisersaschern, Leverkühn's hometown,

> was a practical, rational modern town. — Yet no, it was not modern, it was old; and age is past as presentness, a past merely overlaid with presentness. Rash it may be to say so, but here one could imagine strange things: as for instance a movement for a children's crusade might break out; a St. Vitus's dance; some wandering lunatic with communistic visions, preaching a bonfire of the vanities; miracles of the Cross, fantastic and mystical folk-movements — things like this, one felt, might easily come to pass.[11]

And in talking about the liberal theologian Kumpf:

> I cannot and would not inquire how far he believed in the personal existence of the Great Adversary.... I did say that Kumpf, as a scholar and man of science, made concessions to criticism in the matter of literal faith in the Bible, and at least by fits and starts "abandoned" much, with the air of intellectual respectability. But at bottom he saw the Arch-Deceiver, the Wicked Fiend capitally at work on the reason itself and seldom referred to him without adding: "*Si Diabolus non esset mendax et homicida!*" He appeared reluctant to name him straight out, preferring to say "divel" or "Debbel"; sometimes "the great old Serpent," or with literary relish, "Timothy Tempter." But just this half-reluctant, half shrinking avoidance had something of a grim and reluctant recognition about it.[12]

In one important aspect, disease in *The Magic Mountain* is like the devil in the above quotation: on the surface both are simply negative; but beneath the surface, both are tempting and yet to be covered over and denied by all sophisticated moderns. Moderns fear the devil and illness alike, in much the same way: not simply because both are destructive but also because both are tempting and therefore need to be resisted. For von Aschenbach in *Death in Venice*, the link between disease and temptation is made explicitly: to succumb to illicit (i.e., "homoerotic," as Mann called it) sex is to die of plague in Venice.

Mann was, to some extent, both participating in and repudiating a long-standing theme of German household literature. Every burgher knew his Goethe and Schiller. Mann knew, as well, Heine and Novalis, and Mann's own obsession with illness can also be seen as foreshadowed by these authors. Novalis, for example, asked "Could disease be a means of higher synthesis?" and attributed his own extreme sensitivity to an illness he suffered as a nine-year-old child; he wrote:

> All diseases resemble sin in that they are transcendencies. All our diseases are phenomena of a heightened sensitivity that is about to be transformed into higher powers. When man wanted to become God, he sinned.

Though this theme is hardly restricted to German romanticism and can be seen in authors and musicians and graphic artists of other nations and eras — one need only think of Keats or Chopin — the theme seems especially congenial for the Germans. Thus Heine denies that a Tyrolese can ever be sickly — because the Tyrolese are too stupid to be ill! Hans Castorp says this exactly about Frau Stöhr: he is perplexed that so "stupid" and "obtuse" a woman could also be ill (293, 170). Settembrini is quick to "correct" the misconception in his enlightened (at times, Mann means us to read "shallow") way, connecting to both romanticism and an older form of religiosity:

> "You suggested that the combination of sickness and stupidity is the most pitiful thing in the world. I will grant you that much. I, too, prefer a clever invalid to a consumptive idiot. But my protest begins at the point where you regard the conjunction of illness and stupidity as a kind of stylistic blunder, as an aberration of taste on the part of nature and a 'dilemma for our human emotions' — as you chose to express it. At the point where, or so it appears, you consider illness to be so elegant or — as you put it — so 'venerable' that there is absolutely 'no rhyme or reason' why it and stupidity should belong together. Those, too, are your words. In that case, no! Illness is definitely not elegant, and certainly not venerable — such a view is itself a sickness, or leads to it. Perhaps I can best arouse your abhorrence of that idea by telling you that it is outdated and ugly. It comes from an era of superstitious contrition, when the idea of humanity was demeaned and distorted into a caricature, a fearful era, when harmony and health were considered suspicious and devilish, whereas infirmity in those days was considered as good as a passport to heaven. Reason and enlightenment, however, have banished those shadows." (96)

> "Permit me, permit me, my good engineer, to tell you something, to lay it upon your heart. The only healthy and noble and indeed, let me expressly point out, the only religious way in which to regard death is to perceive and feel it as a constituent part of life, as life's holy prerequisite, and not to separate it intellectually, to set it up in opposition to life, or, worse, to play it off against life in some disgusting fashion — for that is

indeed the antithesis of a healthy, noble, reasonable, and religious view."(197)

Thus it seems clear that young Hans Castorp, the ordinary man turned visitor, then adventurer among the shades, "romanticizes" illness and links it with creativity. Hofrat Behrens notes that the tendency toward disease, and therefore also toward repressed love and creativity, was present in Castorp long before his arrival at the Berghof:

> "You have a fine, sympathetic cousin there," the director went on, nodding in Joachim's direction and rolling back and forth between the balls of his feet and his heels, "of whom we hope someday soon to say that he was ill at one time, but even when that day comes, he will still have been ill — your fine cousin will. And that, as the philosophers say, casts a certain *a priori* light on your own situation, my good Castorp."
> "But he's only a half cousin Director Behrens."

Thus Castorp. Note also that his reply to Behrens indicates that he, too, accepts the heritable nature of the disease. Note also that Behrens rolls "back and forth" in a manner similar to that described above, in Castorp's reflections on the crypt of Saint Michael's (21). But what can we infer of *Mann's* opinion: does he "romanticize" illness, as well, or is it even possible to draw an inference on this question? By the time Hans Castorp (or Mann) was born, the notion that the ill, especially the ill with tuberculosis, were sensitive and creative had become stock, not to say stale. Yes, the notion retained some currency, but it was currency with a musty odor. We can today divest this notion of its glamour and demystify it — after all, haven't we all come to view the sensitive plant, the oversensitive would-be artiste as a bit of a poseur? These poseurs, for whom pathological sensitivity and illness is a stock-in-trade, seem to us to have stepped out of a past age. Hans Castorp did not travel to the heights — or, as he and Settembrini often put it, the depths, as in hell — of the magic mountain only to revisit eighteenth- and nineteenth-century clichés. And yet, on the other hand, Mann could also not possibly have truck with this George Bernard Shaw when he writes that "Crime, like disease is not interesting. It is something to be done away with by general consent, and that is all about it."[13] The author of *Felix Krull*, who wrote this story at least three times, could not possibly simply dismiss illness any more than he could dismiss criminality. The darkness of criminality and illness was too congenial to Mann, cliché or not, for him to dispense with it altogether. In the end, Mann might — no, did — reject illness and criminality as modes of being, but only after a long debate in which the darkness was not so much vanquished by the light, but destroyed by its own impossible logic: "Death, thou shalt die" — and did.

The weird character of Naphta gives us an insight into this darkness run amok. He is a character who necessarily ends in his own elimination. A Jewish Jesuit, a luxuriant ascetic, a reactionary communist, he is contradiction "in essence."[14] Or rather, he embodies contradiction in the sense that his attitudes cannot possibly be contained in one body — and he is conflicted even about that (literal) body. He rejects umbrellas as the paragon of bourgeois mediocrity and softness — and yet he is ill, too weak to live even the physically undemanding life of the academic, and as for this illness, he seems to delight in having it and in living in a "silken cell."[15] Naphta strikes some readers (including myself) as being grotesque, and grotesquerie is one face of illness throughout *The Magic Mountain*. In the same context, one might mention the Half-Lung Club: those patients who have had a portion of their lungs removed[16] and can whistle, a bit obscenely, through the holes in their chests. Mann, especially in his early stories, seemed especially fond of turning sentimental household literature on its head by making it grotesque, even cruel — see, for example, "Little Herr Friedmann," "Tobias Mindernickel," "Little Lizzy," and "The Way to the Churchyard." But what, exactly, is grotesquerie? Grotesquerie is comic (though by "comic," we hardly refer to belly laughs) because refined people can recognize the gross impropriety of it. The word arose in early modern French, with parallels in other languages, to refer to certain crude paintings made on unpolished walls, i.e., "painting appropriate to grottos," according to the OED. The term evolved to refer to comic distortion or exaggeration; in the words of Sir Thomas Browne, "There are no Grotesques in nature"[17] — implying, therefore, that when grotesques are found, they are somehow unnatural and out of joint. Naphta is certainly a monster, albeit an intelligent one, and his monstrosity reminds us of the connection between the word "monster" and the words *montrer* (to show) and "demonstrate": Mann shows us the moral lesson that dark and monstrous characters will always have a stony end. Naphta shoots himself in the head. Even more ominously, a séance, late in the novel, is a foray beyond nature and conjures an image of Joachim, dead and in the guise of the Universal Soldier, wearing the odd and unrecognizable (to the characters, but perfectly recognizable to the reader) uniform of the soldier of World War I — a portent of things to come. In the same vein, one world war later, Adrian Leverkühn commits the ultimate unnatural act of selling his soul to the devil — and, significantly to Mann, of becoming homosexual — for which, after a period of intense musical creativity, he pays with his life. An earlier contact with a prostitute — referred to as Hetæra to connect her with both the butterflies (*Hetæra esmeralda*) Adrian's naturalist father used to study, and the twelve-tone scale of Schönberg (the notes H-E-A-E-A-S) — gave Adrian syphilis. Adrian's syphilis is coextensive with his term of creativity, much as Castorps (lesser) creativity is coextensive with his stay in the sanatorium. The older, grimmer Mann has Leverkühn die, while Castorp is freed from the mountain with the outbreak of the First World War at the end of the novel — and his fate is unknown to readers and the author alike.

This, then, is the unnatural and improper aspect of disease: it is nature gone awry, or it is simply outside of nature, dark and immoral, a shameful thing, and connected therefore with other shameful things. Castorp, however, also recognizes another side of this story: it is also a way to understand the human spirit. When he climbs the mountain, we are frequently reminded, he is also entering the depths. Settembrini refers to Hofrat Behrens as Radamanthus, the guardian of the underworld: in using this sobriquet, Settembrini is making the playful, whining, somewhat shallow allusion to the fact that Behrens sentences him to "prison terms" away from work, as if in hell. But the underworld is also where heroes go to face their greatest dangers: think, for example, of Horus the sun-god in the Egyptian Book of the Dead, or of Jesus's harrowing of hell. In "The Making of *The Magic Mountain*," the short essay often appended to the novel, Mann coyly answers the then-young scholar, Howard Nemerov, who proposed that Hans Castorp is a Quester Hero, by saying, "Perhaps he is right." In common with other Quester Heroes, Castorp faces chaos and possible dissolution, both literally and figuratively, in facing death in its many guises. In the chapter "Snow," he faces the inorganic world, further up the mountain, of "manifold, symmetrical crystals," "the subtlest variation and embellishment of one basic design: the equilateral, equiangular hexagon" (470, 471).[18] We are reminded several times that this ski trip, like all athletic activities, is strictly forbidden to patients, yet Castorp *dares*, and enters this forbidden land, and here he "dreams" his dream of civilization. In an unnamed, highly civilized Mediterranean park — which he *recognizes* despite never having been to the Mediterranean — he sees the blood sacrifice at the heart of it:

> The bronze door of the sanctuary stood open, and the poor soul's knees all but gave way beneath him at the sight within. Two grey old women, witchlike, with hanging breasts and dugs of finger-length, were busy there, between flaming braziers, most horribly. They were dismembering a child. In dreadful silence they tore it apart with their bare hands — Hans Castorp saw the bright hair blood-smeared — and cracked the tender bones between their jaws, their dreadful lips dripped blood. An icy coldness held him. He would have covered his eyes and fled, but could not. They at their gory business had already seen him, they shook their reeking fists and uttered curses — soundlessly, most vilely, with the last obscenity, and in the dialect of Hans Castorp's native Hamburg. It made

him sick, sick as never before. He tried desperately to escape; knocked into a column with his shoulder — and found himself, with the sound of that dreadful whispered brawling still in his ears, still wrapped in the cold horror of it, lying by his hut, in the snow, leaning against one arm, with his head upon it, his legs in their skis stretched out before him. (495)

The lovely detail that the witches are cursing in the dialect of Hans's native Hamburg informs us that their curses were meant only for him, much like the guard addressing the protagonist in Kafka's "Before the Law." The blood sacrifice at the heart of the temple of civilization perhaps signifies the stain of evil on the body politic, as disease is a taint on the body physical, and as sin is on the soul. Yet, to say this only begs the question of the nature of evil in all these cases. Settembrini puts the matter urgently and eloquently to his charge, Hans Castorp (and Ziemssen, as well), in the chapter significantly entitled "The City of God and Evil Deliverance":

"Gentlemen," Herr Settembrini continued now, stepping very near the young men, spreading the thumb and middle finger of his left hand into a wide fork, as if to concentrate their attention, and raising the forefinger of his right hand in warning, "imprint this on your minds: the intellect is sovereign, its will is free, it defines the moral world. If it isolates death in a dualistic fashion, then by that act of intellectual will, death becomes real in actual fact — *actu*, do you understand?"

No longer only the absence of life — as evil is privation of the good — death becomes *actu*: a Manichaean representation of evil. Settembrini continues:

"It becomes a force of its own opposed to life, an antagonistic principle, the great seduction...."

This paragon of enlightenment is often belittled by Hans Castorp — and, one suspects, by Mann as well — for being "a windbag" and an "organ-grinder," forever tootling on his pennywhistle of reason and progress. It is clear from the above citation, however, that in calling him names like that, Settembrini — like Voltaire, Diderot, and Settembrini's beloved Carducci — is not being treated very fairly, and the reports of his intellectual demise are greatly exaggerated. Indeed, in the chapter "The Great Petulance," Hans is presented with the binary choice of Naphta or Settembrini; and given the need to choose, harmless and pacific and rational Settembrini will triumph over self-destructive Naphta, whose ways, we are led to conclude, lead to war.

The issue, presented both passionately *and* clearly in the above citation, is the nature of evil — or rather, *whether* evil has a nature. Settembrini, in discussing death, finds himself in odd agreement with Saints

Thomas Aquinas and Augustine, who argued that evil is nothing, *i.e.*, *no thing*, the privation of the good.[19] The issue Settembrini address in this citation, in other words, is whether death — and more generally, evil — has "*actu*, do you understand?": according to Saints Thomas and Augustine, evil is *not* actual; indeed, it is the very absence of Act in the Aristotelian sense. For St. Augustine, in fact, the recognition that evil does not have a nature or essence[20] was central for his conversion to Christianity. But we could never imagine Hans Castorp expressing, however more lumpishly, this same sentiment. This image of Castorp paraphrasing Augustine in Hamburg German is incongruous not merely because of the language and rapture of Augustine, but also because of the attitude toward evil. Castorp's view of evil and the devil is not only more concrete than his sense of good and God, but his implied concept of evil is also more manichean than Augustine's or Aquinas's. The century that has produced Stalin, Hitler, Pol Pot, and Idi Amin seems to have no difficulty conjuring a concrete notion of the devil, even if the devil is rarely called by that name. We might object, trying to take Augustine's part, that in treating evil so concretely, as if a thing, we are yet still seeing only privations; yet we moderns are sorely tempted to regard evil as a thing: to many, or in any case to Hans Castorp, the notion that evil is *not* a thing is somewhat counterintuitive — for what can be more concrete and (seemingly) actual than the stench of disease and death? It seems inevitable that Hans Castorp will *not* understand Settembrini ("*actu*, do you understand?") and that he, like his fellow countrymen and other Europeans, will rush headlong into the darkness of World War I — to say nothing of the Second World War.

Naphta might well quote Augustine's statement "I believe that I may understand," and Mann does seem to delight in having Naphta and Settembrini, like Tweedledee and Tweedledum, sometimes change intellectual positions with each other. But not always; Settembrini insists: "Gentlemen — I would like to warn you." When Hans Castorp coyly pretends not to understand to what (i.e., to whom) Settembrini is referring, Settembrini responds with another instant of clarity and perspicacity:

> "About the person whose guests we just were," Herr Settembrini replied, "and to whom I introduced you, very much against my will and intentions. As you know, chance wished it otherwise. I could not help it, but I bear the responsibility and it weighs heavily on me. It is at the very least my duty to point out to you as young people certain intellectual risks you run in associating with that man and to beg you, moreover, to keep your relations with him within certain prudent limits. His form is logic, but his nature is confusion." (399)

Castorp's coyness derives, of course, from his attraction to that very darkness and confusion. Indeed, Naphta's arrival coincides exactly with the departure of Clavdia Chauchat, the previous person against whom Settembrini had warned his student: both, perhaps, represent a departure from the light of reason, albeit in very different ways. Yet, for all of Naphta's self-proclaimed spirituality, Settembrini seems to have the better grasp of the fact, so often and amply demonstrated by Saint Thomas, that faith need not, indeed, cannot be in conflict with reason. And so it is Settembrini who, at the end of this chapter, argues to this effect, in the paragraph part of which is quoted above.

And yet, after Settembrini issues his warning, we the readers are told — significantly, in indirect dialogue, rather than direct:

> One could not speak in finer, clearer, more rounded phrases than Herr Settembrini. Hans Castorp and Joachim Ziemssen expressed their warmest thanks for what he had told them, took their leave, and climbed the stairs to the main entrance of the Berghof; and Herr Settembrini returned to his humanist's lectern, one floor above Naphta's silken cell.

Mann, too, by using indirect dialogue, and not merely Castorp, praises Settembrini's language and thanks him for the warm concern — and then omits to say "You are right, Herr Settembrini" — a loud silence. Instead, we see the cousins depart, and Settembrini and Naphta each return to their stations in topological and, it is implied, moral equivalence. Indeed, there is more than a little of Castorp in Mann, more than a little of the nonverbal, musical man-of-the-middle — the middle being Germany — in Mann, who, even knowing in 1922 that his story would end with the thunderbolt could not allow Castorp such a presentiment. And why should Mann have allowed this ordinary German any extraordinary degree of perspicacity, which in all likelihood Mann, so much more than ordinary, did not possess himself?

The love of duality was announced earlier in the chapter on Grandfather in his two guises, but is applied directly to the body and its diseases in the chapter "Walpurgis Night." In a more humorous vein, Felix Krull observes:

> The stage was above my head — an open balcony of the *bel étage* of the great Hotel zum Frankfurter Hof. Onto it stepped one afternoon — it was so simple that I apologize — two young people, as young as myself, obviously a brother and sister, possibly twins — they looked very much alike — a young man and a young woman moving out together into the wintry weather. They did so out of pure high spirits, hatless, without protection of any kind. . . .
>
> Dreams of love, dreams of delight, and a longing for union — I cannot name them otherwise, though they concerned not a single image but

> a double creature, a pair fleetingly but profoundly glimpsed, a brother and sister — a representative of my own sex and of the other, the fair one. But the beauty lay here in the duality, in the charming doubleness, and if it seems more than doubtful that the appearance of the youth alone on the balcony would have inflamed me in the slightest, apart perhaps from the pearl in his shirt, I am almost equally sure that the image of the girl alone, without her fraternal complement, would never have lapped my spirit in such sweet dreams. Dreams of love, dreams that I loved precisely because — I firmly believe — they were of primal indivisibility and indeterminateness, double."[21]

And why does Krull love duality so much? His love of duality is of the essence to his criminality: dualities deceive, and Krull rightly calls them duplicities. Dualities are abhorrent because they multiply reality into illusion. The connection of duality/criminality to both Art and Disease is made explicitly when the young Krull accompanies his father backstage to visit his father's old, dubious friend, Müller-Rosé. Müller-Rosé's name itself is impossible: the combination of the lumpish German word for dullard and the sparkling French word redolent of roses and wine. Müller-Rosé has just given a dazzling, elegant performance of a dance; yet here is the disgusting sight that greets young Felix backstage:

> Müller-Rosé was seated at a grubby dressing-table in front of a dusty, speckled mirror. He had nothing on but a pair of grey cotton drawers, and a man in shirt-sleeves was massaging his back, the sweat running down his own face. Meanwhile the actor was busy wiping face and neck with a towel already stiff with rouge and grease-paint. Half of his countenance still had the rosy coating that had made him radiant on the stage but now looked merely pink and silly in contrast to the cheese-like pallor of his natural complexion. He had taken off the chestnut wig and I saw that his own hair was red. One of his eyes still had deep black shadows beneath it and metallic dust clung to the lashes; the other was inflamed and watery and squinted at us impudently. All this I might have borne. But not the pustules with which Müller-Rosé's back, chest, shoulders, and upper arms were thickly covered. They were horrible pustules, red-rimmed, suppurating, some of them even bleeding; even today I cannot repress a shudder at the thought of them."[22]

These pustules might or might not be stigmata of secondary syphilis, but what is clear is the disparity between Müller-Rosé's glitter onstage and his repulsiveness offstage — concretely reflected in the smeared greasepaint on half his face. Müller-Rosé — and it is comically implied, any artist — is a fraud. But Mann's brilliant twist is that Krull is not therefore discouraged from his career of Crime/Art: on the contrary, how wondrous it is that someone as repulsive as Müller-Rosé could create so delightful an illusion on the stage! Krull, then, is the affective opposite of Tonio Kröger, who is disgusted by the sloven and wayward habits of artists, including himself.

Hans Castorp's declaration of his love of duality is more directly related to the body and disease, and in one of the unique love scenes in all of literature, this love is ligated to the declaration of his love for Clavdia Chauchat; but it is not even so straightforward as this. He uses the pretext of Carnival (Walpurgis Night, Shrove Tuesday) to become familiar to Clavdia which (his own) propriety would not otherwise have allowed. The word "Carnival," like "Walpurgis Night" is about leavetaking. "Carnival" derives from *carnem levare*, the giving up of meat: it is the feast, the Fat Tuesday which comes before Ash Wednesday, in which the priest crosses the forehead with ashes and says, "Man, you are of ashes, and to ashes you will return." The giving up of meat is both the concrete example and the metaphor for the giving up of the world: we must die in order that we may live. In this way, we imitate Christ; Lent ends with the death and resurrection, and when we again take flesh, it is the flesh of the resurrected lamb of God.

The "Walpurgis Night" chapter ostensibly shows us a carnival divertissement for the patients: there are party games, music, and the usual mild flirtations, augmented for the occasion. Settembrini does not seem to approve of these goings-on, but he's there, nevertheless. Several of the games seem to concern pigs; there is, in fact, a lot of pig iconography in this chapter. One of the games is to close one's eyes and try to draw a pig. At one point in the chapter, Settembrini walks past his protégé and quips: "'See beldam Baubo riding now,' quoted Settembrini, as [Frau Stöhr] appeared; and gave the next line, in his clear and 'plastic' delivery."[23] In quoting this line from the Walpurgis Night scene of Goethe's *Faust*, Settembrini expects, as presumably Mann did, that his audience would readily recognize the quote. It continues: "She rides upon a farrow sow." Earlier, Settembrini had passed a note around Hans Castorp's table which read:

> But, mind, the mountain's magic-mad to-night,
> And if you choose a will-o'-wisp decide to light
> Your path, take care, 'twill lead you all astray.[24]

When the mountain is magic-mad, the witches come out and ride on demon-pigs, and it is these with whom the denizens of the mountain consort on Carnival night.

As we have said before, in connection with devil-fear in *Doctor Faustus*, to treat this matter humorously is to distance oneself from the actual hold of magic and deviltry upon Hans Castorp and the other patients. For Castorp, Carnival night is a pretext to speak to Clavdia — but a fortiori it is a pretext to speak to her in French. The attentive reader will have realized that the text has been peppered all along with bits of French — a leitmotif. Here, Hans Castorp insists on speaking to her in French and using the familiar pronoun *tu*.[25] Then she drops the bombshell: she will be leaving the next day.

> "Laisse moi rêver de nouveau, après m'avoir réveillé si cruellement par cette cloche d'alarme de ton départ. Sept mois sous tes yeux — et à présent, où en réalité j'ai fait ta connaissance, tu me parles de départ!"
> "Je te répète, que nous aurions pu causer plus tôt."
> "Would you have liked it?"
> "Moi? Tu ne m'échapperas, mon petit. Il s'agit de tes intérêts, à toi. Est-ce que tu étais trop timide pour t'approcher d'une femme à qui tu parles en rêve maintenant, ou est-ce qu'il y avait quelqu'un qui t'en a empêché?"
> "Je te l'ai dit. Je ne voulais pas te dire 'vous.'"[26]

On other days, that is, he would have needed to speak to her in conventional language, including the use of the formal pronoun. He is, in fact, slightly chafing under the discontents of civilization, and language, so congenial to Settembrini, strikes Castorp as woefully inadequate to his more musical purposes. Thus, he speaks in French. He states:

> "Parler, discourir, c'est une chose bien republicaine, je le concède.... Moi, tu le remarques bien, je ne parle guère le français. Pourtant, avec toi je préfère cette langue à la mienne, car pour moi, parler français, c'est parler sans parler, en quelque manière, — sans responsabilité, ou comme nous parlons en rêve. Tu comprends?"
> "A peu près."
> "Ça suffit... Parler," continued Hans Castorp, " — pauvre affaire! Dans l'éternité, on ne parle point. Dans l'éternité, tu sais, on fait comme en dessinant un petit cochon: on penche la tête en arrière et on ferme les yeux."[27]

At this point a wag might comment that Castorp protected himself well from intimacy by waiting an awfully long time to turn to the subject of sex — waiting, that is, til the day before Clavdia's departure (did he "know," unconsciously?) to speak to her at all, and even then speaking mainly about language and pigs. Nevertheless, whatever ambivalence he might have had, he does finally get around to wooing his lady, and, in one of the strangest love scenes ever written, this is melded with a paean to the body. As we noted earlier, Castorp has been studying medicine (detailed in the chapter "Research").[28] He has been learning anatomy and physiology, the study of "organic matter," "life and its sacred, yet impure mystery," "the warmth produced by instability attempting to preserve form."

As is evident even from these brief quotations, and as was common at the time — or so it would seem from Mann's unexplained use of terms such as "organic matter" and "living matter" and the like — the discussion of "Life" is redolent of vitalism. In "Walpurgis Night," he applies those lessons in Medicine. His love song culminates in a discursus on practical anatomy, as applied to the structure of Clavdia's body:

> "Oh, l'amour, tu sais... Le corps, l'amour, la mort, ces trois ne font qu'un. Car le corps, c'est la maladie et la volupté, et c'est lui qui fait la mort, oui, ils sont charnels tous deux, l'amour et la mort, et voilà leur terreur et leur grande magie! Mais la mort, tu comprends, c'est d'une part une chose mal famée, impudente qui fait rougir de honte; et d'autre part c'cst une puissance très solennelle et très majestueuse, — beaucoup plus haute que la vie riante gagnant de la monnaie et farcissant sa panse, — beaucoup plus vénérable que le progrès qui bavarde par les temps, — parce qu'elle est l'histoire et la noblesse et la piété et l'éternel et le sacré qui nous fait tirer le chapeau et marcher sur la pointe des pieds... Or, de même, le corps, lui aussi, et l'amour du corps, sont une affaire indécente et fâcheuse, et le corps rougit et pâlit à sa surface par frayeur et honte de lui-même. Mais aussi il est une grande gloire adorable, image miraculeuse de la vie organique, sainte merveille de la forme et de la beauté, et l'amour pour lui, pour le corps humain, c'est de même un intérêt extrêmement humanitaire et une puissance plus éducative que toute la pédagogie du monde!... Oh, enchantante beauté organique qui ne se compose ni de teinture à l'huile ni de pierre, mais de matière vivante et corruptible, pleine du secret fébrile de la vie et de la pourriture! Regarde la symétrie merveilleuse de l'édifice humain, les épaules et les hanches et les mamelons fleurissants de part et d'autre sur la poitrine, et les côtes arrangées par paires, et le nombril au milieu dans la mollesse du ventre, et le sexe obscur entre les cuisses! Regarde les omoplates se remuer sous la peau soyeuse du dos, et l'échine qui descend vers la luxuriance double et fraiche des fesses, et les grandes branches des vases et des nerfs qui passent du tronc aux rameaux par les aisselles, et comme la structure des bras correspond à celle des jambes. Oh, les douces régions de la jointure intérieure du coude et du jarret avec leur abondance de délicatesses organiques sous leurs coussins de chair! Quelle fête immense de les caresser ces endroits délicieux du corps humain! Fête à mourir sans plainte après! Oui, mon dieu, laisse-moi sentir l'odeur de la peau de ta rotule, sous laquelle l'ingénieuse capsule articulaire sécrète son huile glissante! Laisse-moi toucher dévotement de ma bouche l'Arteria femoralis qui bat au front de ta cuisse et qui se devise plus bas en les deux artères du tibia! Laisse-moi ressentir l'exhalation de tes pores et tater ton duvet, image humaine d'eau et d'albumine, destinée pour l'anatomie du tombeau, et laisse-moi périr, mes lèvres aux tiennes!"[29]

For someone who claimed not to speak much French, he did exceptionally well here. We might start by reading the paragraph anatomically: it proceeds caudally, seeming to tend, like sexual development, toward the genitals. What are we to make of this weird combination: the melding of sexual desire, leave-taking, medicine and disease, pig icons and witchcraft? The chapter ends with an event that conflates all of the above: an implicit invitation to Clavdia's room and, we must assume, unsafe sex — unsafe, because it will result, as Clavdia warns, in "une mauvaise ligne de fièvre ce soir." But at the same time, the "excuse" to come to Clavdia's room is more than a mere excuse: Hans has borrowed a pencil, and for Mann, the writer, the acquisition of a pencil is more than a coincidental choice. Clavdia, with her "Kirghiz eyes" like a "prairie wolf," is a later manifestation of a type; the other version, also Eastern, also having the oblique eyes of the Asian steppes, was a male named Pribislav Hippe. The pubescent Hans, we learn in the chapter bearing Hippe's name, was also the object of Hans's desire (and spying), which is broadly hinted to be sexual as well, albeit unconsciously so. But Castorp in both cases borrows a pencil, and in both cases, is shown how to use it — in the latter case, with the execrable pun, "C'est à visser, tu sais" (It is to be screwed, you know). And in both cases the approach to the loved one entails the development or exacerbation of his tuberculosis. In the chapter "Hippe," Hans has been singing loudly about love and has a severe nosebleed — again art (music) and illness are linked together, and with love. After stanching the hemorrhage, he is barely strong enough to hail a farmer passing by with a wagon to bring him back to the Berghof. He staggers from the wagon and arrives, speckled with blood, to a lecture by the psychoanalyst Dr. Krokowski, entitled "Love as a Force Contributory to Disease." It is difficult to know what kind of psychoanalysis Dr. Krokowski practices — because he is partly, but *only partly*, a charlatan. But the gist of the lecture is vaguely Freudian: that when love was kept down, "chastity only apparently triumphed, its victory was a Pyrrhic victory, because the demands of love could not be fettered, or coerced; suppressed love was not dead, it continued to live on in the dark, secret depths, straining for fulfillment — and broke the bounds of chastity and reappeared, though in transmuted, unrecognizable form. And in what form or mask did suppressed and unsanctioned love reappear? . . . And Dr. Krokowski said: In the form of illness! Any symptom of illness was a masked form of love in action, and illness was merely transformed love" (124). We might render the following free-form Freudian translation of the previous sentences: A sexual drive can lead to conflict; our awareness of the urge is repressed, and it becomes unconscious; if the conflict is not resolved, a neurosis develops. Mann's Krokowski seems to suggest that tuberculosis, like neurosis, is a malformation of the character — and indeed, Castorp echoes this notion in "Walpurgis Night" when he says,

"Oh, l'amour n'est rien, s'il n'est pas de la folie, une chose insensée, défendue et une aventure dans le mal. Autrement c'est une banalité agréable, bonne pour en faire de petites chansons paisibles dans les plaines. Mais quant à ce que je t'ai reconnue et que j'ai reconnu mon amour pour toi, — oui, c'est vrai, je t'ai déjà connue, anciennement, toi et tes yeux merveilleusement obliques et ta bouche et ta voix, avec laquelle tu parles, — une fois déjà, lorsque j'étais collégien, je t'ai demandé ton crayon, pour faire enfin ta connaissance mondaine, parce que je t'aimais irraisonnablement, et c'est de là, sans doute, c'est de mon ancien amour pour toi que ces marques me restent que Behrens a trouvées dans mon corps, et qui indiquent que jadis j'étais malade...."[30]

Here is another *re*-cognition, as in "Snow." Literally deep in his bosom, if one can use such purple prose, is a defect, in some sense inherited, that Castorp maintains is the sign of both an early infection and an early love, of Hippe; and furthermore, that these two affections — the affection for Hippe and the "affection," as diseases used to be called, of tuberculosis — can be equated. It is also possible to read this stain in the soul as a palpable sign of Original Sin. The German man-of-the-middle, conflicted between the stern morality of the West and the moral laxity of the East, yearns for Clavdia as he did for Hippe, a yearning which originates in his thorax and is manifested by exacerbations in the thorax.

Of course, to look upon "Walpurgis Night" as a culmination in any sense is to overlook that it occurs in the middle of the novel — in fact, literally so by page count, though this night occurs only within the first year of Castorp's stay on the mountain. As noted, Clavdia's departure coincides with the arrival of Naphta; and furthermore, Clavdia will return in the company of the buffoonish Mynheer Peeperkorn.[31] After Clavdia leaves and Naphta arrives, time accelerates, and much of the focus of the novel shifts to the debate between Settembrini and Naphta. As we have noted, these characters do not maintain consistent positions, and at times they exchange positions with each other. As time accelerates, their debate gains entropy and eventually degenerates into nonsense and babble. For Castorp, their debate constitutes a duality — or, to use Krull's word, a duplicity: neither pole of the duality is adequate in itself, but rather, what is needed is the entirety, the warring dialectic synthesized into a whole. In much the same way, Castorp's vision in "Snow" encompasses both ego and animus: neither Settembrini nor Naphta, neither the civilized denizens of the Mediterranean park nor the witches at the heart of the temple: but both; and neither disease and death as "actu" nor the body as entirely spiritualized: but both, always both as the synthesis of a dialectic.

But though we can use highfalutin statements like "synthesis of a dialectic," such statements are anodyne. Indeed, the phrase "synthesis of the dialectic" may well be the essence of Castorp's vision in the snow, and yet, like Hans's vision which begins to fade in the comfort and warmth of the Berghof, such phrases lose their force when we try to posit them as "Author's Message" — especially when that author is so often ironical. In fact, it is debatable how much, if any, of the philosophizing should be taken seriously. One of the pitfalls in writing with frequent or constant irony is that any and all points which are meant to be taken seriously get undercut. And so we can ask what, if anything, we should hold onto in the debate between Naphta and Settembrini. This is surely an open question, but one answer can be gleaned from the chapter "A Good Soldier." In fact, the transition which occurs midway through the chapter speaks volumes. In the first half of the chapter, the degeneration of Settembrini and Naphta's debate is in full glory, and its further degeneration will lead to violence. Here, Mann summarizes this mockery of intellectual debate:

> For progress was pure nihilism, and the liberal bourgeois was in truth a man of nothingness and the Devil — yes, he denied God, the conservative positive Absolute, and instead pledged allegiance to the devilish Anti-Absolute, and in his deadly pacifism marveled at how devout he was. Yet he was anything but devout, was a traitor to life, who deserved to be brought before the Inquisition and the Fehme, to be put to the painful question — et cetera. (515)

If, by some miracle, the reader had been following their debate previously, he is only too glad, at this point, to leave its noise behind with the dismissive "et cetera." The "et cetera" also signals a dramatic transition: we step from guazzabuglio and rotomontade to something serious — and in contrast to the previous irony, something of genuine affect. Sweet, gentle, honorable Joachim is dying. Mann writes:

> And indeed Naphta was clever at making his points, turning a hymn of praise into something diabolical and presenting himself as the incarnation of abiding, disciplined love, so that once again it had become a pure impossibility to decide where God and the Devil, life and death, were to be found. The reader can believe us when we say, however, that his opponent was man enough to respond with a brilliant comeback, which he then received in kind; and so it went for a while and the conversation flowed on into issues previously touched upon. But Hans Castorp was no longer listening, because at one point Joachim had mentioned that he was feeling feverish, almost certainly from his cold, but did not know what he should do, since colds were hardly *reçus* here. (515)

The last statement is a gem of concision: without Mann saying so explicitly, we know that Joachim is seriously ill, indeed, he may be dying — this stoical character would not complain without cause. Hans is no longer listening to the debate, and neither are we. And indeed, though colds may not be "*reçus*" at the sanatorium, Joachim agrees "that official channels should be opened to deal with his cold and sore throat," and he is seen by Head Nurse Adriana von Mylendonk. She clumsily asks Joachim, "Man alive, tell me — have you ever swallowed the wrong way?"

The question is clumsy because it bespeaks her awkwardness and ambivalence about revealing what plainly (as we soon learn) she has seen when she looked down Joachim's throat:

> What did you answer to that? . . . Of course he had swallowed the wrong way now and then eating or drinking something. That was the common fate of humanity — that couldn't be what she meant by her question. So he asked her why she had asked, said he couldn't remember the last time it happened.
> Well, fine; it was just something that occurred to her. He had caught a cold, she said — to the amazement of both cousins, since the word "cold" was taboo here at the Berghof. (516)

The conspiracy of silence is carried forth by Behrens and Joachim alike. A previously made October date for Joachim to return to his regiment passes without mention. Joachim is to continue with his cure, in the interest of returning to his duty in the flatlands. "This was the watchword, with which everyone pretended to be in silent agreement." Such silent agreement is the essence of denial — akin to Ivan Ilyich's denial and consequent anger toward his family — but little or no such (overt) anger is to be found in dutiful Joachim. On the contrary:

> The truth was, however, that no one was quite certain whether anyone else believed this watchword in the depths of his soul; and because of their doubts the cousins would turn their downcast eyes away — but only after their eyes had first *met*. This had happened often since the colloquy on literature, the day when Hans Castorp had first noticed a new light and *ominous* expression deep in Joachim's eyes. It happened once at the dinner table — when Joachim, still hoarse, quite unexpectedly choked on something, so violently he could hardly get his breath. (517)

Their eyes would meet and they would *know*; but they would *turn away* in silence: denial. To define what denial consists of: the splitting of intellectual knowledge of the facts from the affect — terror, anger, grief. The progression of symptoms of laryngeal and epiglottal tuberculosis, always rapidly fatal at that time, would not, of course, allow the denial to persist; but the tendency to deny, indeed, the denial proper, as just defined, remains very strong. For example, Joachim makes conscious efforts not to choke on his food — not simply because of the physical pain and discomfort of this symptom of laryngeal disease, nor even simply because of the terror of being unable to breathe, terrible though this truly is; but also because of the shame and dishonor of a social gaffe with all of its ominous implications: for *this* is why he "lowered his eyes, hid his face in his napkin, and left the table and the dining hall to cough himself out elsewhere." This shame is, to some extent, the shameful aspect of the body and disease, but even more so, this is an attempt to deny and distance himself from his own affect. When, a few days later, he chokes not on a sumptuous dinner but at second breakfast, Hans Castorp merely averts his eyes, continues to eat, and pretends not to notice, while Joachim curses (curses!) "that damned woman, Fräulein Mylendonk who had put a bug in his ear with that question of hers out of nowhere" (517).

When Joachim is summoned, "out of turn," to see the doctor, Mann refers to Behrens by his sobriquet, Rhadamanthus, for here he is truly at his most Rhadamanthine, presiding over lost and departed souls. Joachim reports on the results of the laryngoscopy, saying:

> All Behrens had done was babble on about inflammation of this and that, had said that the throat would have to be painted every day and that he would start the procedure the next morning, since he first had to prepare the cauterant. So, then, inflammation, cauterization. (518)

Again, one is reminded of Ivan Ilyich, where the physicians argue kidney versus vermiform appendix, and do not ever quite get to the fact that Ivan is dying. So Behrens, too, is a denier, and this is, of course, a universal trait, and hardly confined to physicians. Castorp comments: "Behrens was a brick of a fellow and would come up with a cure." Castorp's denial is further translated into repeated, unsuccessful attempts to find and speak to the director: a twofold denial because the facts were obvious, and furthermore (as Mann makes abundantly clear), his failure to speak to Behrens was parapraxis, pure and simple: "That did not explain why, try as he might, he could not lay his hands on Rhadamanthus."

But, finally, he did succeed, and "asks" Rhadamanthus: "It is harmless, isn't it, if I may ask?" And Behrens replies, letting Castorp be the recipient of his frustrated, if partly justified, fury:

> "You want everything to be harmless, Castorp, that's the sort of fellow you are. You're not at all averse to getting involved in things that are not harmless, but then you treat them as if they were, and you think it will ingratiate you with God and man. You're something of a coward, man, a phony, and if your cousin calls you a civilian, that's merely a euphemistic way of putting it."
>
> "That may well be, Herr Behrens. There can be no question that I have many weaknesses of character. But that's the point — there can be no question of that at the moment, and what I've been trying to get from you for three days is simply — "
>
> "For me to tell you the sweet, sugary, diluted truth. You want to badger and bore me, until I reinforce your damn phoniness so that you

can enjoy your innocent sleep, while others wake and watch and let the gale winds blow."

"My, but you are being hard on me, Herr Behrens. It's just the opposite, I wanted to — "

"Yes, hard on you — and that's not up your alley. Your cousin is quite a different sort of fellow, a man cut from different cloth. He knows and says *nothing*, do you understand?" (519–520)

Joachim is admired, in no small part, for his stoicism in the face of death, a very military stoicism. Behrens's rebuke of Castorp is stinging and direct, appropriate to the severe judge of the underworld: for we know and are repeatedly told that Behrens is *not* the owner of the sanatorium, but actually an employee, so that his edicts are merely the enforcement of a law from on high, of divine law, as it were, a law not of his own making.

Yet this is not Greek divinity but a Christian one, and once the (deserved) rebuke has been delivered, Castorp and Behrens can get down to the actual matter at hand:

"You're fond of your cousin, aren't you, Hans Castorp?" the director asked, suddenly grasping the young man's hand and gazing down at him from his blue, bloodshot, protruding eyes with their white lashes.

"What can I say, Herr Behrens? Such a close relative and such a good friend and my comrade up here." Hans Castorp gave a little sob. (520)

Eventually Hans has to write to Joachim's mother — another set of veiled statements whose meanings are abundantly clear. Joachim and Hans go for walks together; they take their meals together, soon in Joachim's room rather than the dining hall: Hans loves Joachim. The cousins' attitude toward Joachim's approaching death is summarized thus:

Joachim walked beside him, his head bent low. He stared at the ground as if examining the soil. It was so strange. Here he walked, so proper and orderly, greeted passersby in his chivalrous way, paying strict attention, as always, to his appearance and *bienséance* — and he belonged to the earth. Well, we all will belong to it sooner or later. But to belong to it when one is so young and has served the colors for such a short time and with such goodwill and joy, that is bitter — even more bitter and incomprehensible for Hans Castorp walking beside him, knowing everything, than for the man who belongs to the earth — whose proper, silent knowledge is actually more academic and less real to him, is less his concern than his companion's. In fact, our dying is more a concern to those who survive us than to ourselves: for as a wise man once cleverly put it, as long as we are, death is not, and when death is, we are not; and even if we are unfamiliar with that adage, it retains its psychological validity. There is no relationship between us and death; it is something that does not apply to us at all, but at best to nature and the world at large — which is why all creatures can contemplate it with composure, indifference, irresponsibility and egoistic innocence. Hans Castorp saw a great deal of this innocence and irresponsibility in Joachim's character during these weeks and understood that although his cousin knew, that did not mean it was difficult for him to observe a decorous silence about his knowledge, for his inner relationship to it was loose and merely theoretical; and in terms of any practical considerations, it was all ordered and governed by a healthy sense of propriety, which no more permitted a discussion of such knowledge than it does of any of the many indelicate functions we are quite aware condition life, but do not prevent us from preserving *bienséance.* (521–522)

Joachim the solider is soon confined to bed; it is early November, and the snow is already deep. Before he is confined, he engages in a seemingly incongruous, final — and indeed, first — explicit flirtation with Marusya. Hans sees this incident as the final proof of Joachim's deterioration:

And it shocked Hans Castorp more than any other sign of his poor cousin's failing strength that he had noticed over the past weeks. "Yes, he is lost," he thought and sat quietly for a while in the music room to give Joachim time for whatever he was allowing himself out there in the lobby on his last evening. (523)

Joachim, though worlds apart from either Thomas Buddenbrook or Gustav von Aschenbach, has this much in common with them: to live "life" — in Joachim's case, the military life — is a strain of which he eventually tires. The tendency to "give in," to give up the battle and strain of life, had been marked previously in Joachim only by the mottling that came over his face whenever Marusya was near and by the occasional sneer that passed across his face when he discussed his own stay at the Berghof: both of these were the rare exception to the otherwise strictly obeyed military rule of his character. To Castorp, this ordinary flirtation is a sign that all is lost: we may see it as a sign of panic — if not now, when will he taste the delights of the flesh? — but also, as Castorp sees it, as a sign that he has ceased to fight the fight, has ceased to maintain the strain that is life. Like Thomas Buddenbrook, Joachim is beginning to resign himself and perhaps even welcome death.

When Joachim assumes "a permanent horizontal position" and is bedfast, his mother is summoned. Standing beside Joachim's mother, Hans finally recognizes, as if through her eyes, the changes that have occurred in Joachim: he is now a moribundus.

Luise Ziemssen was a brave woman. She did not go to pieces at the sight of her fine son. As composed and restrained as the almost invisible hairnet holding her hair in place, as detached and energetic as the people of her native land were known to be, she took charge of Joachim's care. (525)

Earlier, Hans was permitted only "a little sob"; Mann also seems to praise the detachment of Luise Ziemssen.[32] Be that as it may, Joachim's mind wanders in his last days: he imagines that he will soon return to his regiment and take part in maneuvers. In this context, Mann revisits two of his earlier themes:

> Even the most manly men succumb to credulous, oblivious self-deceptions; the phenomenon is as natural as it is melancholy when the process approaches its fatal end — natural and impersonal and beyond all individual conscious effort, much as the temptation to wander in circles overcomes someone who is lost or sleep ensnares someone freezing to death. Hans Castorp's grief and worry did not prevent him from focussing objectively on this phenomenon, and he formulated awkward but clearheaded observations about it in his conversations with Naphta and Settembrini, when he would report to them about his cousin's condition; he was rebuked by the Italian, however, for observing that there was an underlying error in the conventional notion that philosophical credulity and sanguine trust in the good are the expressions of health, whereas pessimism and condemnation of the world are signs of illness. (526)

The allusion to "the temptation to wander in circles" and "sleep ensnar[ing] someone freezing to death" are a re-sounding of motifs from the "Snow" chapter: Hans here, as in "Snow," is visiting the abyss of chaos and death. The other theme revisited here is that, once again, Settembrini rebukes Castorp for associating illness with profundity and health with stupidity. Obviously the lad will never learn this particular lesson.

In the end, there are very few things, especially sentiments, which escape Mann's ironic gaze, but Joachim's death is one of them. The chapter ends:

> We let the curtain fall now, to rise but one more time. But while it rustles to the floor, we wish to join Hans Castorp, left behind on those distant heights, as he gazes down on a wet garden of crosses in the lowlands, watches a sword flash and then lower, hears barked commands and the three volleys that follow, the three fervent rounds of honor bursting above Joachim Ziemssen's soldier's grave, thick with matted roots. (530)

Joachim's spirit will be invoked one last time, in a demonic séance, as a harbinger of war, in the chapter "Highly Questionable." Nevertheless, Mann seems to mourn along with his readers the death of this simple, honorable soul — mourns, that is, with straightforward sadness and ordinary grief; like Hans Castorp, he is left behind on the distant heights, and like Hans Castorp, Mann is the one who survives and therefore bears the burden of living with the loved one's death. In grieving for Ziemssen, he reminds us that illness and death, whatever else they may be, remain illness and death, and that these are overcome not by a clever intellect but only by love.

Notes

[1] "The Making of *The Magic Mountain*" by Thomas Mann; in *The Magic Mountain* by Thomas Mann, translated by H. T. Lowe-Porter (New York: Vintage Books, 1992), 720–721. This older translation of *The Magic Mountain* will be referred to as MM1.

[2] As an example of the lengths to which Mann carries his disease metaphors, consider this innocuous appearing description from *Doctor Faustus*: "His eyes, in his former state half overhung by the drooping lids, were now almost exaggeratedly open, and above the iris one saw a strip of white. That might perhaps alarm me, the more because there was about the widened gaze a fixity — or shall I say it was a stare? — the nature of which I puzzled over until it occurred to me that it depended on the unvarying size of the not quite round, rather irregularly lengthened pupils, as though they remained unaffected by any alteration in the lighting." *Doctor Faustus* (New York: Knopf, 1948), 484. This is, in fact, a textbook description of the Argyll-Robertson pupil, a sign of tertiary syphilis.

[3] This is not, however, true of immunologists who actually study the subject in earnest and have defined many genetic loci rendering animals (humans included) susceptible or resistant to infectious disease.

[4] And in many other diseases, as well. For a review of the role of cytokines in tuberculosis, see Chapter 12, "Cytokines," in Abul K. Abbas, Andrew H. Lichtman, and Jordan S. Pober, *Cellular and Molecular Immunology*, 3d ed. (Philadelphia: W. S. Saunders, 1997).

[5] *Buddenbrooks*, trans. H. T. Lowe-Porter (New York: Vintage Books, 1961), 337.

[6] At least, to himself. He did bid a farewell of a sort to Settembrini, his teacher.

[7] The German word for H_2CO is *Methylaldehyd*, which can be translated as "methylaldehyde" but is more commonly called formaldehyde.

[8] This statement leaves aside whether the loss of such "inhibitions" and "modesty" before death is a change for better or worse. Here I am noting only that doctors now are apparently more "open" and straightforward with dying patients than the doctors of twenty-five and fifty years ago. When I was in medical school, roughly twenty years ago, the notion that one should circumlocute about death was just starting to be challenged.

[9] We might also cite the motto of Prussian reformers of the bureaucracy: "Tot, krank oder dienstfähig." Joachim seems to believe this — except that he might omit the word "krank."

[10] I would like to believe that Mann intended this Spenglerian East-West construct to be read in a jocose manner.

[11] *Doctor Faustus*, 36.

[12] *Doctor Faustus*, 97.

[13] George Bernard Shaw, Preface to *Saint Joan* (Harmondsworth: Penguin, 1959), 59.

[14] The phrase "in essence" is in quotation marks since "contradiction in essence" would be contradictio in adjecto. Evil has no essence; and contradiction, by the same token, is the absence of logos.

[15] He and Settembrini both are unable to work on account of their illness. Ostensibly, Settembrini regrets this interruption (though we might look skeptically upon this regret), but Naphta appears not to mind being ill, even ostensibly. The issue of secondary gain from an illness is well illustrated by both Settembrini and Naphta. Settembrini complains long and loud about being unable to work: we therefore suspect him of malingering even though he is actually ill. Naphta, on the other hand, talks less about any regrets he might have about being unable to work. We learn about how illness interrupted his career not so much from his own words as from Settembrini's. Yet he, too, is able to live (at the expense of his Order!) on account of his illness: more secondary gain. Indeed, the whole seven-year sojourn of Hans Castorp on the mountain is a great monument to secondary gain: he seems only too delighted to inform his uncle James Tienappel that his stay on the mountain must be prolonged again and again.

[16] The rationale for this therapy was to deaerate the infected portion of lung, since that portion was not of use in respiration anyway, and the organism (*Mycobacterium tuberculosis*) is a strict aerobe. This type of therapy was not often successful. The resulting cavity — the pneumothorax — was filled with inert gas (nitrogen), and the opening of the chest could be manipulated so that the gas was forcefully expelled through a narrow opening. To paraphrase Lauren Bacall: you put your rib cage together and blow.

[17] Religioso Medici, 1643.

[18] The conjunction of witches and crystals in this chapter is reminiscent of E.T.A. Hoffmann's story "The Golden Pot," in which another witch curses another student, Anselmus, with these words: "Ay, run, run your way, Devil's Bird! You'll end up in the crystal! The crystal!"

[19] From Saint Thomas: Privatio est negatio in subjecto (*Summa Theologica* I-I:Q48a3): Privation is negation in a subject. This statement emphasizes the distinction between privation of good and its simple absence. "Absence of good, taken negatively, is not evil. For instance, a man would not be evil because he did not have the swiftness of a roe, or the strength of a lion. But the absence of a good, taken in the privative sense, is an evil; as, for instance, the privation of sight is called blindness."

[20] This is a difficult-to-translate term. For Aristotle's term οὐσια (entity), Aquinas gives "quod quid erat esse," which we might translate as "what a thing was (meant) to be, and hence similar to Plato's τα τι ην ειναι. Latin writers, including Augustine and Aquinas, often used the terms "essentia," "substantia," and

"quidditas," which are often translated into English as "essence," "nature" or "substance," and "whatness." The point, here, is that Aquinas and Augustine argue that evil doesn't have any of the above: nature, substance, essence, whatness.

[21] *The Confessions of Felix Krull, Confidence Man (The Early Years)*, trans. Denver Lindley (New York: Vintage International), 79–80.

[22] *Felix Krull*, 28.

[23] The original text reads: "'Die alte Baubo kommt allein,' rezitierte Settembrini bei ihrem Anblick und fügte auch den Reimvers hinzu, klar und plastisch." The translation given here is the older one (MM1, 326), by H.T. Lowe-Porter, which uses the more literal translation of "plastisch" as "plastic."

[24] "Allein bedenkt! Der Berg ist heute zaubertoll / Und wenn ein Irrlicht Euch die Wege weisen soll, / So müßt Ihr's so genau nicht nehmen."

[25] The older translation by Lowe-Porter retains the "shock" to the reader of having text suddenly appear in a foreign language, French. The newer translation by John E. Woods translates the French but uses italic type for any text that was in French in the original — a compromise, one surmises, made on behalf of American readers who were less likely than German readers to know some French. I am not qualified to judge the relative merits of the two translations from German to English; I have given my own translations of the French, however, because I believe some parts of the translation from French to English are debatable.

[26] "Let me dream anew, after having awoken me so cruelly with the alarm clock of your departure. Seven months under your eyes — and at present, when I have, in fact, made your acquaintance, you speak to me of your departure!"

"I repeat to you, that we could have chatted earlier."

"Would you have liked it?"

"Me? You will not escape me, mon pétit. This is about *your* interests, about *you*. Are you too timid to approach a woman to whom you now speak in dream, or was there someone else who prevented you?"

"I have told you so. I did not wish to say 'vous.'"

[27] MM1, 336–337. The French can be translated as: "To speak, to discourse, it is a very republican thing, I concede it.... I, you note well, I hardly speak French. However, with you I prefer this language to my own, because for me, to speak French, it is to speak without speaking, in a way — without responsibility, or as we speak in dreams. Do you understand?"

"A little bit."

"That will suffice ... To speak," continued Hans Castorp, "a poor affair! In eternity, one does *not* speak at all. In eternity, you know, one makes as if to draw a little pig: one leans one's head back and closes one's eyes."

[28] For a representation of medical practice and healing as the sublimation of (unconscious) sexual attraction, see William Carlos Williams's superb story "The Girl with the Pimply Face."

[29] This type of passage makes one admire anyone who dares to be a professional translator. In rendering the following, I have tried to stress the odd mixture of clinical anatomy (of the period) with the wooing, by Hans, of Clavdia: "Oh, love, you know . . . The body, love, death, these three are but one. For the body, it is illness and voluptuousness, and it is that which makes for death, yes, both of these are carnal, love and death, and there is their terror and great magic! But death, you understand, is in one way an infamous and impudent thing, which makes one blush with shame; and in another way it is a solemn and majestic power — much higher than the laughing life of making money and stuffing one's pockets — much more venerable than progress of which one chatters these days — because it is history and nobility and piety and the eternal and the sacred which make us take off our hat and walk on the tips of our toes. . . . Yet, at the same time, the body, that too, and the love of the body, are an indecent offensive affair, and the body reddens and pales at its surface in fright and shame at itself. But also it is a great and adorable glory, miraculous image of organic life, sanctified marvel of form and beauty, and the love of it, for the human body, it is at the same time a most humanitarian interest and a more educative power than all of the pedagogy in the world! . . . Oh, enchanting organic beauty, which is not composed of oil paint nor of stone, but of living and corruptible matter, full of the secret fever of life and of decay! Look at the marvelous symmetry of the human edifice, the shoulders and hips and nipples flowering on both sides of the chest, the ribs arranged in pairs, and the navel in the middle of the softness of the belly, and the obscure sexual organ between the thighs! Look at the shoulderblade stirring beneath the silken skin of the back, the spine which descends toward the double luxuriance of the buttocks, and the great branches of the vessels and nerves which ramify from the trunk through the armpits, and how the structure of the arms corresponds to that of the legs. Oh, the sweet regions of the inner joints of the elbow and of the knee with their abundant organic delicacies under their cushions of flesh! What an immense feast to caress them, these delicious sites of the human body! A feast after which one dies with pleasure! Yes, my God, let me smell the odor of the skin of your kneecap, beneath which the ingenious articular capsule secretes its glistening oil! Let me touch devotedly with my mouth the Arteria femoralis which beats at the front of your thigh and which divides below into the two arteries of the tibia! Let me experience the exhalation of your pores, human image of water and albumin, destined for the anatomy of the tomb, and let me perish, my lips on yours!"

[30] "Oh, love is nothing, if it is not madness, a senseless forbidden thing, and an adventure in evil. Otherwise it is an agreeable banality, good for making little ditties in the flatlands. But as for the fact that I recognized you and that I have recognized my love for you — yes, it's true, I knew you already, formerly, you and your marvelous oblique eyes and your mouth and your voice with which you speak — once already, when I was a schoolboy, I asked you for your pencil in order to get to make your acquaintance in this world, because I loved you with an irrational love, and it is from that no doubt, it is from my ancient love for you

that these scars stay with me, which Behrens has found in my body, and which indicate that I was already ill back then. . . ."

[31] Peeperkorn might or might not be a parody of Gerhart Hauptmann or Leo Tolstoy: charismatic, plethoric of the lifeforce — but not especially bright, and completely incoherent, he commits suicide because he is impotent. Opinion is divided as to whether this late accretion to the text adds to or detracts from the novel's unity.

[32] Who is Spanish — the "stern West": in the Spenglerian construct.

MICHAEL BRENNER

8: Beyond Naphta: Thomas Mann's Jews and German-Jewish Writing

IN ONE OF THE MOST INSIGHTFUL AND CRITICAL analyses of the topic, Ruth Klüger summarizes Thomas Mann's depiction of Jewish characters as follows: "If we want to learn about the perception of the Jew in the non-Jewish Western world, Thomas Mann is, to my mind, the most significant as well as the most frustrating and paradoxical single literary source."[1] There can, indeed, be little doubt that Thomas Mann's oeuvre is a unique source for the study of the complex attitudes German intellectuals held about Jews and Judaism. I would, however, argue that Mann's views about the Jews were less paradoxical and more consistent than most critics admitted. There was no necessary contradiction between Mann's outspoken negative feelings — ranging from condescension to disdain — for what he considered the incompletely assimilated German Jew and his respect and, at times, admiration for the "authentic" oriental Jew. In this respect Mann shared the conviction of many of his contemporaries, among them quite a few German-Jewish writers, who made similar distinctions in their work. As we will see, however, Mann went one step further and claimed that Jewishness and Judaism, while not negative categories themselves, belonged to a world entirely different from that of German culture and literature.

Between Animosity and Admiration: Fictional Jews in Thomas Mann's World

The company of Thomas Mann's Jewish characters begins with the portrait of a family of converted Jews, that of the upstart Baron von Stein in his 1896 short story, "Der Wille zum Glück," and sets the tone for much of his later writings on Jews. Stein's wife was "simply an ugly little Jewess.

Large diamonds sparkled at her ears."[2] We find this milieu again a few years later in his scandalous short story, "The Blood of the Walsungs," which the author withdrew from publication in the last moment before it was supposed to appear in *Die Neue Rundschau* in 1905. Sixteen years later he authorized the publication of a limited luxury edition with illustrations by Thomas Theodor Heine, which could not be purchased in bookstores. The public was able to read the German text (an unauthorized French translation had appeared in 1931 under the title *Sang reservé*) only after Mann's death, when a revised version was printed as part of his collected writings in 1958.

The reason for the suppression of this story was its content, which was open to anti-Semitic interpretation. The twins, Sieglinde and Siegmund Aarenhold, come from an assimilated Jewish home of enthusiastic Wagnerians (Mann's wife, Katia, had a twin brother, Klaus, and their father, Alfred Pringsheim, was one of the best-known Wagnerians in Munich), who, despite all efforts, are unable to leave behind their Jewishness. It lurks not only behind their physical appearance and their mother's Yiddish accent, but also behind the disdain the family carries toward Sieglinde's Gentile husband. The Aarenholds represent the stereotypical Jewish upstarts; they are witty but shallow and live in ostentatious luxury. As if this were not enough, the end of the story reveals their incestuous relationship. The most serious obstacle to publication for the editors of the *Neue Rundschau*, however, was the final sentence, which reads in its original: "Beganeft haben wir ihn, — den Goy!" (We really stuck it to him, the goy!). Mann agreed to change this sentence, and with a harmless new ending the story appeared both in 1921 and 1958.[3]

In "The Blood of the Walsungs" we confront for the first time a major Jewish character type that would become prominent in Mann's further work: the incompletely assimilated Jew whose Jewishness shines through his efforts to become fully German. His endeavors to assimilate are characterized by overcompensating for his Jewishness, in this case by adoring the most German music of Wagner. While most critics concentrated on Mann's text, little has been said about the illustrations of Thomas Theodor Heine. A founder of the satirical magazine *Simplicissimus* and himself of partly Jewish origins, Heine drew Negroid images of the Jewish twins, perhaps unconsciously internalizing the closeness of anti-black and anti-Jewish stereotypes of the "other." At one point, Heine depicts a Jewish family member as a monkey dressed in an elegant suit, recalling Kafka's "Report for an Academy."

While "The Blood of the Walsungs" remains Mann's only "Judengeschichte," Jews are present in most of his great works. The two outstanding Jewish characters in Mann's oeuvre are Leo Naphta in *The Magic*

Mountain and Chaim Breisacher in *Doctor Faustus*. Both fit the anti-Jewish stereotype of the assimilated (or converted) Jews unable or unwilling to leave their Jewish character traits behind: they are depicted as ugly, dangerous, and alien figures, and both are Jewish proponents of totalitarian ideologies. Naphta appears late in *The Magic Mountain*, but he becomes a central figure in its last chapters. He is a Jew and a Jesuit, a Communist and a Fascist, an intellectual nihilist without moral values. Born in Poland to a ritual slaughterer, Naphta converted to Catholicism but retained the typical physiognomy we will meet again in Mann's descriptions of his classmates: "He was a small, skinny, clean-shaven man, and so ugly — caustically, one could almost say corrosively, ugly — that the cousins were astonished. Somehow everything about him was caustic: the aquiline nose dominating the face; the small, pursed mouth; the pale gray eyes behind thick lenses," and his drawling manner of speech.[4] Even after Naphta's suicide as the consequence of his duel with his liberal counterpart Settembrini, when Hans Castorp and Settembrini gaze at the corpse, they "looked into a face that it was best to cover with a silk handkerchief" (696).

The story of Naphta's father is cruel in more than one respect. Elia Naphta, "a brooding introvert . . . , a scholar of the Torah" becomes the victim of a pogrom in his Galician shtetl and is crucified by the vandals. Brutality does not only affect Elia Naphta from the outside but is an integral part of his daily life. His profession of a *shohet*, a ritual slaughterer, is described in detail. As a young child Naphta would watch his father "flourish the large butcher knife and cut deep into the neck vertebrae of the bound and hobbled, but fully conscious, animal, had seen the assistant catch the spurting, steaming blood in basins that filled rapidly." Two conflicting ideas, which should later be spiritualized, begin to crystallize at this early age in the boy Leib Naphta observing his father's work: "the idea of piety became bound up with cruelty, just as the sight and smell of spurting blood was bound up in his mind with the idea of what is holy and spiritual" (433). It should not be overlooked that when those lines first appeared they met with an audience caught in the middle of a fierce political debate in anti-Semitic journals and state parliaments about kosher slaughtering, which led to its prohibition in Bavaria in 1930 by an unusual alliance of National Socialists, Social Democrats, and animal-protection societies.

Ruth Klüger once remarked about Naphta, whom she called "one of the great and greatly successful figures in Mann's work":

> The figure of Naphta remains tinged by anti-Semitism (and, to my mind, flawed by it), but he is not contained by that label. Like Shylock, he remains one of the most fascinating fantasies with which the Western, non-

Jewish, mind has projected its fears and nightmares onto the allegedly dangerous, potentially destructive.[5]

The combination of his Orthodox Jewish upbringing and Jesuit rigidity make Naphta not only a prophet of *Entbürgerlichung* (depriving Jews of their citizenship) and illiberalism but also a harbinger of the looming political totalitarianism. It may surprise contemporary readers that it was a Jew who, more than anyone else, is associated in this central novel of the Weimar Republic with the destruction of democratic and liberal values.

There is, of course, more reason to be astonished that this association is made even more explicit in a work published after the war, *Doctor Faustus*, in the figure of Dr. Chaim Breisacher, clearly modeled on the mystical Oskar Goldberg. Like Naphta, Breisacher was of "fascinating ugliness," and his illiberal credentials are certainly not less outstanding than Naphta's. Goldberg was, indeed, an obscure figure, whose magical speculations, Gershom Scholem said, were "uncommonly incisive and presumptuous, and they had a certain Luciferian luster."[6] Even if Breisacher reflected the dubious figure of Goldberg correctly, the question remains: why choose Goldberg as the prototype for a major Jewish character in a post-Holocaust novel? As Klüger points out, the book "does not refer to mass murder but instead presents a Jew with fascist leanings. At the very least this is a case of almost perversely bad taste, at worst it is a whitewash of German intellectuals."[7]

The Joseph tetralogy, which Mann considered his magnum opus, stands between *The Magic Mountain* and *Doctor Faustus*, but the portrait of Jewish characters here has nothing in common with the despicable likes of Naphta and Breisacher. Mann's biblical figures are not only distinctly Jewish — they are positive characters even in their Jewishness. While the epos serves Mann as an "abbreviated history of mankind,"[8] and while he is inspired by the "Panbabylonian" research discoveries of his generation, he did not de-Judaize and universalize his heroes. Just as his German Jews are despicable as Jewish characters, those biblical characters are admirable also as Jews. A brief analysis will reveal that, in this juxtaposition, Mann was aligned with many German-Jewish writers.

Naphta's Cousins: Trebitsch, Waremme, and Wendriner

German-Jewish literature in the early twentieth century often distinguished between the half-hearted, "inauthentic" assimilated German Jew, on the one hand, and the "authentic" Jew of biblical times or of contemporary eastern Europe on the other. Some Jewish writers depicted German-Jewish characters not that different from a Naphta or a Breisacher. Take, for example, Dr. Trebitsch in Joseph Roth's first novel, *The Spider's Web* (1923); Gregor Waremme (alias Georg Warschauer) in Jakob Wassermann's best-selling novel *The Maurizius Case* (1928); Alfred Engländer in Franz Werfel's *Barbara oder die Frömmigkeit* (1929; untranslated); and, perhaps most poignantly, Herr Wendriner in Kurt Tucholsky's famed *Weltbühne* satires. Those figures count among the most prominent fictional German-Jewish images in the Weimar years, and all represented negative characters. Instead of accusing their authors of Jewish self-hatred (as Scholem and others did), we should realize that they attacked not just "the Jew" but rather the assimilated self-hating Jew — an attack that often contained a substantial measure of self-criticism. After all, Tucholsky had converted to Protestantism, while Roth and Werfel became close to Catholicism.

Despite the disagreement about the threat of anti-Semitism, the Jewish figures in the works of Wassermann and Mann reveal a certain kinship. Like Naphta, Wassermann's Gregor Waremme was of East European background (although born in Germany) but had undergone a major identity shift when coming in contact with the West, culminating in his conversion to Christianity. He invented for himself a new Christian childhood and strove, albeit unsuccessfully, to be recognized as a German ultranationalist.

What Wassermann wrote about Waremme could well have been a characterization of Leo Naphta's personality: "When more closely examined, Waremme amounts to a personification of the Ahasuerus idea; the double motto he inscribes beneath his torn existence is: From East to West, Then, From West to East; his soul, cursed with the need to wander, demands the sedentary, but his mind, as destructive element, makes him rootless and measurelessly alone."[9]

Joseph Roth's Trebitsch is an even more obscure character, modeled on Arthur Trebitsch, an Austrian Jew who considered himself a follower of Otto Weininger and who figured prominently in the development of the Austrian Nazi movement. Dr. Trebitsch was the leader of a secret right-wing anti-Semitic organization. Surprisingly, most of the leading figures within this anti-Semitic organization were Jews. When the fictional Trebitsch flees to America, just as Waremme, in *The Maurizius Case*, he is succeeded as leader of the secret terror organization by the East European Jew, Benjamin Lenz. His true motivation for joining this group was not his great love for Germanness, but his hatred of European civilization. The work of destruction, begun by Lenz, is completed by his brother Lazar, who developed explosives strong enough to blow up the entire European continent.

Franz Werfel's novel *Barbara oder die Frömmigkeit* (1929), his most successful book published before 1933, portrays another Jewish protagonist who tries to escape his Jewishness. Like Werfel himself, his protagonist Alfred Engländer is convinced of the truth of Christianity without, however, taking the formal step of conversion. While Waremme and Trebitsch had given up their Jewishness to fight the cause of German ultranationalists, Engländer finds his new identity in Catholicism. Wassermann and Werfel were not alone in drawing rather negative portraits of German Jews. One is reminded of the Aarenhold family in the description of Stefan Zweig's assimilated Jewish family, the Salomonsohns, in the novella *Untergang eines Herzens* (1926; untranslated). With his assimilation and social rise, Salomonsohn accumulates wealth and supports the luxurious life of his wife and daughter. Intellectually, however, he becomes a "ridiculous clown," as one reviewer had it. He finds no sense in life and dies in total loneliness.[10]

Perhaps the most widely known and most detestable Jewish character to emerge form a Jew's pen in the Weimar period was Tucholsky's "Herr Wendriner." Between 1922 and 1930 Tucholsky published sixteen Wendriner essays in Germany's leading left-wing magazine, *Die Weltbühne*, under one of his many pen names, Kaspar Hauser. In his long monologues in Berlin dialect, mixed with Yiddish expressions, Wendriner advocated a more authoritarian education, complained about rising meat prices, and expressed his outrage that a national mourning was ordered to honor the assassinated Walther Rathenau. In his last and most biting piece Tucholsky envisioned, in 1930, Herr Wendriner "under dictatorship," easily accommodating Nazi rule. Although as a Jew he has to carry a "yellow card," he welcomes the "order" created by the new regime and favors their discriminatory policies toward the East European Jews: "you know, when it's against *them* anti-Semitism really is justified."[11]

Anti-Semitism was a major topic for German-Jewish writers of this time. Perhaps more eloquently and more desperately than anyone else, Jakob Wassermann, who was steadfast in his loyalty to Judaism, expressed serious doubts about the compatibility of Jewishness and Germanness. In his moving confession, *My Life as German and Jew* (1921), he recalled that while he always strove to be seen as a German writer, he was often portrayed as a Jewish author. His complaints about his reception among Germans culminated in the outcry that all his efforts were hopeless: "Vain to live for them [the Germans] and die for them. They say: he is a Jew."[12]

After the appearance of *My Life as German and Jew*, Thomas Mann immediately addressed Wassermann to refute his unease: "Isn't there really quite a bit of artistic hypochondria in play?" And he concludes with a remarkably short-sighted prophecy:

This Germany: cosmopolitan, one that absorbs what it can, seeks creatively to assimilate everything; a people [*Volkstum*] in which the paganism of the north does eternal battle with the yearning of the south, in which western burgherdom mingles with eastern mysticism — is this to be the soil [*Boden*] in which the tiny plant "anti-Semitism" can strike deep roots?[13]

Wassermann did not agree — he intended to elaborate further on the issue of anti-Semitism, which figures prominently in *Etzel Andergast*, the continuation of the Maurizius story. In 1926 he conceived a novel, *Ahasver*, about the "eternal Jew," and in 1932 he made notes for a novella about the anti-Jewish riots of Alsace in 1338, but none of those projects materialized.

While there is no doubt that Mann was always opposed to political anti-Semitism, he hardly took it seriously as a threat to Jewish existence. That may explain why — in contrast to the many Jewish characters in his work — he only portrayed one outspoken anti-Semite: Wiedemann in *The Magic Mountain*. As Ruth Klüger has observed, this marginal figure was not perceived as a serious threat to the Jews but, rather, as merely childish. To fight against him means to descend to his own level of infantile behavior, an attitude that recalls Mann's view of Wassermann as a hypochondriac:

> In this somewhat comical context the anti-Semite Wiedemann and the Jewish patient Sonnenschein literally get into each other's hair and come to blows, rolling on the floor in public, scratching and kicking like little boys: anti-Semitism as well as the fight against it as puerile, ridiculous enterprise. Mature adults will ignore both.[14]

The term "Jewish Self-Hatred" was established in these years with the publication of Theodor Lessing's character study of that name in 1930. Lessing admitted that he himself "had in his youth gone through a phase of exclusive dedication to 'Germanness,' exclusive resistance to 'Jewishness.'"[15] Thomas Mann had his place in the affair to which Lessing refers. Lessing had, in 1903, written a rather vicious attack (he called it "a little satire") against Samuel Lublinski, the critic who had praised *Buddenbrooks* and predicted its enormous success. Lessing's piece was not without anti-Semitic references. Mann's outrage was not less tempestuous and contained anti-Semitic stereotypes against Lessing similar to those that Lessing had directed against Lublinski. Lessing would never overcome his rage against Mann and recalled in his memoirs:

> Only one antagonism ever really hurt me — its hidden malice and secret venom were without comparison — and came close to destroying my outward life. It was with the then already famous writer Thomas Mann,

to whom I had various contacts since 1903. What he did to me, with unyielding insistence and for reasons I will not go into here, by means of meticulously poisoned articles that made me look contemptible in the public eye . . . was the most humanly low experience of my life.[16]

Neither Wassermann nor Werfel, neither Tucholsky nor Roth were themselves self-hating Jews only because they depict self-hating Jews. Their fictional characters are negative because all the authors mentioned here despised futile attempts at assimilation. Consequently, these figures often contain a measure of self-criticism. It is, indeed, difficult to find positive depictions of German Jews in German-Jewish literature during this period. On the eve of the First World War the editor of the most prestigious Jewish newspaper in Imperial Germany, the *Allgemeine Zeitung des Judentums*, Ludwig Geiger, had called for the creation of a positive German Jew in literature, a "German Jew, as we would like him to be: assiduous, solid, diligent, always aiming at the highest, working only for others, never pushing himself forward, faithful, abstinent, but still able to enjoy the happiness that he always longed for, without having fought for it recklessly."[17] Such a fictional character remained a desideratum in German-Jewish literature after the First World War, when German Jews were usually depicted as products of craven assimilation and Jewish self-denial.

There was, however, another figure in German-Jewish literature of the 1920s: the authentic, often exotic, Jew who remained faithful to the world of his fathers and who lived within a genuine Jewish setting. He could appear as East European Jew, Oriental Jew, rural Jew of a bygone generation, or medieval Jewish adventurer. These positive Jewish stereotypes were not new creations of the Weimar period, but now they seemed more prominent than ever. Tucholsky, who was so critical of German Jews (in his Swedish exile he wrote later: "Undoubtedly the German Jews were the worst of all — because they have adapted all the bad characteristics of the *boches*. The Germans are not Judaized — but the Jews *verbocht*."),[18] praised in his first article for *Die Schaubühne* (which later became *Die Weltbühne*) Yiddish theater in Berlin. In much more enthusiastic terms Franz Kafka, who found little attraction in the German-Jewish world of his father, was to do the same in Prague. His close friend, Max Brod, wrote a successful novel concerning a Jewish adventurer in Renaissance Portugal, David Reubeni, thus bringing to life a colorful world of the Jewish past. Similarly, Jewish writers published quite a few novels and dramas on the false messiah from seventeenth-century Izmir, Shabbetai Tzvi. Brod and his fellow Zionist, Arnold Zweig, portrayed the Jewish society in Palestine in two novels. Other Jewish writers turned to the *Ostjuden*, the "authentic" Jews in the East. Joseph Roth was among them, both with his masterful novel *Job* (1930) and with an earlier travel report,

Jews on Wanderings (1927), a response to Alfred Döblin's *Journey in Poland* (1925). The most glowing of these reports was produced by Arnold Zweig and the artist Hermann Struck in 1919, *The Eastern Jewish Countenance*. All these writers agree that the authentic "Jewish Jews" they had discovered in the East were much preferable to the "non-Jewish Jews" in the West, including themselves. "The Jew in the West was on his way to a tepid denomination, a feeble, desperate Piety . . . which threatened to decline daily and crumble away gradually. . . . The old Jew of the East, however, preserved his face," wrote Arnold Zweig, and Döblin went so far as to state: "I discovered I did not really know Jews. I could not label my friends, who called themselves Jews, as Jews. . . . Yes, I was there, and [it was there, in Poland that] for the first time I saw Jews."[19]

The stereotype of the proud oriental Jew served, perhaps more than any other image, as a positive counterpart to the assimilated German Jew. It was Jakob Wassermann who, in a reply to Martin Buber's Prague lecture, "The Spirit of the Orient and Judaism," delineated the contrast between those two basic types of Jews:

> The Jew as Oriental . . . is certain of himself, of the world, of humankind. . . . He is free, while they [the Western Jews] are slaves. He speaks the truth, while they are lying. He knows the sources, he lives with the mothers, he rests and creates, while they are eternally wandering unchangeables.

And again, one might think of Naphta in the following description of Wassermann's Western Jew: "We know them well, my dear friend, we know them and suffer from them, these thousands of so-called modern Jews, Jews who gnaw at the foundations because they are themselves without foundation; Jews who despise what they only yesterday achieved, who sully today what the loved yesterday, Jews for whom betrayal is a voluptuous pleasure, lack of dignity a jewel, and negation a goal. They commit themselves where they can only fail, venerate only where they are rebuffed. . . . But they themselves suffer, and their suffering is a fatal one — they know this as well as we do, we who need only look in their faces to see the death that is there."[20]

While Buber and Wassermann provided the theoretical basis for the distinction between assimilated Western Jew and authentic Oriental Jew, other Jewish writers filled those models with life. Else Lasker-Schüler left no doubt about the disdain she felt for her German-Jewish contemporaries with their "Zwergerei und Gemauschel." But in her *Hebrew Ballads* (1913) she created the images of proud Hebrews of the Bible, projecting herself back into biblical times and identifying with the figure of Joseph. She signed letters with the name "Prince Jussuf of Thebes." In her novel,

Der Malik (1919) she portrayed herself as the belligerent emperor Jussuf Abigail I, who led seven other wild Jews to conquer Moscow. It is this kind of authentic oriental Jew that Mann described in his biblical epic, just as did some of his Jewish contemporaries.

Mann's Joseph is hardly less Jewish than the Patriarchs in a contemporary biblical drama written by an Austrian Jew and much admired by Zionists at the time, Richard Beer-Hofmann's *Jacob's Dream*. Published in 1921, the first part of Beer-Hofmann's drama was performed in Hebrew (a performance by which the author was fascinated — without, however, understanding a word) by the Moscow-based Hebrew theater Habimah in all major cities of Europe and admired as an authentic Jewish play even by the assimilated Jewish critic Alfred Kerr. In Berlin the first editor of *Die Weltbühne*, Siegfried Jacobsohn — anything but a Zionist — reported enthusiastically in his journal: "I am enough of a Jew to perceive *Jacob's Dream* as Bible substitute [*Bibel-Ersatz*], and to admit that I was totally spellbound by it. . . . Especially in our time I welcome a kind of literature for which one has to be a Jew in order to understand it and sympathize with it."[21]

One wonders if Jacobsohn, had he lived to see it, would have perceived Mann's *Joseph and His Brothers* in a similar vein and thus revised his opinion. After all, just as Beer-Hofmann's story of Jacob, Mann's biblical epos was embedded in ancient Jewish culture, the names spelled according to their Hebrew originals (Jaakov and Jitschak, rather than the familiar German Jakob and Isaak), and the story enriched on the basis of later Jewish legends (taken mainly from Micha Josef Bin Gorion's [i.e., Berdyczewski's] multivolume work published a few years earlier). Beer-Hofmann did not have more access to the original sources than Mann had. On the other hand, Mann's biblical Jews are no lesser heroes than Beer-Hofmann's, only because he himself was Protestant. Couldn't *Joseph and His Brothers* serve in the same way as a "Bibel-Ersatz" as did *Jacob's Dream*? If any work by a non-Jewish author would qualify at all under the category of "Jewish literature," few German novels would come as close as Mann's biblical epic.

Mann's negative descriptions of German-Jewish characters have to be seen in this broader context of German-Jewish writing. Many German-Jewish writers constructed quite similar images to Mann's Jewish characters. They, too, juxtaposed the negative German-Jewish figures with heroic images of Oriental or East European Jews. There remained, however, one basic difference. German-Jewish writers looked inside themselves with their negative depiction of contemporary Jews; it served them as a form of self-criticism, not condescension. The same cannot be claimed for Thomas Mann, who viewed the Jew as the "other." In order fully to understand his literary remarks it is therefore necessary to look at his private writings. While the first have their parallel in German-Jewish literature, the latter stand by themselves.

From Fiction to Reality: Where the Parallels Divide

"One has no thought of Jewishness in regard to these people; one senses only culture."[22] So Thomas Mann informs his brother with relief after his first visit to the home of his future father-in-law in 1904. His position that there was a clear-cut distinction between Judaism and culture changed little over the years. After his marriage to Katja Pringsheim, the daughter of a prominent Munich family of Jewish descent, he seems to have felt an ever stronger need to stress the differences between Jewishness and European culture. Obviously, Mann did not share the racists' conviction that Jews could never leave behind their innate peculiarities; this would have excluded his own wife from being German. But, in his view, only very few Jews could become genuinely German, and a radical transformation, perhaps even conversion, was a necessary precondition for this step.

Mann's arguments, most clearly articulated in his 1907 essay, "Solving the Jewish Question," which was undertaken from what he called a position of a "convinced and undoubting philosemite," stand in the tradition of liberal German advocates of Jewish emancipation. In his call for a "Europanization of Jewry" Mann notes the sad state of present Jewry but expresses hope for the future, given rapid assimilation, conversion, and the increase of mixed marriages. His goal is "a re-elevation and ennobling of the Jewish type which would remove all that is objectionable for good Europeans and which must be the first goal to strive for." The recipe for the necessary transformation consists of a rather conventional medication: "The increase of mixed marriage will depend on the improvement and Europeanization of the Jewish type; and the practical importance of baptism is not to be underestimated."[23]

In his famous call, "Concerning the Amelioration of the Civil Status of the Jews," the Prussian civil servant Christian Wilhelm Dohm made similar remarks about the deplorable moral and physical conditions of the Jews (which he blamed on persecution and exclusion from Christian society) and recommended their gradual transformation so that they become useful citizens of the state. Dohm published his treatise in 1781, and the reader of Mann's remarks cannot help but wonder that no basic transformation among the Jews was perceived after a period of 120 years, in which Jews had to a large extent given up their own culture in order to become an integral part of their surrounding culture and society. This argumentation, stretching from Dohm to Mann, had a long chain of tradition among liberal German authors, including Hegel and Humboldt. In their view Jews could truly integrate into German society once they had renounced their Judaism. In other words, they could become Germans as ex-Jews, but not as Jews. In 1879 the most prominent liberal defender of the Jews against the reactionary anti-Semitism in the late nineteenth century, the historian Theodor Mommsen, expressed a similar position:

> The word "Christendom" no longer fully means what it once did; but it remains the only word that summarizes the character of contemporary international civilization and in which millions and millions can feel solidarity on this globe so rich in peoples. To stand outside these limits yet within a nation is possible, but difficult and dangerous. Whoever follows a conscience, whether good or bad, that forbids him to renounce Judaism and instead to profess Christianity, that man will have to accept the consequences.[24]

There was no lack of prominent Jews who would heed those recommendations and convert. In Mann's own lifetime one may just think of names such as Gustav Mahler, Arnold Schoenberg, Kurt Tucholsky, and Karl Kraus. Others, such as Walther Rathenau, sought their salvation in a total assimilation without conversion. In his essay "Hear, Oh Israel," the future German foreign minster wrote, after rejecting the possibility of conversion as a mere exterior change: "What, then, ought to be done? Something without historical precedent: the conscious self-education and adaptation of the Jews to the expectations of the Gentiles. Adaptation not as 'mimicry' in the Darwinian sense . . . but a shedding of tribal attributes which, whether they be good or bad in themselves, are known to be odious to our countrymen, and a replacement of these attributes by more appropriate ones. . . . The final result of the process should not be Germans by imitation, but Jews of German character and education."[25] Thomas Mann would have been the last to object.

The Berlin Jewish entrepreneur Rathenau and the Lübeck Protestant patrician Mann shared the conviction that Jews had to change their physiognomy as a first precondition of acceptance into German society. "Look yourselves in the mirror!" Rathenau called on his fellow Jews, "This is the first step toward self-criticism. . . . You should be . . . careful not to walk about in a loose and lethargic manner, and thus become the laughingstock of a race brought up in a strictly military fashion. As soon as you have recognized your unaesthetic build, your narrow shoulders, your clumsy feet, your sloppy roundish shape, you will resolve to dedicate a few generations to the renewal of your outer appearance."[26]

In Thomas Mann's words, a few years later, the need for physical change reads as follows: "Of course it is not a necessity that the Jew always retain his hunched posture, bowlegs, and red, gesticulating [*mauschelnde*] hands along with a showy, suffering, insolent manner and an on the whole alien, oily character . . . . It will not be long until it no longer seems impossible to be a Jew and at the same time a fine human being in body and soul. To have reached this parity within three generations will soon be a matter of course. . . ."[27]

When Thomas Mann, already in Weimar days, recalled his Jewish childhood friends in an essay, "On the Jewish Question" (1921), his description focuses mainly on their physiognomy, reflecting the popular stereotypes. Young Simson Carlebach (confounded by Mann with his brother Ephraim) was "quick, wenn auch eben sehr reinlich nicht" (lively, even if not exactly clean); a Hungarian Jew called Feher was of "a type, pronounced to the point of ugliness"; and the son of a kosher slaughterer was a lean fellow, "so that his lips were the only fullness in his appearance."[28]

Two years earlier, during the revolutionary unrest of 1918 and 1919 in Munich, he had confided to his diary some of his strongest anti-Jewish sentiments, concentrating not only on the Jews' physical appearance but also on their moral faults. Mann frequently expressed his disgust at the prominent role of Jews and the "großstädtische Scheißeleganz der Judenbengel" (snotty elegance of big-city Jewboys) which led to a "Judenregiment." As early as 8 November 1918, the very first day of the Revolution, he claims: "Munich, as Bavaria, ruled by Jewish writers. How long will she put up with it?" A few days later he planned to defend himself in case of an attack against him with the following words: "Listen, I am not a Jew, a victor in the war, or anything else bad."[29]

Jews were "Literaten" (writers), but could they become an integral part of German literature, to the same extent as the Lübeck patrician? Hardly, since they were "ubiquitously recognizable as outsiders," in politics as well as in literature.[30] How else can one interpret Mann's reply to the accusation of the anti-Semitic literary historian, Adolf Bartels, who had accused Mann himself of being Jewish: "If I were to qualify as a Jew, all my writings would take on a different, false face. What about the book that made my name, what would *Buddenbrooks* be if it came from a Jew? A snob's book."[31] This was long before he wrote *The Magic Mountain* or *Doctor Faustus*. But in this respect his view of the Jews did not change over time. In October 1945 he singled out Jewish writers and critics as a separate category in German literature, when he noted in his diary: "'Race' is completely compromised. What should it be called? For something is different about them, and not just Mediterranean. Heine, Kerr,

Harden, Kraus on up to the fascist Goldberg-type — it's all *one* blood. Could Hölderlin or Eichendorff have been Jews? Not even Lessing, Mendelssohn notwithstanding."[32] Was it coincidental that, after objections of his family (in the first instance his father-in-law, in the second his wife) he had to withdraw both his "Judengeschichte" ("The Blood of the Walsungs") of 1905 and his central essay "On the Jewish Question" of 1921 before publication?

At the same time, Mann was well aware that he owed much of his fame to Jews who had discovered him and who admired him. Reminiscent of Theodor Fontane's ironic lines about the well-wishers at his seventy-fifth birthday, Mann remarked: "Jews 'discovered' me, Jews have published and promoted me, Jews put on my impossible theater play, a Jew — it was poor old Lublinski who, when *Buddenbrooks* produced only sour faces in response, divined in a left-liberal [!] paper that *Buddenbrooks* will grow with time and be read for generations. When I go out into the world and visit cities, it is almost without exception the Jews who receive me, shelter me, cosset me, wine and dine me, and not only in Berlin and Vienna." In the same passage he notes, "In the course of the years it has come to serious conflicts between my nature and that of the Jews. This bad blood was probably inevitable."[33]

Perhaps most revealing both in its negative and its positive aspects was a brief reflection in his diary on the Nazi persecution of the Jews: "I could to some extent go along with the rebellion against the Jewish element were it not that the Jewish spirit exercises a necessary control over the German element, the withdrawal of which is dangerous ... and Germandom is not stupid enough to toss my type into the same pot and drive me out, too."[34] What is most striking in all these passages is that Mann had no doubt that something like a collective "Jewish element" or "Jewish spirit" existed. Lion Feuchtwanger's scornful remarks about the anti-Semites' efforts to single out a "Jewish element" in German literature could well have applied to Thomas Mann, even though, in contrast to the anti-Semites, Mann regarded this element as an essentially positive force and necessary counterbalance to the German mind: "The upshot," Feuchtwanger wrote in 1920, "was, it goes without saying, a Tower of Babel, an arbitrary, senseless construct. They may just as well have construed a literature of people with black hair or of short-sighted types."[35]

In summary of Thomas Mann's views on Jews as recorded in his private notes and essays, it is fair to say that he distinguished three different types. First, there were those who had ceased to be Jews and had become true Germans. They constituted the ideal case. As in his wife's family, among them nothing reminded him of Judaism, "one feels nothing but culture." Next were the "Jewish Jews," those who remained authentic

Jews with a somewhat exotic but always fascinating note, just as the "not very clean" rabbi's son Simson Carlebach, whose name was "filled with the desert poetry" of the Bible; the ugly Neher, whose "alien, drawling dialect . . . struck my ear as more interesting than our usual northern German [*Wasserkantisch*]"; and the local slaughterer's son who represented "the type of the thoroughly pleased Jew."[36]

To the third category belonged the Jews for whom he had the least sympathy: those who unsuccessfully strove to become Germans and in the end were neither "authentic" Germans nor "authentic" Jews — the Heines and Kerrs, the Hardens and Krauses, the revolutionaries Eisner and Leviné, or even worse, intellectuals such as Theodor Lessing and Oskar Goldberg. It must be noted that Mann attacked all who belonged to this category not just as individuals but explicitly as Jews. His conflict was with the "Jewish nature," the "Jewish spirit." It cannot be seen except in terms of a personal obsession that, of all Germans, it is German Jews, such as Chaim Breisacher in *Doctor Faustus*, whom the novelist Mann depicts as allies and harbingers of National Socialism even after the Holocaust.

Notes

[1] Ruth Angress-Kluger, "Jewish Characters in Thomas Mann's Fiction," *Horizonte: Festschrift für Herbert Lehnert zum 65. Geburtstag*, eds. H. Mundt, Egon Schwarz, and William J. Lillyman (Tübingen: Niemeyer, 1970), 172.

[2] Mann, *Gesammelte Werke in zwölf Bänden* (Frankfurt am Main: S. Fischer, 1960), 8:49. Cited henceforth as *GW*. [Translations from the German by S. Dowden.]

[3] See Hans Rudolf Vaget, "*Sang reservé* in Deutschland: Zur Rezeption von Thomas Manns *Wälsungenblut*," *German Quarterly* 57.3 (1984): 367–376.

[4] Thomas Mann, *The Magic Mountain*, trans. John E. Woods (New York: Knopf, 1995), 366. Henceforth citations from this edition will be cited parenthetically.

[5] Angress-Kluger, "Jewish Characters," 167.

[6] Gershom Scholem, *Walter Benjamin: The Story of a Friendship* (Philadelphia: Jewish Publication Society, 1981), 97. For a different view of Goldberg, see Manfred Voigts, *Oskar Goldberg: Der mythische Experimentalwissenschaftler. Ein verdrängtes Kapitel jüdischer Geschichte* (Berlin: Argon, 1992).

[7] Angress-Kluger, 162.

[8] Mann, *Briefe 1889–1936*, ed. Erika Mann (Frankfurt am Main: S. Fischer, 1961), 1:390 (to Louise Vervicen, 23 May 1935).

[9] Jakob Wassermann, *Deutscher und Jude: Reden und Schriften, 1904–1933*, ed. Dierk Rodewald (Heidelberg: Lambert Schneider, 1984). For more details concerning the depiction of Jews in German-Jewish literature see my book, *The Renaissance of Jewish Culture in Weimar Germany* (New Haven: Yale UP, 1997), 129–152.

[10] See Manfred Sturmann, "Studie über Stefan Zweig," *Jüdische Rundschau*, 1 December 1928, p. 97.

[11] Kurt Tucholsky, *Gesammelte Werke 1929–1932* (Reinbek: Rowohlt, 1960), 3:548.

[12] Jakob Wassermann, *My Life as German and Jew* (New York: Coward and McCann, 1933), 226–227.

[13] *GW* 13:465.

[14] Angress-Kluger, 165.

[15] Theodor Lessing, *Der jüdische Selbsthaß* (Berlin: Jüdischer Verlag, 1930), 40.

[16] Theodor Lessing, *Einmal und nie wieder: Lebenserinnerungen, Gesammelte Schriften*, vol. 1 (Prague: Heinr. Mercy, 1935), 320.

[17] *Allgemeine Zeitung des Judentums* 75 (1911): 101–102.

[18] Tucholsky, *Politische Briefe*, ed. Fritz J. Raddatz (Reinbek: Rowohlt, 1969), 109–110.

[19] Alfred Döblin, *Autobiographische Schriften und letzte Aufzeichnungen* (Olten and Freiburg: Walter, 1985), 211.

[20] Wassermann, *Deutscher und Jude*, 31.

[21] S.J., "Bibel-Ersatz," *Die Weltbühne* 15.2 (1919), 641.

[22] Thomas Mann to Heinrich Mann, 27 February 1904. *Letters of Heinrich and Thomas Mann, 1900–1949*, ed. Hans Wysling, trans. Don Reneau (Berkeley: U of California P, 1997), 66.

[23] *GW (Nachtrag)*, 13:461–462.

[24] Theodor Mommsen, "Auch ein Wort über unser Judenthum," *Der Berliner Antisemitismusstreit*, ed. Walter Boehlich (Frankfurt am Main: Insel, 1965), 224.

[25] Walther Rathenau, "Höre Israel!" in his *Schriften*, eds. Arnold Hartung et al. (Berlin: Berlin Verlag, 1965), 91.

[26] Rathenau, 92.

[27] *GW* 13:461–462.

[28] *GW* 13:466–468. On Simson and Ephraim Carlebach see Kurt Loewenstein, "Thomas Mann zur jüdischen Frage," *Bulletin des Leo Baeck Instituts* 10 (1967), 20.

[29] Thomas Mann, *Tagebücher 1918–1921*, ed. Peter de Mendelssohn (Frankfurt am Main: S. Fischer, 1979), 63, 81, 85.

[30] *GW* 13:459.

[31] Cited in Klaus Harpprecht, *Thomas Mann: Eine Biographie* (Reinbek: Rowohlt, 1995), 280.

[32] Thomas Mann, *Tagebücher 1944–1.4.1946,* ed. Inge Jens (Frankfurt am Main: S. Fischer, 1986), 269.

[33] *GW* 13:470. The Fontane poem ironically marks the dominance of the Jewish names among those to congratulate him:

Die auf "berg" und "heim" sind gar nicht zu fassen,
Sie stürmen ein in ganzen Massen,
Meyers kommen in Bataillonen,
Pollacks und die noch östlicher wohnen;
Abram, Isack, Israel,
Alle Patriarchen sind zur Stell...
Jedem bin ich was gewesen,
Alle haben sie mich gelesen,
Alle kannten mich lange schon,
Und das ist die Hauptsache..., "*kommen Sie, Cohn.*"

[34] Thomas Mann, *Tagebücher 1933–34,* ed. Peter de Mendelssohn (Frankfurt am Main: S. Fischer, 1977), 54.

[35] Lion Feuchtwanger, "Die Verjudung der abendländischen Literatur," *Centum Opuscula: Eine Auswahl* (Rudolstadt: Greifenverlag, 1956), 443.

[36] *GW* 13:467–468.

KARLA SCHULTZ

9: Technology as Desire: X-Ray Vision in *The Magic Mountain*

> *Dem Übergang von der Petroleum-lampe, der Gasflamme, die das Rampen-licht der Theater abgab, dem weiß-leuchtenden Gas-Glühlichtstrumpf zum elektrischen Licht — ich war davon Zeuge.*
> —Thomas Mann, *Meine Zeit*

> *Alles klar, aber auch alles zu Ende.*
> —Friedrich Nietzsche, *Briefe*

Taking a Look

WHEN I BEGAN WRITING THIS ESSAY, IT happened that the power went out. Several distant, quasi-musical bangs, a ragged-edged flicker across the screen — and my magic PC window went blank. Agitated as to whether the text had been saved (it wasn't), I decided to make use of the remaining daylight and read an essay I previously had put aside. It really had nothing to do with my topic. But then, all the electricity had left the neighborhood. When it would return (it did) no one knew.

I felt pleasurably isolated. So I reached for the small S. Fischer volume with its dusty-green, flexible linen cover that feels so good to the touch and opened to page 218, Thomas Mann's personal recollection, "Occult Experiences."[1] Of course I had read the episode about the "highly questionable" séance in *The Magic Mountain*, but, being interested in technical matters — if only to wean myself, finally, from the fluffier dimensions of the novel — I had resolved not to waste any energy on it. But this was a break. Sunday afternoon without power.

So I began, immediately put out by Mann's class- and gender-conscious split between high and low metaphysics. The man had a nerve: praising Schopenhauer and calling the low kind a "metaphysics-for-maids," a "Sunday-afternoon-diversion-for-cooks" . . . Sunday afternoon?! A few pages further I settled down. Right there, on page 222, was a passage about "the famous Mr. Einstein," of whose theory, Mann writes, he understands very little except that all things possess time as a fourth dimension and consist of matter that, ultimately, is nothing but energy. I continued reading. "Nicely put," my mind flashed as I read that with Einstein "the border between mathematical physics and metaphysics has become fluid." My leisure was turning legitimate. Hadn't I checked Mann's diaries for references to his famous neighbor at Princeton (few but inconclusive) to see whether the creator of Hans Castorp, with his detailed studies of chemistry and biology, had something to say about physics? Hadn't I consulted *The Britannica Online* on the history of technology, especially in regard to X-rays? A history leading to the special theory of relativity, vacuum tubes, electronics, the transistor . . . all the way home to my PC?

Technology. Enlightenment. So I was right in how I was using this non-electronic time, after all. A few pages later the smugness crumbled. "There are university professors," Mann writes, having stated his skepsis vis-à-vis the occult, "who, by taking a renegade advantage of Munich's insufficient street lighting, sneak under cloak and cover to Mr. von Schrenck's evening sessions in order to see what isn't good for them." Oy vey. Here I was reading in the day's waning light what under the electric light, in right mind and pursuit, I had meant not to read — an eyewitness account of good-for-nothing, supernatural phenomena. But the essay's parlando kept seducing me. Not just that. I, too, like those Munich professors of the early twenties ("Occult Experiences" dates from 1924), suffer from bouts with that vulgar, spider-spun proclivity toward media and ghosts. The power was still out.

I kept on reading, flipping the pages so vividly filled with long-dead people, with pompous ruminations, with tramcars, with tangible, eye-winking gothic: "It was a spacious room, full of disorder and photographic implements, also some apparatus for magnesium-flashes, chairs and tables covered with motley objects like a music box, a rolled-up table cloth, a typewriter, several white felt pads, etc." My bio-pad marked the technical props. And then — then I let go, fully engrossed in the forced chatter of the participants, in Mr. Mann holding hands with Willi-the-medium, in the medium's trance, his contortions, moanings, whispers, his dull exhaustion, the entire male labor room scene: "All the light that was left was a dark-reddish shimmer . . . Who writes on the typewriter? No-one ... We shall listen to you, and then we'll have the writing as a token that we're not just hallucinating." *Gaukelei. Seekrankheit.* How clever. How conventional. How delightful.

And the ending, downright devious. First he hooks Hegel up to Einstein to bring the spirit up to date ("It was Hegel who said that the idea, the spirit must be considered the ultimate source for all phenomena"), then he stages a mock dialogue with himself. What about? Nothing. About never going to Mr. von Schrenck-Notzing's again, no, never again, just one more time. And he retrieves from that labor room, to our mock and his satisfaction, that ghost-propelled handkerchief rising, rising, in dark red light, to his mind's eye moist with mirth. . . What was that line about the cook? The power is on again. Almost dark. The wiliest of bourgeois writers not only knew how to have and eat his cake, he knew how to feed it to us, too.[2]

Einstein's Train

THE AGE into which Hans Castorp is born is the era of exploding science and accelerating speed, of measuring light and penetrating matter. It is the age in which the study of electricity is transformed into the study of electrons. But not quite yet. In the opening scene of the novel, the hero still travels by steam engine and across perceptible dimensions. Or does he? "Two days of travel separate . . . Space, as it rolls and tumbles away between him and his native soil . . . brings about changes very like those time produces."[3]

As space and time slip past and away from the train window, Hans Castorp is being primed for new ways of perception. He will see and hear differently, develop broader and thinner, loftier and deeper views. He will be far away. Like the needle tracing the disk on the turntable of a gramophone, his train, gobbling up the dimensions, is heading dead center. To complicate matters, the time that elapses for the passenger *in* the train relative to that for observers *outside* the train (positioned, say, at the beginning and end of the journey) is shorter, that is, it moves more slowly. Certainly as measured by the speed of light.[4]

We catch a first glimpse of him when he, motionless himself, is transported to the Swiss mountains, the engine huffing and puffing like an exhausted, antediluvian dragon: "the train was winding through a narrow pass; you could see the forward cars and the laboring engine, emitting great straggling tatters of brown, green, and black smoke" (4). That the train, having replaced the horse and soon to be powered by electricity, might be sick we gather hundreds of pages later when Castorp tells his visiting uncle from the flatlands about the "galloping form" that tuberculosis may assume, in severe cases, like that of the Scotswoman, a kind of gangrene of the lungs, "a blackish-green infection" that forces the patient "to breathe a vaporized solution of powdered carbolic acid all day" (424). The concatenation of human illness with technology will propel the novel all the way to its crash.[5]

But as yet the train labors along. It has crossed the flatlands, the undulating hills, the carefully constructed bridges across the chasms in the rising mountains. "It is a long trip from Hamburg to those elevations" (3). From Landquart — a small alpine station — it will carry its passenger to novel heights, to a new field of gravity where temperatures rise and the body is pierced by invisible rays. That will be deep in the bowels of the sanatorium. For now, the journey upward results in a dizzy-spell for the protagonist:

> Hans Castorp thought about how he had left hardwood forests far below him, and songbirds, too, he presumed; and the idea that such things could cease, the sense of a world made poorer without them, brought on a slight attack of dizziness and nausea, and he covered his eyes with his hand a second or two. (5)

Sharp Drop

"MY GOD, I see," he exclaims as he gazes at his cousin's skeleton made visible by the X-ray machine. And, as he watches the flesh fall away from his own hand on the screen, the seal ring inherited from his grandfather hovering black around the joint of his ringfinger (just as his creator had seen Katja Mann's fingers stripped during *his* visit to Davos in 1912,[6] and, before him, Wilhelm Röntgen, who sent prints of an X-rayed hand to colleagues and friends on New Year's Day, 1896[7]), he understands that he will die: "And he made the same face he usually made when listening to music — a rather dull, sleepy, and devout face, his head tilted toward one shoulder, his mouth half-open." Dr. Behrens, shaman and scientist in one, shakes him awake: "Spooky, isn't it? Yes, there's no mistaking that whiff of spookiness." Hans Castorp has trouble tearing himself away from the vision. He remembers a distant relative occasionally mentioned in his family, who had been cursed by clairvoyancy, of having people about to die appear to her eyes in the form of skeletons. But the doctor, not unlike Settembrini in many respects, closes off the current, and the natural world reappears: "The floor grew quiet, the spectacle of lights faded, the magic window wrapped itself in darkness. The ceiling lamp went on" (216).

Cut to the last chapter, the gramophone episode. The hero has studied the human body, its chemical composition, its psychic analysis; he has tasted the flesh of Clavdia Chauchat, kept the plate showing its interior, watched the bones of devoured children fly through the air in his snow dream. Soon he will turn on the ceiling light himself to stop his fellow patients from continuing their ghostly séance. But before he does, his narrator makes him fall under yet another technological spell, this time not of the electromagnetic but of the electromechanical kind. Hans Castorp listens to the record player, to "the lush achievements of this little truncated coffin of fiddlewood, this small dull-black temple with its doors flung wide, before which he would sit in an armchair, hands folded, head on one shoulder, mouth open. . . ." His trance is induced by the vivid physicality of the apparatus, the soundwaves washing over him more tangibly than in a concert hall: "The vibrations produced amazing effects near their source, but like all ghostly things, quickly languished with distance, grew feeble, their power merely illusory" (633).

Steady Now

IN THE EQUATIONS of the novel, indeed, its equivocations, technology is magic and magic — well, magic is duplicitous. While it dazzles the senses it splits them from their synthetic function, leaving the body they belong to as if it were dead. Technology's new magic, the novel is at pains to demonstrate, is dangerous. But it also is effective. It thins the flesh as it stretches the human vision, puffs up the soul as it purifies sound. It must be resisted. No: it must be embraced.

The Magic Mountain, we read in the massive literature on Thomas Mann, is a novel of education, of initiation, of the adventures of the spirit; it is the story of pre-World War I Europe, of the transformation of Unpolitical Man, of the tricks of narration and the alchemy of time.[8] Looked at in terms of technology, it also is an exercise in containment. Hans-the-medium is introduced to a number of new inventions, and it is the narrator's task to steer him toward integrating them into a holistic worldview, that is, toward a clarity not technical but humanistic. But the medium gets out of hand. Infected by the new optics, he tumbles from his mountain "toward a heaven darkened by sulfurous fumes" (702). At the end of the novel (which Thomas Mann fervently wished he had finished ten years earlier[9]) Hans Castorp, the song from his record session on his lips, is lost from sight in the world's first technological war.

This would be half of an interpretation. The other half is that *The Magic Mountain* is an exercise in competition. The new technology that dazzles the senses is highly desirable. It teaches the power of the moment, brings the old magic of storytelling up to date. And it permits conflating an individual's class perception with universal categories. Hans-the-medium is the only one who sees and hears in the novel; he is the bourgeois subject teased and cajoled by his narrator into refining his vision, distending his soul. In fact, it is this narrator who colludes, in the *pluralis maiestatis*, not only with his medium but also with an imaginary reader who is just like himself: perceptive and spectral. "And we are reluctant shades by the roadside, ashamed of our own shadowy security" (703). In terms of competition, then, it is not just technology but "the spirit of our story" that must trample over corpses — so it can produce (since it is better than technology) "a dream of love rising up out of death and this carnal body" (706). As in "Occult Experiences," not even the handkerchief is missing in the end, or rather, it is the twice-mentioned finger that dabs both the humanist Settembrini's and the narrator's eyes.

Mann's strategies of containment and competition are indirect. They are embedded in an organicist, mythologizing worldview that is expansive enough to accommodate demonizing as well as appropriating technology, criticizing its soul-lessness as well as sentimentalizing its practicality, battling its streamlining as well as emulating its marketability. What he borrows from technology (precision, repetition, norm-orientation; the assembly, rearrangement, and exchangeability of parts) is infused with pathos and irony, with the wishful omnipotence of the child as well as the savvy of the producer of bestsellers.

Technique Macabre

HE MAKES the machines that provide for the new ways of seeing and hearing all wear a ghostly patina. They are agents of negativity, heightening the senses and honing them to a pitch as if they, too, partook of fever and thin air. They let the eyes see what is obscured, the ears hear what is no longer there; they make the skin burn and the flesh fade away. Naphta would applaud: they are Lucifer incarnate. Or so it seems. When Hans Castorp is introduced to the X-ray machine, a hellish spectacle breaks loose:

> For two seconds the dreadful forces necessary to penetrate matter were let loose ... Discharges exploded like gunshots. The gauges sizzled with blue light. Long sparks crackled along the wall. Somewhere a red light blinked, like a silent, threatening eye, and a vial behind Joachim's back was filled with a green glow. (212)

Colors flash, sounds explode, ozone spreads — yet the body, Hans Castorp notes with astonishment, feels nothing. The senses are bombarded yet cannnot make any sense of the show. Settembrini, we may be sure, would *not* applaud. Mann's description is the stuff of which demons are made: powerful forces are unleashed ("thousands of volts, one hundred thousand, Hans Castorp thought he had heard somewhere"), a lifeless apparatus stirs, a piercing eye that looks past the human flesh hovers in the dark. Technology (and the story) as spook.

Unlike the big machine in the cellar, the dainty gramophone is openly on display in the salon. It is a magnet for social gatherings, providing first-class entertainment instead of a startling memento mori. With its appeal to the ear it should have less of a specular effect, but it doesn't. Elegantly shaped, it flaunts the perfect commodity form, soul-specter included:[10]

> "The newest model," said the director, who now entered the room. "The latest achievement, children, top-notch, A-1, nothing better in the warehouse . . . Music most faithful, in its modern, mechanical form. The German soul, up-to-date. . . . Shall we give a disk a try, let her rip and roar?" (627–628)

Dr. Behrens is in charge of all the levers. He flips the switch for the current, waits for the turntable to spin, lifts the "club-shaped, nickel-plated arm with its flexible joints,"[11] and places the steel point on the rim of the disk: a catchy tune making the legs move and spirits soar bursts from the coffin-shaped box. Like the ultraviolet tanning lamp, the gramophone makes the patients feel younger, sexier, and light of step; like the bioskop down in the village, it brings to life what has been framed and fixed. Technology (and the story) as animation:

> The body of sound, though not in any way distorted, had suffered a diminution in perspective; it was, if one may use a visual comparison for an audible phenomenon, as if one were gazing at a painting through the wrong end of opera glasses, so that it looked distant and small, but without forfeiting any definition of line or brilliance of color. (628)

When Thomas Edison first recorded "Mary had a little lamb" on his phonograph in December 1877, he was convinced that the machine would be much more than the ephemeral toy it appeared to be. He described its future function as a keeper of invaluable records, of preserving the last words of dying persons, of preserving languages by reproducing their exact pronunciation. In contrast to the telephone of his competitor Bell, it was not a device to transmit momentary, fleeting communication but, "a brilliant, almost otherwordly conception,"[12] to enshrine the living voice with fidelity. Technology (and the story) as quality control.

The peering eye and the faithful ear, modeled after the new inventions, become part of the medium Hans. But in him they appear part of an organic whole. As he leans over Joachim's shoulder in the darkness of Dr. Behrens's laboratory, he gazes at the architecture of his cousin's interior, harmoniously proportioned and illuminated by the milky shine of faded flesh: the column of the spine, the scaffolding of the ribs, the floating roof of the clavicles. "The collarbone curved upward on both sides, and the bones of the shoulder, the joint where Joachim's arm began, looked lean and angular against the soft halo of flesh. The chest cavity was bright" (214). By its light he also discerns the heart, a half-obscured, baggy creature that moves, off-center, in primal rhythm. The scene stages classical lines with a baroque vanishing point, shows a visual depth that triggers an aural fantasy.

The gramophone episode illustrates the reverse, i.e., he learns to combine aural depth with visual fantasy. The patients, along with Hans (who will soon claim control over the machine's operation), stand marveling at its capabilities as they listen to the voice of the fabled Caruso: "The splendid vocal organ swelled to its full natural range and power, and indeed if you walked into an adjoining room, leaving the doors open but staying out of the line of sight, it was exactly as if the artist were physically present, as if he were standing there in the salon singing, music in hand" (629). The two scenes together demonstrate a concerted effort to synthesize what is falling apart: presence and sensation.

Placet Experiri

The voice split from the body, the bones bared from the flesh give Hans Castorp much to think about. But he doesn't examine the mechanics, let alone the physics of these phenomena, as one might expect from someone trained in engineering — it might reveal the operations of his creator (who, after all, is a model constructivist). So Hans turns to the study of the biological sciences instead. He concentrates on life, on its composition and evolution, its cyclical nature of matter dying and being reborn. His studies lead him to envision a mythical correspondence between the atom and the starry sky above, between the microcosm of the cell and the macrocosm of the universe: "Had not one researcher in his visionary boldness spoken of the 'beasts of the milky way' — cosmic monsters whose flesh, bones, and brains were formed from solar systems?" (279–280). He designs, over and against the ghostly displays by the X-ray machine and the music-shrine, a vibrant, comforting view of the world — with himself, the observer, its innermost, mystically dividing cell:

> Hans Castorp believed . . . [that] at the very moment when one thought one had reached the outermost edge, everything began all over again. But that meant, did it not, that perhaps in inner world after inner world within his own nature he was present over and over again — a hundred young Hans Castorps, all wrapped up warmly, but with numbed fingers and flushed face, gazing out from a balcony onto a frosty, moonlit night

high in the Alps and studying, out of humanistic and medical interest, the life of the human body? (280)

His ruminations are grandiose and circular; once they detach from the body, they invariably return to it. They also manage to turn an image of industrial reproduction into one of self-same metaphysics.[13] While the machines wear the sheen of death, the human body, Hans insists, harbors an internal glow. Sick as it may be, it must be charged by divine energy, he concludes as his studies arrive at the atom, for "indeed, the gap between matter and nonmatter demanded — at least as urgently as the one between organic and inorganic nature — that there be something to fill it" (279). This "it," for him, has a body. It even has lips and arms, as the dreamed figure bends over Hans, who has fallen asleep from all his exhausting research: "He felt an embrace, hot and tender around his neck. Melting with lust and dismay, he laid his hand on her upper arms, there where the skin stretched taut over the triceps and was blissfully cool to the touch. He felt the moist suckle of her kiss on his lips" (281).

Dry science is no match for such desire — but it did illuminate the body whose spectral apparition made Hans Castorp fall in love with death. X-rays were discovered during experiments which the physicist Wilhelm Röntgen was conducting to further study the properties of cathode rays, or "negative" light issuing from the negative electrical pole. Emanating from the charged induction coil in an evacuated glass tube, the rays were assumed to travel along the straight band of pale bluish light that turned a spot on the glass wall directly opposite into a fluorescent green; if allowed to exit via a metal plate encased in the glass, the rays' effect disappeared, passing a slight electric charge to the immediate air.[14] (The image would have made a fine phallic emblem for Mann's novel — too bad he didn't include it.)

While in his laboratory in late December 1885, Röntgen noticed that a piece of cardboard lying nearby, painted with barium platinocyanide, gave off a greenish glow. He wrapped the glass tube entirely in black cardboard to stop any light from escaping, but whenever the tube received a charge, the piece glowed. It even glowed when he positioned a 1,000-page book between it and the tube. He tried a sheet of rubber, a chunk of wood, a pack of whist cards — nothing stopped the invisible rays from lighting the screen. They could not be deflected, as cathode rays could be by a magnet, nor were they reflected from objects, as were light rays. But most wondrous of all, in the sober words of his report, was their penetrating power: "If one holds the hand between the discharge apparatus and the screen, one sees the darker shadows of the bones within the much fainter shadow picture of the hand itself."[15]

The discovery caused a sensation in Europe and abroad. Reactions reported in the newspapers ranged from cautious hope for the diagnosis of injuries and diseases to an immediate, if somewhat startling, application: "At the college of Physicians and Surgeons the roentgen rays were used to reflect anatomic diagrams directly into the brains of students, making a much more enduring impression than the ordinary methods of learning anatomical details."[16] Even the potential for quick economic gain was recognized right away: "Edison himself has been having a severe attack of Röntgenmania . . . we learn that last week Mr. Edison and his staff worked through seventy hours without intermission."[17] And pundits, poetically inclined, succumbed to the urge to poke fun at the new vision in verse:

> Around her ribs, those beauteous 24,
> Her flesh a halo makes, misty in line,
> Her noseless, eyeless face looks into mine,
> And I but whisper, "Sweetheart, je t'adore."[18]

Historically, the X-ray provided the first glimpse of virtual reality. It also articulated, in the idiom of science, the baroque topos of graveyard bones stripped of ephemeral flesh. Technically, of course, it prepared the way for our television and computer screens some fifty years later — the image tubes of both, fluorescent like Röntgen's little cardboard screen, being activated by the negative light of the cathode ray.

While Röntgen had discovered the X-rays, Einstein discovered why they worked.[19] In his paper on the photoelectric effect, published concurrently with his special theory of relativity (1905), he proposed a revolutionary theory about the nature of light, which until then had been considered a continuous affair. But X-rays, produced when incident electrons knock an inner orbital electron out of an atom,[20] proved that this was not so, that the propagation of light, under certain conditions, moved staccatolike in small energy packets or quanta. In other words, Röntgen's radiation experiment ushered in the age of quantum mechanics and, along with it — to Einstein's chagrin — the principle of uncertainty: the more precise the position of a particle, the more indeterminate its momentum.[21] Translated into lay terms and applied to Hans Castorp's plight, this means that if we capture an object, it is dead; if we figure out its movement, it is gone.

Ways of Seeing

Hans Castorp's path toward a new optics of the body is not as sudden as I initially suggested. It meanders from an acuity for the "porous" via mechanical diversions to the clarity of the X-ray, then shifts, inspired, to artistic and metaphysical visions.

He proves his receptivity for the porous (and the phosphorescent) as soon as he arrives. When he first sees the sanatorium in the distance, with its balconied facade, it appears to him a perforated sponge, just as he hears, a first impression, the horrible cough of the Austrian aristocrat in visually penetrating terms: "It's as if you were looking right down inside and could see it all — the mucus and the slime..." (12). And before he meets anyone else of the sanatorium's personnel, he is startled by the psychoanalyst Dr. Krokowski's extraordinary paleness: "there was almost a translucence, even phosphorescence, to his pallor" (16).[22]

A consumer of the amenities, he also peers through three little video machines offering diversion in the salon; they prime him for the qualitative difference of the X-ray machine. The first, a stereoscope, allows for binocular vision of the photograph that is propped up inside, "a Venetian gondolier for example, in all his bloodless and rigid substantiality" (82). The second is a kaleidoscope. Instead of a still figure it shows mobile abstractions, conjuring up "a magical fluctuation of colorful stars and arabesques." The zoetrope, finally, primitive forerunner of the bioskop/movie house in the village, consists of a rotating drum containing a cinematographic strip. It demonstrates the "natural" mobility of filmed human figures, in this case beating each other up and dancing together.

The review suggests a history of some "dead" or mechanical aesthetics: mimetic, abstract, kinematic. The gondolier's "rigid substantiality," for example, recalls little Hans' intuition of his grandfather's corpse, the sheer, waxy "stuff out of which this life-size dead figure was made" (27). The kaleidoscopic display, like the snow crystals whirling before his eyes during the snow episode, exhibits equally lifeless "stuff," albeit stylized and in motion, while the film strip is merely the photograph multiplied and speeded up. The X-ray image, on the other hand, shows the live body elucidated from within. It is the photograph doubly inverted, i.e. translucent and negative, as well as the stereoscopic and kinematic promises made good: it reveals the body's internal structure, the kinesis of the heart.

It is not difficult to detect Thomas Mann's aversion to both photographic realism and abstract modernism, one being outdated, the other tough to sell. But how about an X-ray aesthetics, this win-win combination of a vitalism made sheer by up-to-date technology? *The Magic Mountain* proves to be just like Behrens's basement office housing the machine: "You couldn't tell if you were in a photographer's studio, a darkroom, or an inventor's workshop and sorcerer's laboratory" (211). Its aesthetics is progressive and occult, experimental and nostalgic in one.

When Hans Castorp has recovered from his X-ray confrontation, his visual acuity is at its peak. There are to two portraits of Clavdia Chauchat, the glass plate with her X-ray photo which he keeps close to his heart, and the painting that hangs between the windows in Dr. Behrens' living room. One exhibits her illuminated interior, the other her luminous skin. Both are described in detail, and both harbor a secret ingredient. Behrens, the Sunday-afternoon painter with a scientific eye and a stark way of putting things, expounds on his method: "That human hide there ... you can examine it under a microscope for organic accuracy. And you'll see not just the horny and mucous layers of the outer skin, but along them, the imagined reticular layer with its sebaceous glands, sweat glands, blood vessels, papillae" (255).

As the doctor points out, the object Chauchat in the painting has the skin of everywoman — layered, glandular, grainy — yet to the love-struck Hans Castorp this skin appears as special as his own: "you could imagine that you saw perspiration, the invisible vapors of life, rising from the flesh, that if you were to press your lips against the surface, you would smell a human body, not paint and varnish" (254). He looks so closely that he sees what isn't there. But that is, paradoxically, also the way advocated by the shaman-scientist Behrens, for he concludes his lecture on stereoscopic vision with a defense of the invisible that must accompany exactitude: "And what is thought and imagined is important, too. It flows into your hand and has its effect. It isn't there and yet it is" (255).

Similarly, Clavdia's interior portrait, on one hand no different from Hans' own or from Joachim's, is described with reverent attention, the glass plate containing it made bright by the celestial light:

> a little rectangle, which when held parallel to the ground was a black, opaque, reflective surface, but when held up to the light of heaven, grew light and revealed very humanistic things: the transparent picture of a human body, with rib cage, the outline of the heart, the curve of the diaphragm, the bellows of the lungs, plus scapulae and humeri, all surrounded by a pale, hazy halo, the flesh — of which, against all reason, Hans Castorp had tasted on Mardi Gras. (382)

Universal and special in one, this human memento/divine signifier reminds Castorp of his adventures: his heterosexual and homoerotic passion, his research into life and ruminations about death, his memories of flatlandish opaqueness and the cosmic clarity gained on his mountaintop.

But his enlightenment is brought about by a twist. The light caught *in* the plate is different from the light that shines *through* the plate; it is artificially produced. It is "dark" light, caused by electrons hitting a tungsten screen inside a vacuum tube and aimed at a second screen behind the body, whose variously dense layers of matter are projected onto it via the invisible rays, and from where the image is transferred to yet a third screen to be permanently fixed and framed. While these mediations may seem tedious, they show what Mann's novel is playing with: the ability to see and the inability to touch. Technology (and the story) as desire.

The Dream-Machine

Is it really the Clavdia-in-the-flesh who so agitates Hans?[23] Is it not rather her negative interior, placed under glass? Her framed, scientifically layered skin? Or, to shift from art to androgyny, her Pribislav-Hippe-eyes, her collarbone (or was it Joachim's?), her dusty voice with its odd vocalization so in tune with the elliptic diction of Mynheer Peeperkorn?[24]

It is all of these and more. Hans-the-medium is a fetishist if ever there was one. He, the lover and engineer, likes the parts. He likes testing their various functions, rearranging, even jumbling them. As befits a technologist he is especially hooked on arms — or are they levers, as in the operation of the gramophone? Levers that let the sound rise from the box, let it lift and push the air in waves of seemingly immaterial, celestial music? *"Da' mi il bracchio, mia piccina"* (632). Are they limbs that embrace? Arms that move the hand that lifts the pencil?[25] During the *Walpurgisnacht* he is confronted with Mme. Chauchat's new dress, a shimmery, quasi-fluorescent affair:

> it left Clavdia's arms bare all the way to the shoulder — her arms, so tender and full at the same time, and cool, one could only presume — so that they stood out extraordinarily white against the dark shadows of silk. The effect was so overwhelming that Hans Castorp closed his eyes and whispered to himself, "My God!" (319)

Clavdia's arms, up to now spied on from so many angles, veiled under so many more or less transparent covers, are a revelation. Under his gaze they freeze into their own inverted X-ray image, perversely fleshy and ghostly in one. He has become the medium par excellence, having learned his lesson in the darkroom well.

What is more, he has become media-conscious himself. When he pours forth his hymn to the fleeting beauty of the body electric[26] to Mme. Chauchat, he stammers it in French — which is his German under cover, a kind of speaking without speaking.[27] His poetry is almost as bad as the verse about the Röntgen-rays I cited earlier, though considerably more touching. This is how it ends: "Laisse-moi ressentir l'exhalation de tes pores et tâter ton duvet, image humaine d'eau et d'albumine, destinée pour l'anatomie du tombeau, et laisse-moi périr, mes lèvres auz tiennes!"[28]

While the arm is the lever for the writer's passion, lips — or, more precisely, the mouthing of sounds — are his desire. On some occasions when Hans Castorp falls into a trance (vis-à-vis the skeletal body, or the musical coffin), he remains speechless, his mouth forming a slightly slack *O*. But on two other occasions the words, their sounds unstopped by labialization, tumble and drop from his mouth. It is as if his speech incorporated Chauchat's open vowels and Peeperkorn's disdain for closure. I am referring to his exhortations to revive himself during the snow episode, and his delirious address to Clavdia in her new dress. In both instances his medium, language, is stripped down to bare essentials, to an articulation unchecked by consonants. When he asks Clavdia for the notorious pencil, he looks like death himself, "his bloodless lips were open, and they stayed open, unused" (327). Likewise, during the snow adventure, "his lips were so numb that he did not bother to use them and spoke without the consonants that they help form" (475). In both instances the fleshy, consonantal differentiation of language fades to exhibit its skeletal vocality: cameos of Mann's X-ray vision of regressive speech.[29]

The scenes, showing Hans at moments of gravest danger and hottest pursuit, recall the lallations of an infant or a dreamer — and, of course, those uttered by Willi-the-medium in "Occult Experiences." It is a language not yet (or no longer) conscious of itself. But on paper and in the story it is conscious language, controlled and directed by a savvy writer. And he knows that he will sell first-class entertainment to an audience that *wants* to regress — to a better time and place, better yet, to a no-time and no-place: "Who writes on the typewriter? No-one.... We shall listen to you, and then we'll have the writing as a token that we're not just hallucinating...." It is the bourgeois audience after World War I, longing to escape to the time "before," thereby cultivating, infatuated with its own demise, a love for death and a talking spirit. Another audience, this time after World War II (and after the spirit had gruesomely materialized), also longed for the "time before," a trip that Mann's novel seems to facilitate once again today.

But a writer shouldn't be blamed for his readers, nor should he be held responsible for his medium. Thomas Mann was remarkably clearheaded about both, satisfying one while pursuing the other.[30] Whenever he openly experimented, he posted warnings, even had them printed in cursive (i.e. the moral in the snow chapter). That is why his texts, perennially popular, toe the line between humanism and hightech.

Coda

We have come full circle. In "Occult Experiences," which dealt tongue-in-cheek with the new physics and the puzzlement over perception, Mann asks the question posed by charlatans and metaphysicians alike. It concerns the coordinates by which the energy invested in a dream gains a body, becomes stable and visible: "Where is the point, the magic turn, when a dream image objectifies itself and becomes, in space and the eyes of others, real?"[31] There is no answer by mathematical physics, but I think that the media specialist Mann knew it by using a pencil, as do his latter-day colleagues by using the electron: it is desire on paper, negative light hitting the screen.

Notes

[1] Thomas Mann, "Meine Zeit," in *Über mich selbst: Autobiographische Schriften* (Frankfurt am Main: S. Fischer, 1983), 218–255. The spin-off of "Okkulte Erlebnisse," the séance in *The Magic Mountain*, was most recently addressed by John S. King, "'Most Dubious': Myth, the Occult, and Politics in the *Zauberberg*," *Monatshefte* 88.2 (1996), and Richard Koc, "Magical Enactments: Reflections on 'Highly Questionable' Matters in *Der Zauberberg*," *Germanic Review* 68.3 (1993). See also chapters XI and XII in Michael Maar's "philological thriller" on Thomas Mann and Hans Christian Andersen, *Geister und Kunst: Neuigkeiten aus dem Zauberberg* (Munich: Hanser, 1995).

[2] Walter Benjamin, who was fascinated by *The Magic Mountain*, speaks of the "schlechthin souveräne Mache" of the novel. See Benjamin, *Briefe I* (Frankfurt am Main: Suhrkamp, 1966), 374.

[3] Thomas Mann, *The Magic Mountain* (New York: Vintage, 1996), 4. All subsequent quotations except two (see notes 11 and 28) are from this new translation by John E. Woods, with page numbers indicated in the text.

[4] Einstein's special theory of relativity not only shifted the independent status of time and space to one dependent on matter, it also proved mathematically that one of the few constants known to physics, the velocity of light, was the absolute limit of matter (other constants being the charge on an electron, the Planck constant, and the electric and the magnetic constants). The theory combined two principles: the relativity of inertial systems of reference in regard to each other (we can measure time as the *difference* between these systems), and the constancy of the velocity of light (we can *measure* this difference because of light). A physical phenomenon, light thus borders on the metaphysical (or divine) because of its arbiter status. It is this arbiter status that the metaphors "light" and "enlightenment" invoke, both in Mann's novel and my essay.

Few commentators have focused on Mann's novel in regard to the new physics and its attendant technologies. I have found Rudi Prusock, "Science in

Mann's *Zauberberg*: The Concept of Space," *PMLA* 88 (1973), very helpful, also Valerie D. Greenberg's "Literature and the Discourse of Science: The Paradigm of Thomas Mann's *The Magic Mountain*," *South Atlantic Review* 50.1 (1985). Both advocate further investigation of the links between literature and science, and both consider Mann's novel an exemplary text for such study. More pointedly political as concerns the category of class is Raimar Zons, "Naphta," *Zeitschrift für Deutsche Philologie* 112.2 (1993). Its polemic is directed on one level at the "Großschriftsteller" Mann (who acquired a shiny new car from the novel's stellar proceeds) and other Weimar intellectuals like him who retreated from the "Mediengewitter" of the era into "high" culture. On an another level, the essay separates the grand-bourgeois essayist Mann, who defends this culture, from Mann the "politicized" romancier, who transforms his media fascination into a truly democratic, polyphonic novel.

[5] Mann's use of a highly complex metaphorical "system" (denser and more encompassing than the Wagnerian technique of the leitmotif) has been argued by Walter Weiss, who also points out the novel's metaphorical linkage of the train with lung disease, among myriad of other connections. See Weiss, "Thomas Manns Metaphorik. Zwischenergebnisse eines Forschungsprojekts," in *Thomas-Mann-Studien* 7 (Bern: Francke, 1987). The resulting thick texture promotes the multi-directional, "simultaneous" reading that Mann advocated.

[6] Thomas Mann, "The Making of *The Magic Mountain*," in *The Magic Mountain*, trans. H. T. Lowe-Porter (New York: Vintage, 1969), 718–719.

[7] Otto Glasser, *Dr. W. C. Röntgen* (Springfield, Ill.: Charles C. Thomas, 1945), 54.

[8] Some titles since 1970 concerning "adventure," "education," and "initiation" are Eckhard Heftrich, *Zauberbergmusik* (Frankfurt am Main: Klostermann, 1975); Jochen Vogt, "Thomas Mann I," in Erhard Schütz and Jochen Vogt, eds., *Einführung in die deutsche Literatur des 20. Jahrhunderts*, 2 (Opladen Wiesbaden: Westdeutscher Verlag, 1977), 43–55; Henry Hatfield, *From "The Magic Mountain"* (Ithaca and London: Cornell UP, 1979) 34–67; Helmut Koopmann, *Der klassisch-moderne Roman in Deutschland* (Stuttgart: Kohlhammer, 1983) 26–76, and Borge Kristiansen, *Thomas Manns Zauberberg und Schopenhauers Metaphysik* (Bonn: Bouvier, 1986). Regarding "time" and "an era," there are Ulrich Karthaus, "*Der Zauberberg*— ein Zeitroman," *DVjs* 44 (1970); Roman Struc, "*The Magic Mountain*: Time and Timelessness," *Research Studies* 39.2 (1971); Terence Reed, *Thomas Mann and the Uses of Tradition* (Oxford: Clarendon Press, 1974); Erhard Schütz, "'Wohin verschlug uns der Traum? ' Thomas Mann: *Der Zauberberg*" in *Romane der Weimarer Republik* (Munich: Fink, 1986): 52–69, Eva Wessell, "*Der Zauberberg* als Chronik der Dekadenz," Volkmar Hansen, ed., *Interpretationen: Thomas Mann. Romane und Erzählungen* (Stuttgart: Reclam, 1993), 121–149, and the Zons article mentioned in note 3. Horst Fritz, *Instrumentelle Vernunft als Gegenstand von Literatur* (Munich: Fink, 1982) delves into the socio-mythic dimension, Frederick A. Lubich, "Thomas Manns *Der Zauberberg*: Spukschloß der Großen Mutter

oder Die Männerdämmerung des Abendlandes," *DVjs* 67 (1993), into the psycho-mythic.

[9] The diary of March 3, 1920, in a self-congratulatory yet frustrated entry, refers to Einstein's theory and "the problem of time . . . that I anticipated in my conception of *The Magic Mountain*, just as I had anticipated the political antitheses leading up to the war. My satisfaction at my seismographic sensitivity in more than one respect in those days is diminished, even nullified by the recognition, constantly absolutely confirmed, that this novel . . . should have been finished in 1914." Hermann Kesten, ed., Richard and Clara Winston, trans., *Thomas Mann: Diaries 1918–1939* (New York: Harry N. Abrams, 1982), 87–88.

[10] In the section on commodity fetishism in *Capital*, Marx explains how such a specter is produced: "A commodity is therefore a mysterious thing, simply because in it the social character of men's labour appears to them as an objective character stamped upon the product of that labour. . . . The form of wood, for instance, is altered by making a table out of it. Yet, for all that the table continues to be that common, everyday thing, wood. But, so soon as it steps forth as a commodity, it is changed into something transcendent. It not only stands with its feet on the ground, but, in relation to all other commodities, it stands on its head, and evolves out of its wooden brain grotesque ideas, far more wonderful than if it were to start dancing on its own accord." Eugene Kamenka, ed., *The Portable Karl Marx* (New York: Viking Penguin, 1983), 445–446. Mann's equally mocking description of the gramophone stamps it for what it is: a product of labor by one class for the entertainment of another.

[11] I use here the Lowe-Porter translation, because it alludes, like the original ("den gewunden keulenförmigen, in weichen Gelenken beweglichen Hohlarm aus Nickel"), more directly to the fetishization of "arms" found throughout the novel. *The Magic Mountain*, trans. H.T. Lowe-Porter (New York: Vintage, 1969), 636. By comparison, John E. Woods's new translation refers to a "sinuous, club-shaped nickel tube."

[12] James R. Smart and Jon W. Newson, *"A Wonderful Invention": A Brief History of the Phonograph from Tinfoil to the LP* (Washington, D.C.: Library of Congress, 1977), 8.

[13] As of this writing, actual—not just wishful—cloning has been accomplished. The front page of my local newspaper this morning (*The Register Guard*, February 24, 1997) carried a report from *The New York Times* about geneticists having cloned a lamb using adult DNA: "In a feat that may be the one bit of genetic engineering that has been anticipated and dreaded more than any other, researchers in Britain are reporting that they have cloned an adult mammal for the first time."

[14] For a contemporary account of the details of the experiment see Dr. R. Fürstenau, *Röntgen* (Neurode in Schlesien: Verlagsanstalt Dr. Ed. Rose, 1912), 6–7. This little volume, part of an *Illustrierte Heldenbibliothek*, may well have inspired the description of the wonders Hans Castorp sees on the X-ray screen. On page 9, Fürstenau describes an image familiar from the novel: "Von diesem hellen

Hintergrunde hoben sich dunkel das Knochengerüst, welches die Lunge umgiebt und einhüllt, die Schlüsselbeine, die Rippen, die Wirbelsäule, das Brustbein, ab. . . . Nach weiter unten hin wuchs ein sehr kräftiger, dunkler Schatten, breiter und breiter werdend, heraus, und dieser Schatten vergrößerte und verkleinerte sich taktmäßig, dehnte sich aus und zog sich wieder zusammen: das arbeitende Menschenherz, die Pumpe, die den ganzen Organismus in Tätigkeit erhält. Seinem geheimnisvollen Wirken konnte man mit den Wunderstrahlen nachspüren." Translated into literature, *The Magic Mountain* is just such a "tracing of the heart."

[15] W. C. Röntgen, "On a New Kind of Rays (Preliminary Communication)," trans. G.F. Barker, 1896, reprinted in Glasser, *Dr. W. C. Röntgen*, 41–52.

[16] Quoted in Glasser, 83.

[17] *The Electrical World*, quoted in Glasser, 83.

[18] *Life*, March 12, 1896 (quoted in Glasser, 81).

[19] I am indebted for this concise phrasing to one of my students, Eric Abel, who is majoring in German and physics at the University of Oregon.

[20] "X-rays," in Alan Isaacs, ed., *A Dictionary of Physics* (Oxford: Oxford UP, 1996), 465.

[21] "Uncertainty principle (Heisenberg uncertainty principle, principle of indeterminism)" in *A Dictionary of Physics*, 446.

[22] According to my *Dictionary of Physics*, 239, both fluorescence and phosphorescence belong to the same phenomenon of luminescence, i.e., the emission of light by a substance due to a nonthermal excitation of energy. They are arbitrarily distinguished by their duration (phosphorescence lasting longer once the exciting cause is removed). The irony in Dr. Krokowski's appearance is his lasting "after" glow caused by the excitements of his profession.

[23] For an extensive discussion of the Clavdia figure see Karl Werner Böhm, "Die homosexuellen Elemente in Thomas Manns *Der Zauberberg*," in Hermann Kurzke, ed., *Stationen der Thomas-Mann-Forschung: Aufsätze seit 1970* (Würzburg: Königshausen + Neumann, 1985), 145–165.

[24] Peeperkorn's diction receives detailed attention by Philip Sicker, "Babel Revisited: Mann's Myth of Language in *The Magic Mountain*," *Mosaic* 19/2 (1986):12–20.

[25] The phallic pencil has figured centrally in many interpretations; see especially Böhm's essay (note 23) and Walter Jens, "Inferno mit paradiesischen Wonnen: Thomas Manns *Der Zauberberg*," *Frankfurter Allgemeine Zeitung*, August 5, 1987. The pencil also draws attention to writing as a gendered activity, traditionally understood as male.

[26] On the intimate correspondence between this passage and Walt Whitman's "I Sing to the Body Electric" in Hans Reisiger's German translation of 1922 see Henry Hatfield, "Drei Randglossen zu Thomas Manns *Zauberberg*," *Euphorion* 56 (1962). The connection is elaborated in homoerotic terms (without men-

tioning Hatfield's discovery) by Claus Sommerhage, *Eros und Poesis: Über das Erotische im Werk Thomas Manns* (Bonn: Bouvier, 1983), 118–124.

[27] In the German (French) version the narrator has Castorp say, "pour moi, parler français, c'est parler sans parler, en quelque manière, — sans responsibilité, ou comme nous parlons en rêve." Thomas Mann, *Der Zauberberg* (Frankfurt am Main: Fischer, 1967), 356. It is noteworthy that the new English translation (unlike the old) does not retain the French.

[28] I use the 'original' French here for its estrangement effect (in my German edition on p. 362). In the new English translation, p. 337, it appears as "Let me take in the exhalation of your pores and brush the down — oh my human image made of water and protein, destined for the contours of the grave, let me perish, my lips against yours!"

[29] The image is an eerie reminder of Joachim's face in death, which, showing "honorable" composure at first, "began to smile" after two days: "Hans Castorp could not help admitting that this smile bore within it the seeds of degeneration" (530).

[30] Sicker's article (note 24) investigates the novel's "simultaneous multiplication and breakdown of language" from a mystical-theological perspective. Another approach is taken by Ulrich Karthaus, "Zu Thomas Manns Ironie," *Thomas Mann Jahrbuch* 1 (1988), 89, which sees, along with Mann, in the very syntax of the novel the desire to say everything at once, while Erhard Schütz comments on the matter of "rhetoric and sensuality," with the fear of death and sexual desire prompting a speaking-without-end (Schütz 61–65, note 8).

[31] Mann, "Okkulte Erlebnisse," in *Über mich selbst*, 245, my translation. This may also be the place to add a note about a written dream's persistence. Forty years after the publication of *The Magic Mountain*, in 1964, a well-known critic wrote a tongue-in-cheek account of his run-in at a famous Hamburg hotel with an elderly, distinguished gentleman. Director Hans Castorp, now head of the shipbuilding firm he had been about to enter when he left on his trip to Switzerland, is being called to the telephone. As he steps out of the booth, he exchanges a knowing glance with his observer/accomplice and dissolves into air: "Ob er die Röntgenplatte vom Thorax der lieblichen Clawdia noch besaß, stand sie vielleicht gar auf seinem Schreibtisch bei Tunder und Wilms? ... Da trat er auch schon wieder aus seiner Telefonzelle, und als er mich erblickte, kniff er sein rechtes Auge komplizenhaft und mit fast schockierender Schelmerei zusammen ... während er sich vor mir auflöste." Friedrich Sieburg, "Dauer eines Traumes," in *Gemischte Gefühle: Notizen zum Lauf der Zeit* (Stuttgart: Deutsche Verlagsanstalt, 1964), 198. Far less charming, indeed depressing, is Professor Saueressig's reported report that the real Hans Castorp died in 1933 and left six children (Hans Scherer, "Die achtundzwanzig Fischsaucen der Frau Stöhr: Ein Leser-Symposium über den *Zauberberg* in Davos," *Frankfurter Allgemeine Zeitung*, August 25, 1994).

KENNETH WEISINGER

10: Distant Oil Rigs and Other Erections

GEOGRAPHIC SIGNIFICATION AS CODE for political and psychological allegory is only one of a legion of strategies of referentiality employed by Thomas Mann in his monument to overdetermination, *The Magic Mountain*,[1] but it is certainly one of the most important. The wide scope of geographic allusion, from South America to Java to Ethiopia, serves to intensify the claustrophobic atmosphere of the actual site of the novel's action and to point to the global implications of the affairs in the mountain sanatorium. The novel is above all a meditation on the origins of the First World War, and it is not surprising that the whole world is implicated in its narrative. Virtually no character in the novel is without some geographic specificity, and, more often than not, these explicit locational coordinates supply a great deal about the character's allegorical potential: Leo Naphta, for example, comes from the border between Galicia and Volhynia (432); Lodovico Settembrini is from Padua and has studied in Bologna; Herr Wehsal is from Mannheim; Dr. Behrens is from northwest Germany and has a fraternity cap hanging on his wall (252); the narrator seems so eager to furnish geographic details, we feel that if we could interrogate him more closely he would undoubtedly disclose to us the specific fraternity (*Germania* perhaps?) and the university (Heidelberg? Marburg?) where Behrens had studied medicine. International geography is everywhere: the dining hall is divided by nationalities and class; there are, for example, a "good" Russian table and a "bad" Russian table, and, late in Hans Castorp's stay, when fights break out among the guests at the Berghof, these conflicts inevitably have their origin in national, or geographic differences, as in the dispute between Wenzel the Czech and Magnus the German beer brewer from Halle (418).

Settembrini repeatedly delineates his political concepts under the shorthand guise of geographic denomination. For him, "Asia" and "Vienna" are the polar opposites of the Western mode of thought: "I am thinking here of a sentimentality, a trancelike self-hypnosis that is not European, that is foreign and hostile to our active hemisphere's form of life.... My friend, that is Asia" (507). For Settembrini Vienna is "the vital center point" of that Asiatic principle of bondage and obduracy" (154). It is, for him, the moral duty of the West to "deal a fatal blow to Austria and crush her" and all the Asian philosophy she represents (154). The Italian nationalist Settembrini still smolders under the memory of Austrian domination over Italy and generalizes that experience of political oppression into a larger philosophical geographic concept, even though such an abstraction brings conflicting intellectual complications along with it. There is, for example, a hidden irony in Settembrini's equating Asia with Vienna, for, historically, it was the very Vienna that Settembrini castigates that dealt the "fatal blow" to the Turkish (Asian) invasion of Europe in 1697. It was then that, thanks to Prince Eugene of Savoy, the battle of Zenta fell to the Viennese and from that point Western Europe was free to develop its characteristic modes of thought unthreatened by further influence from the East. This irony, to which Settembrini seems entirely oblivious, is just one example among many of the inconsistencies and contradictions that teem in the novel's use of geography as allegorical insignia. Settembrini never seems to recognize the slipperiness of his terms, just as he never recognizes the peculiar use to which the theories of Darwin are put in his "League for the Organization of Progress," with its doctrine that "humankind's innermost natural purpose is its own self-perfection" (241). To construe Darwin as a prophet of human perfection takes as great a leap of intellectual daring as to equate Vienna and Asia philosophically.

In addition to geographic bearings, almost every character, place, even many physical things in the novel also have associated with them a mythic mode of nomenclature: Behrens and Krokowski, the presiding doctors at the sanatorium, are labeled the "Minos and Rhadamanthus" of the Berghof (55); Hans Castorp and his cousin Joachim Ziemssen are described, in their acts of visiting the dying, as the "Dioscuri" (212); Settembrini is associated with Satan (54) and Mephistopheles (318). The thermometer Hans Castorp purchases is associated with the god Mercury, and the Berghof itself at times looks like the Olympian hall of the gods for which the novel is named: "the entire dining hall ... burst into Homeric laughter" (292).[2] The novel abounds in such mythic parallels and interpretations, and by enrolling every person, thing, or event simultaneously on at least two registers (here, for example, those of geography and classical myth), the narrator presents the reader with a multiplicity of interpretative directions which immediately demands further interrogation.[3] In the case of the two doctors, for example, if we search for a relationship between the two allegorical systems, are we justified in saying syncretically that the narrator is suggesting something nether-worldish or diabolic about the study of medicine in Germany in the years before World War I? In other words, do the interpretative possibilities of one register blur over into those of the other register? And, as for the two cousins, is there something salvatory and divine in their nature, since the Dioscuri, whose name is applied to them, were semidivine beings known particularly for their power to rescue sailors in peril? And since the two cousins are so clearly representatives of a specific class of northern Germans, is this sense of salvational purpose intended to spill over into their generic type? Are we to coordinate these two fields of reference (the geographic and the mythological), and infer the possibility that there is something salvational about the area of Germany from which the cousins come? Certainly, at times Hamburg does seem to be a lost paradise for Hans. But if the narrator does invite us to accept the possibility of that paradise, we are also cautioned by the fact that Hamburg's representative in the novel is the last of his line; that is, his is the last name on the baptismal bowl of the Castorps. Since there will be no more Castorps, it would seem that the role of avatar from paradise is up for reappointment. At the time the novel takes place, Hamburg and northern Germany in general are making their bid to become the major economic force in the world, and the question remains open whether the enterprise will succeed. Would this economic success mean something redeeming for the world? The possibility is there, but there is also something ominous in the fact that Hans Castorp has no young Felix Meister on his shoulders, no one to insure that his redemptive education will play a role in a future, better world. His education, with the redemption it promises, will remain suspended in irony. This fact alone should make any attempt to interpret the novel strictly as a *Bildungsroman* suspect, despite Mann's own much reiterated statements to that effect.[4]

The temptation to interpret in this syncretic fashion along two lines simultaneously is frequently held out to us as readers, and we can either resist the intoxication such interpretative flight promises, or we can act more soberly and simply recognize our susceptibility to the temptation and acknowledge that this very narrative temptation must be an important constituent in our account of what the novel can mean.[5] Hans Castorp himself is tempted on every front in the novel, and our temptations run along the same lines as his, but we at least are in a position to heed the warning the narrator offers us on the first page of the novel. He tells us explicitly that we must be careful of reading too much into geography. The landscape through which we and Hans are traveling is no longer what it once was, or even still seems to be; that is, this landscape is no longer mythic: "The journey leads through many a landscape . . . from the high plain of southern Germany to the shores of Swabia's sea, and proceeds by boat across its skipping waves, passing over abysses once thought unfathomable" (3). If an abyss is unsoundable, it may have mythic dimensions (Loch Ness comes to mind) and, therefore, be open to certain forms of interpretation; but if its measure can be taken and quantified, then it no longer carries with it a sense of mystery and wonder. In that case, another form of interpretation must replace the mythic. In the first pages of the novel, then, we are traveling through a landscape that was *once* mythical, and that still *seems* mythical (the "springenden Wellen") but is mythical no more. This loss of the mythic or spiritual dimension is also shown on the human level in Hans Castorp's habit of "clasp[ing] his freshly washed hands together and rub[bing] them in congenial expectation, a habit of his whenever he sat down to eat — *perhaps because his forebears had prayed before every meal*" (13, emphasis mine). The gesture remains, but it has lost its religious or mythic meaning. Similarly, Naphta's father ritually slaughters animals with "a solemnity *recalling* ancient times when the slaughtering of animals had indeed been the duty of priests" (432, emphasis mine). In geography and psychological gesture, then, traces of myth remain, but their meanings have become overshadowed by a newer, more "scientific" mode of interpretation.

    The world through which Hans Castorp is traveling is, in fact, as depleted of wonder as Hamburg is depleted of Castorps. It is the world described by the Madman in Nietzsche's *Joyful Science* who asks of his fellow countrymen, "How were we able to drink up the sea? Who gave us the sponge to wipe away the horizon?"[6] By the time Mann takes up work on the novel, he has realized that science is determined to quantify the world around us and that the resulting loss of mystery is perhaps not entirely compensated by the advances in human health and prosperity. The novel is set at precisely that point in which the old world is becoming demythologized: "It takes place . . . in the old days of the world before the Great War, with whose beginning so many things began" (ix). It is emblematic that Castorp is traveling over ancient abysses once deemed unfathomable carrying with him the latest in technological publications — *Ocean Steamships*[7] (the book is in English) — as his guide. And yet the old world calls out to be read in all its former mystery: "at one point a single peak jutted heavenward out of the fog — it looked supernatural, like something from Valhalla, distant, sacred, inaccessible" (684). The world of the novel is an antebellum world where every place and fact is still top-heavy with potential readable meaning and where no detail is irrelevant. Yet the old modes of understanding are under assault from every side. Hans, and the rest of us, are tempted by the new possibilities but are at the same time reluctant to abandon the past altogether.

Indeed, a world that provides such a wealth of interpretable detail while at the same time discrediting the very means of interpretation (that is, a world that appears mythic at the very time when science is discrediting myth) could be described as decadent or perverse.[8] I will give only one example of such perverse superfluity of interpretable detail, one to which I will return later. The world around Hans Castorp is literally filled with phallic icons, sexual surrogates that stridently call out for simple Freudian interpretation: Hippe's pencil and the little shavings from that pencil that Hans keeps carefully preserved in his desk for years (120); Hans's cigars with their "organic, living quality . . . tiny pores along the edges . . . and veins that seemed almost to throb. . ." (249–50); Herr Albin's knife, which is of such interest to the women at the Berghof: "You ladies will surely allow me to play with my knife a little. I bought it in Calcutta from a blind magician. He would swallow it" (77); Herr Albin's pistol: "Look how small it is . . . but if I press right here — it will bite" (77); the reddish-brown flagpole Hans tries to climb in his dream (89); finally, the thermometer that registers Hans's body temperature by an act of oral insertion.[9] These details and the narrative elaboration lavished on them make them unavoidable objects for psychoanalytic interrogation, but the narrator frustrates, or at least compromises, any such instinct by introducing early in the plot a character, Dr. Krokowski, who is an elaborate parody of Freud and the Freudian system of interpretation.[10] So, just as we are presented with a world that seems mythic while myth is discredited as a way of knowing, so, too, the world is filled with sexual signs, the reading of which is simultaneously encouraged and frustrated by a comic discrediting of the dominant mode of understanding such symbols. How are we to interpret this?[11]

Furthermore, the novel is perverse in its tendency to dwell at numbing lengths on issues that seem to be irrelevant red herrings or philosophical tail-chasing, such as the debates between Naphta and Settembrini about the nature of culture, or the long disquisitions on the nature of time.[12] (This is not to say that these debates are not highly entertaining.) These elements of the "intellectual novel" often seem more like psychological subterfuge or further clever narrative temptations to diversionary exploration, elements that serve as substitutes for more pressing or tempting interrogations.[13] For example, in the most critical chapter of the novel ("Snow"), Hans Castorp has a vision of Greece and we are told that, although he had never visited that geographic region of the world, he remembered it (481). That is virtually all that is said about this very important act. How was Hans able to remember something he had never seen? Of course, we can supply some tentative answers, referring to the communal and anonymous nature of dream or to the pervasive influence of Classicism on Germany's educational system prior to the war, but the text does not give us a great deal of help. To know more about this act of remembering would be far more valuable in terms of the psychological narrative than to hear the endless nipping and sniping that takes place between Hans's two intellectual mentors. It might help us, for instance, to understand the other crucial act of memory in the novel, when Hans remembers (significantly, after a severe nosebleed) his infatuation with his young classmate Pribislav Hippe. But these acts of "memory" are never examined by the narrator in the detail they deserve, and we are left with the task of interpreting them. To cite yet another example: when Herr Peeperkorn dies, his Malaysian servant dresses in his traditional Javanese folk costume to stand watch over the body. What has prompted this return to atavistic display? We know virtually nothing of the mind of this intriguing representative of the colonial world, and yet he makes one of the most dramatic and compelling gestures in the novel. All we are given is a rather detailed description of the costume, but as for the motives that lie behind its emergence we are thrown entirely upon ourselves to interpret. Even though Mann claims that the novel is not a *"roman à clef*,"[14] there are clearly secrets embedded in its fabric that readers are invited to unravel; the number seven is just the most obvious of these. To understand these larger and hidden issues, we must examine the details with greater scrutiny.[15]

Let us begin with one geographical detail that slips by the reader practically unnoticed. This is the casual reference to the Caucasus region called Daghestan. When Hans first begins his research on Madame Chauchat, he learns from Fräulein Engelhart that she is Russian and that "Perhaps her husband is French, or of French extraction" (75). When he asks if a certain person at the Good Russian table is M. Chauchat, he learns that Clavdia's husband "has never been here even once, he's quite unknown to us." Later, in another foray of research, Hans learns, again from Fräulein Engelhart, that M. Chauchat is "a civil servant, an administrator for the Russian government in some remote province, Daghestan" (134–135). At the Walpurgisnacht celebration, in his conversation with Clavdia Chauchat (in French, a linguistic appropriation that may place Hans in the position of a surrogate for the missing French husband), Hans learns that she is going away: "Very far away." "To Daghestan?" he asks. "You are not badly informed. Perhaps — for now at least" (332). Hans has quietly obtained this information about M. Chauchat and now finds it confirmed by Clavdia herself. Clavdia tells him that she is obsessed with independence, to which he replies, "And your husband in Daghestan consents to — your liberty?" (332).

Who is this husband who is unknown to the guests at the Ber and why, if geographic details have such importance, is he in Daghestan? If he is, indeed, French, such a placement would appear at first glance to be unusual. Why would a Frenchman be acting as a Russian administrator in Daghestan in 1907? Is this odd detail motivated in some deeper level of the narrative's meaning?

Many readers of literature would probably know of the Caucasus region mainly through Mikhail Lermontov's *A Hero of Our Time*, a work whose title might remind us of Mann's own description of Hans Castorp. Hans is "a perfectly ordinary, if engaging young man" (ix), in other words, a normal, national representative, a hero for *his* time. Certainly Mann, who was an avid reader of Russian literature,[16] was well acquainted with Lermontov's novel. In 1841, a few months before his death (in a pistol duel with a fellow officer at the foot of Mount Mashuk in the Caucasus), Lermontov wrote a poem that eerily anticipates his own death; the poem reads (in Vladimir and Dmitri Nabokov's translation):

> In noon's heat, in a dale of Dagestan,
> With lead inside my breast, stirless I lay;
> The deep wound still smoked on; my blood
> Kept trickling drop by drop away.
>
> On the dale's sand alone I lay. The cliffs
> Crowded around in ledges steep,
> And the sun scorched their tawny tops
> And scorched me — but I slept death's sleep.
>
> And in a dream I saw an evening feast
> That in my native land with bright lights shone;
> Among young women crowned with flowers,
> A merry talk concerning me went on.
>
> But in the merry talk not joining,
> One of them sat there lost in thought,
> And in a melancholy dream
> Her young soul was immersed — God knows by what.
>
> And in a dale in Dagestan she dreamt;
> In that dale lay the corpse of one she knew;
> Within his breast a smoking wound showed black,
> And blood ran in a stream that colder grew.[17]

Susan Layton has shown the enormous cultural investment that nineteenth-century Russia had in the Caucasus region and the "rigidly dichotomous cultural mythology that surrounded the place, largely drawn from the works of Lermontov, Pushkin, and Bestuzhev-Marlinsky."[18] For the creators of this "literary Caucasus,"[19] the Daghestani hero is "both the Islamic other and the surrogate self."[20] Following the lead given by Lermontov, Daghestan becomes the location of the martyred lover, the location of the self's isolation, and of a cold and lonely death. It is the dream of redemption from just such a death that prompts Hans Castorp to listen over and over to the aria from *Aïda* — "Tu? In questa tomba?" (634–635), where a stunned Rhadames realizes that his beloved Aïda has chosen to join him in his death by suffocation. Such companionship in death can only be a dream for Hans, for he has never experienced love so profound. And who knows what kind of love M. Chauchat has had from Clavdia? Perhaps M. Chauchat is even now dreaming of his beloved Clavdia as she sits at the "merry feast" (the Berghof) where the talk centers on him (the conversation between Fräulein Engelhardt and Hans). And such a dreamer, who at the point of death hallucinates about a bright feast, might remind us of Hans himself and his own crystal-clear vision in the deathlike snow (480). Moreover, Lermontov's own death, which is foreshadowed by the poem, is a death by duel, a theme which runs through the novel and culminates in the duel between Settembrini and Naphta. This antiquated way of settling scores is perhaps the most pervasive image of the honor-bound antebellum society and points inexorably to the suicidal war that is to come, with its myths of glory and national pride. The theme of the duel also points to the two crossed swords hanging conspicuously in Dr. Behrens's apartment (252).

But one would not have to have read Lermontov or the other Russians to know what was of greatest significance in Daghestan in the years preceding the Great War. The importance of Daghestan was then, and largely is today, oil. In fact, Azerbaijan and the neighboring Daghestan can claim one of the world's oldest oil industries. The country's Zoroastrian religious sect held sacred an "eternal flame" fueled by a natural gas seep long before Azerbaijan was conquered in the eigthth century by followers of Islam.[21] In the modern era, as early as 1875 Alfred Nobel's brothers Robert and Ludwig had laid an oil pipeline in this area of the Caucasus for shipping oil to the port of Baku in nearby Azerbaijan.[22] By 1901 Russia, thanks to oil fields like those exploited in Daghestan, was by far the world's largest producer of petroleum products, representing in the years 1900–1905 almost 40 percent of the world's total production.[23] Since the sixteenth century, Russia had sporadically attempted to conquer Daghestan; it finally did come into Russian possession under Peter the Great, was later ceded to Persia, but returned to Russia in 1813 under Czar Alexander. In 1853 a fortress called Petrovskii was built in the area to secure the ties to Russia, and in 1921 the autonomous region became part of the Soviet Union. With the discovery of its vast oil reserves in the late nineteenth century, Daghestan was to become a crucial element in Russia's ability to conduct a modern war.

Therefore, if M. Chauchat is a Frenchman and is hanging around in Daghestan in 1907, the implications are fairly clear that he is there because of that oil, and his presence further hints at the kind of cooperation between Russia and France that had in fact been negotiated in 1892 and would later be the basis of the Triple Entente. By the terms of the Franco-Russian agreement, it was mandated that, if Germany should attack France, Russia would attack Germany and that if Germany (or Austria-Hungary with German backing) should attack Russia, France would attack Germany. Ratification by the two states (winter 1893–1894) converted this agreement into the formal Franco-Russian Alliance. Eventually, this would grow into the Triple Entente, which included Great Britain and formed the nucleus of allied opposition to Germany and Austria-Hungary in the war to come.[24] As we have seen, Mann carefully laid out his narrative in the "old days of the world before the Great War" (ix), and certainly one of the most important aspects of life in those days was the constantly shifting negotiations and alliances between the great European powers, nations whose representatives we see at the dining tables in the Berghof. It would have been impossible for a reader of any newspaper of the times to be unaware of this growing problem, and it is indeed to this unstable and threatening aspect of European life that Mann had earlier alluded in the opening sentence of his *Death in Venice*: that story opens on "a spring afternoon in 19 — , the year in which for months on end so grave a threat seemed to hang over the peace of Europe."[25] And it is against this background pattern of shifting agreements and filiations that many of the details of *The Magic Mountain* become resonant.

Although Mann refuses to call his novel a roman à clef, the very name of the mysterious Clavdia has to be seen as suggesting herself as the key to some questions. In terms of the novel's psychological complexity, she is the key to Hans's growing sexuality, and if we could ascertain what she meant, we might be able to interpret the young man's sexuality accordingly. Clavdia (or Clawdia in German) is the Russian form of Claudia, but in its adoption of the "v" sound the name begins to resonate with the possibilities of the Latin *clavis* (key) but equally with *claudere* and its connotations of "closed" or inaccessible. If Clavdia is true to the potential held within her name, then, she is the inaccessible key by which questions of sexual desire would be understood. And her last name, Chauchat, is perhaps even more intriguing with its resemblance to the word Caucasus and the autonomous Russian region where her husband is serving as a government administrator.[26]

If M. Chauchat is a reference to the confluence of Russian and French interests that represented such a threat to Germany and was of such critical importance in the eventual configuration of combatants in the war, what might the novel reveal about the equally important relationship between Germany and England? Germany, having definitely abandoned Russia as an ally by the last decade of the nineteenth century, was, at the beginning of the new century, making ostentatious but ambiguous overtures toward Great Britain, an alliance with whom Kaiser Wilhelm felt was a natural one since he and the king of England were cousins. (This familial argument, of course, could only be applied with caution, since most of the crowned heads of Europe were in one or another way related to each other, and if one were to put a portrait of King George of England next to a portrait of Czar Nicholas of Russia, it would be hard not to believe that they were brothers, even twins.) Germany, with the encouragement of the Kaiser, attempted several times to come to an understanding with Great Britain, but all these attempts failed, largely for two reasons: Germany insisted on increasing the size of her navy despite England's fears and protests, and Germany was following her own quest for oil by an aggressive policy toward the Middle East that centered on the building of the Berlin-to-Baghdad Railway. Both of these international movements are figured in the novel.

First of all, with the major figure in the novel, Mann takes his usual Lübecker out of his native city and makes him a citizen of Hamburg. Where Lübeck faces the Baltic and the Hanseatic cities of the east, Hamburg clearly faces west, looking onto arenas of trade and competition with, above all, England and Holland. Where Lübeck represents the past commercial life of northern Germany, Hamburg represents the future. If Hans Castorp were simply to be a representative of northern German culture, Mann could have easily kept his hero within the familiar context of his own native city; but he chooses instead to make him very specifically a representative of Hamburg. In a rather apologetic article published in 1926, "Lübeck als geistige Lebensform," Mann speaks of that particular element of Hans's background that is his "Hanseatentum," a heritage that is important primarily because of its "höheres Seeräubertum."[27] Hamburg's sphere of piracy faces west. Its very name points toward England, with its resemblance to the "homburg," the hat that becomes an essential element in the costume of the gentleman in the early decades of the century. And Hans Castorp is in many ways a would-be Englishman. His blankets are English (93); he likes to speak English (43, 58); above all, he is reading an English book about naval engineering, *Ocean Steamships* (in a few years, if

Hans had remained with the firm Tunder and Wilms — whose names could easily pass for English — the book would undoubtedly be *Ocean Battleships*).

Since Hans has never actually been on a long ocean voyage, there is something hypothetical about his profession; and one might say that in this, too, he is a representative German: there was something definitely experimental and hypothetical about the German naval enlargement since Germany had never in the past been a particularly important seagoing nation outside the Baltic region. There was something tentative and exploratory about the entire enterprise, an alien quality that is characterized by the fact that the textbooks on the subject are in a foreign language (English). In its relationship with Britain, Germany was displaying two of the most important aspects of a traditional male-male relationship: rivalry and admiration. Hans definitely admires the English and is trying to look like one of them. His very name, with its initial *C* is somewhat removed from the usual German orthography and sounds like the English *castoff* which is precisely what Hans is in many ways — a castoff lover, a castoff family member, a castoff of destiny when he joins the war. And a "castor" is a small vessel for spices, the diminutiveness and ordinariness of which accords well with just those qualities in Mann's repeated description of Hans. The word *Castor* is frequently used with oil (*Kastoröl*) and is a bitter pill to swallow, but above all "Castor" is the name of the brother of Pollux in the celebrated pair of twins, the Dioscuri, to whom Hans and his cousin are compared. (Are the cousins Hans and Joachim in this way representatives of the royal cousins mentioned before, the one ersatz-English and the other German?) There are of course other possible readings of Hans Castorp's name which point in more sexual directions — *castus* (chaste) or *castrato* (castrated). Siegmar Tyroff sees in the name a resonance of Hans's avocation, that of "pastor," and notes that the name contains the magical seven letters.[28]

If Hans Castorp's attempts to be English are a prefiguration of the naval aspects of the Anglo-German competition which was to ignite World War I, we would expect to find traces of the other great source of conflict at the time: the rush for oil in the Middle East and here "Daghestan" is the first clue. Of course, the race for oil was not isolated from the Anglo-German naval escalation. In fact, much of the reason Germany was intent upon having a large navy was to secure and maintain a colonial empire which would rival the empires of her contemporary European powers, especially that of Britain. Because Germany at the end of the nineteenth century did not possess a large navy, much of the commerce with her few colonies was actually carried out by the British, and Germany was definitely eager to have her share of this trade:

British traders [had] actually secured a very considerable share of the commerce of the German colonies — which was largely attributed to the lack of discriminatory tariffs, unlike the colonial empires of other powers — and British appreciation of this fact was more than matched by German industry's own reliance upon imported raw materials from British Empire territories. Moreover, the post-1900 phase of German overseas expansion was chiefly characterized by her *pénétration pacifique* — in Turkey and the Euphrates valley, in Latin America, in the Dutch East Indies, and in the Belgian and Portuguese colonies in Africa, all of which appeared to offer greater economic rewards than the formal German colonial empire itself.[29]

Britain had to fear that Germany, while building its own impressive naval power, would also begin to "demand . . . colonial concessions under the threat of taking military action in Europe."[30] But it was not immediately clear to the more experienced British colonial administrators just what Germany wanted; Germany was expanding in every direction at once, at times threatening Britain and at times seeking reconciliation with her. Perhaps it was her very inexperience at such colonial expansion (reminiscent of Hans Castorp's inexperience of the open sea as an actual lane of commerce) that made her so dangerous: "Such vagueness of aim was . . . a typical characteristic of a new power conscious that it is expanding, but unwilling or unable to specify the future limits of that expansion."[31] Whatever her intentions toward Britain, it was, in any case, clear that Germany wanted to be in a position to say with Winston Churchill: "We have got all we want in territory, and our claim to be left in unmolested enjoyment of vast and splendid possessions, mainly acquired by violence, largely maintained by force, often seems less reasonable to others than to us."[32] Churchill was a master of conciseness, brusque and to the point; one could hardly find a more frank expression of colonial desire than this phrase.

THE QUEST FOR COLONIES and for the raw materials they could provide are also figured in the novel — most explicitly in the figure of Mynheer Peeperkorn, who enters the world of the Berghof late in the novel; he is "a colonial Dutchman, a man from Java, a coffee-planter" (538) who brings in his train a Malaysian servant. He enters the scene at the same time as an Egyptian princess, whose sexual mystery and ambiguity make her a superb representative of that "Orientalism" which so intrigued the colonial powers and sparked whole aesthetic tendencies in Europe. I will return to Mynheer Peeperkorn but first I want to trace out the lines of the Middle Eastern involvement in the novel, which is only hintingly represented by the Egyptian princess. This historical aspect is less clearly delineated than the English engagement, but it lies there in the details.[33] As a network of symbolic references, it is as clear as Hans Castorp's act of English imitation and offers the same field of interpretative possibilities. Perhaps the most intriguing of these details is again, like Daghestan, a geographic one, and that is Hofrat Behrens's little smoking alcove, decked out in "Turkish" style. It is to this architectural niche that Dr. Behrens invites the two cousins for a visit. The chapter in which this occurs, "Humaniora," is worth examining in some detail because it puts the matter of the Middle Eastern adventure into several contexts.

The chapter begins with the cousins sitting in the garden after one of the Gargantuan dinners served at the Berghof. Hans is inwardly fighting against Joachim for leading him away from the other Berghof residents (and Clavdia Chauchat); he protests: "Joachim was acting like a tyrant. As far as that went [*genaugenommen*], they weren't Siamese twins. They could go their separate ways if they were of different minds" (248). *Genaugenommen*, that is, "strictly speaking": of course, they are not *Siamese* twins, but the formulation, more evident in the German, leaves open other twinning possibilities. And by having referred to them earlier as the "Dioscuri," the narrator has already affirmed at least part of Hans's recalcitrant but half-accurate description of the two men. They *are* in some sense twins. And it remains an open question why Hans has *allowed* his cousin to exert this power over him; why is his free will thus diminished in the presence of his cousin? And it is true that Joachim does exercise a tyrant's power over Hans's emotions, as we see demonstrated time and again. Following Hans's vain inner protest, as a kind of erotic joke at the expense of the intimate relationship between the two cousins the narrator immediately continues with a long description of Hans's supply of cigars. Specifically, Hans tells himself that he can hold out against such tyranny as long as he can take comfort in his own cigar. It is not gratuitous that Hans thinks of his own cigars immediately after he has questioned his rebellious but submissive attitude toward his cousin; cigar smoking is certainly more than a mildly narcotic pastime for Hans. A cigar is literally an extension of Hans's personality and phyical body; he can never really quite believe that Joachim is *not* a smoker: "I don't understand how someone can not be a smoker — why it's like robbing oneself of the best part of life" (46). And so, Hans, when confronted by an unpleasant situation, turns to his own cigar, as he might turn to another part of his body, as a source of comfort and pleasure. Cigars will continue to play an important role in this scene.

While Hans is thus smoldering between the conflicting desires of being with Joachim or with Clavdia, Dr. Behrens emerges and greets the cousins with an odd expression, "Behold, behold, Timotheus!" (249), and goes on to express his blessing on their metabolisms ("Segenswünschen für ihren Stoffwechsel"). Who is Timothy? Behrens often makes obscure literary references, but this address to the cousins is particularly strange; on the one hand, because it is first directed to just one of the two (Timothy), and then is expanded to encompass both cousins in the blessing on *their* metabolisms. The very ambiguity of number is illustrative of the ambiguous relationship between the cousins — are they one or are they two, are they twins or not? And, on the other hand, the greeting is curious for its reference to Hans as Timothy. Who is this Timothy, of whom we have heard nothing so far? Because of the biblical tone of the greeting ("Sieh da, sieh da," "Behold, behold") the most obvious reference would seem to be to the saint named Timothy, the recipient of two letters from the apostle Paul.[34] (Timothy is, incidentally, from the town of Lystra, in present-day Turkey, and his remains are reputedly still to be found in Istanbul; he is one of the few major saints from Asia Minor to have remained physically in Turkey, and thus obliquely he introduces us to the Turkish theme that will emerge more fully in the course of the chapter.)

In his letters to Timothy, Paul, like Dr. Behrens, seems to take an unusual interest in the metabolism of his disciple, sounding almost like a doctor: "You should give up drinking only water and have a little wine for the sake of your digestion" (1 Tim. 5:23). And commentators have been puzzled by the emotional attachment Paul seems to show for Timothy (2 Tim. 1:4, "I remember your tears and long to see you again to complete my happiness").[35] This intimate tone of the letters to Timothy are stylistically so different from Paul's other letters that many commentators, mostly Protestant, have been convinced that the writer of these two letters could not be the historical Paul.[36] (The Roman Church, on the other hand, symbolically celebrates the close connection between the two men by placing the feast of Saint Timothy on the eve of the feast of Saint Paul's Conversion, January 24 and 25. One might say that, liturgically speaking, Saint Paul's conversion is traditionally seen as a "morning-after" affair.)

But even if one ignores the arguably erotic tone of the letters, they still contain many of the themes important for *The Magic Mountain*: the admonition to avoid false teachers (1 Timothy ends with this advice: "Have nothing to do with the pointless philosophical discussions and antagonistic beliefs of the 'knowledge' which is not knowledge at all"); the call for women to act modestly (that is, not to slam doors; Clavdia will rebel against this stricture and gain Hans's attention by doing so); the mystery of the spiritual life made manifest in flesh; the "good soldier"; spiritual discipline and physical exercise; finally, sexual stoicism. In his relationship to Paul, Timothy reenacts the relationship of John to Jesus, that is, the role of the "beloved disciple," and in this regard we must remember that

Hans's real name is Johannes and that he will himself re-enact the very role of John to his master Peeperkorn in the scene that is so clearly modeled, if parodistically, on the Last Supper.[37]

Saint Paul is but another of the many guises of the paternal figure that Dr. Behrens assumes in his relationship to Hans. Paul's paternal position to Timothy is clear from the fact that it was Paul himself who performed the rite of circumcision on Timothy (Acts 16:1–3); this perhaps lends a sly note of humor to Behrens's request to see Hans's cigar to see how it is burning: "Let me have a look. I'm a connoisseur" (249). The German is more erotic: "Lassen Sie mal sehen, ich bin Kenner und Liebhaber." Missing the erotic dimensions of "lover," both translators of the novel collapse the two terms of recognition and endearment into the far less sexual single term "connoisseur." But Behrens means what he says; he is a passionate lover, as well as someone who knows what he is looking at.[38] And so the two men pore over their cigars; they compare their cigars in taste and the ability to burn evenly. Hans says of his, "[It is] quite spicy, but light on the tongue." Hofrat Behrens suggests that they exchange cigars, a proposal Hans accepts, and "Each rolled his gift between his fingers, examining the slender body with expert eye." A reader does not need to consult a theoretical discussion of metonymic tropes to understand the implications of the scene. Even if the cigars are given feminine names such as Maria Mancini, the act of exchange is charged with male erotic significance. It is worth noting that the name of the Bremen-produced cigar, Maria Mancini, is hardly German; perhaps here the native product is coquettishly posing as an import. The name is so preposterously foreign sounding that it only calls greater attention to its role as feminine protection. Perhaps the exchange is *only* possible when the cigars are given apotropaic and euphemistic feminine names, but even if these slender bodies are well-protected, an actual exchange does take place between the men.[39] At this point, if we are to imagine Dr. Behrens as Hans Castorp's paternal lover, it is pertinent to remember that Hans was orphaned early in life and never really knew his own father (18). That Hofrat Behrens acts so clearly as a surrogate father is evidence that Hans Castorp's sexual quest is not simply that of seeking the Universal Mother, as has recently been suggested.[40]

Hans and Behrens exchange more than their cigars; there is also a temporary exchange in roles as Hofrat Behrens tells Hans and his cousin of his experience smoking a heavy Havana cigar, and the tone now is that of patient to doctor. The cigar was too strong for him, caused an erratic heartbeat, and brought on a strong sense of fear and ecstasy simultaneously: "But fear and euphoria aren't mutually exclusive, everybody knows that" (250). Behrens then compares this smoking experience to a sexual experience: "Some scalawag who's about to have a girl for the first time is afraid too. So is she. But they simply melt together for euphoria. Well, I was close to melting myself." The scalawag ("der Bengel") the doctor refers to could well be a young man like Hans himself, for, so far as we know, Hans, too, has had no sexual experience[41] and it is this very innocence that may well attract Behrens to the younger man. Interestingly, the name of the Havana cigar that nearly did the doctor in was "Henry Clay," a dramatic shift in gender from the Maria Mancinis Hans has to offer. (Here we have the colonial import parading as a native or at least as a domestic American product). Continuing in the role of patient to doctor, Behrens's eyes fill with tears as he recounts his "import" experience for Hans and Joachim, an experience that lets us know that the imported cigar he smoked (whose name was Henry) had emotional, as well as medical repercussions. Fortunately for the affection Behrens has for the younger man, Hans Castorp's cigar is not an exotic imported variety but is a domestic product from Bremen. Behrens can smoke Hans's cigar as much as he likes, with complete assurance that the experience will not cost him his life.[42] But why is the imported variety so dangerous? I will return shortly to the role of the imported product in the novel.

Hans next mentions that he has heard that the Hofrat is a painter. Hans knows that there is a portrait of Clavdia somewhere in the doctor's possession and is calculatedly preparing the path to see that portrait. When he asks if he might view the Hofrat's paintings, Behrens becomes visibly excited by the request: "Behrens was so pleased and flattered that he was almost ebullient. He even turned red with delight, and by now his eyes seemed close to shedding actual tears" (251).[43] This doctor certainly breaks into tears very easily. When Behrens learns that Hans, too, is a painter of sorts, he asks, "The real thing in oils?" (Ganz solide in Öl?) and Hans must answer with some embarrassment that he is as yet only a watercolorist. Oil is a medium for the mature, and Hans is not yet at that level (just as he is an apprentice naval engineer with no real sea experience behind him, and just as he is playing the role of disciple to the older man). Oil exploration in the novel is a major concern of this essay, and so it is a happy coincidence that oil makes its appearance here following so closely upon the very explicit scene of sexual revelation through the exchange of cigars. Oil is the sign of a mature art, and it is also the sign of a mature industrial state. When Hans achieves his professional goal, will his ships be oil tankers, bringing the necessary oil to Germany for her industrial needs and will he, as a mature man, begin to paint ("ganz solide") in oils?

As Behrens takes the cousins into his private apartment, he becomes exuberant; he even pulls them from the bench in his haste to get them into his private realm. As he fumbles with the many keys on his keychain,

"His hand trembled as he did it; he was definitely nervous" (251). Once again, important information is suppressed. Why is Behrens so nervous? Is his nervousness a reflection of the excitement Hans felt when he first put the thermometer into his mouth? Is Behrens conscious of the sexual significance of the act of bringing Hans into his apartment? Did Zeus tremble when he brought the young Ganymede into his Olympian home? Is there a Hera in Behrens's life who will punish him for his escapades (perhaps the medieval Adriatica von Mylendonck)?[44] The questions come naturally, for nothing less than a seduction is taking place here, but under the excuse that they are going into the older man's home to look at pictures. (Perhaps this is a joke on the old line of approach, "Come up and see my etchings.")

The rooms inhabited by Hofrat Behrens are, like the man himself, an odd mixture: two rooms in "banal-bourgeois" style, the first a dining room done up in "altdeutsch" fashion, then a living room-cum-office where a fraternity cap and crossed swords are conspicuously placed. Next to that is a smoking alcove done up in "Turkish" style. Interior decoration is always an extremely important marker for Mann. In the short story "Tristan," which also takes place in a sanatorium, the aesthete Detlev Spinell cannot "live" without the Empire style of the health institute, and it is unclear if he is at the sanatorium for its decorative style or for its curative powers.[45] And here in *The Magic Mountain,* too, interior decoration is revealing, especially the conjunction of the "Old-German" style with its emblems of military training in the form of the crossed swords (a reminder that the duel is a leitmotif in the novel) and student fraternity life in the form of the cap; next to that is the imported "Turkish" style of the smoking alcove. By way of contrast, the style of the rest of the sanatorium seems to be severely modern and coldly functional (10). But here we have two very distinct styles, one native or national, deeply rooted in the German tradition, and the other "Oriental" and exotic. When we remember Dr. Behrens's vulnerability for imported cigars, the inclusion of this "Turkish" alcove for the act of smoking in the heart of his living arrangements seems questionable or even rather risky. Is this inclusion of the foreign and imported not an act of living dangerously? In the latter part of the book, the toxicity of the foreign and imported will take on an intensified tangibility in the form of the poison that kills Mynheer Peeperkorn, a poison he has brought with him from Malaysia. What is the role of foreign imports in this novel and why are they so dangerous?

In the last quarter of the nineteenth century, German interest in Turkey became acute as Germany began work on the Berlin-to-Baghdad railway, an enormous engineering project that was to become of even greater importance after the discovery of oil in Mesopotamia. Indeed, the very discovery of that oil was closely linked to the German presence in the area and was not unrelated to the oil known to be in abundance in the Baku-Daghestan area. Calouste Gulbenkian's father and uncle had earlier exported Russian oil (from Baku and Dagestan) to Turkey. After these oil fields were set on fire during the 1905 revolution, and when it had became clear that the Russian government was unable to maintain control over its raw materials, Calouste Gulbenkian made a deal (1912) with Turkey, Shell Oil, and the German government to explore for petroleum in Baghdad, then a part of the Ottoman empire.[46] In fact, as early as 1891 two officials of the Turkish Sultan had asked Goulbenkian to investigate the possibilities of oil production in Mesopotamia; and while he had not visited the area himself, he was able to put together a competent report based on earlier reports and on discussions held with German railway engineers.[47] Goulbenkian reported back to the Sultan that the region had very great petroleum potential.[48] All this led to a greater sense of urgency for the railway project which naturally had to pass through Turkey. The German emperor himself made a journey to the Turkish capital to promote German interests, particularly those of the railway, and to parade his image as friend and protector of the Islamic world.[49] These high-level negotiations and flirtations caused considerable alarm among the British government and other European powers who were also struggling to acquire the requisite oil from abroad:

> One player in the prewar years was a German group, led by the Deutsche Bank, which aimed to project German influence and ambitions into the Middle East. Arrayed against it was a rival group, sponsored by William Knox D'Arcy and eventually merged into the Anglo-Persian Oil Company. It was championed by the British government as a counterweight to Germany. Then, in 1912, the British government was alarmed to discover a new player on the scene. It was called the Turkish Petroleum Company, and it turned out that the Deutsche Bank had transferred its claims for a concession to this entity. The Deutsche Bank and Royal Dutch/Shell each held a quarter of the new company. The largest share, half of the total equity, was held by the Turkish National Bank, which, ironically, happened to be a British-controlled bank set up in Turkey to advance British economic and political interests.[50]

It was in this same year (1912) that the British Admiralty decided to start converting some of its fleet from coal to oil fuel and to construct new oil-fired dreadnoughts. Already by 1914, 25,000 tons of oil a month were being imported from south Persia into Britain for this purpose.[51] The success of the Berlin-to-Baghdad Railway would threaten this British supply and insure that Germany itself would be "ganz solide in Öl." And geography being what it is in the novel, it comes as no surprise that the little

Turkish alcove is described as an annex to the "altdeutsche" rooms that dominate the apartment, for it is by economic annexation that Germany was to pursue her goal of securing the rail's right of way.

Hofrat Behrens is making "Turkish" coffee for the cousins, using a coffee-grinder whose phallic form makes Hans Castorp blush (it can be assumed that in the days before electric grinders, a certain manual rotation was required); Behrens tells him that it is a "tool for single gentlemen," and just as Hans turned Behrens's cigar between his fingers, so now he manipulates the coffee grinder: "Hans Castorp rolled the cylindrical coffee mill between his palms" (258). The coffee grinder and coffee utensils were a gift from the Egyptian princess whose return to the Berghof coincides with that of Mynheer Peeperkorn; once again, a woman provides the occasion for the men to enjoy themselves. But the little smoking alcove in which these "single gentlemen" are sitting, enjoying their coffee is more than just a representative annexation of Turkish style; the room is, in fact, a collation of the entire East. In style it is, we learn, actually "more Indian or Persian than Turkish" (258); they are using an Egyptian coffee service; and they are seated at a little bamboo table that must have come from even further east in Asia. Joachim sits on an ottoman, or "Ottoman" to give the word its full symbolic potential, and it is worth noting that all the parts of the world mentioned in connection with this alcove's style are territories within the English colonial economic sphere — India, Persia (recall the Anglo-Persian Oil Company), China, and Egypt. Some are outright colonies, some are protectorates, but all are definitely part of the "splendid possessions" Churchill referred to with such pride. It is curious, then, that what looks like a Turkish alcove begins to resemble the entire portion of the Orient controlled by England, as if this small smoking room were a representation of the growing German desire to expand its own colonies along the lines of Britain's already established empire.

Ultimately, the conversation for these three single gentlemen sitting together under the twin aegis of the German fraternity cap and crossed swords turns to the topic of women and sex. This is not unexpected, since they are playing with a phallus in the form of a coffee-grinder. Women are discussed here in the most factual, biological way.[52] And what is it, the question arises, that makes women so beautiful? Behrens explains that the softness of female tissue is the result of oil, specifically, three substances: palmitin, stearin, and olein. All three are types of fatty oil derived from various metabolic processes. Thus, the search for female beauty beneath the skin, like the search for wealth beneath the surface of the earth, becomes a search for oil. Any thought of romantic idealism is thrown out by Behrens's cynical question, "What did you think it was? Ambrosia, perhaps?" (257). Like fraternity men sharing their intimate sexual experiences, the three go on to discuss skin and its erectile properties. Skin is, according to the Hofrat, "your external brain . . . ontologically speaking, it has the same origin as the apparatus for the so-called higher sensory organs up there in your skull" (259). But there are mysteries connected with this tissue. We do not know, for example, why the cock's comb swells, nor why we blush with shame. The conversation turns to other erectile properties of the skin, namely goosebumps, and Hans recalls that he has the same reaction to the scratching of metal on glass as he does to beautiful music — he gets goosebumps: "What amazes me is that these glands go erect under such a variety of circumstances" (260). Finally, the conversation comes to the final form of erection or rigidity: rigor mortis, and with that the doctor and his disciple have discussed practically every form of human erection possible with the exception of the most obvious one, the one that lies as the key to the entire interest Hans Castorp has in Clavdia Chauchat and the one that has been driven home to the reader through the phallic images of the cylindrical cigars and coffee mill. It seems that erectile tissue can react characteristicaly in a variety of contexts, even a variety of sexual contexts. Nature has made the male, it seems, profoundly bi- or omnisexual.

This very lability of erections is at the heart of the conversation between Hans and the doctor, and it is as if in recognition of their having stepped over boundaries of propriety that Hofrat Behrens brings the conversation abruptly to an end: "You're in very bold and daring form today, yourself. Literally kicking over the traces. But I'm fading quickly here").[53] Hans has proven to be as enterprising and as boundary-crossing in his sexual research as the German spirit of science that is engaged in building the Turkish railway. Earlier, Behrens asked Hans Castorp why he became an engineer, to which Hans replies that it was an accident; but perhaps it was an historically determined accident, one that makes of its romantic young men the avant-guard of an intellectual and territorial expansion the likes of which Germany had never seen before.[54] Behrens admits that he has to call an end to the visit because he is beginning to fall into a fit of melancholy: "I'm fading quickly here . . . suddenly it just comes over me and I get melancholy" (263). Undoubtedly the reasons for this melancholy are as difficult to locate precisely as the reasons for the responses of the erectile tissue, but certainly, the final mood here has something of the sadness that, according to Aristotle, settles on all animals after sex.[55] As sign of this melancholy, Dr. Behrens's face wears "a mournful look" (263). Hans replaces the portrait of Clavdia to the wall, and the cousins retire to their rest cures. Joachim, who has played the faithful acolyte to the erotic rituals between Behrens and his cousin, is not unaware that boundaries have been crossed; he notes that Hans has begun to explore new territory.

Certainly, boundaries have been crossed. There is no chapter in literature so filled with marginally covert homoeroticism except perhaps the ninety-fourth chapter of *Moby-Dick* ("A Squeeze of the Hand"), where the sailors of the *Pequod* find themselves working with their hands in buckets of sperm-whale oil, catching each others' slippery fingers and gazing soulfully into each others' eyes with desires of friendship and love.[56] The emblems hanging on the walls of Behrens's study suggest an initial direction for further interrogation: does the fraternity cap mean that the encounter taking place beneath it has been nothing but an adolescent discussion of sex, a typical student experience? Or does it mean that there is a truer and more mature fraternity (a genuine "Verbindung") between the participants of the discussion?[57] Do the crossed swords suggest that the conversation has actually been a duel between Hans and the doctor as rivals for the possession of Clavdia? Or are the crossed swords simply a supplement to the cigars that have been exchanged, and is the crossing of swords the inevitable consequence of having exchanged (or crossed) the less significant cigars; in other words, do they represent a kind of remorseful homophobic reaction to the intimacy shared earlier? We must not lose sight here that these emblems also have a strong nationalistic connotation, implying that the "Verbindung" encoded in the discussion could perhaps *only* be a German kind of fraternity.[58]

SWORDS DISPLACE CIGARS. Here we are confronted with a critical problem in the interpretation of the novel, that of displacement: how does one thing or person come to replace another? We see this theme fully developed as early as the second part of Chapter One, "Number 34," where Hans Castorp meditates on the fact that he has displaced the American woman who died in the room just before his arrival. The novel thus begins with the theme of displacement, and it ends with a graphic description of displacement as one mania follows another among the increasingly impatient patients at the Berghof. As the novel draws to a close, the entire sanatorium goes mad for photography, then for stamp collecting, then for the many varieties of chocolate. And as the Great War looms ever nearer, the very pace of displacement seems to accelerate. What do these social and personal displacements mean? What does it mean that Hans Castorp's love for Pribislav Hippe has been displaced by his love for Clavdia Chauchat? Is this displacement intended to be read as a sign of maturation — out of adolescent, homosexual love arises a love between the sexes? Or is the love for Clavdia simply an extension of that earlier love? Or is love, like the erectile tissue the men have been discussing, capable of responding to a variety of stimuli? Again, it would seem that Freud could be of help, because displacement and transference are major modes of psychoanalytic interpretation; but we are more or less constrained from turning to him, since his theories have been reduced to parody in Krokowski's proposal to regard disease as repressed love (126). Mann himself suggested alchemy as a mode of understanding these displacements; in the novel he writes, "there is a great deal said of an alchemistic, hermetic pedagogy, of *transubstantiation*. And I, myself, a guileless fool, was guided by a mysterious tradition."[59] Alchemy would draw us closer to the interpretative strategies of Jung, whose school of psychiatric studies had opened in 1911 in nearby Zurich. But whatever mode we choose to guide our understanding of the scene between Behrens and the two cousins, it must be admitted that the actions of the three men have confused the usual opposition between homo- and heterosexuality. Eve Sedgwick's formula is useful here; it is her aim in *Between Men*, she writes, "to question, rather than to reinforce . . . the presumptively symmetrical opposition between homo- and heterosexuality."[60] It seems to be Mann's aim, as well, to blur these same distinctions and to question the apparent polarity between sexual modes.

In her reading of the work of René Girard, Sedgwick finds that "what is most interesting for [our] purposes . . . is [Girard's] insistence that, in any erotic rivalry, the bond that links the two rivals is as intense and potent as the bond that links either of the rivals to the beloved: that the bonds of 'rivalry' and 'love,' differently as they are experienced, are equally powerful and in many senses equivalent."[61] Sedgwick advances this insight through various works of English literature from the late eighteenth to the mid-nineteenth century; and the same terms of investigation could be applied to Mann's novel, but with the necessary acknowledgment that a further complicating element appears to be present in the equation: the fact that Mann is *aware* that he is creating just such an erotic triangle, and that he is doing so precisely because such triangles are an indispensable element of the earlier literary tradition (mostly English) that he is parodying. Where earlier English (and German) authors more or less unconsciously depict the similarities between male rivalry and attraction in the erotic triangle, Mann explores this element of male psychology with a full awareness of that earlier literature. This self-conscious parodistic element gives Mann's triangles a degree of ambiguity and humor that are less apparent in the originals of the type.[62] Perhaps Mann himself was engaging in the same syndrome of admiration and rivalry with his literary predecessors, and his engagement with that tradition reflects Hans Castorp's own ambivalent attitude toward the English; in other words, just as Hans is trying to develop a German navy equal to that of Britain, so, too, his author is trying to beat them at their own literary game. It is, then, this very intertextual awareness that prompts Mann to give his main character his ersatz Englishness; Hans Castorp is in fact a comic extension of that nineteenth-century novelistic tradition where such love triangles are common coin. Mann himself even alludes to such an influence when describing the style he adopted in the novel: "The humorous and expansive English style, itself a relief from the austerity of *Death in Venice*, took up space and time."[63] Earlier, in a letter to Julius Bab, Mann had acknowledged his conception of the novel in general as that of a social genre: "Sicher, Roman, das heißt Gesellschaftsroman, und ein solcher ist der Zgb. bis zu einem Grade ja auch ganz von selbst geworden."[64] For Mann in 1925, a novel had to be by its very nature a representation of society, and such gendered triangles as we find in *The Magic Mountain* are a constitutive part of the social world as Mann found it represented before him. A novel such as James's *Washington Square* comes easily to mind, where Dr. Sloper and Morris Townsend exercise their rivalry (and, I would suggest, their mutual attraction) through the body and person of Sloper's daughter Catherine. Here, it is Clavdia who is the proving ground of the attraction between Behrens and Hans. In a later triangle, Mynheer Peeperkorn will displace Behrens in both his roles, as father figure for Hans and lover for Clavdia.

Inherent in Sedgwick's project is the historicization of the triangle; she aligns herself with earlier theorists to offer such triangles not "as an ahistorical, Platonic form, a deadly symmetry from which the historical accidents of gender, language, class and power detract, but as a sensitive register precisely for delineating relationships of power and meaning, and for making graphically intelligible the play of desire and identification by which individuals negotiate with their societies for empowerment."[65] Definitely, the triangle as configured by Mann among Behrens, Hans and Clavdia is one that has to do with just such social empowerment; in his letter to Bab, Mann touches on this topic: "Einige Kritik des vorkriegerischen Kapitalismus läuft mit unter."[66] The specific form of Mann's critique of capitalism is part of the figuration of the triangle we observe in the scene at Hofrat Behrens's apartment, and it can be read as a reference to a specific relationship between German colonial aims and the search to understand (and therefore possess) the woman. Prewar capitalism could not be honestly depicted if it did not include reference to the colonial empire-building which was so great a part of the economic and political life in the powers that would soon be at war over that very issue. In his English essay on the making of the novel, Mann says that the life he describes in *The Magic Mountain*, especially in light of its luxury and carefree timelessness, was "only possible in a capitalistic economy that was still functioning well and normally. Only under such a system was it possible for patients to remain there year after year."[67] And the literary triangle as he figures it is also bound by time and location. This is a triangle such as could only have been found in the years the novel depicts.

Further in the same essay Mann describes his project as presenting "a simple-minded hero, in conflict between bourgeois decorum and macabre adventure."[68] The macabre adventures are many, and certainly the coffee and cigars with Hofrat Behrens could be construed as one; but these adventures are not his alone, for Hans Castorp is also a representative of young German men in 1907 and as such he is being subjected to an adventure far more macabre than a thinly veiled sexual encounter with an older man. He is also reenacting, symbolically, the strange adventure his country was undergoing in the antebellum years: colonial expansion and vigorous military development. Hans only needs to look at his cousin sitting on the ottoman to see a symbol of that adventure, with all its resonance of domination, complacency and luxury: a soldier (sick to the core it turns out, but healthy in appearance[69]) sits in complete unawareness that his comfort (including his health-benefits package) is supported by an ancient and sumptuous empire that is at that very moment being brought ever more securely within the boundaries of the German economic interests. In the same essay Mann writes that a fundamental theme of the book was that of "heightening" or "enhancement"[70] ("Steigerung," which in this context might better be translated as "intensification"), by which he is primarily referring to the heightening of Hans Castorp's sensibilities to the point at which he is capable of undertaking his own adventures in the moral and sensual realms. But the word can hardly be used of the antebellum world of Europe in the first decade of the century without thinking of the most obvious "heightening" taking place at the time: the accelerating crises (such as the intensification of the naval race between Germany and Britain and the increasingly frequent minor skirmishes that took place between the major powers or their second-string allies, such as Serbia) that would ultimately lead to the outbreak of war.

Indeed, Mann shows his awareness of *this* form of heightening in the chapter "The Great Petulance," in which the patients of the Berghof are seen developing quarrels and antagonisms among themselves that in their own way, reflect the point to which European negotiations and alliances had come and which would determine the point at which actual warfare began:

> What was it then? What was in the air? A love of quarrels. Acute petulance. Nameless impatience. A universal penchant for nasty verbal exchanges and outbursts of rage, even for fisticuffs. Every day fierce arguments, out-of-control shouting matches would erupt between individuals and among entire groups; but the distinguishing mark was that

bystanders, instead of being disgusted by those caught up in it or trying to intervene, found their sympathies aroused and abandoned themselves emotionally to the frenzy. (673)

And in the midst of all this turmoil is Hans Castorp, listening to his music. Hans is literally in the middle of all the polarities of the book; he is the German caught between East and West, passionate Russian mysticism and Mediterranean rationality. He is caught between homosexual and heterosexual love, between the duties of life and the attractions of death. Yet Hans never makes a clear decision for either side. It is this very undecidability that attracted Mann to his character: "He doesn't want to be pinned down. As soon as Settembrini presses him, he becomes evasive — and not without a certain guile. This attitude seems to me to correspond to Germany's in-betweenness, and in this regard there is something most deeply German about Hans Castorp."[71] Hans is also positioned between the attractions of the foreign colonial import and the attractions of the native domestic product. Both sides have their sexual aspects; this is perhaps more obvious in the seductive eyes of Clavdia and Hippe, with their call to the German to quest abroad for sensual gratification. But the domestic has its sexual appeal, as well, which Hans would recognize if only he could understand why his heart beats "like a man in love" when he is near Joachim and why he experiences such hope and joy when he thinks of Joachim as Marusya's lover. Joachim, too, despite his attraction to Marusya, has unrecognized emotional and homosexual depths. There is hardly a more charged moment in the novel than the parting between the two cousins; Joachim, breaking the code of avoiding first names, says "'Hans' . . . and in desperate anguish he squeezed his cousin's hand, and the latter noticed Joachim's head trembling from lack of sleep and the excitement of the trip . . . 'Hans,' he said imploringly, 'come soon'" (417). As much as he loves Hans, Joachim is determined to join the military and the regimental dinners that are called so ambiguously in German "Liebesmahle" ("love-feasts," 490).

IN THE NARRATIVE, Hans Castorp's intermediate position is nowhere more elaborately detailed than in his relationship to his two mentors, Naphta and Settembrini; it is surely this aspect of Hans Castorp's character that Mann is referring to when he calls his character "mittelmäßig," meaning not so much that Hans is mediocre in talent but, rather, that he is positioned in the middle between what seem to be oppositions. Far too many of the novel's polarities are embodied in the intellectual positions represented by these two men to go into them fully here; let it suffice to say that as Hans learns more and more about each man, he is forced to see an underlying sameness in their apparent opposition to one another. For example, he comes to see that Settembrini's membership in the Freemasons is not entirely different from Naphta's membership in the Jesuits. On the surface, the two seem worlds apart, but as the novel progresses their arguments seem to become lost in one another and to lose the sharpness of differentiation that initially characterized them; like the homo- and heterosexuality of the Turkish alcove scene, the intellectual oppositions begin to blur into one another. But beyond representing apparently opposing intellectual systems, the two men also represent another, less obvious opposition, that between the homoerotic Western tradition and the consequences of violent colonialism. But, once again, we will find that even these two opposing terms have a curiously symbiotic relationship with each other.

If we begin with his name, "Settembrini" immediately reminds one of the number seven, which lies encoded in so many of the book's details (seven tables, seven months, Room no. 7, Room no. 34, etc.[72]), and of the month September. His usual propaganda is an ironic September song that is filled with an autumnal nostalgia for the Western culture he raggedly represents. Hans reminds us of this number when he makes the mistake of calling him "Herr Septem— " (55) on their meeting. We know that Spengler's *Decline of the West* was high on Mann's reading list while working on the earlier phases of the novel,[73] and it is not improbable that the name is somehow intended to cast a shadow of impending decline over the tradition of Western Humanism. We also know that Mann modeled much of Settembrini on his own brother, Heinrich, whom he had earlier designated as the type of *Zivilisationsliterat* described unflatteringly in the *Reflections of a Nonpolitical Man*.[74] Whether the depiction of Settembrini is ultimately to be interpreted as vengeful sibling retribution or loving acknowledgment is not entirely clear, especially in the light of the changes that take place in Mann's treatment of the character in the course of writing the novel, but there is always a definite familial relationship present between Hans and his mentor. If Hofrat Behrens takes on the semblance of a father to Hans, Settembrini is easily seen as an older brother. This closeness of relationship is further emphasized when we learn that Settembrini's grandfather was, in his way, like Hans's own grandfather: "And so they had both worn black, the grandfather in the North and the one in the South, and both for the purpose of drawing a strict line between themselves and the evil present" (151). In a sense, the two men share a common grandfather, and the family resemblance between them leads to the common rivalry-admiration syndrome so often found among brothers.

In the relationship of Hans with Settembrini, as in his relationship with Behrens, there is an ambiguous kind of sexuality. On the one hand, while the Italian constantly berates Hans for not escaping the Berghof and for dwelling on paradoxes instead of clear-headed reason ("Paradox is the poison flower of quietism, the iridescent sheen of a putrefied mind, the greatest depravity of all" [219]), he is himself, as we have seen, full of such paradoxes. Consider that Settembrini holds the poet Leopardi up to Hans as a kind of hero despite the fact that he "lacked the love of a woman, and that [lack] was what made him incapable of preventing his soul from being stunted" (98). But of course it is precisely for his stunted soul that Settembrini loves Leopardi. If Leopardi were to have had the love of a woman, he would not have been the kind of poet he was. There is, in other words, beneath the sunny Italian persona more of the German Romantic than at first meets the eye. His identification with life and health is not so seamless as he would want us to believe. And his adherence to the cult of the Freemasons is in its own way not entirely different from Naphta's membership in the Society of Jesus (both orders reject women from their numbers, have degrees of commitment and advancement, work for a sense of betterment for humanity, and were largely expelled from European society for their political activities).

Lodovico is the Italian form of the German name Ludwig, and perhaps the cold northern winds, the *tramontane*, which blew into his father's study in Padua (94) carried with them a spirit of German Romanticism that has now infected the old scholar's son. Settembrini, under the guise of advising Hans to embrace convention and heterosexuality, is at the same time importing into his message a high regard for the very opposite of that message. And, furthering his fraternal role in the complication of Hans's sexual identity, it is Settembrini who suggests a feminine category within which Hans might see himself reflected: "you almost remind me more of a young nun than a monk, one of those innocent young brides of Christ, her hair newly shorn, with great martyr's eyes" (191). The curious visual inspection to which Settembrini so often subjects Hans Castorp is a reflection of the pedagogic desires which Aschenbach bestows on his would-be pupil Tadzio, and it is perhaps not a coincidence that Settembrini appears to Hans Castorp in the recreation room just after a stereoscopic view of a Venetian gondolier has been described (82). Settembrini is associated with Venice and all that Venice had come to mean in the course of Mann's earlier and related novel.

In 1932 Mann wrote to thank Benedetto Croce for sending a copy of Luigi Settembrini's memoirs, remarking that "I have observed with pleasure that not only as certain likeness of viewpoint but also a similarity of character exists between the hero of this book and my Settembrini."[75] It is on the basis of this letter that the editors of Mann's correspondence have surmised that Mann actually had Luigi in mind when he created Lodovico,[76] but Mann's phrase is cagily and politely poised to give that impression but not to confirm it. Heilbut offers a more interesting note on the provenance of Settembrini's name: "This author recently learned that 'Settembrini' is Venetian dialect for the 'September men,' the pederasts who arrive once the season is over and buy the local boys at half-price. If Mann knew this, Settembrini lives up to his name to the extent that his 'pedagogy' is 'happily/painfully' erotic."[77] If we accept this Venetian attribution of the name, which is modestly supported by the fact that he is indeed from nearby Padua, Settembrini could be read as a colorfully disguised Aschenbach, in whose character are combined an allegory of the decline of the West with the dreamy city on the Adriatic. The idea of the old pedagogue who has a sexual interest in his pupil renders Hans Castorp's comment that he is receiving Settembrini's tutelage "*sine pecunia*," (323) rather comical. Who should be paying whom?

It is within this context of the homoerotic Western tradition, which Mann has already explored in *Death in Venice*, that Settembrini's love for Brunetto Latini is to be placed. For Settembrini, Latini was "the great master who had first given the Florentines their polish and taught them both how to speak and the fine art of guiding their republic by the rules of politics" (156). Settembrini's admiration for Latini finds its intended mark on his pupil Hans, for later in the novel, Hans will remember this phrase about Latini, and will recite it to himself, an ironic epic repetition, word for word (348). Settembrini proposes himself as a teacher for Hans, and Brunetto Latini provides the classical model for this pedagogic position; he is remembered by Dante as his beloved teacher:

> e chinando la mano alla sua faccia,
> rispuosi: "Siete voi qui, ser Brunetto?"
>
> E quelli: "O figliuol mio, non ti dispiaccia
> se Brunetto Latino un poco teco
> ritorna in dietro e lascia andar la traccia."
>
> (And to his face inclining down my own,
> I answered, "Ser Brunetto, are you here?")
>
> And he: "May it not displease thee, O my son,
> If Brunetto Latini turn with thee
> A little back, and let his troop go on."
>
> (trans. Lawrence Binyon)[78]

In the *Inferno* Latini can only accompany his former pupil for a little while, a companionable walk in hell that is echoed in Settembrini's accompanying Hans as he embarks on his skiing trip in the snow. Settembrini goes with Hans to buy the skis: "I would gladly accompany you into the mountains, moving alongside you with wings on my heels" (465). But, like Latini with his pupil Dante, Settembrini can only go so far, can only say so much ("Di più direi; ma 'l venire e 'l sermone / più lungo esser non può" [I would say more, but must not be deferred / My going, and speech must end now]). Both pupils leave their mentors behind them as they move on to new experiences; Hans disappears in a cloud of white fog, just as Latini sees his pupil Dante disappear in a "Smoke of new dust from the sand." In other words, Settembrini reenacts in significant ways and details the role of Brunetto Latini to his pupil Hans Castorp.

Brunetto Latini was the great Florentine teacher, just as Settembrini tells Hans, but Settembrini fails to tell the entire story. Latini is known to most readers through his appearance in Dante's *Inferno*, where he appears among those being punished for having been "sodomites." It has been argued that the sins of Sodom, as Dante understood them, include many that have nothing to do with sex, and that Latini is being punished for these less sensual transgressions.[79] And the city of Sodom may, indeed, stand for a number of nonsexual sins political and spiritual, but for Proust and for Mann, the primary interest in the city is surely its sexual orientation. In fact, except for scholars determined to redeem the sexual reputation of the great Florentine, his homosexuality is simply taken for granted. Thus, the founder of Florentine eloquence was also a homosexual, and Settembrini reflects all aspects of his model pedagogue including that one. In his *De vulgari eloquentia*, Dante divided the vernacular languages of his day into the "lingua d'oïl" (French), the "lingua d'oc" (Provençal, or as we say now, Occitan), and the "lingua di si" (Italian), according to the words used in them to mean "yes." (*Oïl* comes from the Latin *hoc ille*.) Brunetto Latini chose to write his major work, the *Livre du trésor*, in what we now call Old French, or "lingua d oïl." Like Hans Castorp, he considered French the most appropriate language for certain types of linguistic endeavor.

And with the mention of the language of "Oïl," we must turn to the character of Naphta, whose name is the Russian word for petroleum. Indeed, the very area from which Naphta comes, the borderlands between Galicia and Volhynia, is the only region in Poland that has oil reserves.[80] The limited Polish oil production is entirely centered in the area south of the Vistula and east of Krakow, between the towns of Bochnia and Sanok and centered around the city of Krosno. This is the area of Galicia that borders on the old duchy of Volhynia, and in view of its petroleum potential it could be seen as the northern complement of Daghestan. The name Naphta then links the character with the petroleum and petroleum by-products which were the goal of much of German and Russian colonial expansion in the years before the First World War. In English, as in German, *naphtha* is a word for any of various volatile, often highly flammable liquid hydrocarbon mixtures that are used mainly as solvents and dilutents. These mixtures are also the raw material used for conversion into gasoline. The Greek word *naphtha*, which is perhaps of "Oriental" origin (according to the *Oxford English Dictionary*), was applied to the more volatile kinds of petroleum issuing naturally from the ground in the Baku district of the Caucasus, and it was naphtha that was an essential ingredient in "Greek fire," the secret weapon of the Byzantine Empire, which from as early as the seventh century was credited for much of the military advantage exercised by the Byzantines and which for centuries kept the enemy out of Byzantine cities.[81] Living up to his name, Naphta is himself a highly volatile missile sent out by his religious order and a fiery advocate of his adopted philosophical ideologies. He is so volatile, in fact, that he cannot tolerate the presence of natures less flammable than his own; in the duel with Settembrini, in which the Italian refuses to shoot, Naphta implodes with rage and kills himself with his own pistol.

In the volatility and anger directed toward the self, Naphta is the novel's best insight into the world of the subjugated colonial. Again, Naphta's name is a clue to the character's meaning; his name was Leib before he changed it to the more Christian Leo,[82] and Leib is a name that suggests the importance of the body as the site of colonial violence and suppression. Indeed, no one in the novel comes from a more persecuted background. Born in a community of devout Jews, Naphta early on sees the deeply spiritual meaning of life for these people, and he learns to distinguish their sense of piety from the Christians' world, which seems, in contrast, devoid of holy meaning. At the same time, he learns from his father's scrupulous acts of animal slaying (he is the village *shoket* or ritual slaughterer) a profound reverence for "the sight and smell of blood," which for him are bound up with ideas of what is holy and spiritual (433).

How, then, does he react to his father's gruesome death by crucifixion during a pogrom? We are not told precisely, but in the eventual and enthusiastic conversion Naphta makes to militant Christianity we can only surmise that after his father's bloody death the young Jewish scholar converts not just to a new religion but to a level of aggression he recognized in his father's murderers. For him, the execution of bloody acts becomes identified with the father; and when the father himself is the victim of a vicious, bloody act, young Naphta, by an act of staggering transference, sees in that act simply an escalation of what he has already been predisposed to acknowledge as holy and spiritual. By converting to the Christianity of the Jesuits, he accepts what he perceives to be a higher form of the holy spirit that he has already known. Or, we may surmise that the young Naphta is so traumatized by his father's murder that he will do anything to avoid such a fate for himself. Whichever of these two reasons for conversion is the dominant one (and they are not mutually exclusive), Naphta finds a new and more powerful father to protect him and to legitimize his own visions of bloody revolution and world conversion. That he will eventually turn his pistol to his own brain is just one more instance of his ultimate nature of turning against what is native to the self: first by rejecting his own father, family and religion, and then by turning against his own body. Naphta becomes Leo to escape being the Jewish Leib but finds in the end that his original name was to be his fate.

By adopting the Jesuit order as the foundation for his life, Naphta has internalized the essence of the group that had been his family's oppressor; and he aligns himself completely with his new allegiance. Yet the powerful father that Naphta adopts as his own is an amalgam compounded of a variety of sources that Leo will prove incapable of bringing into a sense of unity: Catholicism, revolution, Communism, Epicurean life. He is a walking paradox; he is "by instinct both a revolutionary and an aristocrat — a socialist, yet obsessed with the dream of participating in a proud, elegant, exclusive, closely circumscribed world" (436). He has been adopted into the world of the Jesuits along with others similarly elected from out of the colonial world: "The cosmopolitanism of the [school] prevented his racial traits from being noticed. There were other young foreigners — Portuguese South Americans, who looked more 'Jewish' than he. . . . The Ethiopian prince who had been admitted at the same time as Naphta was a very elegant-looking Moor with woolly hair" (437). With students from Africa and South America, the Jesuit school is an international collection of compradors, colonials who have been taken in by the grace of the conqueror and who can be used in further offensives against the people from which they have come. The Jesuits had been expelled from Portugal and its empire in 1759 and only reluctantly readmitted to those countries in the ninettenth century. Roman Catholicism is not the form of Christianity practised in Ethiopia, so in some sense these young novices have engaged in a double compromise with their own heritage. To advance in such a group requires the intellectual dexterity to square oneself with the foreign ideologies and rituals antithetical to one's origins, but it also takes, if we are to judge by the example of Naphta, a certain amount of self-aggrandizement and self-promotion. There is no doubt that there is much of this in Naphta's personality; he has shown from early on "vaunting ambition, and an aching desire for more elegant surroundings, a passionate need to move beyond the world of his origins" (434). In a word, he wants to live well, and the life of the colonial subaltern is acceptable to him for the satisfaction of this goal: "He was grateful beyond bounds for the respect shown his origins, his infant Christian faith, his personal status in general" (437). This gratitude is perhaps the hardest aspect of Naphta to grasp, but it accords well with his role as the adopted colonial. He is supremely glad to have escaped the fate to which his origins would have condemned him (a death like that of his father) and is grateful to the Christians for having provided him with a life of elegance and form. But Naphta's adopted fathers are a jealous pack who allow no unconverted fragments to remain, and there are parts of Naphta's person that resist conversion — namely, his body, his "Leib," his original self.

Naphta's logic and argumentative skills are robust, but the Leib on which Christianity has been passionately imprinted is a sick body, and it has been sick from the very start, for within Naphta's body there is a growing weakness that is not, we are told explicitly, the result of the severity of the discipline expected of the young novice. The sickness was there when he entered the order and it only grows worse, because for him it is only "physical ruin" that could bring his troubled soul the peace others in the order find in religious faith (438). To this degree, the disease he suffers is both volitional and congenital. The disease is the means by which Leib refuses to become Leo, to become wholly one with his new mission; and it is his disease that provides him with the only escape from the impossibility of the contradictions and paradoxes that enclose him. Ultimately, however, disease is not enough, and it is only through suicide that he can find the final escape, because suicide is the greatest assertion of the body over its constraints. His is the fate of the comprador who has enjoyed too deeply the pleasures of eating at the conquerors' table, and, like Tantalus eating with the gods, the pleasures prove to be fatal, if not tragic. The violence which spawned his conversion ultimately becomes transformed into the violence exercised against the self. And violence (as we heard Churchill proclaim) is an inherent part of the colonial experience. Naphta embodies this violence completely. He is incapable of understanding the compassion in Settembrini's tattered and dated philosophy, nor can he understand why the humanist refuses to shoot at him in the duel. The colonial mind inexorably falls victim to the violence that enabled its existence in the first place.

And so we have in the duel an allegorical tableau vivant with Hans Castorp, once again undecided, between Naphta and Settembrini, between the representative of the Western tradition with its homoerotic dimensions and the representative of the colonial mind with its violence, immense wealth and luxury. Either side brings with it enormous dangers, but love is always better than hate (Settembrini's room, modest though it is, hovers *above* Naphta's apartment), and self-hate can be as violent as any hatred of the other. But the apparent opposition between Settembrini and Naphta is also not a clean polarity. Just as each of the two mentors proves to have much in common with the other, while at the same time fighting the other with every intellectual weapon available, so, too, the realms of homoeroticism and the colonial are not exclusive of each other. To begin with, the homoerotic desire for the other which Hans displays is not entirely without its colonizing potential. In Hans Castorp's fascination with the Kirghiz eyes of Pribeslav Hippe, which is eventually displaced by his fascination for Mme. Chauchat, there may be the beckoning call of colonial expansion. Once again, it is oil which lurks in the geographic designation by which Hippe is recognized: the Ferghana valley which runs through Kirghizia, Turkestan, and Uzbekistan is another long-known repository of oil reserves. During the years of the Russian empire, the area was called Turkestan; however, the people in that region were and are Kirghiz.[83]

Why should Pribislav's eyes be called "Kirghiz eyes"? Young Hippe is by no means of Kirghiz extraction; we know that he is a mixture of German and Wendisch blood. But in his attraction to his classmate, Hans fantasizes something much more to the East and much more open to colonial expansion. The Wends were, after all, already colonized in the early modern era as Prussia expanded eastward. By the end of the nineteenth century they had long been subsumed into a greater Germany. To cast his feelings into desire, Hans transforms Pribislav into an exotic import; he sees in the blue eyes of his beloved, distant Asian mountains. There are, of course, no mountains in Mecklenburg which is Hippe's actual home. The foreign import is much more appealing than the national product, and it is far more dangerous, as we have seen in Dr. Behrens's cigar. But from his earliest youth Hans has, in fact, been attracted to the foreign and to commercial expansion: "The atmosphere of the metropolitan seaport, the damp atmosphere of global shopkeeping and prosperity, had been the air of life itself for his forefathers. . . . His nose took in the fumes of the harbor, of coal and tar, the pungent odors of the world's produce piled high" (29). The German text is more explicit; what Hans takes in are "Kolonialwaren." And since childhood Hans has liked to pretend that he is in control, to play king of the roost; the German word Mann uses is "regieren." If the British Empire was won on the playing fields of Eton, Hans Castorp has emulated this aspect of English life too. His childhood is filled with games of rule, which, as colonial he will easily transfer to the rule of the colony. And like many a colonialist before him, Hans has transferred his penchant for rule and commercial expansion into the realm of sexual desire.

But territorial colonialism is not the only imperative we find in Hans Castorp's desires. In his sexual composition there is also a definite psychological element that corresponds to a colonizing impetus. In his relationship to his cousin, Hans finds one of his most satisfying emotions by vicariously living through the feelings of Joachim. Hans, lying on his back in Room 34, thinks of Joachim and the expression on Joachim's face earlier in the evening when Hans mentioned "Marusya's physical attributes." Now, having thought of that, Hans is so excited that he cannot fall asleep: "Now that he had such a view, vivid understanding of why Joachim had blushed, the whole world seemed new, and that sense of extravagant joy and hope stirred again deep within him. But he was still waiting for something else, too, although he did not really ask himself what it was" (88).[84] Since, as we learn in the chapter "Humaniora," the blush is yet another example of the behavioral possibilities of erectile tissue, we may read into Hans's interest in Joachim's blush a sexual overtone.

What is Hans waiting for but closer contact with his cousin? The love story of the magic mountain is as much Hans's love for his cousin as it is his love for Clavdia, and there again we find a clear opposition between the imported and the domestic product. Hans may not be able to articulate his love for Joachim, but the evidence is there. When Hans first arrives on the mountain he feels as though his face is burning, perhaps another form of the blush, perhaps something even more significant. He even asks his cousin to touch him: "my face feels awfully flushed — here, feel it, it's burning up" (12). He is immediately embarrassed by the request since he and Joachim do not even use first names with one another. But Hans's deep feelings for Joachim are always with him and they express themselves in an interest in his blush, his erectile tissue, and in the beauty of Joachim's body. At Joachim's medical examination, Hans "was soon lost in thought as he regarded Joachim's upper body . . . the youthful torso, with black hair at the breastbone and along the still powerful arms. . . . Look at him, a perfect adult male, an absolute Apollo Belvedere" (175). From his first appearance at the sanatorium Hans's heart has been pounding, even before he meets Clavdia, and his gesture indicates the emotional resonance of this pounding: "'If I only knew,' Hans Castorp continued, pressing his hands to his breast like a man in love, 'why my heart keeps pounding'" (69). He is speaking to his cousin and they have just been discussing thermometers.

In a recent book, Christopher Lane has cogently drawn the connections between homoeroticism and colonial allegory in British literature of the late nineteenth and early twentieth centuries. He locates two "structural and conceptual" frontiers: "the first lies between the nation and its enemies . . . the second falls between masculine identification and homosexual desire."[85] In attempting to trace these two frontiers along the same lines, Lane suggests that empire only becomes possible when ungovernable sexual desires are transferred onto the colonial other and are steadfastly held in check. But because these suppressions of desire, at home and abroad, are always unstable, the impetus to colonial domination will always be threatened from within. This is the same territory that Mann, some eighty years earlier, was already exploring in *The Magic Mountain*. And in that novel he has presented us a clear choice of desires: that for the colonial and that for the domestic. The fate of colonial involvement is evident in the text from both sides: Naphta, the colonized body, turns upon itself and commits suicide; Mynheer Peeperkorn, when he no longer feels adequate, administers to himself a poison he has brought with him from the colonies and is another suicide. Hans, with his ocean steamships, is precariously poised to engage in colonial adventure comparable to the British experience. But Mann clearly shows the consequences of this imported love. We can only speculate what the outcome might have been had Hans Castorp been able to express his love for Joachim. Perhaps World War I would have been averted.

Notes

[1] Thomas Mann, *The Magic Mountain*, translated by John E. Woods (New York: Knopf, 1995). All page numbers cited in the text refer to this edition. When the German text is necessary, I have quoted from Mann, *Der Zauberberg* (Frankfurt am Main: Fischer, 1963).

[2] As far as I can determine, the title of the novel comes from Nietzsche's *Birth of Tragedy*, § 3, in which Nietzsche describes the home of the Olympian deities.

[3] My choice of the two coordinates is a more limited application of what Vernon Venable ("Structural Elements in *Death in Venice*," in *Thomas Mann: Modern Critical Views*, ed. Harold Bloom [New York: Chelsea House, 1986], 23–24) has described as Mann's more general use of polarities: "The clue to [Mann's] technique lies in the dualism or polarity which always characterizes [his] subject-matter. Such large antitheses as life and death, time and individuality, fertility and decay, flesh and spirit, invariably constitute the themes of his novels. Mann never allows this dualism to become vitiated, for it is the formal and operative principle of his aesthetic. He never prefers one term of his antithesis to the other, for his interest is not in arguing theses but in developing themes. Hence we misunderstand his fiction if we isolate individual symbols from their dualistic context."

[4] An early example of such a claim, from a letter to Max Rychner (August 22, 1922): "das Buch als ein Versuch verstanden werden kann, die Linie des Bildungs- und Entwicklungsromans, die Wilhelm Meister-Linie fortzusetzen."

In *Dichter über ihre Dichtungen,* eds. Hans Wysling and Marianne Fischer, (Passau: Heimeran/Fischer Verlag, 1975). This edition is hereafter referred to as *Dichtungen.*

[5] Mann himself saw the genesis of the book as temptation resisted. When he was visiting his wife at a sanatorium in Switzerland, it was suggested to Mann that he, too, had a weak spot in his lungs: "wenn ich Hans Castorp gewesen wäre, vielleicht meinem ganzen Leben eine andere Wendung gegeben hätte" (*Dichtungen,* 555). In resisting the temptation to see himself as sick, Mann creates a surrogate for himself to explore the possibilities of being seduced.

[6] Friedrich Nietzsche, *The Gay Science,* § 125.

[7] Curiously, the title of the book Hans is reading is given as *Ocean steamships.* If the title were genuinely English, it would have to be *Ocean Steamships.* In the alteration of the proper English format, is there already a hint of a one-word title and a sense of a pending German appropriation of the English contents?

[8] In his own approach to religion, Mann formulated a skepticism that could be extended to the interpretation of the world: "Glaube? Unglaube? Ich weiß kaum, was das eine ist und was das andere. Ich wüßte tatsächlich nicht zu sagen, ob ich mich für einen gläubigen Menschen halte oder für einen ungläubigen. Tiefste Skepsis in Bezug auf beides... ist all mein Ausweis, wenn man mich katechisiert.... Die Stellung des Menschen im Kosmos, sein Anfang, seine Herkunft, sein Ziel, das ist das große Geheimnis... ich bin nicht weit entfernt, [*Der Zauberberg*] ein religiöses Buch zu nennen..." (in "Fragment über das Religiöse" [1931], *Dichtungen,* 535–536.)

[9] It seems that Mann, when invited to read from his novel, liked particularly to read the chapter "The Thermometer" which records Hans's first oral encounter with the instrument: "He picked up the red case with a smile and opened it. The glass instrument lay bedded like a precious gem in its red velvet cushion... the lower, tapered end was filled with lustrous, glistening mercury.... He took the instrument from its case, examined it and walked restlessly with it back and forth in the room a few times. His heart was beating fast and strong.... [He had] the idea of looking in on Joachim, but then gave that up... and quickly stuck the thermometer in his mouth, the mercury tip under his tongue... his lips tucked tightly around it to keep air out" (164–165). Hans's nervous act may be a coy method of relaying Mann's own sexual interests to his audience: "Thomas Mann hatte das Kapitel 'Das Thermometer' am 19.1.1921 im Lesezirkel Hottingen, Zürich, und am 19.2.1921 in der Aula des Werner-Siemens-Gymnasiums in Berlin gelesen" (*Dichtungen,* 462–463). We must bear in mind Mann's tendency to be attracted to the young men who came to his readings; Anthony Heilbut, *Thomas Mann: Eros and Literature* (New York: Knopf, 1995) records one such instance: "In March 1919, he becomes aroused by a young man who attends one of his readings. He is a 'Hermes-like dandy' with 'a slight, youthful figure... a prettiness and foolishness that amounts to a real classical 'godlike' look. I don't know his name and it doesn't matter" (312). For Mann, reading aloud

Hans Castorp's experience with the thermometer in the presence of such young men must have been a savored act of tongue in cheek.

[10] The relationship of Mann to Freud is a volume unto itself; let it suffice here to say that at the time of publication of *The Magic Mountain*, Mann showed a general skepticism about the uses of psychoanalysis: "Auch in meinem eben herausgegebenen Zeitroman *Der Zauberberg* spielt [Psychoanalyse] ihre Rolle. Dr. Krokowski, wie ihr Agent heißt, ist zwar ein bißchen komisch. Aber seine Komik ist vielleicht nur eine Schadloshaltung für tiefere Zugeständnisse, die der Autor im Inneren seiner Werke der Psychoanalyse macht" (*Dichtungen*, 499).

[11] Mann coyly shows his own perverse recalcitrance to be interpreted in this fashion in his reply to Harry Slochower's reading of sexual meaning into Peeperkorn's finger gestures: "Die Auffassung von Peeperkorns Finger-Gebärde als Phallus-symbolisch ist meinem Bewußtsein fremd. Sie haben die Interpretation schon in Ihrem Büchlein gebracht [*Three Ways of Modern Man*, New York, 1937], und ich habe sie als Über-Interpretation empfunden" (*Dichtungen*, 551). This from the man who gave us Hippe's pencil and its treasured shavings!

[12] Perhaps only an English critic such as T. J. Reed would have an empirical bias strong enough to question the long discussions of time: "The limitations of his [Hans Castorp's] learning are made plain — in the hoariness of his philosophical musings (the universe repeated in the atoms of a dog's leg) or in his very commonplace reflections on the nature of time." Reed finds a companion in Ziolkowski, who is "rare in being ready to dismiss these [discussions of time] as 'not really very original.' The usual response is to be deferentially awe-struck" (249). I side with these two critics.

[13] In his otherwise excellent study of the novel, Helmut Koopmann in his *Die Entwicklung des "Intellektuellen Romans" bei Thomas Mann: Untersuchungen zur Struktur von "Buddenbrooks," "Königliche Hoheit," und "Der Zauberberg"* (Bonn: Bouvier Verlag Herbert Grundmann, 1980) shows the traditional reverence: "Die Zeit, Urelement des epischen Erzählens, wird — etwa wie im 'Zauberberg' — in sich selbst problematisch, da sie zugleich Gegenstand und Mittel der Erzählung ist" (35).

[14] "... ebenso fern wie bei der Benutzung gewisser Portraitähnlichkeiten [ist] der Gedanke an die Wirkungen des 'Schlüsselromans'" (*Dichtungen*, 555).

[15] In writing to an American reader, Mann apologized for putting much of the dialogue of the "Walpurgisnacht" chapter in French; his explanation could be taken as applying to the whole book: "Quite particular reasons were necessary to induce me to do [this]. This scene needed the veil of a foreign idiom" (*Dichtungen*, 563). The French language is not the only veil in the novel.

[16] "Du hast recht mit der Annahme, daß ich schon in meiner Jugendnovelle *Tonio Kröger*, die 'heilige russische Literatur' genannt habe, von jeher aufs dankbarste verbunden bin" (*Dichtungen*, 569).

[17] Mihail Lermontov, *A Hero of Our Time*, translated by Vladimir and Dmitri Nabokov (New York: Doubleday, 1958).

[18] Susan Layton, *Russian Literature and Empire: Conquest of the Caucasus from Pushkin to Tolstoy* (Cambridge: Cambridge UP, 1994), 192. Layton remarks that this "frontier territory quickly acquired a stylized character to become the 'Caucasian Alps.'" She gives eloquent evidence to the fact that Daghestan was, for the Russian colonist, a "land of fruit," a "paradise on earth" (178).

[19] Layton, 193.

[20] Layton, p. 114.

[21] "These Baku springs were originally worshiped, the natives believing them to be manifestations of the gods.... There is still in Baku a temple, or rather the remains of a temple, where the sacred fire has never ceased to burn," according to John Mitzakis, *The Russian Oil Fields and Petroleum Industry* (London: Pall Mall Press, 1911), 22. One could say that for Clavdia, Daghestan is the site of her "old flame."

[22] Mitzakis notes the location of Daghestani oil reserves and cites 1893 as the date when fields in nearby Grosny were brought into production (28–29). At the time Mitzakis was writing, many sites in the south Caucasus were known to exist but had not yet been brought into modern production, which implies that oil exploration was active in Daghestan in the decade 1900–1910.

[23] Reinhold Nimptsch, *Beiträge zum russischen Erdölproblem*, Neue Folge, Heft 3 of *Quellen und Studien, Abteilung Wirtschaft of the Osteuropa-Institut in Breslau* (Berlin: Hermann Sack, 1925). Nimptsch summarizes: "Der sehr erhebliche Anteil Rußlands an der Gesamtproduktion läßt für die Vorkriegszeit eine entsprechende Bedeutung Rußlands für die Versorgung der Welt mit Erdölproduktion vermuten" (7).

[24] In 1918, while writing *The Magic Mountain*, Mann requested an article he had read earlier about the Entente, "Der Artikel muß von Hofmiller gewesen sein und behandelte das europäische u. im Besonderen das Entente-Mauerertum in seinem Verhältnis zu Deutschland, zum Krieg, zum Kriege gegen Deutschland" (*Dichtungen*, 457). The walls of the Entente around Germany are associated with the *Freimaurer* of which Settembrini is a representative.

[25] Thomas Mann, *Death in Venice and Other Stories*, translated by David Luke (New York: Bantam, 1988), 195. *The Magic Mountain* began as a comic piece complementary to *Death in Venice*, and it is not surprising that they share a common historical setting.

[26] The name of Clavdia as "key" becomes even more crucial when we remember the musical nature of the novel's structure. Music must exist in a given key; is she then the key or clef in which the music is to be played? Of course, "Chauchat" sounds like the French for a "hot cat," but I am more intrigued by other linguistic possibilities, such as the Russian adaptation of the name and its linguistic symmetricality with "Caucasus." Clavdia's return to the Caucasus is, then, a return to her own name, a circularity which fits well with her role as inaccessible key.

[27] *Dichtungen*, 517.

[28] Siegmar Tyroff, *Namen bei Thomas Mann in den Erzählungen und den Romanen "Buddenbrooks", "Königliche Hoheit," "Der Zauberberg"* (Frankfurt am Main: Herbert Lang, 1975), 178. Tyroff's motto for his work is from a letter Mann wrote June 29, 1918 to his friend Ernst Bertram and which fairly sums up Mann's great attention to names: "Ich brauche Namen!"

[29] Paul M. Kennedy, *The Rise of the Anglo-German Antagonism, 1860–1914* (London: George Allen and Unwin, 1982), 413.

[30] Kennedy, 317.

[31] Kennedy, 431, quotes Spring-Rice, a contemporary British politician: "Germany is a mystery. Does she simply want the destruction of England, pure and simple, as is advocated in her press and by the university teachers, from Treitschke downwards — or does she want definite things which England can help her to get?" This ambiguous attitude toward England is seen in Castorp's ambiguous character as English but not English.

[32] In a speech delivered at the time of the 1913–1914 quarrels over the naval estimates, quoted in Kennedy, 467.

[33] When discussing the novel Mann had several pat formulas to which he returned time and again, referring to the large themes of love, death, music, disease, etc., but at least once he gives a tantalizing glimpse into his more craftsmanlike preoccupation with details; on that occasion, when asked about his relationship to Proust, he replied, "Das liegt wohl an der Proustschen Art, den Alltag zu romantisieren, das nichtige Detail zu heben und merkwürdig zu machen. Auch ich bin weniger für die großen als für die kleinen Dinge. Daher das Mikroskopische bei Proust und mir" (*Dichtungen*, 507). It is a refreshing confession in the light of the usual more expansive explanations.

[34] See, for example, Acts 16:1 in Luther's translation: "Er kam aber gen Derben und Lustran. Und sihe, ein Jünger war da selbs, mit namen Timotheus."

[35] John Boswell, *Christianity, Social Tolerance and Homosexuality: Gay People in Western Europe from the Beginning of the Christian Era to the Fourteenth Century* (Chicago: U of Chicago P, 1980), 106–108, offers a discussion of the possible interpretations of words used by Paul in 1 Corinthians 6:9 and 1 Timothy 1:10 that might allude to homosexuality. Martin DiBelius and Hans Conzelmann in the *Pastoral Epistles* (Philadelphia: Fortress Press, 1972) are surprisingly uncurious about the passionate tone Paul (or the pseudo-Paul) adopts here: "The paradoxical coupling of mourning and joy is an attempt to recapture Paul's feelings.... But the change from one to the other is more abrupt here" (98). We would like to know more about Paul's feelings for Timothy.

[36] See DiBelius and Conzelmann, especially pp. 1–10, for a review of the arguments for and against Pauline authorship.

[37] See Oscar Seidlin, "Mynheer Peeperkorn and the Lofty Game of Numbers," in Harold Bloom, ed., *Thomas Mann: Modern Critical Views* (New York: Chelsea House, 1986), 189.

[38] The Pauline circumcision also reminds us of Hans's shaving Hippe's pencil. Given Paul's personal role in the act of Timothy's circumcision, it is a wonder that Mann does not mention here the cigar clippers which must inevitably initiate any session of smoking.

[39] It would be worth considering whether the entire scene is in fact a playful meditation on the comment of Freud, "Sometimes a cigar is just a cigar." Mann renders an entire ontology and taxonomy of cigar smoking, with every suggestion of sexual meaning and innuendo, only to scurry back to Freud's dictum for fatherly protection from dirty-minded critics.

[40] See Frederick A. Lubich, "Thomas Manns *Der Zauberberg*: Spukschloß der Großen Mutter oder Die Männerdämmerung des Abendlandes," *DVjs* (1993): 729–763. Lubich argues that the novel is "repräsentativster Rückzug der machtgeschützten Innerlichkeit ins hermetisch verschlosssene Mutterreich" (731). Claudia Chauchat is ultimately the great representative of this sought-after "spectral Mother," but Clavdia, as Karl Werner Böhm has shown (*Zwischen Selbstzucht und Verlangen: Thomas Mann und das Stigma der Homosexualität* [Würzburg: Königshausen und Neumann, 1991]), displays far too many traits of gender ambiguity to be considered a serious candidate for the role of a Magna Mater: "Clavdia Chauchat bringt Castorps Re-homo-sexualisiserungsprozeß in Gang. Sie und Hippe verschmelzen auf der Leitmotivebene zu einem hermaphroditischen Wesen mit männlichen... und weiblichen·Determinanten, einem Pseudoandrogyn, denn was die beiden Figuren verbindet ist kein 'androgynes Mysterium', sondern die Traumlogik von Verdichtungen und Verschiebung" (355).

[41] In one of the few fragments of the *Zauberberg* manuscript which survive, we can see that Mann originally made allusion to Hans Castorp's earlier sexual experience (and that experience was cautiously left without a specifically gendered partner); but in the final version Mann carefully deleted this passage. See James F. White, *The Yale Zauberberg Manuscript: Rejected Sheets Once Part of Thomas Mann's Novel* (Bern and Munich: Francke, 1980), C-39.

[42] An amusing event took place in 1925, shortly after the publication of the novel, when a cigar firm from Mannheim asked Mann to endorse its cigars and to allow his name and picture, as well as the word *Zauberberg*, to appear in advertisements for the brand. Mann agreed but was glad when nothing came of the enterprise since he had begun to fear that the product might be of inferior quality.

[43] The German is far more intense and suggestive: "Behrens war entzückt, geschmeichelt bis zur Begeisterung. Er wurde sogar rot vor Vergnügen, und seine Augen schienen ihre Tränen diesmal vergießen zu wollen."

[44] In fact, in the same manuscript fragment we find that originally Mann had planned to give Behrens a living and domineering wife with the medieval name "Irmentrudis," but she, like Hans Castorp's sexual experience, is deleted from the final text. See White, xvi.

[45] Mann, *Death in Venice and Other Stories*. "Treatment? . . . Oh, I am having a little electrical treatment. It's really nothing worth mentioning. I will tell you, dear madame, why I am here: it is on account of the style" (102).

[46] Ralph Hewins, *Mr. Five Per Cent: The Biography of Calouste Gulbenkian* (New York: Rhinehart, 1958), 47–49. In September of 1918 Turkey actually took over the oil fields of Baku, cf. Robert E. Ebel, *Communist Trade in Oil and Gas* (New York: Praeger, 1970), 14.

[47] James Joll recounts the history of the railway: "In 1889 a German group headed by the Deutsche Bank had won a concession to build the first section of a railway across Anatolia; and in 1899 they had obtained from the Ottoman government approval for the next stage. In 1903 the German promoters were backed by the German government and the Kaiser, . . . but they were short of capital for such a large and expensive project and tried to raise money in London and Paris." (James Joll, *The Origins of the First World War* [London and New York: Longman, 1984], 158–159).

[48] Daniel Yergin, *The Prize: The Epic Quest for Oil, Money and Power* (New York: Simon and Schuster, 1991), 186.

[49] Joll, 189.

[50] Yergin, 185.

[51] Joll, 160–161.

[52] The graphic tone of the scene is too much for translators to accept at face value; when Hans drags Clavdia's portrait along with him into another part of the room, Hofrat Behrens says: "Was machen Sie denn, was schleppen Sie sich denn mit dem Schinken?" Woods translates blandly, "Dragging my daubings around with you?," while Lowe-Porter uncharacteristically leaves the ham in: "Hullo, where are you going with the ham?" But the "Hullo" maintains her usual vitiating Victorianization of the dialogue.

[53] Again, the German is more sexual, with its undertones of penetration: "Förmlich was Durchdrängerisches." And "durchdrängerisch" is the word Joachim uses to describe Hans Castorp's new inquisitive mode. Hans is penetrating areas which have until now remained closed to him. Translating this penetration as "kicking over the traces" is accurate but misleadingly quaint.

[54] Hans's choice of a career is indeed a sign of the times: "A human being lives out not only his personal life as an individual, but also, consciously or subconsciously, the lives of his epoch and contemporaries" (31).

[55] Aristotle, *De generatione animalium*, Book I, chapter 18.

[56] It is well known that a reading of Walt Whitman helped Mann to turn the direction of *Der Zauberberg* toward a greater acceptance of Western democracy. It would be interesting to know if Mann read further in classic American literature. The whiteness of the whale is as grand a landscape for mystical insight as the snow at the heart of *Der Zauberberg*.

[57] Cf. George Byron Bridges, *Homoeroticism and the Father-Son Relation in the Principal Works of Herman Melville and Thomas Mann* (diss., Urbana, Illinois, 1983): "To some extent, Hans Castorp's story confirms the oedipal conflict theory as an inexorable law. The significance of the *Bruderbund* can be grasped only in the context of a 'universal' hostility and rivalry between father and son. . . . By springing over a generation the author spares his Protagonist the conflict that other boys must experience and resolve one way or another to acquire their identity as males" (259).

[58] It was in the university fraternities that the German nationalist movement found its most fervent, even fanatical expression at the time of German unification.

[59] "The Making of the Magic Mountain," in Lowe-Porter's translation of *The Magic Mountain* (New York: Vintage, 1992), 728. Henceforth referred to as Lowe-Porter.

[60] Eve Sedgwick, *Between Men: English Literature and Male Homosocial Desire* (New York: Columbia UP, 1985), 219.

[61] Sedgwick, 21.

[62] A more recent and hilarious use of this traditional triangle is Fassbinder's *Querelle*, where the triangle man-woman-man is completely collapsed as one sailor sexually attacks another by telling him, "This is what I'd do if your sister were here." The "triangle" is reduced to the most implausible subterfuge and, indeed, proves to be really no triangle at all, just two men having sex.

[63] Lowe-Porter, 723.

[64] *Dichtungen*, 496 (23.4.1925).

[65] Sedgwick, 27.

[66] *Dichtungen*, 496.

[67] Lowe-Porter, 721. Mann goes to great lengths to describe precisely the financial underpinnings of Hans Castorp's stay at the sanatorium. We know his exact income, the exact cost of a month at the Berghof, what interest Hans is deriving from his capital investment, how much money he needs beyond his inheritance to live the life he chooses for himself, etc. These economic details are perhaps another inheritance from the English style of novel as represented by, for example, Jane Austen, where a precise knowledge of income and investment is intimately bound up with a close examination of personality. By contrast, look at the imprecise idea we have of Aschenbach's financial affairs.

[68] Lowe-Porter, 722.

[69] Hans Wisskirchen, *Zeitgeschichte im Roman: Zu Thomas Manns "Zauberberg" und "Doktor Faustus,"* Thomas-Mann-Studien, 6 (Bern: Francke, 1986), quotes Mann on this subject: "In konsequenter Druchführung der Lehre Schopenhauers, die das historisch sich Vollziehende als einen Fingerzieg des Schicksals bewertet, heißt es am 19.11.1918 im Tagebuch: 'Wirklich bereue ich zur Zeit

alle Wünsche, die ich in Betreff deutscher Herrschaft hegte. Dies Volk hat sich als tief ungeeignet zur Macht erwiesen'" (43).

[70] Lowe-Porter, 725.

[71] *Dichtungen*, 506.

[72] See Seidlin, 184.

[73] Heilbut, 313 and 369.

[74] Heilbut, 420.

[75] *Dichtungen*, 538.

[76] "Bei der Konzeption der Figur . . . hatte Thomas Mann wohl u.a. an die Gestalt des neapolitanischen Revolutionärs Luigi Settembrini gedacht. Vermutlich hat er aber dessen Memoiren, die 1881 . . . erschienen waren, nicht gekannt" (*Dichtungen*, 543). *Luigi* is, of course, like *Lodovico*, another Italian form of the same *Ludwig*.

[77] Heilbut, 434.

[78] Dante's *Inferno*, translated by Laurence Binyon (London: Macmillan, 1933), canto 15. The relationship between the *Inferno* and *The Magic Mountain* may be more than casual. James White (Yale Manuscript, p. xv.) points out that the numerical arrangement of the sections of the novel's first volume (Vorsatz + 33) are the same as Dante's arrangement in the Inferno (1+33). White believes that this structure was part of the composition of the novel from the first.

[79] Richard Kay, "The Sin(s) of Brunetto Latini," *Dante Studies* 112 (1994): "In the Bible . . . Sodom is the image of a community that has been perverted by its leaders, and moreover the perversion attributed to Sodom in the Bible is not primarily sexual and in fact may not be sexual at all . . . I suggest . . . that the sin of Brunetto Latini consisted of misleading Florence and other Italian communities in a form of political life that Dante regarded as being contrary to nature" (19). And Peter Amour, "*Inferno XV* in *Dante's 'Divine Comedy': Introductory Readings, I: Inferno*, ed. Tibor Wlassics (Charlottesville: U of Virginia P, 1990): "Of course, if one interpolates an exclusively homosexual definition of the sin of Sodom from canto xi, one can find hidden references to it *ad libitum*" (196). Such a libidinal search might in fact prove to be an intriguing project.

[80] Mitzakis (1911) ends his survey of Russian oil production by quoting a few lines from J. D. Henry's remarkable book *Baku*. In this long and poetic passage, Henry says that there is no place on earth as rich in oil as Baku; he compares Baku to other sites renowned for their oil: "In oil, Baku is incomparable. I know of no oil city that will compare with it, either in subterranean wealth, or, to leave the commercial for a moment, in wealth of history and tradition, legend and story. Los Angeles, chief town in the oil fields of far-away California; Petrolea, Canada's petroleum capital; Beaumont, the four-year-old creation of Texas oil; Boryslaw, chief of the widely scattered group of oil fields in *Galicia, home of the ancient Poles*" (28, emphasis mine). Clearly, by 1911 Galicia was well known for its oil and petroleum industry.

[81] Robert James Forbes, *Bitumen and Petroleum in Antiquity* (Leiden: E. J. Brill, 1936), 96–109.

[82] Leo was one of the most important of the late Classical popes, consecrated in 440 and responsible for greatly increasing the power of the papacy. It is a name, in other words, that conjures the more militant side of Christian faith.

[83] Mitzakis (1911) describes Ferghana: "Russian Turkestan. The Province of Ferghana, situated in the very heart of Central Asia, comprises many known oil-bearing districts, of which Maily-Say, near the town of Namangam, is probably the most important. This district, if properly developed, promises to become in the near future an important producer" (32).

[84] "Extravagant joy and hope" are the feelings, too, of Aschenbach when he learns that he is forced to remain in Venice and when he begins to feel that Tadzio is not indifferent to his interest (*Death in Venice and Other Stories*, 228, 237).

[85] Christopher Lane, *The Ruling Passion: British Colonial Allegory and the Paradox of Homosexual Desire* (Durham, NC: Duke UP, 1995), 213.

SUSAN SONTAG

11: Pilgrimage

EVERYTHING THAT SURROUNDS MY MEETING with him has the color of shame.

December, 1947. I was fourteen, steeped in vehement admirations and impatience for the reality to which I would travel once released from that long prison sentence, my childhood.

End almost in sight. Already in my junior year, I'd finish high school while still fifteen. And then, and then . . . all would unfold. Meanwhile I was waiting, I was doing time (still fourteen!), recently transferred from the desert of southern Arizona to the coastland of Southern California. Another new setting, with fresh possibilities of escape — I welcomed that. My peripatetic widowed mother's remarriage, in 1945, to a handsome, bemedalled and beshrapnelled Army Air Forces ace who'd been sent to the healing desert to cap a year-long hospitalization (he'd been shot down five days after D Day) appeared to have grounded *her*. The following year our newly assembled family — mother, stepfather, kid sister, dog, notionally salaried Irish nanny left over from the old days, plus the resident alien, myself — had vacated the stucco bungalow on a dirt road on the outskirts of Tucson where we'd been joined by Captain Sontag for a cozy shuttered cottage with rosebush hedges and three birch trees at the entrance of the San Fernando Valley, where I was currently pretending to sit still for a facsimile of family life and the remainder of my unconvincing childhood. On weekends my now out-of-uniform but still militarily perky stepfather marshalled sirloins and butter-brushed corn tightly wrapped in tinfoil on the patio barbecue; I ate and ate — how could I not, as I watched my morose, bony mother fiddling with her food? His animation was as threatening as her apathy. They couldn't start playing family now — too late! I was off and running, even if I looked every inch the baby-faced, overgrown elder daughter effusively munching her fourth ear of corn; I was already gone. (In French one can announce, while lingering unconscionably, *Je suis moralement partie*.) There was just this last bit of childhood to get past. For the duration, that wartime locution that gave me my first model of condescending to present time in favor of the better future, for the duration it was permissible to appear to enjoy their recreations, avoid conflict, gobble their food. The truth was, I dreaded conflict. And I was always hungry.

I felt I was slumming, in my own life. My task was to ward off the drivel (I felt I was drowning in drivel) — the jovial claptrap of classmates and teachers, the maddening bromides I heard at home. And the weekly comedy shows festooned with canned laughter, the treacly Hit Parade, the hysterical narratings of baseball games and prize fights — radio, whose racket filled the living room on weekday evenings and much of Saturday and Sunday, was an endless torment. I ground my teeth, I twirled my hair, I gnawed at my nails, I was polite. Though untempted by the new, tribal delights of suburban childhood that had quickly absorbed my sister, I didn't think of myself as a misfit, for I assumed my casing of affability was being accepted at face value. (Here the fact that I was a girl seeps through.) What other people thought of me remained a dim consideration, since other people seemed to me astonishingly unseeing as well as uncurious, while I longed to learn everything: the exasperating difference between me and everyone I'd ever met — so far. I was certain there was a multitude like me, elsewhere. And it never occurred to me that I could be stopped.

If I didn't mope or sulk, it was not just because I thought complaining wouldn't do any good. It was because the flip side of my discontent — what, indeed, throughout my childhood had made me so discontented — was rapture. Rapture I couldn't share. And whose volume was increasing steadily: since this last move I was having near-nightly bouts of jubilation. For in the eight houses and apartments of my life before this one I had never had a bedroom to myself. Now I had it, and without asking. A door of my own. Now I could read for hours by flashlight after being sent to bed and told to turn off the light, not inside a tent of bedclothes but outside the covers.

I'd been a demon reader from earliest childhood (to read was to drive a knife into their lives), and therefore a promiscuous one: fairy tales and comics (my comics collection was vast), Compton's Encyclopedia, the Bobbsey Twins and other Stratemeyer series, books about astronomy, chemistry, China, biographies of scientists, all of Richard Halliburton's travel books, and a fair number of mostly Victorian-era classics. Then, drifting to the rear of a stationery and greeting-card store in the village that was downtown Tucson in the mid-nineteen-forties, I toppled into the deep well of the Modern Library. Here were standards, and here, at the back of each book, was my first list. I had only to acquire and read (ninety-five cents for the small ones, a dollar twenty-five for the Giants) —

my sense of possibility unfolding, with each book, like a carpenter's rule. And within a month of arriving in Los Angeles I tracked down a real bookstore, the first of my bookstore-besotted life: the Pickwick, on Hollywood Boulevard, where I went every few days after school to read on my feet through some more of world literature — buying when I could, stealing when I dared. Each of my occasional thefts cost me weeks of self-revilement and dread of future humiliation, but what could I do, given my puny allowance? Odd that I never thought of going to a library. I had to acquire them, see them in rows along a wall of my tiny bedroom. My household deities. My spaceships.

Afternoons I went hunting for treasure: I'd always disliked going home directly from school. But in Tucson, visits to the stationery store excepted, the most cheering postponement I'd come up with was a walk out along the Old Spanish Trail toward the Tanque Verde foothills, where I could examine close up the fiercest saguaros and prickly pears, scrutinize the ground for arrowheads and snakes, pocket pretty rocks, imagine being lost or a sole survivor, wish I were an Indian. Or the Lone Ranger. Here in California there was a different space to roam and I had become a different Lone Ranger. Most days after school I boarded the trolley on Chandler Avenue to hasten into, not away from, town. Within a few blocks of the enchanted crossroads of Hollywood Boulevard and Highland Avenue lay my little agora of one- and two-story buildings: the Pickwick; a record store whose proprietors let me spend hours each week in the listening booths, gorging myself on their wares; an international newsstand where militant browsing yielded me *Partisan Review, Kenyon Review, Sewanee Review, Politics, Accent, Tiger's Eye, Horizon*; and a storefront through whose open door one afternoon I unselfconsciously trailed two people who were beautiful in a way I'd never seen, thinking I was entering a gym, which turned out to be the rehearsal quarters of the dance company of Lester Horton and Bella Lewitzky. O golden age! It not only was, I knew it was. Soon I was sipping at a hundred straws. In my room I wrote imitation stories and kept real journals; made lists of words to fatten my vocabulary, made lists of all kinds; played conductor to my records; read myself sore-eyed each night.

And soon I had friends, too, and not very much older than myself — to my surprise. Friends with whom I could speak of some of what absorbed and enraptured me. I didn't expect them to have read as much as I had; it was enough that they were willing to read the books I lent them. And in music, even better, I was the novice — what bliss! It was my desire to be taught, even more thwarted than my desire to share, that made me my first friends: two seniors at whom I flung myself soon after entering this new school as a sophomore, whose taste in music was far superior to mine. Not only were they each proficient on an instrument — Elaine played the flute, Mel the piano — but they had done all their growing up here, in Southern California, with its infusion of refugee virtuosi, employed in the full symphony orchestras maintained by the major film studios, who could be heard at night playing the canonical and the contemporary chamber repertory to small gatherings scattered across a hundred miles. Elaine and Mel were part of that audience, with tastes elevated and made eccentrically rigorous by the distinct bias of high musical culture in Los Angeles in the nineteen-forties — there was chamber music, and then there was everything else. (Opera was so low on the scale of musical goodness it was not worth mentioning.)

Each friend was a best friend — I knew no other way. Besides my music mentors, who started at U.C.L.A. the following autumn, there was a fellow-sophomore, my romantic comrade for the remaining two years of high school, who was to accompany me to the college I had already elected at thirteen as my destiny — the College of the University of Chicago. Peter, fatherless and a refugee (he was part Hungarian, part French), had had a life even more marked by displacements than my own. His father had been arrested by the Gestapo, and Peter and his mother escaped Paris to the South of France and from there, via Lisbon, to New York in 1941; after a spell in a Connecticut boarding school, he was now reunited here with the very single, tanned, red-haired Henya (whom I acknowledged to be as young-looking, if not as beautiful, as my own mother). Our friendship started in the school cafeteria with an exchange of boastful anecdotes about our glamorously dead fathers. Peter was the one with whom I argued about socialism and Henry Wallace, and with whom I held hands and wept through *Open City, Symphonie Pastorale, The Children of Paradise, Mädchen in Uniform, The Baker's Wife, Brief Encounter*, and *Beauty and the Beast* at the Laurel, the theatre we'd discovered that showed foreign movies. We went bicycling in the canyons and in Griffith Park and rolled about, embracing, in the weeds — Peter's great loves, as I remember, were his mother, me, and his racing bicycle. He was dark-haired, skinny, nervous, tall. I, though always the youngest, was invariably the tallest girl in the class and taller than most of the boys and, for all my outlandish independence of judgment on matters Olympian, on the matter of height had the most abjectly conventional view. A boyfriend had to be not just a best friend but taller, and only Peter qualified.

The other best friend I made, also a sophomore, though at another high school, and also to enter the University of Chicago with me, was Merrill. Cool and chunky and blond, he had all the trappings of "cute," a "dish," a "dreamboat," but I, with my unerring eye for loners (under all disguises), had promptly seen that he was smart, too. Really smart.

Therefore capable of separateness. He had a low sweet voice and a shy smile and eyes that smiled sometimes without his mouth — Merrill was the only one of my friends I doted on. I loved to look at him. I wanted to merge with him or for him to merge with me, but I had to respect the insuperable barrier: he was several inches shorter than I was. The other barriers were harder to think about. He could be secretive, calculating (even literally so: numbers figured often in his conversation), and sometimes, to me, insufficiently moved by what I found moving. I was impressed by how practical he was, and how calm he remained when I got flustered. I couldn't tell what he really felt about the quite plausible family — mother, real father, younger brother (who was something of a math prodigy), even grandparents — with which he came equipped. Merrill didn't like to talk about feelings, while I was seething with the desire to express mine, preferably by focusing feeling away from myself onto something I admired or felt indignant about.

We loved in tandem. Music first — he'd had years of piano. (His brother played the violin, which made me equally envious, though it was for piano lessons that I'd implored my mother — rather, stopped imploring my mother — years before.) He introduced me to getting into concerts free by ushering (at the Hollywood Bowl in the summer), and I made him a regular at the Monday chamber-music series "Evenings on the Roof," to which I'd been brought by Elaine and Mel. We were building our nearly identical, ideal record collections (on 78s, happily unaware that this was the last year before L.P.s), and joined forces often in the cool, dark listening booths of the Highland Record Store. Sometimes he came to my house, even if my parents were there. Or I went to his house; the name of his frumpy, hospitable mother — I remember finding this embarrassing — was Honey.

Our privacy was in cars. Merrill had a real driver's license, while mine was the "junior" license one could hold from fourteen to sixteen in California then, entitling me to drive my parents' cars only. Since parents' cars were the only ones available to us, the difference was moot. In his parents' blue Chevy or my mother's green Pontiac we perched at night on the rim of Mulholland Drive, the great plain of twinkling lights below like an endless airport, oblivious of the mating couples in cars parked around us, pursuing our own pleasures. We pitched themes at each other in our inexact treble voices — "O.K., listen. Now, what's this?" We quizzed each other's memory of Köchel listings, knowing by heart long stretches of the six hundred and twenty-six. We debated the merits of the Busch and the Budapest Quartets (I'd become an intolerant partisan of the Budapest); discussed whether it would be immoral, after what I'd heard from Elaine and Mel about Gieseking's Nazi past, to buy his Debussy recordings; tried to convince ourselves that we had liked the pieces played on the prepared piano by John Cage at last Monday's "Evenings on the Roof" concert; and talked about how many years to give Stravinsky.

This last was one of our recurrent problems. Toward John Cage's squawks and thumps we were deferential — we knew we were supposed to appreciate ugly music; and we listened devoutly to the Toch, the Krenek, the Hindemith, the Webern, the Schoenberg, whatever: we had enormous appetites and strong stomachs. But it was Stravinsky's music we sincerely loved. And since Stravinsky seemed grotesquely old (we had actually seen him on two Mondays in the small auditorium of the Wilshire Ebell, when Ingolf Dahl was conducting something of his), our fears for his life had given rise to a compelling fantasy à deux about dying for our idol. The question, a question we discussed often, was: what were the terms of the sacrifice we so relished contemplating? How many more years of life for Stravinsky would justify our dying now, on the spot?

Twenty years? Obviously. But that was easy and, we agreed, too good to hope for. Twenty years granted to the ancient homely person we saw Stravinsky to be — that was simply an unimaginably large number of years to the fourteen-year-old I was and the sixteen-year-old Merrill was in 1947. (How lovely that I.S. lived even longer than this.) To insist on getting Stravinsky twenty more years in exchange for our lives hardly seemed to show our fervor.

Fifteen more years? Of course.

Ten? You bet.

Five? We began to waver. But not to agree seemed like a failure of respect, of love. What was my life or Merrill's — not just our paltry California-high-school students' lives but the useful, achievement-strewn lives we thought were awaiting us — compared to making it possible for the world to enjoy five years more of Stravinsky's creations? Five years, O.K.

Four? I sighed. Merrill, let's go on.

Three? To die for only three additional years?

Usually we settled on four — a minimum of four. Yes, to give Stravinsky four more years either one of us was prepared right then and there to die.

READING AND LISTENING TO MUSIC: the triumphs of being not myself. That nearly everything I admired was produced by people who were dead (or very old) or from elsewhere, ideally Europe, seemed inevitable to me.

I accumulated gods. What Stravinsky was for music Thomas Mann became for literature. At my Aladdin's cave, at the Pickwick, on November 11, 1947 — taking the book down from the shelf just now, I find the date written on the flyleaf in the italic script I was then practicing — I bought *The Magic Mountain*.

I began it that night, and for the first few nights had trouble breathing as I read. For this was not just another book I would love but a transforming book, a source of discoveries and recognitions. All of Europe fell into my head — though on condition that I start mourning for it. And tuberculosis, the faintly shameful disease (so my mother had intimated) of which my hard-to-imagine real father had died so long ago and exotically elsewhere, but which seemed, once we moved to Tucson, to be a commonplace misfortune — tuberculosis was revealed as the very epitome of pathetic and spiritual interest! The mountain-high community of invalids with afflicted lungs was a version — an exalted version — of that picturesque, climate-conscious resort town in the desert with its thirty-odd hospitals and sanatoriums to which my mother had been obliged to relocate because of an asthma-disabled child: me. There on the mountain, characters were ideas and ideas were passions, exactly as I'd always felt. But the ideas themselves stretched me, enrolled me in turn: Settembrini's humanitarian élan but also Naphta's gloom and scorn. And mild, good-natured, chaste Hans Castorp, Mann's orphaned protagonist, was a hero after my own unprotected heart, not least because he was an orphan and because of the chastity of my own imagination. I loved the tenderness, however diluted by condescension, with which Mann portrays him as a bit simple, overearnest, docile, mediocre (what I considered myself to be, judged by real standards). Tenderness. What if Hans Castorp was a Goody Two-Shoes (appalling accusation my mother had once let fly at me)? That was what made him not like but unlike the others. I recognized his vocation for piety; his portable solitude, lived politely among others; his life of onerous routines (that guardians deem good for you) interspersed with free, passionate conversations — a glorious transposition of my own current agenda.

For a month the book was where I lived. I read it through almost at a run, my excitement winning out over my wish to go slowly and savor. I did have to slow down for pages 334 to 343, when Hans Castorp and Clavdia Chauchat finally speak of love, but in French, which I'd never studied: unwilling to skip anything, I bought a French-English dictionary and looked up their conversation word by word. After finishing the last page, I was so reluctant to be separated from the book that I started back at the beginning and, to hold myself to the pace the book merited, reread it aloud, a chapter each night.

The next step was to lend it to a friend, to feel someone else's pleasure in the book — to love it with someone else, and be able to talk about it. In early December I lent *The Magic Mountain* to Merrill. And Merrill, who would read immediately whatever I pressed on him, loved it, too. Good.

Then Merrill said, "Why don't we go see him?" And that's when my joy turned to shame.

OF COURSE I knew he lived here. Southern California in the nineteen-forties was electric with celebrity presences for all tastes, and my friends and I were aware not only of Stravinsky and Schoenberg but of Mann, of Brecht (I'd recently seen *Galileo*, with Charles Laughton, in a Beverly Hills theatre), and also of Isherwood and Huxley. But it was as inconceivable that I could be in contact with any of them as that I could strike up a conversation with Ingrid Bergman or Gary Cooper, who also lived in the vicinity. Actually, it was even less possible. The stars stepped out of their limos onto the klieg-lighted sidewalk of Hollywood Boulevard for the movie-palace première, braving the surge of besieging fans penned in by police sawhorses; I saw newsreels of these apparitions. The gods of high culture had disembarked from Europe to dwell, almost incognito, among the lemon trees and beach boys and neo-Bauhaus architecture and fantasy hamburgers; they weren't, I was sure, supposed to have something like fans, who would seek to intrude on their privacy. Of course, Mann, unlike the other exiles, was also a public presence. To have been as officially honored in America as Thomas Mann was in the late nineteen-thirties and early nineteen-forties was probably more anomalous than to have been the most famous writer in the world. A guest at the White House, introduced by the Vice-President when he gave a speech at the Library of Congress, for years indefatigable on the lecture circuit, Mann had the stature of an oracle in Roosevelt's *bien-pensant* America, proclaiming the absolute evil of Hitler's Germany and the coming victory of the democracies. Emigration had not dampened his taste, or his talent, for being a representative figure. If there was such a thing as a good Germany, it was now to be found in this country (proof of America's goodness), embodied in his person; if there was a Great Writer, not at all an American notion of what a writer is, it was he.

But when I was borne aloft by *The Magic Mountain*, I wasn't thinking that he was also, literally, "here." To say that at this time I lived in Southern California and Thomas Mann lived in Southern California — that was a different sense of "lived," of "in." Wherever he was, it was where-I-was-not. Europe. Or the world beyond childhood, the world of seriousness. No, not even that. For me, he was a book. Books, rather — I was now deep in *Stories of Three Decades*. When I was nine, which I did consider childhood, I'd lived for months of grief and suspense in *Les Misérables*. (It was the chapter in which Fantine is obliged to sell her hair that had made a conscious socialist of me.) As far as I was concerned, Thomas Mann — being, simply, immortal — was as dead as Victor Hugo.

Why would I want to meet him? I had his books.

I didn't want to meet him. Merrill was at my house, it was Sunday, my parents were out, and we were in their bedroom sprawled on their white satin bedspread. Despite my pleas, he'd brought in a telephone book and was looking under "M."

"You see? He's in the telephone book."

"I don't want to see!"

"Look!" He made me look. Horrified, I saw: 1550 San Remo Drive, Pacific Palisades.

"This is ridiculous. Come on — stop it!" I clambered off the bed. I couldn't believe Merrill was doing this, but he was.

"I'm going to call." The phone was on the night table on my mother's side of the bed.

"Merrill, please!"

He picked up the receiver. I bolted through the house, out the always unlocked front door, across the lawn, beyond the curb to the far side of the Pontiac, parked with the key in the ignition (where else would you keep the car keys?), to stand in the middle of the street and press my hands to my ears, as if from there I could have heard Merrill making the mortifying, unthinkable telephone call.

What a coward I am, I thought, hardly for the first or the last time in my life; but I took a few moments, hyperventilating, trying to regain control of myself, before I uncovered my ears and retraced my steps. Slowly.

The front door opened right into the small living room, done up with Early American "pieces," as my mother called them, that she was now collecting. Silence. I crossed the room into the dining area, then turned into the short hall that went past my own room and the door of my parents' bathroom into their bedroom.

The receiver was on the hook. Merrill was sitting on the bed's edge, grinning.

"Listen, that's not funny," I said. "I thought you were really going to do it."

He waved his hand. "I did."

"Did what?"

"I did it." He was still smiling.

"Called?"

"He's expecting us for tea next Sunday at four."

"You didn't actually call!"

"Why not?" he said. "It went fine."

"And you spoke to him?" I was close to tears. "How could you?"

"No," he said, "it was his wife who answered."

I extracted a mental picture of Katia Mann from the photographs I'd seen of Mann with his family. Did she, too, exist? Perhaps, as long as Merrill hadn't actually spoken to Thomas Mann, it wasn't so bad. "But what did you say?"

"I said we were two high-school students who had read Thomas Mann's books and would like to meet him."

No, this was even worse than I imagined — but what had I imagined? "That's so . . . so dumb!"

"What's dumb about it? It sounded good."

"Oh, Merrill. . . ." I couldn't even protest anymore. "What did she say?"

"She said, 'Just a minute, I'll get my daughter,'" Merrill continued, "and then the daughter got on, and I repeated — "

"Go slower," I interrupted. "His wife left the phone. Then there was a pause. Then you heard another voice . . ."

"Yeah, another woman's voice — they both had accents — saying, 'This is Miss Mann, what do you want?'"

"Is that what she said? It sounds as if she was angry."

"No, no, she didn't sound angry. Maybe she said, 'Miss Mann speaking.' I don't remember, but, honest, she didn't sound angry. Then she said, 'What do you want?' No, wait, it was 'What is it that you want?'"

"Then what?"

"And then I said . . . you know, that we were two high-school students who had read Thomas Mann's books and wanted to meet him — "

"But I don't want to meet him!" I wailed.

"And she said," he pushed on stubbornly, "'Just a minute, I will ask my father.' Maybe it was 'Just a moment, I will ask my father.' She wasn't gone very long . . . and then she came back to the phone and said — these were her words exactly — 'My father is expecting you for tea next Sunday at four.'"

"And then?"

"She asked if I knew the address."

"And then?"

"That was all. Oh . . . and she said goodbye."

I contemplated this finality for a moment before saying, once more, "Oh, Merrill, how could you?"

"I told you I would," he said.

Getting through the week, awash in shame and dread. It seemed a vast impertinence that I should be forced to meet Thomas Mann. And grotesque that he should waste his time meeting me.

Of course I could refuse to go. But I was afraid this brash Caliban I'd mistaken for an Ariel would call on the magician without me. Whatever the usual deference I had from Merrill, it seemed he now considered himself my equal in Thomas Mann worship. I couldn't let Merrill inflict himself unmediated on my idol. At least, if I went along I might limit the damage, head off the more callow of Merrill's remarks. I had the impression (and this is the part of my recollection that is most touching to me) that Thomas Mann could be injured by Merrill's stupidity or mine ... that stupidity was always injuring, and that as I revered Mann it was my duty to protect him from this injury.

Merrill and I met twice during the week after school. I had stopped reproving him. I was less angry; increasingly, I was just miserable. I was trapped. Since I would have to go, I needed to feel close to him, make common cause, so we would not disgrace ourselves.

Sunday came. It was Merrill who collected me in the Chevy, at one exactly, in front of my house at the curb (I hadn't told my mother or anyone else of this invitation to tea in Pacific Palisades), and by two o'clock we were on broad, empty San Remo Drive, with a view of the ocean and Catalina Island in the distance, parked some two hundred feet up from (and out of sight of) the house at 1550.

We had already agreed on how we would start. I would talk first, about *The Magic Mountain,* then Merrill would ask the question about what Thomas Mann was writing at present. The rest we were going to work out now, in the two hours we'd allotted to rehearse. But after a few minutes, unable to entertain any idea of how he might respond to what we were considering saying, we ran out of inspiration. What does a god say? Impossible to imagine.

So we compared two recordings of "Death and the Maiden" and then veered to a favorite notion of Merrill's about the way Schnabel played the "Hammerklavier," a notion which I found wonderfully clever. Merrill seemed hardly to be anxious at all. He appeared to think that we had a perfect right to bother Thomas Mann. He thought that we were interesting — two precocious kids, minor-league prodigies (we knew neither of us was a real prodigy, which was someone like the young Menuhin; we were prodigies of appetite, of respect, not of accomplishment); that we could be interesting to Thomas Mann. I did not. I thought we were ... pure potentiality. By real standards, I thought, we hardly existed.

The sun was strong and the street deserted. In two hours only a few cars passed. Then, at five minutes to four, Merrill released the brake and we coasted silently down the hill and reparked in front of 1550. We got out, stretched, made encouraging mock-groaning sounds to each other, closed the car doors as softly as we could, went up the pathway, and rang the bell. Cute chimes. Oh.

A very old woman with white hair in a bun opened the door, didn't seem surprised to see us, invited us in, asked us to wait a minute in the dim entryway — there was a living room off to the right — and went down a long corridor and out of sight.

"Katia Mann," I whispered.

"I wonder if we'll see Erika," Merrill whispered back.

Absolute silence in the house. She was returning now. "Come with me, please. My husband will receive you in his study."

We followed, almost to the end of the narrow dark passageway, just before the staircase. There was a door on the left, which she opened. We followed her in, turning left once more before we were really inside. In Thomas Mann's study.

I saw the room — it seemed large and had a big window with a big view — before I realized it was he, sitting behind a massive, ornate, dark table. Katia Mann presented us. Here are the two students, she said to him, while referring to him as Dr. Thomas Mann; he nodded and said some words of welcome. He was wearing a bow tie and a beige suit, as in the frontispiece of *Essays of Three Decades* — and that was the first shock, that he so resembled the formally posed photograph. The resemblance seemed uncanny, a marvel. It wasn't, I think now, just because this was the first time I'd met someone whose appearance I had already formed a strong idea of through photographs. I'd never met anyone who didn't affect being relaxed. His resemblance to the photograph seemed like a feat, as if he were posing now. But the full-figure picture had not made me imagine him as frail; it had not made me see the sparseness of the mustache, the whiteness of the skin, the mottled hands, the unpleasantly visible veins, the smallness and amber color of the eyes behind his glasses. He sat very erectly and seemed to be very, very old. He was in fact seventy-two.

I heard the door behind us close. Thomas Mann indicated that we were to sit in the two stiff-backed chairs in front of the table. He lit a cigarette and leaned back in his chair.

And we were on our way.

HE TALKED without prompting. I remember his gravity, his accent, the slowness of his speech: I had never heard anyone speak so slowly.

I said how much I loved *The Magic Mountain*.

He said it was a very European book, that it portrayed the conflicts at the heart of European civilization.

I said I understood that.

What had he been writing, Merrill asked.

"I have recently completed a novel which is partly based on the life of Nietzsche," he said, with huge disquieting pauses between each word. "My protagonist, however, is not a philosopher. He is a great composer."

"I know how important music is for you," I ventured, hoping to fuel the conversation for a good stretch.

"Both the heights and the depths of the German soul are reflected in its music," he said.

"Wagner," I said, worried that I was risking disaster, since I'd never heard an opera by Wagner, though I'd read Thomas Mann's essay on him.

"Yes," he said, picking up, hefting, closing (with his thumb marking the place), then laying down, open again, a book that was on his worktable. "As you see, at this very moment I am consulting Volume IV of Ernest Newman's excellent biography of Wagner." I craned my neck to let the words of the title and the author's name actually hit my eyeballs. I'd seen the Newman biography at the Pickwick.

"But the music of my composer is not like Wagner's music. It is related to the twelve-tone system, or row, of Schoenberg."

Merrill said we were both very interested in Schoenberg. He made no response to this. Intercepting a perplexed look on Merrill's face, I widened my eyes encouragingly.

"Will your novel appear soon?" Merrill asked.

"My faithful translator is at work on it now," he said.

"H. T. Lowe-Porter," I murmured — the first time I'd actually said this entrancing name, with its opaque initials and showy hyphen.

"For the translator this is, perhaps, my most difficult book," he said. "Never, I think, has Mrs. Lowe-Porter been confronted with such a challenging task."

"Oh," I said, having not imagined H. T. L.-P. to be anything in particular but surprised to learn that the name belonged to a woman.

"A deep knowledge of German is required, and much ingenuity, for some of my characters converse in dialect. And the Devil — for, yes, the Devil himself is a character in my book — speaks in the German of the sixteenth century," Thomas Mann said, slowly, slowly. A thin-lipped smile. "I am afraid this will mean little to my American readers."

I longed to say something reassuring, but didn't dare.

Was he speaking so slowly, I wondered, because that was the way he talked? Or because he thought he had to speak slowly — assuming (because we were Americans? because we were children?) that otherwise we wouldn't understand what he was saying?

"I regard this as the most daring book I have written." He nodded at us. "My wildest book."

"We look forward very much to reading it," I said. I was still hoping he'd talk about *The Magic Mountain*.

"But it is as well the book of my old age," he went on. A long, long pause. "My *Parsifal*," he said. "And, of course, my *Faust*."

He seemed distracted for a moment, as if recalling something. He lit another cigarette and turned slightly in his chair. Then he laid the cigarette in an ashtray and rubbed his mustache with his index finger; I remember I thought his mustache (I didn't know anyone with a mustache) looked like a little hat over his mouth. I wondered if this meant the conversation was over.

But, no, he went on. I remember "the fate of Germany" . . . "the demonic" and "the abyss" . . . and "the Faustian bargain with the Devil." Hitler recurred several times. (Did he bring up the Wagner-Hitler problem? I think not.) We did our best to show him that his words were not wholly lost on us.

At first I had seen only him, awe at his physical presence blinding me to the room's contents. Now I was starting to see more. For instance, what was on the rather cluttered table: pens, inkstand, books, papers, and a nest of small photographs in silver frames, which I saw from the back. Of the many pictures on the walls, I recognized only a signed photograph of F.D.R. with someone else — I seem to remember a man in uniform — in the picture. And books, books, books in the floor-to-ceiling shelves that covered two of the walls. To be in the same room with Thomas Mann was thrilling, enormous, astounding. But I was also hearing the siren call of the first private library I had ever seen.

While Merrill carried the ball, showing that he was not entirely ignorant of the Faust legend, I was trying, without making the divagations of my glance too obvious, to case the library. As I expected, almost all the books were German, many in sets, leather-bound; the puzzle was that I could not decipher most of the titles (I didn't know of the existence of *Fraktur*). The few American books, all recent-looking, were easy to identify in their bright, waxy jackets.

Now he was talking about Goethe . . . .

As if we had indeed rehearsed what we would say, Merrill and I had found a nice, unstrained rhythm of putting questions whenever Thomas Mann's glacial flow of words seemed to be drying up, and of showing our respectful appreciation of whatever he was saying. Merrill was being the Merrill I was so fond of: calm, charming, not stupid at all. I felt ashamed that I'd assumed he would disgrace himself, and therefore me, in front of Thomas Mann. Merrill was doing fine. I was, I thought, doing so-so. The surprise was Thomas Mann, that he wasn't harder to understand.

I wouldn't have minded if he had talked like a book. I wanted him to talk like a book. What I was obscurely starting to mind was that (as I couldn't have put it then) he talked like a book review.

Now he was talking about the artist and society, and he was using phrases I remembered from interviews with him I had read in *The Saturday Review of Literature*, a magazine I felt I'd outgrown since discovering the fancy prose and convoluted arguments of *Partisan Review*, which I had just started buying at the newsstand on Las Palmas. But, I reasoned, if I found what he said now a little familiar it was because I had read his books. He couldn't know he had in me such a fervent reader. Why should he say anything he hadn't already said? I refused to be disappointed.

I considered telling him that I loved *The Magic Mountain* so much that I had read it twice, but that seemed silly. I also feared he might ask me about some book of his which I had not read, though so far he hadn't asked a single question. "*The Magic Mountain* has meant so much to me," I finally ventured, feeling that it was now or never.

"It sometimes happens," he said, "that I am asked which I consider to be my greatest novel."

"Oh," I said.

"Yes," said Merrill.

"I would say, and have so replied recently in interviews..." He paused. I held my breath. "*The Magic Mountain*." I exhaled.

THE DOOR OPENED. Relief had come: the German wife, slow-gaited, bearing a tray with cookies, small cakes, and tea, which she bent over to set down on a low table in front of the sofa against one wall. Thomas Mann stood up, came around the table, and waved us toward the sofa; I saw he was very thin. I longed to sit down again, and did, next to Merrill, where we'd been told to sit, as soon as Thomas Mann occupied a wing chair nearby. Katia Mann was pouring tea from a heavy silver service into three delicate cups. As Thomas Mann put his saucer on his knee and raised the cup to his mouth (we followed, in unison), she said a few words in German to him in a low voice. He shook his head. His reply was in English — something like "It doesn't matter" or "Not now." She sighed audibly, and left the room.

Ah, he said, now we will eat. Unsmiling, he motioned to us to help ourselves to the cakes.

At one end of the low table that held the tray was a small Egyptian statuette, which sits in my memory as a funerary votive figure. It reminded me that Thomas Mann had written a book called *Joseph in Egypt*, which in the course of a cursory browsing at the Pickwick I'd not found enticing. I resolved to give it another try.

No one spoke. I was aware of the intense, dedicated quiet of the house, a quiet I had never experienced anywhere indoors; and of the slowness and self-consciousness of each of my gestures. I sipped my tea, tried to control the crumbs from the cake, and exchanged a furtive glance with Merrill. Maybe it was over now.

Putting down his cup and saucer, then touching the corner of his mouth with the edge of his thick white napkin, Thomas Mann said that he was always pleased to meet American young people, who showed the vigor and health and fundamentally optimistic temper of this great country. My spirits sank. What I had dreaded — he was turning the conversation to us.

He asked us about our studies. Our studies? That was a further embarrassment. I was sure he hadn't the faintest idea what a high school in Southern California was like. Did he know about Drivers' Education (compulsory)? Typing courses? Wouldn't he be surprised by the wrinkled condoms you spotted as you were darting across the lawn for first period (the campus was a favorite nighttime trysting spot) — my own surprise having revealed, the very first week I entered, my being two years younger than my classmates, because I'd witlessly asked someone why there were those little balloons under the trees? And by the "tea" being sold by a pair of pachukes (as the Chicano kids were called) stationed along the left wall of the assembly building every morning recess? Could he imagine George, who, some of us knew, had a gun and got money from gas-station attendants? Ella and Nella, the dwarf sisters, who led the Bible Club boycott that resulted in the withdrawal of our biology textbook? Did he know Latin was gone, and Shakespeare, too, and that for months of tenth-grade English the visibly befuddled teacher handed out copies of the *Reader's Digest* at the beginning of each period — we were to select one article and write a summary of it — then sat out the hour in silence at her desk, nodding and knitting? Could he imagine what a world away from the Gymnasium in his native Lübeck, where fourteen-year-old Tonio Kröger wooed Hans Hansen by trying to get him to read Schiller's *Don Carlos*, was North Hollywood High School, alma mater of Farley Granger and Alan Ladd? He couldn't, and I hoped he would never find out. He had enough to be sad about — Hitler, the destruction of Germany, exile. It was better that he not know how really far he was from Europe.

He was talking about "the value of literature" and "the necessity of protecting civilization against the forces of barbarity," and I said, yes, yes ... my conviction that it was absurd for us to be there — what, all week, I'd expected to feel — at last taking over. Earlier, we could only say something stupid. Actually having tea, the social ritual that gave a name to the whole proceeding, created new opportunities for disgrace. My worry that I would do something clumsy was driving out of my head whatever I might have ventured to say.

I remember beginning to wonder when it would not be awkward to leave. I guessed that Merrill, for all the impression he gave of being at ease, would be glad to go, too.

And Thomas Mann continued to talk, slowly, about literature. I remember my dismay better than what he said. I was trying to keep myself from eating too many cookies, but in a moment of absent-mindedness I did reach over and take one more than I had meant to. He nodded. Have another, he said. It was horrible. How I wished I could just be left alone in his study to look at his books.

He asked us who our favorite authors were, and when I hesitated (I had so many, and I knew I should mention only a few) he went on — and this I remember exactly: "I presume you like Hemingway. He is, such is my impression, the most representative American author."

Merrill mumbled that he had never read Hemingway. Neither had I; but I was too taken aback to reply. How puzzling that Thomas Mann should be interested in Hemingway, who in my vague idea of him was a very popular author of novels that had been made into romantic movies (I loved Ingrid Bergman, I loved Humphrey Bogart) and wrote about fishing and boxing (I hated sports). He'd never sounded to me like a writer I ought to read. Or one my Thomas Mann would take seriously. But then I understood it wasn't that Thomas Mann liked Hemingway but that we were supposed to like him.

Well, Thomas Mann said, what authors do you like?

Merrill said he liked Romain Rolland, meaning *Jean-Christophe*. And Joyce, meaning *Portrait of the Artist*. I said I liked Kafka, meaning *Metamorphosis* and *In the Penal Colony*, and Tolstoy, meaning the late religious writings as much as the novels; and, thinking I must cite an American because he seemed to expect that, threw in Jack London, meaning *Martin Eden*.

He said that we must be very serious young people. More embarrassment. What I remember best is how embarrassing it was.

I was still worrying about Hemingway. Should I read Hemingway?

He seemed to find it perfectly normal that two local high-school students should know who Nietzsche and Schoenberg were ... and up to now I'd simply rejoiced in this first foretaste of the world where such familiarity was taken for granted. But now he seemed also to want us to be two young Americans (as he imagined them); to be, as he was (as, I had no idea why, he thought Hemingway was), representative. I knew that was absurd. The whole point was that we didn't represent anything at all. We didn't even represent ourselves — certainly not very well.

Here I was in the very throne room of the world in which I aspired to live, even as the humblest citizen. (The thought of saying that I wanted to be a writer would no more have occurred to me than to tell him I breathed. I was there if I had to be there as admirer, not as aspirant to his caste.) The man I met had only sententious formulas to deliver, though he was the man who wrote Thomas Mann's books. And I uttered nothing but tongue-tied simplicities, though I was full of complex feeling. We neither of us were at our best.

STRANGE THAT I DON'T RECALL how it ended. Did Katia Mann appear and tell us that time was up? Did Thomas Mann say he must return to his work, receive our thanks for granting this audience, and take us to the study door? I don't remember the goodbyes — how we were released. Our sitting on the sofa having tea and cakes cross-fades in my memory to being out on San Remo Drive again, getting into the car. After the dark study, the waning sun seemed bright: it was just past five-thirty.

Merrill started the car. Like two teen-age boys driving away after their first visit to a brothel, we evaluated our performance. Merrill thought it was a triumph. I was ashamed, depressed, though I agreed that we hadn't made total fools of ourselves.

"Damn, we should have brought the book," Merrill said, as we neared my neighborhood, breaking a long silence. "For him to sign."

I gritted my teeth and said nothing.

"That was great," said Merrill, as I got out of the car in front of my house.

I doubt we spoke of it again.

TEN MONTHS LATER, within days of the appearance of the much-heralded *Doctor Faustus* (Book-of-the-Month Club selection, first printing over a hundred thousand copies), Merrill and I were at the Pickwick, giddily eying the piles of identical books stacked on a metal table in the front of the store. I bought mine and Merrill his; we read it together.

Acclaimed as it was, his book didn't do as well as Thomas Mann expected. The reviewers expressed respectful reservations, his American presence began to deflate slightly. The Roosevelt era was really over and the Cold War had started. He began to think of returning to Europe.

I was now within a few months of my big move, the beginning of real life. After January graduation, I started a term at the University of California at Berkeley, luckless George started doing his one-to-five at San Quentin, and in the fall of 1949 I put Cal behind me and entered the University of Chicago, accompanied by Merrill and by Peter (both of whom had graduated in June), and studied philosophy, and then, and then . . . I went on to my life, which did turn out to be, mostly, just what the child of fourteen had imagined with such certitude.

And Thomas Mann, who had been doing time here, made his move. He and his Katia (who had become American citizens in 1944) were to leave Southern California, returning to the somewhat leveled magic mountain of Europe in 1952. There had been fifteen years in America. He had lived here. But he didn't really live here.

Years later, when I had become a writer, when I knew many other writers, I would learn to be more tolerant of the gap between the person and the work. Yet even now the encounter still feels illicit, improper. In my experience deep memory is, more often than not, the memory of embarrassment.

I still feel the exhilaration, the gratitude for having been liberated from childhood's asphyxations. Admirations set me free. And embarrassment, which is the price of acutely experienced admiration. Then I felt like an adult, forced to live in the body of a child. Since, I feel like a child, privileged to live in the body of an adult. The zealot of seriousness in me, because it was already full-grown in the child, continues to think of reality as yet-to-be. Still sees a big space ahead, a far horizon. Is this the real world? I still ask myself that, forty years later . . . as small children ask repeatedly, in the course of a long tiring journey, "Are we there yet?" Childhood's sense of plenitude was denied me. In compensation, there remains, always, the horizon of plenitude to which I am borne forward by the delights of admiration.

I NEVER TOLD ANYONE of the meeting. Over the years I have kept it a secret, as if it were something shameful. As if it happened between two other people, two phantoms, two provisional beings on their way elsewhere: an embarrassed, fervid, literature-intoxicated child and a god in exile who lived in a house in Pacific Palisades.

Select Bibliography

Bloom, Harold, ed. *Thomas Mann's "The Magic Mountain."* New York: Chelsea House, 1986.

Ezergailis, Inta, ed. *Critical Essays on Thomas Mann.* Boston: G. K. Hall, 1988.

Frizen, Werner. "Die 'bräunliche Schöne': Über Zigarren und Verwandtes in Thomas Manns *Zauberberg,*" *DVjs* 55.1 (1981): 107–118.

Goldman, Harvey. *Max Weber and Thomas Mann: Calling and the Shaping of the Self.* Berkeley: U of California P, 1988.

Grenville, Anthony. "'Linke Leute von rechts': Thomas Mann's Naphta and the Ideological Confluence of Radical Right and Radical Left in the Early Years of the Weimar Republic," *DVjs* 59.4 (1985): 651–675.

Harpprecht, Klaus. *Thomas Mann: Eine Biographie.* [Reinbek]: Rowohlt, 1995.

Hatfield, Henry. *From "The Magic Mountain": Mann's Later Masterpieces.* Ithaca: Cornell UP, 1979.

Heftrich, Eckhard. *Zauberbergmusik: Über Thomas Mann.* Frankfurt am Main: Vittorio Klostermann, 1975.

Heilbut, Anthony. *Thomas Mann: Eros and Literature.* New York: Knopf, 1995.

Heller, Erich. *Thomas Mann: The Ironic German.* Cleveland: Meridian Books, 1961.

King, John S. "'Most Dubious': Myth, the Occult, and Politics in the *Zauberberg,*" *Monatshefte* 8.2 (1996): 217–236.

Koc, Richard. "Magical Enactments: Reflections on 'Highly Questionable' Matters in *Der Zauberberg,*" *Germanic Review* 68.3 (1993): 108–117.

Koopmann, Helmut, ed. *Thomas-Mann-Handbuch.* 2 volumes. Stuttgart: Kröner, 1990.

Kowalik, Jill Anne. "'Sympathy with Death': Hans Castorp's Nietzschean Resentment," *German Quarterly* 58 (1985): 27–48.

Lehnert, Herbert. "Leo Naphta und sein Autor." *Orbis Litterarum* 37 (1982): 47–69.

Lubich, Frederick A. "Thomas Manns *Der Zauberberg*: Spukschloß der Großen Mutter oder Die Männerdämmerung des Abendlandes," *DVjs* 67 (1993): 729–763.

———. "Thomas Mann's Sexual Politics — Lost in Translation," *Comparative Literature Studies* 31.2 (1994): 107–127.

Maar, Michael. *Geister und Kunst: Neuigkeiten aus dem Zauberberg.* Munich: Hanser, 1995.

Mayer, Hans. *Thomas Mann: Werk und Entwicklung.* Berlin: Volk und Welt, 1950.

——— . *Thomas Mann.* Frankfurt am Main: Suhrkamp, 1980.

Müller-Seidel, Walter. "Degeneration und Decadence: Thomas Manns Weg zum *Zauberberg*," in *Poetik und Geschichte*, pp. 118–135. Edited by Dieter Borchmeyer. Tübingen: Niemeyer, 1989.

Nehamas, Alexander. "'Getting Used to Not Getting Used To It': Nietzsche in *The Magic Mountain*," *Philosophy and Literature* 5 (1981): 73–89.

Neider, Charles, ed. *The Stature of Thomas Mann.* New York: New Directions, 1947.

Reed, T. J. *Thomas Mann: The Uses of Tradition.* Oxford: Clarendon Press, 1974.

Ridley, Hugh. *The Problematic Bourgeois: Twentieth-Century Criticism on Thomas Mann's "Buddenbrooks" and "The Magic Mountain."* Columbia: Camden House, 1994.

Rieckmann, Jens. *Der Zauberberg: Eine geistige Autobiographie Thomas Manns.* Stuttgarter Arbeiten zur Germanistik, 24. Stuttgart: Akademischer Verlag Hans-Dieter Heinz, 1979.

Sicker, Philip. "Babel Revisited: Mann's Myth of Language in *The Magic Mountain*," *Mosaic* 9.2 (1986): 1–20.

Stock, Irving. "The Magic Mountain." *Modern Fiction Studies* 32.4 (1986): 487–520.

van Beers, Monique. "Clawdia Chauchat: Die Darstellung einer Frauengestalt im *Zauberberg* von Thomas Mann." *Neophilologus* 70 (1986): 576–591.

Weigand, Hermann John. *Thomas Mann's Novel "Der Zauberberg": A Study.* New York: Appleton-Century, 1933; rpt. Chapel Hill: U of North Carolina P, 1965.

Widdig, Bernd. "Mann unter Männern: Männerbünde und die Angst vor der Masse in der Rede 'Von deutscher Republik,'" *German Quarterly* 66.4 (1993): 524–536.

White, James F., ed. *The Yale Zauberberg Manuscript: Rejected Sheets Once Part of Thomas Mann's Novel.* Thomas-Mann-Studien, vol. 4. Berne and Munich: Francke, 1980.

Notes on the Contributors

Michael Brenner is professor of Jewish History and Culture at the University of Munich. He is the author of *The Renaissance of Jewish Culture in Weimar Germany* (Yale University Press, 1996), *After the Holocaust: Rebuilding Jewish Lives in Postwar Germany* (Princeton University Press, 1997), and co-author and co-editor of the four-volume *German-Jewish History in Modern Times* (Columbia UP, 1996–97).

David Blumberg received his Ph.D. in German Literature from University of California at Berkeley in 1996. His principal research interests include music and literature (with special emphasis on contemporary settings of German poetry), theories of modernity, Expressionist cinema, and lyric poetry. He currently teaches German in Moraga, California.

Stephen D. Dowden has written books and essays on German literature in the twentieth century, most recently *Kafka's Castle and the Critical Imagination*. He teaches German at Brandeis University.

Edward Engelberg, emeritus professor of Comparative Literature at Brandeis University, has written books and essays on topics in English, German, and French literature. He is currently at work on a book about solitude.

Eugene Goodheart, the Edytha Macy Gross Professor of Humanities at Brandeis University, is the author of many books and essays on modern literature and criticism. His most recent volume is *The Reign of Ideology.*

Ülker Gökberk is an associate professor of German and Humanities at Reed College. Apart from her scholarship on Thomas Mann, she explores the theories and representations of alterity and is currently working on a study of literary criticism of "Migrantenliteratur."

Stephen C. Meredith is a biochemist/pathologist by day and a humanist by night, both at the University of Chicago. In his scientific work, he studies protein structure, most recently apolipoprotein E and beta amyloid. He also teaches courses at the university on Thomas Mann, James Joyce, and Thomas Aquinas, among others.

Joseph P. Lawrence has written essays on Plato and Aristotle and on German philosophy from Kant to Heidegger. He has a particular interest in the thought of Schelling. He teaches philosophy at the College of the Holy Cross.

Karla Schultz, professor, teaches German and comparative literature at the University of Oregon. She has written numerous articles on the interface of modernism, critical theory, poetry and gender, as well as a book on Adorno's concept of mimesis. She is currently completing a book about the ethics of literary criticism.

Susan Sontag is the author of three novels, *The Benefactor*, *Death Kit*, and *The Volcano Lover*. She has published a volume of stories, *I, etcetera* and several collections of essays, including *AIDS and Its Metaphors* and the prize-winning *On Photography*. She lives in New York City.

Kenneth Weisinger is professor of German and Comparative Literature at the University of California in Berkeley. He is the author of books and essays dealing with German literature from the age of Goethe to the twentieth century.

Index

Adorno, Theodor W., 53–55, 58, 72–75; on film music, 84–85; on Mahler, 93 n. 7
Aïda, see: Verdi
AIDS, 111
Andersen, Hans C., xvii, 27
androgyny, 170, 209
antebellum Europe, 180
Aquinas, 122
Auden, W. H., 97
Augustine, 122

Barker, Pat, 49
Bartels, Adolf, 153
Baudelaire, Charles, 98, 107 n. 3
Beer-Hofmann, Richard, 150
Bendel, Franz, 86
Benjamin, Walter, xiv, 27
Bergman, Ingrid, 228
Bildungsroman, 179
Bizet, Georges, 87–88
bioskop, 164, 168
boredom, *see*: ennui
Brecht, Bertolt, 228
Britain, oil imports, 194–195
Broch, Hermann, xiv, 27
Brod, Max, 148–149
Browne, Sir Thomas, 119
Buber, Martin, 149

Cage, John, 226
Carlebach, Simson, 153, 155
Caruso, Enrico, 165
Castorp, Hans, xii–xv, 31, 60, 80, 122, 130–133, 161–162, 200, 227; and Asia, 95–108, 115–116; baptismal font of, 114; and Behrens, 190–193; identification with Bizet's Carmen, 87–88, 91; and cinema, 168; courage, 6; dandyism, 20; and England, 186–187; growth into silence, 4; illness, 96, 100, 118; homoeroticism, 86, 182, 191, 197–198, 203; as "life's problem child," 2; model for, 176 n.31; love for Clavdia, 87, 95, 102, 114, 125–127, 162, 169–170, 197–198; love for Joachim, 210; love of music, 81–85, 201; materialism, 20; middling position, 26, 70, 201–202; movies, 85; as mummy, 100; name, 187–188, 191; philosophical education of, 1–13, 173 n.8, 179; at prayer, 180; prudery of, 17, 82; as quester hero, 120; scientific ruminations, 165–166; snobbery, 82, 96; as Timothy, 190–191
Caucasus, *see:* Daghestan
Chauchat, Clavdia, xiv–xv, 24, 26–32, 45, 86, 99, 125; animal imagery, 27, 128; Asiatic features, 27, 95–96, 128; body of, 127, 169–170, 195–196; as cigar, 1–2; and Daghestan, 182–186; husband of, 182–185; illness and freedom, 42; name, 185; portrait, 192–193; and Settembrini, 27–29; witch, 29; x-ray photo, 168
Chopin, Frédéric, 117
Churchill, Winston, 188, 195, 208
cigars, 1–2, 189–193; as colonial import, 209

Cooper, Gary, 228
cinema, 168
Claudius, Matthias, 89
coffee, 195
colonialism, 188, 192, 206–209; expressed as erotic desire, 209; and homoeroticism, 201–202, 210–211
Conrad, Joseph, xiv, 27, 108 n. 5
conservatism, 57
Croce, Benedetto, 203
cytokines, 112

Daghestan, 182–186; setting of martyrdom and isolation, 184; oil production, 184
Dante, *Inferno*, 204–205
Darwin, Charles, 178
Davos, x, 6, 110, 161
death, as theme, xiv–xvi, 2, 5–9, 16, 21–25, 30, 85, 97, 99–100, 109–140, 168; eros, 26–27, 32–36, 46, 49–52, 81–82, 166, 196; evil, 121–122; music, 88
Debussy, Claude, 98, 225
DeLillo, Don, 21–22, 24
De Quincey, Thomas, 98, 107 n. 3
Derrida, Jacques, 4
Döblin, Alfred, 149
Dohm, Christian W., 151
dormouse, xvii–xviii
Dostoyevsky, Fyodor, 101; 48–49; *Brothers Karamazov*, 95, 98; "The German Question," 63–64; *Notes from Underground*, 105
dueling, 184

Edison, Thomas, 164; and x-rays, 167
Einstein, Albert, 159–161; relativity, 172 n.4; and x-rays, 167
Eisler, Hanns, 84–85
Eliot, T. S., 98

Enlightenment, 11, 44, 48, 57, 64, 121, 159
ennui, xi, 35, 99–100
eros, 195–196; *see also*: love
Eugen, Prince of Savoy, 178
evil, 121

Feuchtwanger, Lion, 154
film, 85
Flaubert, Gustave, xii, 51
Fontane, Theodor, 154
Franco-Russian Alliance, 185
Freemasonry, 66
French Revolution, 57, 65
Freud, Sigmund, 7, 35, 41, 44–45, 99, 101, 128, 181, 198; and Schopenhauer, 86
Fussell, Paul, 49

Gass, William, 21
Geiger, Ludwig, 148
German-Jewish writing, 144–151
Germany; conservatism of intellectuals, 57; site of European intellectual oppositions, 67–70; identity of; 53–79; middling position, 70–71
Gieseking, Walter, 225
Girard, René, 198
Goethe, Johann Wolfgang von, 15, 116; *Elective Affinities*, 18, 35; *Faust*, 125, 234; *Italian Journey*, 49; *Wilhelm Meister*, 179; "Siebenschläfer," xvii–xviii
Goldberg, Oskar, 144, 154
Grey, Zane, 25
grotesque, 119
group identity, 54
Gulbenkian, Calouste, 194

Halliburton, Richard, 222
Hamburg, 179
Hegel, G. W. F., 160
Heine, Heinrich, 116
Heine, Thomas Theodor, 142

INDEX   247

Hemingway, Ernest, 237
Hesse, Hermann, xiv, 98
Hindemith, Paul, 226
Hippe, Pribislav, 182, 197, 209
Hitler, Adolf, 234; German identity of, 55
Horton, Lester, 223
hospital, dominant institution of modernity, 49
Hugo, Victor, 228–229
Huxley, Aldous, 22, 228

ideas, destructive power of, 46–49
illness, 6–7, 41–52, 109–140; as comfort, 113; and creativity, 118; and love, 24, 128–129; and sin, 109, 115; and time, 41
irony, 2, 4, 19–20, 22–23, 35–37, 71, 113, 130, 178–179

Jacobsohn, Siegfried, 150
James, Henry, 199
Jell-O, 22
Jewish self-hatred, 147–148; *see* Theodor Lessing
Joyce, James, xiv, 20, 237
Jung, Gustav, 7

Kafka, Franz, xii, 21, 27, 142, 148, 237
Karstedt, Karen, 32, 85
Keats, John, 105, 117
Kerr, Alfred, 150
Kirghiz (Turkestan), oil reserves, 209
Klüger, Ruth, 141, 143
Kraus, Karl, 152
Krenek, Ernst, 226
Kowalik, Jill Anne, 45
Kundera, Milan, 21

Lane, Christopher, 210–211
language, 171, 204–205; exhaustion of; 13

Latini, Brunetto, as "sodomite," 204–205
Lasker-Schüler, Else, 149–150
Laughton, Charles, 228
Lawrence, D. H., 42, 51; "verbal consciousness," 47
Layton, Susan, 183–184
Leopardi, Giacomo, 203
Lermontov, Mikhail, *A Hero of Our Time*, 183–184
Lessing, Theodor, 147–148
Levi, Primo, 50
Lewitzky, Bella, 223
Loch Ness, 180
London, Jack, 237
love, 26–35, 41–42, 82, 127–129, 166, 197–198, 208–210
Lowe-Porter, Helen, 233
Lublinski, Samuel, 147
Lucretius, 8
Lukács, Georg, 68

McClary, Susan, 88
Maar, Michael, xvii
Mahler, Gustav, 83, 152
Mann, Erika, 230
Mann, Katia, ix–x, 55, 151, 230, 232, 235; illness of, 110, 161
Mann, Thomas; appearance of, 232; artist figure, 68; on Bolshevism, xi; depiction of Jewish characters, 141–144; and German identity, 53–79; Goethe, 18, 179; on happiness, xi; homosexuality, 17, 77 n. 19, 116, 119; humanism, 36; Jews, ix, xv, 141–142, 146–147, 150–155; modernism of, 17; and Lübeck, 186; politics, x, 14–16, 19, 21–22, 57–58; relations with Heinrich Mann, x, 58, 202;
Mann, Thomas, works by: *Buddenbrooks*, ix, 1, 25, 111–113, 134, 153;

The Black Swan, 111;
"Blood of the Walsungs," 142–143;
The Confessions of Felix Krull, 123–125;
Death in Venice, ix, 17, 19, 51, 116, 134, 185, 203–204;
Diaries, xix, 17;
Doctor Faustus, 15, 17, 24, 55, 116 119–120, 143, 155, 233–234, 238;
Joseph novels, 144, 150, 236;
The Magic Mountain; composition of, ix–xii, 16, 55, 110; dialectical conception, 81; geography of, 177–178; gramophone episode, 161–165; Mann's view of, 234–235; naming of characters, 178–179, 185; novel of health, 7; phallic imagery, 181, 195; portrayal of reality, 1–13; translation, xvi–xvii, 28, 138 n. 25; use of French, 125–126, 170; and technology, 158–176; Weimar era, 21–22; "Occult Experiences," 158–159, 163, 171–172
Reflections of a Nonpolitical Man, x, xi, 2, 19, 56, 59–75, 202;
Royal Highness, ix, 58
"Tonio Kröger," 69, 112, 124, 236;
"Tristan," 193
Mannheim, Karl, 57, 64
marriage, 17–18, 33–34
mass society, 29, 36
Melville, Herman, *Moby-Dick*, 108 n.5, 197
Methfessel, Albrecht, 89
Modernism, 16, 31, 34, 92
Mommsen, Theodor, 152

music, 65, 80–94; and film, 84–85; and repressed desire, 83
Musil, Robert, xiv, 27

Naphta, Leo, xi, 8, 17, 30–31, 43, 66, 119, 122–123, 130–131, 177, 181, 211; as duelist, 184; illness, 208; as Jesuit, 203, 206–207; as Jew 142–144, 180, 206–207; meaning of name, 205–206; as paradox, 207
Napoleon, 15
Nehamas, Alexander, 48
Nemerov, Howard, 120
Newman, Ernest, 233
Nietzsche, Friedrich, 89, 101, 106, 237; *Birth of Tragedy*, 80–81; *Joyful Science*, 180
Nobel, Alfred 184
Nobel, Robert, 184
Nobel, Ludwig, 184
Novalis, 116–117
novel as form, xv–xvi, 19, 73

orientalism, 107 n.3, 188

Paz, Octavio, 105
Peeperkorn, Pieter, 1, 8, 45, 87–88, 91, 97, 99, 129, 170; as colonialist, 188–189, 211
Pound, Ezra, 20
Pringsheim, Katia; *see* Mann, Katia
progress as shallow ideal; 65
Pushkin, Alexander, 184

Rathenau, Walther, 152
renunciation, theme of, xi, 18–19
ritual, 180
Rolland, Romain, 67, 237
Romanticism, 203
Röntgen, Wilhelm, 161, 166
Roth, Joseph, 145–146, 148
Russia, 184; M. Chauchat's reasons for being in, 185; prewar oil production, 184, 194

St. Paul, 190–191
Schiller, Friedrich, 116
Schoenberg, Arnold, 92, 152, 226, 228, 233, 237
Scholem, Gershom, 144–145
Schopenhauer, Arthur, xii, xiv, 8, 31–32, 113; and Freud, 86; and music, 80–81
Schubert, Franz; "Death and the Maiden," 231; "Lindenbaum," 11, 62, 106
Schulz, Bruno, xvi
Sedgwick, Eve, 198–199
self as theme, x, 6, 10, 26, 69, 90
Settembrini, Lodovico, 30, 43, 65, 91, 100, 115–116, 121–123, 177, 181; Asia and Vienna, 177–178; attraction to Hans Castorp, 29–30, 202–204; as bigot, 28–29, 97, 101; downfall as mentor, 60–61; eugenics, 28; Madame Chauchat, 27–29, 109–110, 125; materialist, 6, 8, 10, 47–48; meaning of name, 202–204; Italian nationalism, 178; as satanic figure, 178
Settembrini, Luigi, 203–204
Shakespeare, William; *King Lear*, 10
Shaw, George Bernard, 118
Socrates, 2, 30
solitude, 95–108
Sontag, Susan; childhood of, 221–239; meets Thomas Mann, 228–239; and music, 225–226; parents of, 221–223; as reader, 222–223; reads *The Magic Mountain*, 227–228
Sontheimer, Kurt, 58
Spengler, Oswald, 202
Stevens, Wallace, 104
Stevenson, Robert Louis, x
Stravinsky, Igor, 226, 229
Strauss, Johann Jr., 84
Struck, Hermann, 149

style, 19, 21–23; and character, 20
supernatural phenomena, 159–160

thermometer, 178, 212 n.9
time, xiii–xiv, 16, 41, 97, 100
Tolstoy, Leo, 27; *Anna Karenina*, 24, 33–36; *The Death of Ivan Ilyich*, 131–132
tragedy, 81
Trebitsch, Arthur, 145
Trilling, Lionel, 16
Triple Entente, 185
tuberculosis, 23, 25–26, 42, 111–113, 160–161; and original sin, 129
Tucholsky, Kurt, 145–146, 152
Turkey, oil production, 193–194

Verdi, Giuseppe, 88–89, 184

Wagner, Richard, 68, 89–90, 142, 233
waltzing as sexual metaphor, 83
war, 35–36, 41, 49–50, 61–62, 65, 171, 180; and technology, 162
Waremme, Gregor, 145
Warschauer, Georg, 145
Wassermann, Jakob, 145–150
Webern, Anton, 226
Weininger, Otto, 145
Werfel, Franz, 145–146
wisdom, 5
Witkiewicz, Stanislaw Ignacy, 22

x-rays, invention of, 161, 166–167

Yourcenar, Marguerite, 14, 16

Zenta, battle of, 178
Ziemssen, Joachim, 23, 26, 32–34, 111, 130–136, 195; and Hans Castorp, 33–35, 178–179, 189, 210; compared with Ivan Ilyich, 131

Zimmermann, Johann Georg, 106
Zweig, Arnold, 149
Zweig, Stefan, 146